A FAMILY AT WAR

The Unofficial and Unauthorised Guide to
Till Death Us Do Part

Mark Ward

First published in England in 2008 by
Telos Publishing Ltd, 5A Church Road, Shortlands, Bromley, Kent BR2 0HP,
United Kingdom.

www.telos.co.uk

This edition 2017

ISBN: 978-1-84583-949-9

Telos Publishing Ltd values feedback. Please e-mail us with any comments
you may have about this book to: feedback@telos.co.uk

With thanks to Ian Pritchard for the Index.

British Library Cataloguing in Publication Data.
A catalogue record for this book is available from the British Library.

With love and gratitude for *my* family – Mom, Dad, Gary and Greg

Contents

Introduction: A Word About Alf ...

Look ... Look ... *Listen!* You might learn somefink. This is not a book about Alf Garnett, that venerated Great British Institution, that racist Cockney bigot, that Falstaff, that Mask of the People. This is a history of the show that spawned him, kicking and screaming, into the public consciousness over 40 years ago, a show called *Till Death Us Do Part*. This is a story of a family at war – with each other, with the world, with religion, with royalty, with politicians, with the BBC, with *everything*. It is a story of life continually imitating art imitating life. While battles were spectacularly fought on-screen, the campaigns and skirmishes continued behind the scenes, the conflicts just as explosive, just as vitriolic. The soldiers in this war were actors Warren Mitchell, Dandy Nichols, Anthony Booth and Una Stubbs, and a cast of many others. The commander was creator and writer Johnny Speight, and his *aide de camp* was producer Dennis Main Wilson, who drew the battle lines and set the tactics. Together, they made an invincible combination; but when they were separated from the field, like old campaigners, they told a good story, but it could never be the same. The excitement and fervour that the Garnetts generated could never be replicated by Alf Garnett alone or by the tales of his own individual battles *In Sickness and in Health*. For me at least, it needed that phalanx to work together in war and disharmony – once it was disbanded in 1975, after ten years of conflict, much of the interest and energy inevitably dissipated. This is the story of the most controversial, most influential sitcom ever made for television, *Till Death Us Do Part*, and that's where I'll stop – although I've covered the spin-offs and follow-ups briefly; and, unlike Alf, I'm willing to consider alternative views ...

All the research for this book is my own, and therefore any mistakes are all mine. I consulted the very sparse programme files and scripts surviving at the BBC Written Archives Centre in Reading; press reviews and features in Birmingham's excellent Central Library; the extant television shows themselves, together with surviving ancillary programmes such as: the BBC's viewer reaction forum *Talkback* (the 1968 show regarding 'The Blood Donor' episode survives, the 1972 show covering Lord Hill's apology to Mrs Whitehouse doesn't); the relevant *Man Alive* documentary (1967); *Late Night Line-Up*'s raucous 1966 interview with Speight; the *This Is Your Life* 1970 and 1972 editions honouring Speight and Mitchell respectively; various '80s interviews with Speight and Mitchell; and so forth.

Since the first edition of this book in 2008 several previously missing episodes of the series have been recovered ('In Sickness and In Health', 'State Visit' and 'Intolerance'), whilst audio recordings of all the missing '60s episodes except for the *Comedy Playhouse* pilot now exist. For the first edition, 'The Puppy'/ 'The Dog' was not available and all of the audios were in poor acoustic quality but the imminent release of the Network DVD Box set should resolve these issues. For example, the quality of the audio of 'In Sickness and In Health' used to complete the synopsis in the first edition was so poor that the crucial line 'Randy Scouse Git' which Mickey Dolenz would assimilate and use to entitle a classic Monkees single was inaudible. The actual television episode recovered in 2009 thankfully restored the insult into its proper context. However, all audios of the show must be treated with caution, as much of the action without dialogue can be deeply confusing, as readers of the first edition of this book will recognise with the synopsis for 'State Visit' for example – I knew from press reaction that Alf threw ink and accidentally hit a picture of the Queen but did not know where this came sequentially until the actual episode was recovered soon after the book was published.

Finally, I read the wonderfully entertaining – if of occasionally dubious accuracy – autobiographies by Speight and Booth, and the excellent 1967 John Burke book on the series, and … oh, I've lost me bloody thread now, 'aven't I?

Before I forget, you may notice a distinct decrease in the amount of information available for the series once the character of Else departs; this is due to the comparative lack of contemporary media interest, and more pertinently to the absence of any surviving BBC written correspondence for the 1975 period. A word about episode titles; for the first two series, these were quoted in *Radio Times* and in the BBC scripts, thanks in no small part to Dennis Main Wilson, who apparently christened Johnny Speight's virtually-illegible teleplays. From then on, the episodes were untitled, but headers for the third series (e.g. 'The Puppy', 'Aunt Maud', 'Football') appeared during the 1968/1969 repeat season. For the others, I have used either the titles given in Speight's 1973 script book or those adopted by general consensus of the people who categorise such things.

I would like to thank Neil Ingoe for his kind and generous assistance in loaning several key programmes, as well as the script for the *Comedy Playhouse* show, which the BBC did not appear to retain. As always, thanks to Dave Auger and to Ian Riley for their wisdom and beer.

Mark Ward

1
A Product Of Its Time

A WAPPING MYTHOLOGY

Alf Garnett's living room. A two piece settee, adorned with antimacassars. Alf's armchair, frazzled newspaper spread unceremoniously across the seat. A battered coffee table. The telly. The aspidistra in the corner. A heavy wooden clock on the sideboard, near an oversized, grotesque terracotta landscape-with-figures. A Bakelite radio. Three flying ducks. A miniature terracotta bust of an Arab. A silver frieze depicting caravels in full sail. Above the scene rests the true heart of Garnett's world, the symbolic centre of his universe – a series of photographs, of dusty deities and sepia statesmen, religious artefacts that reflect the Garnett cosmos, like heavenly bodies beaming down on a joyless, functional world. There's royalty – our current monarch (God bless her) in her Annigoni glory, with the Queen Mum and Dad at her side. Prince Charles lurks somewhere, chatting benignly to the potted plant. Somewhere hangs his sister, smiling with benevolent despotism, alongside her consort Mark, caught by Snowdon at her most radiant moment, now trapped in time, forever peering through a naff colour reproduction. Let's not forget the faded Duke of Windsor, the worker's king, and a personal friend of Alf's father, a noble man who supported a noble team, West Ham. The lads of this team stand, enshrined in evanescence – Bobby, Alan, Gordon, the other Bobby … they what won the World Cup for England that glorious summer of 1966. There's a portrait of Jesus, whose dad created the world in seven days, including the sun, moon and planets, not like the bloody rubbish we have today, smoking fags and hiding in the khazi. There's fellow Londoner Henry Cooper, in his prime, fists outstretched for proud pugilistic mayhem. But place of honour amongst these heroes of Empire and England goes to the Man of the Century himself, Winston Churchill, displaying the Agincourt salute with heartfelt pride. Never, in the field of human … whatever … has so much been owed to … something or other. Yes, these photographs are not merely pictures or portraits; instead they are icons, sacred objects through which our hero venerates the institutions wot made Britain great. They bridge the gap between the monolithic heaven of the past and the ever changing hell of the present, between the blazing sun of a glorious history and the dimming light of an iniquitous today. Alfred Edward Garnett is the last of a kind, a metonym for those sturdy Edwardian ethics and Victorian values that our predecessors cherished and worshipped. He is a man who refused to be circumscribed (even if he knew what it meant), a man who would never submit, a man of strong convictions and limitless horizons, a man who would go anywhere to honour his Queen, his country and his football team …

And now he's going down the pub …

1966 AND ALL THAT …

Think 1966. A Good Thing, as Sellers and Yeatman would have it. A seminal year – England's Greatest Sporting Achievement, winning the World Cup in a life and death struggle with the Hun. Swinging London. Carnaby Street. Minis. Miniskirts. 'Waterloo Sunset'. 'Good Vibrations'. 'River Deep, Mountain High'. 'Revolver'. The Beatles bigger than God (or indeed, Rod), playing their last official concert. *Alfie. The Good, The Bad and The Ugly. Blow Up.* The death of Disney. *Batman.* 'Cathy Come Home'. A new Doctor Who. *Star Trek* premieres in America. The Post Office Tower. Vietnam. The Cultural Revolution. The Moors Murders. The Krays. Aberfan …

Then there's the hidden 1966, the year that we don't recall so well in the sound bites that are aimed at us. It was a different world, for good and for bad. It was a world that most of us have forgotten. There was separation of the public life from the private. The formality of dress and manners when engaged in most social functions. The fact that it was considered bad form to swear in public. Children were better seen and not heard. A quieter, less raucous world devoid of muzak, mobiles, over-exuberant teenagers. The respect for authority, whether in the form of policemen or doctors or lawyers or for the findings of public enquiries that would now merely generate disbelief or further inquest. The visual impact of a world that still consisted mainly of pre-War housing, some of it retaining the scars of the Blitz. The noises and smells and dirt and pollution of the manufacturing industry that still dominated British life and work. The lack of ethnic minorities, and the lack of choice linked to this – few ethnic restaurants or shops, the first ports of call for much of the White majority for meetings with other cultures. The nation of shopkeepers still existed, with half day closing on Wednesdays and all day closing for the Sabbath. There were no shopping malls or massive car parks. When an address included a phrase such as Lakeside or The Paddocks, it generally meant just that, rather than another new stretch of modern, affordable housing. The exigencies of post-War development meant that the citizen had few rights when it came to the councils who could demolish properties with very little recourse to appeal. Nearly two million people lived in slums, and that was a conservative estimate. There was no central heating. There was no air conditioning. More and more homes had integrated bathrooms, but many still had to use the outdoor lavatory or a tin bath in the kitchen, and, even if they had acquired all mod cons, most adults had a memory of those inconveniences. Washing, because of this, because of bigger families and smaller homes, because there was so little money to spend on clothes that did not have the versatility of material that we have today, and because of the use of the mangle and tub to clean clothes rather than today's omnipresent washing machine, meant that standards of hygiene were nowhere near as high as today. Food, and therefore diet, was restricted in terms of variety. Stodgy meals of pies and chips and potatoes and fish were the norm.

Technology was limited. There were no mobile phones, computers, videos, even cassettes. Cars were not affordable to many people. Telephones were rare in working class homes; one had to use the public phone box, with its massive directory kept inside. Money (pounds, shillings, pence) was still tight, despite the fact that the '60s were supposedly swinging. Expensive goods were bought on Hire Purchase, repossessed if payments fell. Credit cards were unknown in the UK – the first was introduced by Barclays in London in May 1966. Few went abroad for their holidays, and if they did it was to Spain or France. Anywhere further afield was still seen as wildly exotic … and full of foreigners … News about foreign climes was restricted. There were problems in Aden, and in Rhodesia where Ian Smith had made a unilateral declaration of independence (UDI). China was in the grip of the Cultural Revolution. Russia – the USSR – was seen as the Cold War enemy. America was involved in Vietnam, a war still considered winnable in the early presidency of Lyndon Johnson. Berlin was divided by a wall only five years old. France, led by De Gaulle, had repeatedly said 'non' to Britain's attempts to join the Common Market (as it was termed in those days). In Britain, a shaky Labour government with a majority of only four had been in power since 1964, but had gone to the polls again on 31 March 1966 to win a more significant majority in order to empower it to deal with the terrifying number of industrial problems that confronted it, as well as to gain a secure mandate for its social reforms. Harold Wilson was a familiar figure with his Gannex mac and pipe and sturdy Northern accent, a politician who knew the value of the media. The main Conservative opposition was led by Edward Heath, an upper-middle-class comedown from a party hitherto dominated by ancient, died-in-the-tweed Scottish aristocrats, such as Macmillan and Home. Bizarrely, two scions of the upper class, Quintin Hogg and Anthony Wedgwood Benn, had recently graciously discarded their lordly status to stand for the Commons, the first as a Conservative, the second for Labour.

Divorce was easier than in the past, but infrequent. Abortion was illegal, homosexuality also. The death penalty had gone, but only recently. People were more aware of their class, buttressed by their dialects and accents, with the cut glass of the BBC still regnant on the airwaves. The Royal Family were still endowed with a sense of mystique, and regarded with affection, a relic from the War only 20 years in the past. Cinema showings, concert performances and each day's TV always ended with the anthem 'God Save the Queen' and pictures of Her Majesty being displayed. People had always paid more lip service to religion than participated in actual devout worship, but it was still a touchy subject, and few would have had the temerity to pronounce themselves atheists or non-believers. Politicians were still respected, in line with the general deference to authority instilled by the Victorians and the Edwardians, although things was changing: from the late '50s onwards, they were increasingly viewed with the kind of healthy scorn they had endured in earlier eras – the free press and media helped here. Although everyone knew that Empire was no more, there was a far greater national consensus than today. This was a unicultural, White society, still industrially based, still focussed on the older male, the breadwinner, rather than the women or the children. Entertainment for this happy breed was limited – the pub, the cinema (then apparently in decline), with the occasional concert and restaurant visit for the better off or the middle class. But the biggest source of entertainment was television. There were only three channels – BBC 1 (no adverts, higher class entertainment), ITV (two to three advert breaks per hour, more lowbrow, and therefore more popular) and BBC 2, which only a limited population could access and which even fewer people watched, and dubbed an 'intellectual ghetto' by one influential writer. Television could bring the news virtually instantaneously to the people; it made the Moors Murderers the most vilified monsters in British history and it could move millions to tears with scenes from the Aberfan disaster. Politicians, especially Wilson, had begun to use television as an integral part of their propaganda. In sport, the BBC's unprecedented coverage of the World Cup – 50 hours of coverage, and the innovation of a new technology imported from America and dubbed 'the action replay' – was to change the perception of football for ever. In other entertainment, soaps (although they weren't called that at the time) such as *Coronation Street* and *Emergency Ward 10* were immensely popular. Individual hour-long plays, sometimes wrapped up in anthology strands, still ruled the drama roost. American imports were popular, because they were shot on film and therefore had greater pace and excitement than similar home-grown shows. The dramatic water-cooler moments (well, all right, whistling kettle moments) of the time were not just the shows celebrated today but series such as *The Power Game* (boardroom shenanigans, starring Patrick Wymark, with one episode becoming so popular it gave the highest ever boost to the National Grid) and *Mrs Thursday* (homely moral issues emanating from a charlady who inherits the business empire of her tycoon boss, starring Kathleen Harrison). Also popular were sitcoms (although, again, they weren't called that then), such as *Marriage Lines*, *Steptoe and Son* and *The Likely Lads*. But the biggest draws were variety shows, providing the 'colour' (although that didn't yet exist on British screens), brightness and blissful relaxation that many men and women craved after a day on the lathe or the conveyor belt. There was no way of recording a programme, so it was no surprise when pubs were emptied as popular shows were transmitted. There were no remote-control handsets, and in any case, the valve-based television sets meant that excessive use of the channel changing switches could mean disaster. Tellies broke down a lot in those days; you even had to wait for them to 'warm up' after they were switched on. They were also very expensive. Dad, the main breadwinner, whose wages had provided the set, had total control over it. And there was sufficient money for only one set, stuck in the living room. The entire family gathered around it to watch whatever Dad wanted to watch. And in 1966, soaring down from Broadcasting House, swooping past the Bakelite radio, sweeping aside the set of flying ducks on the wall, and plunging past the aspidistra in the corner, there arrived the most explosive series of the year …

CREATING THE '60S

It has been said, with considerable perceptiveness, that 100 people invented and ran the '60s. It can be seen indeed as a decade that was nurtured, moulded and shaped by a handful of creative people; the showbiz set, working in London; a cavalcade of accidental meetings, drunken conversations, transmission of individual ideas, romantic liaisons; and business decisions made on impulse rather than long term consideration and generally brazened out in the ineffable style and unusual presentation that seemingly graced that decade. It all merged and fused to forge a conglomeration of creative power that remains unparalleled to this day. The main reason why the architects of the '60s still recall those days as halcyon was their ability to generate such creativity without many of the later constrictions placed on showbiz – demographic budgeting and marketing, the financial limits of technology, or the murky waters of political correctness. Today, most creative ideas have to be rubber stamped by lawyers, accountants and market researchers – a case of creation by committee – whereas in the golden days of the '60s it was creation by cabal, or conversation, or collusion (or at least that is how it was perceived to be – they had accountants and so forth in those days too). But even in 1965, when our story begins, a small core of creative minds was still recognised as paramount in certain aspects of the British media, when Frank Muir could write 'In this country, all our comedy is written by about 24 gentlemen'. And here begins the saga of *Till Death Us Do Part*, a television series that encapsulated all the perceived glories of creativity in the swinging '60s and went on to become, in sickness and in health, for richer and poorer, the most unusual and most successful comedy series ever made.

2
Johnny Speight

ANGRY OF CANNING TOWN

One of Muir's 24 gentlemen was a certain Johnny Speight, and he was the prime mover in the development of the series that was then, in pure '60s style, shaped by chance meetings and drunken (and occasionally sober) conversations that he enjoyed with a handful of people. Speight was born on 2 June 1920 in Canning Town in the East End of London. He joked in later years that his family were 'affluent poor' – at least they had a home, even though it was a two up, two down slum with outside toilet and no garden. In those days, Speight also stated, he didn't know he was poor – his family's world consisted only of the neighbouring streets, and the short route to work, and everyone was in the same demographic boat, so to speak. His father had a job, as a scaler in the dockyards, cleaning hulls and tanks, covered with oil up to his neck. It was secure work, but poorly paid, and Speight's mother was always aware of how little extra money was available, buying Johnny's shoes one size too big so that he could grow into them, while his father used to be proud of the weeds growing in the yard, the only sign of any vegetation that could be conceivably termed a garden.[1] Despite this poverty, it seems Johnny had an idyllic home life; his father was mild mannered and rarely swore, and hardly ever drank alcohol, while his mother was a devout Roman Catholic with firm moral convictions, and they both brought up their children with love and affection. Speight attended the local Roman Catholic Primary School, which he hated, despising a spoon-fed education and the ever present bullying, which he, short in stature and encumbered with a pronounced stammer, bore the brunt of. He left school at 14 with a report confirming that he was 'suited for manual labour', and – according to his later recollection – went on to work in every factory along the road between Canning Town and Woolwich, hating every minute of it. One early job was in a cakemill factory, working with grease and oil that left his clothes saturated. The absence of baths or showers or a laundry at work or at home meant that he had to reuse his saturated clothes every day. On cold nights, they would freeze solid overnight due to the lack of any heating, and in the morning he would have to

---

[1] This memory is recalled in the *Comedy Playhouse* pilot when Rita is being sarcastic about her father's Conservative values.

slide them on and then stagger down the road, zombie like, until he and his overalls had thawed out. He yearned to become a white collar worker, and thus have the opportunity to go out for the evening directly, without having to wash …

Such early experiences imbued in him a deep awareness of the iniquities of a society that wanted to – as he said – 'keep you in the place they preferred you to be … i.e. down a coalmine, or at a workbench or in the dole queue'. He was conscious of his East London accent, as well as his stutter: 'People with an accent like mine usually come to collect the refuse, or mend the drains'. His anger with the class system and the darker side of capitalism impelled him to join the Communist party, but he very quickly tired of the equally ludicrous mindset of that ideology.

Speight was a very likeable figure in real life; a great and charming conversationalist who, according to his agent Alexandra Cann, was never antagonistic to people who upset him, but simply wrote them into his scripts. He was, she said, a man with a tiny bit of cynicism and a great deal of naïveté, like most great comics. Indeed, despite all the frustrations his career caused him, it seems Speight never gave anyone cause to say or write a bad thing about him. But inside him there seems to have been a great deal of anger waiting to come out. He was angry about the poverty he saw all around him during his early days. He detested that aspect of working class life that gave unthinking respect to the aristocracy, whom he dismissed as Britain's first criminal class, having ruled first by physical power, later by the more subtle deployment of mental terror. He disliked the working class ethic that they should remain in their social station, again because they had been told to do so by their so-called betters. He loathed the Conservatives, whom he saw as ruining the nation, but he was also angry at the Labour party for failing to fulfil its social obligations, and irritated that when they had improved the lot of the proletariat, their services were discarded and their help forgotten as the workers began to emulate the middle class. Then he despised the middle class, seeing them as equally stupid, although ensconced in suburbia, but with less justification for their stupidity because of their better education. Reacting against his intense Roman Catholic upbringing, he saw religion as a useless comfort zone that sedated the people rather than stimulated them. Later, he abhorred the dogma of Marx, which started out proclaiming atheism and ended up deifying Marx himself. Thus Speight was an angry young man, trying to find a means to ground the electricity of his inner rage, a means of expressing an anger that was volcanic and needed an outlet.

He found an escape route from the endless industrial grind of manual labour in his affinity for the jazz and big band music he heard on the radio. Loving the sounds of Duke Ellington and Count Basie, he learned to play the drums, eventually performing in a semi-professional jazz band that 'kept him sane'. He formed Johnny Speight and his Hot Shots, and retained the jazzy feel of the Christian name for the rest of his life. In 1939, his world expanded when he joined the army and was posted in the Royal Corps Of Signals, fortunately managing to keep out of the conflict by retaining a post in Britain as an army cook spending most of the War 'making lumpy mashed potatoes'. Here again he noted a class system in operation, preferring to cook for the officers who were too polite to grumble about his food as opposed to the normal servicemen who registered their disapproval by simply throwing it at him. In 1944, he thought that his good fortune may have run out when he was moved to France 60 days after D Day, but again he was blessed with luck, because he stayed behind on the coast while the army moved inland. After VE day, he was on the verge of being sent out to the Far East, but managed to keep quiet in the holding battalion, and then have the foresight to volunteer as a batman to the officer in charge of selecting troops for the transfer – if he gave good service, he knew that the officer would never send *him*, another example of class habits he utilised to his own advantage.

On demobilisation, it was back to Canning Town, factories and drumming, but now at least he had discovered the smoky pleasures of Soho, especially a club in Windmill Street owned by Johnny Dankworth and Ronnie Scott, where he was to meet his future wife, Connie, a typist from Dagenham. The club closed at 11.00 pm in those days, and Speight frequented the local milk and coffee bars, full of colourful figures who were to later to form his database of comic characters. Inspired by jazz, he spent his session money on snappy clothes from Cecil Gee on Tottenham Court Road, wearing American-style suits and emulating his US icons; a very individual fashion sense that he was to retain all his life.[2]

Tired of factory jobs, Speight was to become a milkman and then in November 1952 an insurance salesman, traversing the East End desperately trying to sell policies or collect payments in a world reliant on ready cash and with no real credit facilities. He learned quickly that on Fridays he had to strike fast before the workers' wage packets dissipated in a weekend of booze and cigarettes. Warren Mitchell once asked him how on earth he had fared selling insurance with his pronounced stammer, but Speight replied that he had actually done very well: once he had got his foot in the door, he had played for the sympathy vote and been quite successful. His boss, recounting his tale on *This Is Your Life* in 1970, affirmed this, yet genially remarked that he was always late and it was obvious his heart was not in it, as he was always dreaming about writing and poetry.

---

[2] Warren Mitchell in 1972 was to say of Speight: 'He has extraordinary taste in clothes – very garish, and nothing matches. He has awful taste in everything'. This is also reflected in the episode 'Euthanasia' (see episode guide).

THE INTELLECTUAL TOMMY TRINDER

By this time, Speight had found his aesthetic muse in the unlikely spot of Canning Town Public Library. Venturing in one day, he found a shelf full of books by George Bernard Shaw. Shaw was still active when Speight was young (Shaw died in 1950) and Speight had often read humorous remarks and comments by the author in the newspapers, always believing him to be a stand up comic *a la* Tommy Trinder – he hadn't realised that Shaw wrote books and plays as well … Reading Shaw's first novel, *Immaturity*, he introduced himself to his artistic lodestar, to a new horizon of creative expression. Speight was soon to read every novel and play the man had written. Shaw's works were to provide him with a framework and an inspiration for his own combination of black humour and observational dialogue, and a deep well of artistic obsessions on class, society, politics, ethics and religion, again at once moulding an aesthetic framework and supplying a language for his inner frustrations.

Speight's entire concept of comedy was imbued in him by his discovery and reading of the great playwright. Shaw, for instance, had recalled his father, so drunk sometimes that he kept walking into the garden wall thinking it was a gate, provoking a great deal of laughter and evoking the idea that Shaw was 'clearly not a boy who will make tragedies of trifles instead of making trifles of tragedies'. Shaw saw comedy as having a natural and indissoluble link with tragedy, a form that if '… pursued to a logical conclusion … inevitably resolved itself into comedy'. He also declared that it was the 'highest art form'. Speight was perhaps aware of Shaw's comments on *his* hero, Henrik Ibsen, whom he celebrated as presenting 'the drama of ideas'. Shaw wrote that 'the drama of the individual is seen in the perspective of larger social issues' and believed that characterisation, feeling and situation were paramount; he hated 'well-made drama with absurd sentimental plots', or 'drawing room drama', and he sought, like Ibsen, to question values underlying bourgeois morality. Here for Speight was a paradigm he was to follow in all his work – a love of dialogue and character rather than of plot or structure. And then there were Shaw's father's views on religion: 'Even the worst enemy of religion could say no worse of the Bible than that it was the damnedest parcel of lies ever written'. This was a theme that resonated with his Catholic upbringing and was to recur throughout *Till Death Us Do Part*. But perhaps a key quote by Shaw on his own work can be applied to Speight's view of Alf Garnett – an 'imaginary monster with my name attached to it'.

In January 1966, Speight appeared on the BBC Two programme *Late Night Line Up* as part of a forum discussing television comedy, and he imparted his overview of comedy derived from his worship of Shaw, describing his insistence on some form of social realism to drive the comic ideal, contrasting it to the P G Wodehouse chamber-room comedy then being adapted for television in the BBC's *The World of Wooster* starring Ian Carmichael and Dennis Price. Such highly polished, characteristically 'English' upper-class comedies of manners were not for him, a view devolved from Shaw, who had dismissed such material as socially irrelevant. Speight realised that he could write comedy and satire as an outlet for his own inner frustrations at the world he saw around him; later he was to realise that the comic horse should come before the dramatic cart, as Shaw himself had perceived: 'When a thing is funny, search it for a hidden truth.' And Speight was eventually to realise one of Shaw's most vitriolic observations: 'The secret of success is to offend the greatest number of people.' Speight, the lapsed Catholic, the committed atheist, had now found his God. In 1972, he was to say: 'To me, discovering Shaw had been like meeting God. He was a man who seemed to know all about the world ... [He seemed to be] explaining to me my ill-formed thoughts.'

Speight was soon to avidly digest works by Strindberg, Ibsen, Chekhov, Sean O'Casey (from whom he assimilated an idea of comedy, to write 'with tears in his eyes') and, like many in the epoch before the real scale of Stalin's and Mao's genocides were discovered, Marx and Engels; but it was Shaw who triggered for Speight the idea that he too could become a professional writer, an idea ridiculed by most of his friends, who reflected the old working class ideas that the only way to escape the East End in those days was via football (at which Speight was useless) or by being a boxer or a lifestyle criminal (for both of which Speight admitted he was too cowardly).

'Everyone looked at me as if I was an idiot. Only Connie believed in me. "Why not", she said, "You can do it".'

The works of George Bernard Shaw introduced Speight to a new world, a world of words and ideas, even though he frequently needed to consult a dictionary to discover what his new hero was talking about. He bought an old typewriter with one key missing, and both he and Connie joined the Fabian Society, quoted Shaw's dialogue and attended meetings at school halls all over London. As a member of the Communist Party, he also wrote plays for a writers' collective at the left wing Unity Theatre in Camden Town, 'Writing scripts about evil capitalists and noble working class people. Everything was black and white. What a load of rubbish.' He refused to accept the party line that all non-socialist dogma was worthless and that writers such as Noel Coward and Peter Ustinov were useless, and he was to leave the party after a few months, dismissing its members as 'bloody fools', an early appreciation that rigid thoughts about class and society were a nonsense. '[The Communists] talked so much crap. And the people in the writers' group talked even more crap.' By a strange quirk of fate, Warren Mitchell was to attend the same theatre collective as an actor a short time afterwards. He was later to believe that Communism was crap, too.

20

Speight was still selling insurance and experimenting with writing when, in 1953, he got his first showbiz break. An old army friend and fellow jazz player introduced him to Frankie Howerd, then appearing in *Pardon My French*, a characteristic '50s revue show being performed at the Prince of Wales Theatre in the West End. Speight's friend was working as a masseur, helping to treat the ever-nervous Howerd's stiff neck, when Speight met the star, who immediately 'bought' his first ever joke – 'I'm livid – they're pulling down my house to build a slum.'

Howerd offered to help Speight break into the business and asked him to write for his radio show. 'You don't have to write all those oohs and aaahs,' Frankie said. 'I'll put all those in myself.' Speight was cynically impressed – 'This one can ad lib!', he thought, until Frankie started to return all of his jokes asking that he put all the 'oohs' and 'aahs' in after all …

'He was a big help to me as a writer. I was like a young journalist joining a newspaper and having a marvellous editor … Working for a great stand up like Frankie was the same thing. I mean, Frankie's attitude (toward a new piece of writing) was "Yeah, maybe a nice thought, but is it going to get a *laugh*?" You know … we all had such trust in him. We knew that if he said yes, it was okay, then it *was* okay.'

In 1955, Howerd worked with Eric Sykes on the TV series *The Howerd Crowd*, and he urged Speight to approach Sykes, a member of the writers' cooperative Associated London Scripts (ALS). ALS had been set up the previous year by Sykes, Spike Milligan, Ray Galton and Alan Simpson as a serious attempt to direct comic writing and enable the group to develop their craft by each of them receiving some share of the profits. Initially, the ALS offices were over a greengrocer's on the Uxbridge Road, and visitors had to negotiate various crates of fruit and veg prior to ascending five floors to the offices. A nervous Speight did just this one day in February 1955 to find Galton and Simpson, the young prodigies who were writing groundbreaking comedy for Tony Hancock, lying on the floor motionless, which was the method they used to brainstorm ideas. Because Galton, like Speight, dressed in very flamboyant clothes, Speight almost made off in terror at the sight of them. 'We later discovered that he was convinced that we were homosexuals and that we were going to have our wicked ways with him,' recalled Galton. Nevertheless, Speight handed over a script to Sykes – clad in his camelhair coat, which Speight envied as the ultimate garb of a serious showbiz star – who promised to consider it and asked him to return the following week. Speight obliged, with Connie as support against any possible Galton blandishments, and was overjoyed when Sykes accepted the script. Sykes then asked if the budding writer had any more scripts he could deliver on a regular basis, knowing full well that one good idea did not a comic writer make. Speight said he had, because he had long considered the idea of becoming a professional writer. Sykes helpfully noted that Speight might one day be able to pack in his insurance salesman job and write full time, and was later horrified to hear that Speight had taken him literally at his word and had quit his day job immediately. Thankfully, Speight was never to look back, although his boss insisted that should he ever need to revert to his insurance job, he would be welcomed back – and Speight's insurance pedigree was to stand him in good financial stead in the harsh world of show business.

3
Alf's Comic Roots

MR PENNYFEATHER AND MR NICHOL-ARSE

In his fledgling career as a full-time writer, Johnny Speight supplied radio material for such varied luminaries as Morecambe and Wise, Peter Sellers, Dickie Valentine, Arthur Askey, Tony Hancock, Vic Oliver, Bill Maynard, Cyril Fletcher and bandleader Edmundo Ros. His first television work came on Frankie Howerd's shows in 1955. He then worked on Valentine's shows, but continued supplying jokes for Howerd and also wrote the first television series for Eric Sykes. By the dawn of the '60s, however, he was most prolifically and most profitably employed writing for Arthur Haynes on ITV.

Haynes, born in 1914 in Hammersmith, had developed his comedy routine in ITMA as one of Charlie Chester's crew in *Stand Easy* prior to going solo in the late '40s and following a successful career in music hall and variety. He had been discovered for television in a spotlight show devised by George and Arthur Black for the nascent ITV channel early in 1956. Initially, Nicholas Parsons acted in the role of commentator while Haynes performed sketches written by Sid Colin and Ronnie Wolfe; but when the Blacks recognised Haynes's star potential and provided him further exposure on other shows, the comedian realised that he needed other writers to contribute new material. Speight was to supply jokes for *Get Happy* later in the year, and when Haynes was offered a guest slot on *Star Time* for ATV, he was reluctant to use his stage act for fear that it would be overexposed, so he requested Speight to write new sketches involving him and Parsons. This proved so successful that Haynes was then offered his own show, at first recorded in front of a live audience at Wood Green Empire, with Speight authoring one main sketch and several 'quickies' in each episode. The format was so popular that by 1959 *The Arthur Haynes Show* was transmitted at peak time as a staple part of the schedule of the all-conquering commercial channel. In all, Speight wrote for 14 of Haynes's series between 1957 and 1966.

Haynes was defiantly working class in appearance, ideal for ITV's populist stance, and his onscreen character was one of utter self confidence, whatever the occasion, outwardly bluff but with an inner cunning that could take him through any situation he faced. His most popular alter ego was the insufferably rude Oscar Pennyfeather; a figure not devised by Speight, but from which Speight developed the Haynes persona's unholy trinity of know-all, bluff working man and cunning tramp to its ultimate success. Nicholas Parsons' remarks: '[Speight's] style was clearly suited to Arthur's personality. Arthur, in turn, brought out the best in Johnny's writing.' Speight relished working for Haynes: 'Arthur had a marvellous, immobile face in which only the eyes moved – malicious eyes. You knew that tramp was going to con you the moment you saw him.'

Parsons always played the straight man who suffered various indignities at the hands of the star, who 'played for the laughs through the subtle and conniving way in which he always came out on top'. Because of the comparatively blank canvas he presented to television viewers, in contrast to the established personas of performers such as Frankie Howerd, Haynes gave Speight the opportunity to develop his own style, writing for one character rather than submitting jokes tailored to several stars' individual styles. Speight admired Haynes's apparent effortlessness: 'His art really concealed his art … When he played a character, he gave the impression that he had just walked in off the street.' This effortlessness came at a price, however. Parsons says that Haynes hated rehearsing, because as a music hall comic he could not understand the exigencies of acting for television. Thus, when presented with Speight's scripts, Haynes would read them through twice, make comments and suggest alterations and then try to remember the sense of the lines and run through some of them in his head. Then he would go home and work on his first love, DIY. Parsons thus had to learn not only his own lines but also the star's, in case Haynes's memory failed him. On one sketch, as Parsons was playing a bank manager and Haynes a customer, the latter forgot his lines and gave the former one of his funny looks signifying that he had dried, prompting Parsons to declare, 'Mr Haynes, I think that the word you are searching for is "collateral", and you want to inform me that you don't have any.'

The audience loved this occasional element of danger, and Haynes knew this, so he riposted with a sly play on words, calling the bank manager 'Mr Nichol-arse', thus making it difficult for Parsons to retain a straight face and letting the audience lap this up and feel complicit in the knife-edge atmosphere of the moment. Haynes's aversion to becoming too familiar with the material and thus strangling its spontaneity was always redeemed by his timing, which then produced amazing results. This was to have a marked influence on Speight, as it brought home to him the necessity of having his material interpreted by quality performers. He realised that although he had developed his craft from one-liners to sketches, this more substantial work would nevertheless go through a process of being handed over to performers such as Haynes, who could then be relied upon to mould it into their own individual style. This would later be demonstrated to good effect on *Till Death Us Do Part*, but would also occasionally give rise to problems as, having honed his craft writing sketches, Speight never became comfortable with the discipline of turning in precisely-timed 30-minute scripts; he would fail to clearly delineate his work and would thus cause chaos when he delivered it late or incomplete or overlong to the performers. He refused to review his work once he had written it, because he felt that this discipline might dispel the 'truth' of its spontaneity, a dubious practice that friends such as writer John Antrobus warned him against to no avail. Thus Speight, the autodidact, was to achieve his extraordinarily perverse worldview while eschewing any form of literary or dramatic structure. This was an approach he had seen repeatedly vindicated in his success as a sketch-writer, and he never regarded it as a problem; indeed, he was rather proud of it: 'I don't mind a critic pointing out that my work is of feeble construction and that it lacks concept and style and that other word so loved these days – structure – or that it is poorly written and without any real grasp of language, as long as he's not using those adjectives as a stick just to beat the ideas with … Is it good theatre, does it work, is it exciting, and if it's a comedy, is it *funny*?.' In other words, meticulously-plotted, John Sullivan-style sitcoms with an ingenious pay-off at the end would never be for Speight.

It was also during his stint on *The Arthur Haynes Show* that Speight began to acquire his reputation for late delivery of scripts, intent as he was on keeping them as topical and as relevant as possible. Because he wrote in one continuous session once he was inspired by an idea, and because he always refused to look back over and revise or rewrite his work, he had to wait until his muse visited him. This visitation, according to Nicholas Parsons and to Speight's son Richard, usually occurred in the bath. Parsons had a vision of Speight submerged for hours in the water with a typewriter perched nearby. If any television executive or producer telephoned to enquire as to when the script would be available, Speight was usually 'in the bath' and could not answer. According to Richard Speight, only a select few passed 'the bath test', and these were generally performers rather than programme-makers. The consequent delays were to prove frustrating for executives, cast and crew – and occasionally useful for Speight – for the rest of his career.

Speight felt able to create a far darker vein of comedy for Haynes than for any other comedian he wrote for. Haynes usually appeared as a working man, belligerent, cunning and generally on the winning end of a situation. Early on in the partnership, Speight, in a chance encounter, discovered Haynes's most consistent alter ego, a tramp. Never averse to displaying the trappings of wealth, in a marked contrast to his poverty-stricken beginnings and in an unconscious emulation of the jazz stars he worshipped, Speight had bought a Rolls Royce (although Nicholas Parsons says it was a Bentley) in which he drove to work.[3] One day, stuck in traffic at a red light in central London, he

---

[3] In 1972, Speight was also to buy a Rolls Royce from Max Bygraves and then register it as 'MOO 16'.

saw the passenger door open and a tramp calmly climb onto the upholstered seats, as if it was a perfectly natural thing to do. The tramp's first words were that he was pleased to be in a Rolls Royce (or a Bentley), because he always met a better class of people there. Speight, forced to drive on thanks to a green light, became a willing captive audience for the next hour as the tramp chatted to his driver, attacking his bourgeois lifestyle and at the same time cadging a lift, even asking if Speight might lend him the use of the Rolls to drive his family down for a seaside holiday, for which he'd receive the princely sum of five bob. Amused by this delicious archetype for Haynes, Speight immediately wrote into the show a sketch featuring Haynes as the belligerent, blazingly self-assured yet socially conscious tramp. The tramp, later to feature in the show's title sequence (complete with cheery signature tune), had powerful self-esteem and was utterly unembarrassed by his social status.

Tramps fascinated Speight, because they existed outside the law and society, and here he could use his thoughts and ideas to question such distinctions. In one memorable sketch, Haynes, with Kenneth Griffith as partner (and with his vertically-challenged parents living in a nearby dustbin!), waits outside the Ritz Hotel for the scraps from the rich clientele inside. 'Arthur' convinces 'Ken' that, if he deploys a bit of philosophy, he will see that they are actually quite similar to the toffs inside – after all, don't they both eat caviar? The tramp characters were to recur many times in the show, using such comic foils as Rita Webb (for whom Haynes, as Oscar Pennyfeather, developed his catchphrase insult, 'rat bag') and Patricia Hayes. Speight later wanted to develop a sitcom series featuring Haynes and Dermot Kelly as the tramps, but this fell by the wayside due both to Haynes's misgivings about the artistic drain of working in sitcoms and to their boss Lew Grade's reluctance to change a winning format in Haynes's present shows. The format was to be resurrected by Speight as *Them* for BBC One in 1972, with James Booth and Cyril Cusack as the gentlemen of the road, and then as *The Lady is a Tramp* for Channel 4 in 1983, with Patricia Hayes and Pat Coombs as the itinerant travellers. The essence of the tramp figure – a man (or woman) totally oblivious of his or her lifestyle, totally confident of his or her opinions and, because of this, always gaining the upper hand, was, with modifications, another springboard for the concept of Alf Garnett.

Speight explored other themes using Haynes's characters – the duplicitous car mechanic or the good-for-nothing decorator; the lazy milkman; the thieving workmate; even a Santa Claus acting as a burglar. There was never any pathos or any attempt to leaven the harsh nature of the sketches. George Black once telephoned Speight and asked him to tone down the content and increase Arthur's innate appeal, because – he stated – every comic needed to be loveable. This was anathema to Speight, whose comic hero was the distinctly unloveable W C Fields, but when he told Haynes of the request, his star simply told him to carry on as before, since *he* enjoyed playing these types of characters so much. Speight's subject matter became distinctly odd, and radically different to that of his contemporaries. In one sketch, Haynes wanders up to proud father Parsons, busily trying to console his wailing baby in a pram, and promptly proceeds to take over, insulting Parsons' skills as a father, and, when the baby does not respond to his cajoling, threatening to clobber it. Another sketch centres on a vicar and his girlfriend discussing the merits of Shaw's *Heartbreak House*, and particularly the scene in which the play's protagonists discuss what they would do if they discovered a burglar in the house – not realising that Haynes is inside their own house, stealing the silver. Haynes is discovered as he willingly joins in the conversation, and the vicar and friend are conned into thinking that his motive for his terrible crimes is that he has a wife and 25 children to support. Unlike other socially-committed writers of the time, Speight considered that the working class were rarely victims of society, did not deserve patronising sentimentality and were not to be used as fodder to be ground down by the exigencies of the class war – they were real people, faults and all, existing in a hostile world, displaying all the passion and skills they needed to survive, and also all their prejudices and preoccupations.

THE THEATRE OF ANGER

From this point, a self-confident Speight was to explore similar ideas in his then-burgeoning career as a 'serious' playwright for the stage, concomitant with the increasingly dark palette he was deploying for his television comedy. In the early '60s, Speight's regular work as comic scriptwriter was satisfying for his finances but insufficient for his spiritual creativity. While he always saw the amusing side of life, Speight's upbringing had raised serious ideas about the world he lived in, and he still needed a vehicle to express these, although not necessarily in a serious manner. He sought a framework similar to that in which Shaw had expressed his ideas, but in a more contemporary mode.

'As a writer ... I wanted more and more to delineate characters who would take the blame for their own abysmal ignorance and bigoted prejudice, i.e. the man in the street or in the Big House or the pretentious middle class, who are responsible for some of the most stupid utterances of our time on race, religion, philosophy and politics.'

During one single night in 1961, he wrote *The Compartment*, a short piece devised as a one-act play, which he then showed to his friend and ALS colleague John Antrobus. The latter loved it. Over lunch in a local restaurant as they discussed it, Peter Sellers appeared, and they suggested that he might present the play for television, with himself as the star. This idea fell through, but Elwyn Jones, Head of BBC Drama, suggested a young actor called Michael

Caine, whom Speight saw at the audition and agreed was ideal for the part. The short play was screened on the BBC in July 1961, and was highly praised by the critics. Caine himself was always grateful to Speight for the step up in his career.

The Compartment involves a middle class businessman in a railway carriage finding that his cosy world is upset by the arrival of a manic, borderline psychopathic younger man who terrorises him on his journey. The young man verges schizophrenically between intense self-belief and vivid insecurity, directing this nervous energy in a mischievous, anarchic, highly aggressive manner. His fellow passenger reacts at first with disinterest, then disgust and finally abject terror as the man pulls out a gun. The protagonist then gives his middle class victim the weapon, which he turns to shoot his tormentor, only to discover that the young man has been playing with his emotions all along and that this – a toy gun – is his final humiliation. The entire affair is never given any motive or reason, which makes it all the more disturbing, and there is insufficient time for characterisation; however the few details that emerge from the young man – a love of jazz, boundless confidence constantly overturned by apprehension, and an endless torrent of words that tumble out of him – suggest that Speight may have been presenting a wishful vision of himself, or at least of his inner psyche. The play's lack of structure has perhaps resulted in its merits being overlooked in the long term, but at the time it was regarded as evidence of a new and startling dramatic talent in the mode of Harold Pinter. (It also enabled Speight to meet one of his heroes, Sammy Davis Jnr, who happened to see it on a visit to London and loved it.) The play showed much of Speight's unique individuality, drawn from his genuinely poor upbringing, his disillusionment with the rigid tenets of socialist politics and his social passion. In a typical 'kitchen-sink' or social protest play of the time, the middle class 'victim' would probably have been portrayed as an arrogant bourgeois fool getting his comeuppance, while in a more traditional drama, he would no doubt have been shown fighting back with middle class decency and incipient moral superiority; values that left-wing writers of the time so despised. In *The Compartment*, however, he is merely transformed into a babbling, incoherent mess by his working class nemesis.

We can see here a further step on the path toward Alf Garnett, *The Compartment* linking Speight's pent-up rage and simultaneous self-awareness of the dangers implicit in its expression, with the knowledge that ultimately such violence is useless when applied to society as a whole. It also connects with the overwhelming self-confidence of the Haynes characters versus the empty middle class world of Mr Nichol-arse; indeed, one can see how it might easily have had its origins in a sketch originally devised for Haynes and Parsons but rejected as too nasty for them to perform. The railway carriage compartment itself is a self-enclosed world in which the angry protagonist can vent his inner feelings to his heart's content, an idea mirrored by the Garnetts' living room later. The main difference here is that the protagonist's anger is ultimately revealed as controlled, as a trick to display superiority, whereas Garnett's Neanderthal howl would be shown to be empty bluster reflecting the insecure emptiness of inner convictions being torn down by the progress of the world outside.

The sheer anger displayed in *The Compartment* was replicated the following year, 1962, in *Playmates*, another one-set piece by Speight, with Caine again in the lead part. Here, a manic young man convinces a spinster that her home is actually a hotel. (When in 1969 the BBC remade both this piece and *The Compartment* and combined them to form one 75 minute instalment of *The Wednesday Play*, they actually treated their respective protagonists as the same character, Bill, played in this instance by Marty Feldman.)

1963 saw the debut, at the Arts Theatre in London, of Speight's most ambitious 'serious' play, *The Knackers Yard*, a full three-act piece that one critic called 'one of the nastiest plays ever staged in Britain'. Dermot Kelly, fresh from theatre in Dublin, played a central role, and was soon to be scooped up by Speight as a foil for Arthur Haynes.

Speight had thus carved out for himself a niche that some have described as 'the Theatre of Anger'. Moreover, he had managed to do so in a very short space of time, just as he was enjoying huge success on the commercial channel writing for an actor who displayed similar anger but in a more obviously comic vein. Speight was now writing apparently 'serious' works with dark overtones that were also funny, scabrous and thoroughly unique, using serious actors in comic situations (Frank Finlay and Michael Caine in *The Compartment*) and vice versa (Dermot Kelly, originally a powerful Irish stage actor, but perceived as a comic thanks to his television work, in *The Knacker's Yard*). Despite Speight's success as Haynes's scriptwriter, it was these three plays that made his name one to watch, and convinced him that in order to progress his art, he needed to focus on situation comedy, replete with dramatic characters in comic form. Here he already had a model on which to build, based on the vision and brilliance of two of his good friends and colleagues at ALS, Ray Galton and Alan Simpson. It was a comedy series on BBC TV called *Steptoe and Son*, and it was unlike anything else on the box.

A VISION IN OIL DRUM LANE

Galton and Simpson had already created a vehicle for Tony Hancock, the biggest comic star in Britain at the time, firstly with a series of groundbreaking radio shows and then with the transfer of *Hancock's Half Hour* to television. In 1962, however, they struck platinum with 'The Offer', their contribution to the BBC's *Comedy Playhouse* – a strand of one-off sitcoms that would run until 1974 and that was used to pilot potential new ongoing series. 'The Offer' featured two 'serious' actors, Wilfrid Brambell and Harry H Corbett, in a comedy set in a rag and bone yard. It featured the deadly serious situation of a younger man forced to live in the same house as his father, trapped by poverty and bound by filial obligation; a younger man with dreams of creative expression and a better life that are utterly alien to his father, who carries on with his soulless drudgery regardless, blindly devoted to his awful lifestyle simply because that is all he has ever known and all he has ever been conditioned to have. Albert Steptoe, the father, has rendered himself oblivious to criticism of this lifestyle, happy in a life built on prejudice, half-chewed knowledge and long-eroded myths, now representing a staid, static view of a world that he *has* to uphold, Atlas style, as it perches forever on the verge of dissolution. Harold Steptoe, his long suffering son, yearns for a more cultured, idealistic world, a socialist utopia, yet also a more dynamic, more protean world that offers him a chance to escape not just his poverty but also his father. The 'joke', of course, is that he can't.

Steptoe and Son, the series spawned by 'The Offer', displayed the same blueprint for the expression of Speight's artistic yearnings as Shaw had dazzlingly revealed, this time illustrating the medium that Speight could deploy, but that Shaw had never known: the television sitcom. It contained all the elements that Speight had become obsessed with in his powerful, unconventional mind: those of working-class entrapment in all its political, social and moral bonds. It also conveyed these ideas in a very down-to-earth, realistic form, in its settings, its acting and its language. The earthy language featured was actually quite radical for television, yet all apposite to the drama – and it *was* drama with comic tonings, rather than comedy played purely for laughs. Furthermore, *Steptoe and Son* was a stunning success, quickly going stratospheric in popularity in 1963 and even achieving political status in 1964 when future Labour Prime Minister Harold Wilson asked the BBC to change its scheduling in order that Labour supporters might go out and vote in the General Election instead of sitting in to watch a repeat of the show. A rigid distinction between comedy and drama on television was forever obliterated by Galton and Simpson, just as George Bernard Shaw and Harold Pinter and Edward Albee had destroyed such categorisations in the theatre. Now Speight thought he could develop his own model based on his friends' genius, and using Arthur Haynes's undoubted gifts of comic realism. Speight's success with his 'straight' plays had therefore revealed another direction to try to present all the ideas of society, politics and philosophy that had burned inside him for so long – he now wanted to use this experience in a more directly comic form.[4] Indeed, Speight and Parsons had been trying for some time to persuade Haynes to use a continuous storyline in each of his shows, and

---

[4] It has to be said, however, that Speight himself never cited *Steptoe and Son* as a source of inspiration for *Till Death Us Do Part*.

thereby take his comedy to a more ambitious level. Speight was becoming fed up with the successful but increasingly difficult job of devising new jokes and sketches with different scenes each week. He wanted a sitcom format that would give him greater freedom to express his ideas. Parsons agreed that this would be a logical step forward both for Haynes and for himself. Parsons pointed out to Haynes that a sitcom was in essence no more than a long sketch, except that it featured the same characters each week, in the same environment, but in different situations. Embryonic situations had been considered in 1962, perhaps indicating the influence of *Steptoe and Son* on Speight.

Michael Caine, having appeared in two of Speight's 'serious' plays, was now recruited onto *The Arthur Haynes Show*. In one sketch, he played the part of a young burglar, diametrically opposed in style and motive to an older counterpart, Haynes, whom he meets inadvertently while burglarising the same house. At first adversarial, they soon discover that their 'job' unites them, and they exit the sketch as the best of friends. Speight developed a friendship with Caine that extended to drinking sessions with such luminaries as Sean Connery, Peter O'Toole, Richard Harris, Ronald Fraser and Patrick Wymark at the Queen's Elm pub on Fulham Road – about which, more later – and, as with all of his buddies, he generously allowed them some influence on the show. Speight and Caine were in the ATV canteen together one day when they spotted a blonde '60s chick whom Caine loudly stated would be 'good to have in the show'; thus Wendy Richard became Haynes's working class daughter, engaged to Parsons' upper class boyfriend. In one sketch, Arthur, Wendy and Uncle Les (Leslie Noyes) sit around a table covered in beer bottles in a shabby dilapidated room, being occasionally showered in plaster as Arthur's wife, upstairs in bed suffering from some mysterious illness (we later learn it is the effects of gin), bangs on the ceiling to attract attention. Wendy remembers suddenly that Nicky, her 'Vice-count' boyfriend, is coming to visit, and Arthur, having checked the time by comparing his trusty archaic timepiece to the modern clock on the wall and finding the latter wanting – a joke later to be reworked as a key element in the *Comedy Playhouse* pilot for *Till Death Us Do Part* – throws things at Uncle Les and tells him to clear up the dinner service (the beer bottles) and put something over the table (at which Les obligingly covers it with sheets of newspaper). When Nicky arrives, Arthur offers the decent, unpretentious but hopelessly dippy boyfriend a meal, and Les, much to Nicky's bemusement, provides some winkles and celery, which the family then proceed to devour. Arthur then slyly demands money from Nicky so that he and Les can go down the pub and leave the two lovers in privacy to indulge in some 'slap and tickle'. Arthur, financially replenished, then shouts up to his wife that he's off to the pub, and immediately the wife recovers and (unseen) runs down the stairs and out the back so she can reach the pub before her husband. The set-up for an awful family was thus in place (although the hilarious scenes as first Haynes then Richard and finally Parsons broke into giggles, were unintended – the Garnett version would be far tighter!).

Behind the scenes, the embryonic sitcom was discussed again, using this family set-up of working-class father and daughter and upper-class boyfriend. Richard later stated that the idea was to retain her and Parsons and then embellish Haynes's ambitions as a social climber while he still appeared resolutely left-wing. It is likely that this format derived a lot of inspiration from the wildly successful Boulting Brothers movie *I'm Alright Jack* (1959), starring Peter Sellers as pedantic union official Fred Kite, who at one point discovers that his daughter (played by Liz Fraser) is seeing the frightfully posh, decent, but desperately naïve Stanley Windrush (played by Ian Carmichael). Add Irene Handl as sensible, long suffering Mrs Kite and the situation is similar not just to that of the Haynes idea but also (with revisions) to that of *Till Death Us Do Part*. Parsons in turn has recalled that a situation format was actually set up for *The Arthur Haynes Show*, and that Haynes eventually agreed to consider it during the summer break. This revised scenario envisaged Haynes as an abrasive, working-class man with a supporting wife, living in a dilapidated house in a street where the other properties were, by contrast, well cared-for by their non-working-class owners. Haynes's 'wives' on his show were nearly always put-upon, helpless creatures, vegetables used to supply the indomitable Haynes's every need; in several sketches, Patricia Hayes was the spouse, intellectually challenged, laconic and obviously living in a world of her own: an early prototype of the 'silly moo'. Parsons would be the young, middle-class neighbour, with a good job in the City, who would become enamoured of Haynes's daughter, Richard, but would be resented by Haynes and seen as a class traitor. Parsons would complain about the desperate state of Haynes's property and lifestyle while Haynes would accuses Parsons of exploiting the working classes. This would set up a series of several storylines. At first, the agreement of Haynes seemed to have been clinched, and Speight and Parsons were eager to commence work on the idea, but when Haynes returned from his break, he summarily dismissed the notion and stated that he would adhere to the tried and trusted sketch format. This was probably in the summer of 1964.

There were several problems with the idea of Arthur Haynes making the transition from his own variety and sketch show to working within a sitcom format. Parsons, as a fellow performer, could understand his decision to stick to the former. As Parsons saw it, apart from an embedded reluctance to learn his scripts, Haynes had a distrust of 'acting' as a means of creating comedy. Whereas trained actors such as Patricia Hayes or Dermot Kelly would learn their lines diligently, Haynes, ever mindful of music hall, wanted to remain spontaneous by simply taking the gist of the lines and adapting them to his style. Having achieved fame and fortune relatively late in life, he was very conscious of the transience of success, and thus very reluctant to accept any suggested changes. He was happy with the variety format of his show (quick sketch/specialist act/sketch/singer/main sketch), which was hugely popular – to the satisfaction of head of ATV Lew Grade – and which he regularly repeated onstage at seaside venues every summer when the show itself was off the air. Why should he change the format when it was so successful? Then there was another problem, too. Speight knew that Haynes would not be keen to be portrayed as a left-wing idiot in the context of a sitcom, whereas in the context of his own show, his bullish character was popular and acceptable. In the early '60s, sitcoms were based around the winning personalities of the performers, who generally retained their natural or showbiz names – Tony Hancock, for instance, was referred to by his real name, as was Sid James in *Citizen James*, and as were Hugh Lloyd and Terry Scott in *Hugh and I*; this was naturally also true of Haynes in *The Arthur Haynes Show* itself. Haynes would not relish having his name associated with raucous political views; and, in any case, he felt that Speight was already entering too dark a territory in some of his sketches. The idea of transforming himself into an actor, *a la* Wilfrid Brambell or Harry H Corbett, was too radical for him.

Speight's ambitions were thus temporarily thwarted. He had already submitted via his friend and colleague Dennis Main Wilson a *Comedy Playhouse* script, which became 'Shamrot', transmitted in 1963 and starring Dermot Kelly as a cunning, self deceiving Irish layabout, but this was insufficiently successful to be granted a complete series. Yet Speight kept the Haynes family format in mind, changing the politics of the main protagonist and retaining the idea of Caine rather than Parsons as his youthful mirror image, and this formed the blueprint for what would eventually become the *Comedy Playhouse* pilot of *Till Death Us Do Part*. By 1966, the Speight and Haynes partnership had already begun to drift, ironically at the same time that Haynes's agent was also recommending to his client that his future lay in sitcom. Haynes nevertheless concentrated on his music hall stage performances. It was while on an engagement in the West End in November of that year that he suffered a fatal heart attack at the age of 52, on the night that his former scriptwriter was going to the London Palladium, his new sitcom – which Haynes had turned down – now a major hit.

C-C-CHRIST, SAID THE KING TO THE ONE-ARMED NIGGER

In the '50s, radio and television comedy was still heavy circumscribed by restrictions on content and style; restrictions that scriptwriters Dennis Norden and Frank Muir summed up in one neat aphorism: 'C-C-Christ, said the King to the one-armed nigger.' Swearing and references to disability, religion, royalty and race were strictly taboo; a legacy of the pre-War world of deference and class system. Naturally enough, in a post-War world that now, as Norden once remarked, 'recognised the literacy of the listener', many radio broadcasters saw these restrictions as a challenge and attempted every which way they could to subvert them. Early attempts were thwarted by the establishment – scriptwriter Sid Colin recalled having to excise 'strewth' as an exclamation from one script, while actor Terry-Thomas could not speak the line 'Poke his eyes out' because of its perceived sexual connotations. Norden and Muir – the latter eventually to become BBC TV's Head Of Comedy and the man who allowed Alf Garnett into the world – pursued a more subtle campaign with the likes of *Take It from Here*, their BBC radio show that ran from 1948 to 1960 and that featured a popular family of characters called the Glums, seen by many as a precursor of the Garnetts. The Glums consisted of an overweening patriarch played by Jimmy Edwards, his laconic wife, his awe-inspiringly daft son Ron, and the latter's whining girlfriend Eth. They were effectively an inversion of the wholesome, establishment-approved Huggett family headed by Joe (Jack Warner) and Ethel (Kathleen Harrison) in the popular 1948 movie *Here Come the Huggetts*. After a war in which the working class had given and suffered so much (and until the mid '50s were *still* suffering, in the form of rationing), a media view that would confirm their nice, salt-of-the-earth, backbone-of-the-Empire values and not question their nasty ones (and so make them real people) was seen as paramount. The new-wave broadcasters, who had seen the class divide with their own eyes, wished to shatter such cosy fictions. 'What we also did,' recalled Norden, 'was to send up relationships between people, family relationships, things that were fairly sacrosanct at the time. We wanted to make the father ghastly, an insensitive pig …'

Hence Glum's idea of a proper home: 'You couldn't have a finer front room for a social evening. Put the telly up on the sideboard and there's room for eight people to pass out in comfort.'

Or Ron's view of social class, as revealed in the following exchange:

Eth: 'If Ron doesn't mix with better-class people, how is he going to get on in life? In this world, it's not what you know, it's who you know, isn't it, Ron?'
Ron: 'Yes, Eth. And I don't know either of them.'

Old man Glum was raucous, bullying, loud mouthed and always sure of himself. Eth saw herself as different, as more sophisticated and more tolerant, yet she was ultimately as empty as her prospective father-in-law, while son-of-Glum Ron was merely a shell devoid of any intellect. In 1962, the Glums made their TV debut in one episode of Edwards' *Six More Faces of Jim* series, also starring June Whitfield and Ronnie Barker, and later featured in a sketch entitled *The Christmas Face of Jim* in the *Christmas Night with the*

Stars anthology; their portrait of working class life, with a revisionist view of its prejudices and idiocies, was still unusual for television at that time, although the advent of *Steptoe and Son*, earlier the same year, was already helping to break down barriers in that medium.

The really earth-shattering work in the battle against the prim and proper, benevolent despotism of the media establishment was, however, spearheaded on stage, with the arrival of 'the Angry Young Men' of John Osbourne, Harold Pinter and company in 1956, and, on a more populist level, in 'kitchen-sink' movies such as *A Taste Of Honey*, *The Loneliness Of the Long Distance Runner*, *A Kind Of Loving* and *Saturday Night and Sunday Morning* – and not forgetting movies directly questioning the ideals and values of the working man, such as *The Angry Silence* or the splendid, aforementioned, *I'm All Right Jack*. The working class were now seen in a more realistic light, with their own attitudes, problems, ambitions and fallacies. The taboos were being broken down, and the first barrier to crumble was that of 'bad language'. On television, *Steptoe and Son* pioneered this development, with its 'bloodies' and 'gits', which despite being perfectly apposite in the context of the show were occasionally challenged in the media. Galton and Simpson had to rely on the determination of their boss Tom Sloan, Head of Light Entertainment (Television), to support them when they wrote one 'bleeding' in the episode 'The Piano'. Such language was authentic, and heartfelt, and added to the realism. Whereas *Steptoe and Son* would provide an inspiration for a realistic framework for Speight to build on, another show was to emerge, again in 1962, that was to furnish him with the opportunity of expressing all his social ideas within that framework: the BBC's satirical series *That Was The Week That Was* – thankfully generally abbreviated to *TW3*. Whereas his own work and that of his friends had already begun to crystallise and give confidence and direction to his ideas, this new arrival was to create an environment in which he could embellish them. The man chiefly seen as responsible for its introduction was the Director General of the BBC, Hugh Carleton Greene, appointed in January 1960, a figure who was to recur several times in the story of *Till Death Us Do Part*. The brother of novelist Graham and heir to the Greene King brewery fortune, Greene had served as Head of BBC Overseas Services during the War, and had then become Director of News and Current Affairs. He had vast ambitions:

'I wanted to open the windows and dissipate the ivory tower stuffiness that still clung to some parts of the BBC. I wanted to encourage enterprise and the taking of risks. I wanted to make the BBC a place where talent of all sorts, however unconventional, was recognised and nurtured, and where talented people could work, and, if they wished, take their talents elsewhere, sometimes coming back again to enrich the organisation that they had started. I may have thought at the beginning that I should be dragging the

BBC kicking and screaming into the '60s. But I soon learnt that some urge, some encouraging, was all the immense reserve of youthful talent in the BBC had been waiting for, and from that moment, I was part of a rapidly-flowing stream. Otherwise, the job could never have been done. Most of the best ideas must come from below, not from above.'

An avid admirer of the Berlin political cabarets of the '30s, Greene had himself directed BBC political satire and propaganda speeches against (and, later, inside) Germany. In 1962, following on from the satire explosion in the theatre pioneered by *Beyond the Fringe* and its architects Peter Cook, Dudley Moore, Alan Bennett and Jonathan Miller, producer Ned Sherrin wished to bring the format to television, and he found a willing recipient in Greene, seeking to reproduce the same satirical atmosphere he had seen in the Weimar Republic for a wider audience.

TW3 began transmission in the autumn of 1962. It encapsulated the theatrical revue format that was so popular in the West End at the time, but incorporated political and social satire and presented it to a mass audience. A weekly, weekend-orientated format ensured that the gags remained as topical as they were controversial. To allow it the maximum perimeters of taste, the show was even produced under the aegis of the BBC Current Affairs Department, rather than Light Entertainment. Despite its late night slot, it was soon attracting a huge audience of around ten million. *TW3* was a landmark show in very way. It was the first to regularly show the interior of a TV studio as it actually looked, rather than as a camouflaged setting; it employed a team of writer-performers, using stand-up routines and specially presented sketches; and, most importantly, it transgressed the age-old broadcasting taboos of combining humour with sex, politics, religion and royalty. Headed by David Frost, Millicent Martin, Lance Percival, William Rushton, Bernard Levin and Kenneth Cope, and with writers including Keith Waterhouse, Willis Hall, Kenneth Tynan and John Mortimer, the show presented, at its best, articulate, biting satire that could launch the weapon of humiliation to devastating effect at any kind of figure in the public domain. It crystallised the view that television could be a dangerous, political medium; and this was to have a far-reaching effect in the '60s. It was in the area of political satire that it was most effective; even in the early '60s, the general view of politicians still existed that they were self-sacrificing public servants, honour-bound to direct the nation in a pragmatic, statesmanlike and selfless manner. Frost and Sherrin knew that politicians were in reality just like the rest of us, and were determined to demonstrate this using the barbs of irreverence and the batons of disrespect. Every aspect of current political life was up for grabs, and television (and, indeed, politics) could never be the same again. As Hugh Carleton Greene was later to write, 'Beneath a bland surface, there was a lack of consensus in British society. By mixing comedy and current affairs, *TW3* brought politics and show business closer together, and show business became an increasingly important part of politics.'

It was in the autumn of 1963, with the onset of the political crises surrounding Prime Minister Macmillan's administration, caused in part by the scandal surrounding the Profumo affair, that *TW3* achieved its greatest success. Willie Rushton would parody Macmillan as a decent yet bumbling buffoon, while John Wells portrayed his political rival Harold Wilson as sly and devious. *TW3*'s spoof on October 19 1963 of Henry Brooke, the Home Secretary, and Alec Douglas Home, taking on the mantle of the retiring Macmillan, was a masterpiece of political satire, with David Frost dressed as Disraeli making the following speech:

> 'My Lord, when I say that your acceptance of the Queen's commission to form an administration has proved, and will prove, an unmitigated catastrophe for the Conservative Party, for the constitution, for the nation, and for yourself, it must not be thought that I bear you any personal ill-will … You are the dupe and unwitting tool of a conspiracy – the conspiracy of a tiny band of desperate men who have seen in you their last slippery chance of keeping the levers of power within their privileged circle. For the sake of that prize, which can at best be transitory, these men are prepared to dash all the hopes of the party they profess to serve: or rather, the two nations which by their actions they seek to perpetuate. And so there is the choice for the electorate: on the one hand, Lord Home, and on the other hand, Mr Harold Wilson. Dull Alec versus Smart Alec.'

This provoked a huge response, with 600 phone calls and 300 letters received. Subsequently, the Postmaster General ordered that certain scripts be vetted in advance. At every level, however, *TW3*'s missile attacks of venomous barbs evoked vastly differing and strongly held views. There was religious uproar when it presented a 'Consumer's Guide to Anglicanism': 'This handy little faith … If you want transubstantiation, you can have it; if you don't, you don't have to …' There was political uproar against the constantly disparaging references to Henry Brooke, the harsh but hapless Home Secretary; against Rushton's portrayal of Macmillan as a dunderhead; against Millicent Martin's singing of astonishingly poisonous songs celebrating such taboos as sex before marriage …

As the show soared in the ratings, it attracted as much flak as it did appreciation. William Haley, the former Director General of the BBC and then editor of *The Times*, suggested that the Corporation was 'in a panic flight from all decent values' and lamented its 'televising inanities', 'a sick, sniggering attitude to life'. Others described the series as 'as smutty as a train window in a Crewe railway siding' (*Daily Sketch*); 'adding a new quality to its irresponsible offensiveness – it is now sinister' (*Time & Tide*); and raising 'questions of taste, fairness, propriety and even libel' (*Daily Telegraph*). The show was at the same time viewed reverently by a large, powerful younger, better educated audience, who relished not only the satire and smut but also the ever-present element of danger always associated with a live show; a guilty delight that reached its apogee with the assault by an angry husband on Bernard Levin, who had criticised his wife's latest artistic work a little too cruelly. *TW3* was television as history in the making, and for a short time seemed to be sweeping all before it.

But the show *was* ultimately answerable, and the BBC suddenly decided not to continue with it beyond 28 December 1963. There were many conspiracy theories as to why it was terminated in mid season. Some believe that it was due to worry on the BBC's part about the renewal of its 12-year charter, due for January 1964; others that it was due to concern about the show's influence on an impressionable public in the light of the probability of forthcoming elections. Indeed, the debut of an approved but less trenchant spin-off, *Not So Much a Programme, More a Way Of Life*, was not scheduled until 13 May 1964, after the country's local elections had taken place. Ned Sherrin thought that the introduction of schoolboy smut in the second series had given the establishment the weapon they wanted to kill the series off; falling ratings or declining standards may also have contributed. Ultimately, Greene was the man responsible, and he later admitted that he had wanted it taken off before the General Election. Here he realised that his position of power had a double edge: 'It was in my capacity as a subversive anarchist that I yielded to the enormous pressure from my fellow subversives and put *TW3* on the air; and it was as a pillar of the Establishment that I yielded to the Fascist hyena-like howls to take it off again.' But Greene was later very proud of *TW3*: 'It opened up the possibility of political humour on television; it signalled new kinds of language, thought and wit. This created the culture of creative space within which *Steptoe and Son* and *Till Death Us Do Part* could prosper'.

Johnny Speight could only admire *TW3*'s power and sheer confidence, which conveyed ideas of social and political anger similar to his own; however, these ideas were generated by the upper middle class, Oxbridge-educated elite, rather than the voice of the working class. Inspired by the show, however, it was only a matter of time before he contributed to it. (As we shall see, another key contributor to *Till Death Us Do Part* would also write for Sherrin's programme.) Again, the catalyst here was Frankie Howerd. Howerd had suffered a career lapse with the advent of the new, more strident style of humour, and, having accepted a residency at Peter Cook's club, The Establishment, had requested that Galton, Simpson and Speight help out with dialogue. Speight, eager to repay his debt to the comic, suggested that Howerd deliver his dialogue as if he was a misfit, 'bringing satire to the level of the kitchen sink'. Howerd's act was so successful as to merit a solo spot on *TW3*, which Speight was happy to supply in the form of a monologue satirising Chancellor Reginald Maudling's recent budget. Hence, on 6 April 1963, Howerd and Speight in one swoop dragged all the Oxbridge upper-middle-class satirical barbs down a chatty, populist, resolutely proletarian level:

> 'Everyone blames Macmillan for sacking half the government last year, you see._*Everyone* blames Macmillan. But, you see, I don't. No. I don't blame *him*. I blame *her*. No, I do! It's *Dot*! Yes. *Dot*. Dotty Macmillan. You can see what's happened; she's obviously got her knife into some of their wives and they've had to go, you see, … and you see that's why *Beryl* – Beryl Maudling – was so shrewd, because, I mean, she and Reg have this farm down in the country, this *smallholding* down in the country, you see, and so obviously what Beryl does is, she brings up a few eggs, and a bit of pork, and a bit of … well, you know …, for Dot, you see, and keeps it with her …'

Speight had now managed to convey a demotic form of politics for the masses, politics that could be related to and discussed by the man and woman in the street. The blueprint thus created for Howerd would reverberate throughout *Till Death Us Do Part* as its principal characters discussed what politics meant for *them*.

THE BRAIN DRAIN

As an alternative to comic realism, and as another symbiosis between the various forms of theatre, Speight was working on another 'serious' play in 1964 when he met the second figure who was to help spawn 'The Monstrous Alf'. This time he considered a different style of satire, based on Samuel Beckett and the Theatre of the Absurd, in the provocatively entitled *If There Weren't Any Blacks, You'd Have to Invent Them*, which was to receive its stage premiere in 1965 at the Pitlochry Festival. It covered all of Speight's favoured bases of society, class and religion, with a *dramatis personae* of army officers, physicians, churchmen, politicians and the working class, setting out his grim view of modern society in a series of interconnected tableaux set in a deliberately artificial netherworld. It was distinctly arty, pressed all the right buttons, and suggested a radically different approach to future work. From the first, Speight envisaged a television production of it, but although Rediffusion and then the BBC expressed interest, they thought it either too controversial or too quirky to take it on. Ultimately, Dutch TV would produce it in 1965, and then, when Speight's star had ascended well into the firmament, London Weekend Television would make versions of it in 1968 and in 1973. As it was, the Theatre of the Absurd did not sit comfortably with Speight's Theatre of Anger, and apart from a half-hearted stab in 1967 with *To Lucifer, A Son*, he subsequently abandoned it in favour of seedy social realism. And the key to this was provided when Speight had a few drinks with an old BBC colleague who now entered the scene on a much more permanent basis.

Dennis Main Wilson, possibly the most influential figure in British comedy after the War, and certainly one of the most important figures in the history of *Till Death Us Do Part*, was born in Dulwich on 1 May 1924. The son of an engineer, whilst at school he developed a talent for languages, particularly French and German. This he later used in the field of media propaganda when he was conscripted into the military during the War. He became Controller of German Communications at Nordwest Deutche Rundfunk in Hamburg, working for Hugh Carleton Greene, later BBC Director General. Dennis had developed a taste for satire and comedy in the European Services Division as a record programmes assistant, playing gramophone records and disseminating anti-Nazi propaganda – one example he cited to Barry Took many years later was that of the characters Kurt and Willy, who had regular chats about the current state of Germany under the Third Reich, one of them fiercely pro-Hitler, the other considerably more doubtful about the Fuhrer, the expositions between them bringing out satirical barbs employed in a fashion that *Till Death Us Do Part* was to maintain over 20 years later. In 1947 he was in charge of the BBC audit for potential entertainers following military demobilisation, and in the process was instrumental in highlighting the talents of Frankie Howerd and Bob Monkhouse, further nurtured by stints at the Nuffield Centre coffee bar in the Strand, where Bill Kerr, Michael Bentine and Tony Hancock developed their acts. Then Wilson took over BBC Radio Variety, and besides developing shows such as *Opportunity Knocks!* and George Mitchell's *Glee Club*, he also encouraged and publicised Harry Secombe and Graham Stark before creating *The Goon Show* (which, he later admitted, only really took off under the aegis of a stronger producer). In essence, Wilson, in the space of ten years, set the landscape for post-War British radio and TV comedy, 'discovering' performers such as Terry Thomas, Kenneth Williams and Leslie Mitchell and writers such as Sid Colin, Talbot Rothwell, Dick Clement, Ian La Frenais and, after a particularly harrowing episode when another producer had a nervous breakdown, Ray Galton and Alan Simpson, who thus gained the opportunity to write for Tony Hancock, changing British comedy forever.

In the early '60s, having developed British TV's first youth programme, the *6 5 Special*, Wilson produced Eric Sykes' television series, on which he worked extensively with Johnny Speight, and then launched the highly successful working-class ensemble sitcom *The Rag Trade*. By the middle of the decade, he was renowned for having an uncanny ability to spot gifted artists and writers. He was also adept at dealing with their eccentricities and idiosyncrasies, such as on one occasion when Hancock suddenly walked out of the recording of a show, forcing Wilson to search desperately for a replacement, which he found in the form of Harry Secombe. He had an unerring ability to improvise quickly and successfully when calamities struck – witness the Galton and Simpson incident mentioned above. Furthermore, he loved dangerous, iconoclastic and satirical material, as evidenced by his development of the anarchy of *The Goons* and by his delight at the consternation of BBC senior management over the amount of flesh on view in *The Rag Trade*. All of this would prove a crucial asset to the frantic world of *Till Death Us Do Part*; it was, indeed, a marriage made in heaven.

Wilson's peers were full of admiration for him. Took described him as 'enthusiastic to the end, often over-zealous, nevertheless a stimulating man to work with'. Galton called him 'remarkable … very supportive and extremely talented'. Simpson said: 'He was very manic. For a 100% result he put in 120% effort. Sometimes he would overwork, become over enthusiastic … but … whatever you wanted from Dennis in terms of the programme, you got.' It was indeed Wilson who urged Galton and Simpson to initiate a new style of comedy based on greater realism, even adding greater authenticity to the radio broadcasts with Hancock by employing real guest stars or announcers, such as commentators Brian Johnson and Colin Cowdrey in a cricketing sketch. This was an approach he was to use extensively in the 1974 series of *Till Death Us Do Part*.

The more eccentric side of Wilson was seen by Frank Muir, who affectionately dubbed him '80% idiot and 20% genius', and by Sammy Davis Jnr, who called him 'Dame May Whitty' when he worked with him in the '60s. Took recalls the time that Wilson blew the entire budget for a series featuring Marty Feldman on the exterior filming alone, forcing the scriptwriters to confine the remainder of the series to a handful of studio sets. Anthony Booth called him 'Brain Drain' and described him as 'a nice man, really, but a bit of a prat'. Wilson had introduced himself to Booth with the line, 'I used to be a nutter, but I'm cured now' … His endless enthusiasm could prove overbearing; when Tommy Cooper, Johnny Speight and Wilson shared a train carriage together one day in the early '70s, Cooper locked himself away in a toilet for an hour just to get away from his producer's endless chatter.

Wilson had worked with Speight on both radio and television. One BBC producer thought him a madman and equated him to one of the proverbial wise monkeys when he made a radio show linking up Speight ('who couldn't talk') with Eric Sykes ('who couldn't hear'). Speight himself dubbed Wilson 'a unique kind of madman that the BBC seems to specialise in (and without whom they would not be able to properly function – they're its life blood in many ways)'. The two men often used to meet socially over a liquid lunch, either at a BBC club or at Speight's favourite restaurant, The White Elephant in Curzon Street, a celebrated showbiz haunt, where they would discuss the state of television and the shortcomings of certain programmes in particular – 'space fillers' such as soap operas *Peyton Place* and *Coronation Street*, then (as now) the most popular show on the box. They disliked the latter show's depiction of uplifting working class virtues and cosy homilies, and favoured a far bleaker archetype of the British working class male – 'a liar, a cheat, a bigot, a materialistic, greedy bastard' as Wilson was to put it in 1991 – a portrait that of course Speight had already been attempting to paint with Haynes. Wilson recalled that, having agreed over a few drinks[5] that they both 'sought a form of comedy that would truthfully depict the shambles that homo sapiens had made out of what God created in those six days (or what evolution created in a rather longer time)' and that they mutually hated *Coronation Street*'s cod working class values and fake families, they 'decided to write about a street and a family that would show *Coronation Street* what writing for streets and families was about. We started with one idea – to knock *Coronation Street* out of the ratings. What resulted came out of Johnny Speight's gift, out of his genius. Nobody sat in an office'.

Then, as now, the Holy Grail for the BBC was to create the show that would dislodge the *Street* from the top ten listings. Speight already had the basic idea for a format, based on the one that Haynes had rejected. This involved a Cockney family headed by a raucous, opinionated, right-wing father with a downtrodden wife, a still-innocent daughter and a loud-mouthed Cockney son-in-law. The attraction of this seemed obvious to the two men. Speight's idea offered polemics, whereas the *Street* offered platitudes; brown-papered reality versus gift-wrapped myth – the ideal contrast, yet also the ideal complement. Initially, Wilson suggested depicting several families in the street, to make the duality doubly delicious, but Speight came back in 12 days with a five page, three minute treatment featuring just one, particularly obnoxious, East End family, with the father named – at that stage – Joe Ramsey. Beryl Vertue, ALS's chief mover and shaker, recalled how infectious his enthusiasm was: 'I remember him coming into my office one day, and he said, "I've got an idea about doing something with a family. A father who's always arguing with his son-in-law."' It would be very, very unusual, but at the same time, quite familiar …

---

[5] Wilson was later to joke that 'the Great Whisky Drought of '64' was down to him and Speight.

4
A Monster Is Born

RAMSEY STREET

Joe – later, Alf – Ramsey is a man in his fifties, who has worked all his life in the same area doing the same job, as a dockhand in the East End. His entire world is centred around the streets he walks on and the house he lives in. He sees himself as affluent poor. His home, of which he is intensely proud, is a two up, two down hovel with an outside toilet and a backyard full of weeds rather than a garden. The wider world is filtered in to this man through a combination of half truths, semi-digested bar room debates and unquestioned mythical origins, all of which he holds dear and clings to with utter dedication while never questioning why. The outside world infringes on this compartment via his obnoxious son in law, and Ramsey stands like a rock, defiant to the vortex of change that is going on around him, threatening his self-enclosed world. As D A N Jones was to note in *The Listener*, he 'sees himself, against all the evidence, as an independent fellow, neither slave nor stooge, having lived through world wars which he sees as the high watermarks of civilisation, the zenith of national greatness, a form of racial and moral superiority maintained by British military power and safely led by a hereditary ruling class'.

He does not regard himself as a member of the working class, whom he despises. But at the same time, he sees his perceived utopia as being in danger of dissolution. 'The peers claim to be lefties,'continued Jones, 'the Queen takes tea with low born Labourites, the authorities whom Alf wants to respect seem more sympathetic to the skivers and the "rubbish" laid-off workers and non-White immigrants than they do to Alf, the last man to notice the change in tone of his masters' voice.'

The only constants in this world of change are his home, his job, his daughter and his wife, to whom he is married 'Till death us do part'. But here the Anglican vow has become a threat, an entrapment, and his wife cares nothing about the changing world, unless it impinges on the minutiae of homemaking, or if it can be used as a weapon to beat her husband. Their marriage may be fixed for eternity, but it is truly bereft of love, sustained only by obligation and tradition. In contrast to this we have the fresh, vibrant, natural love of Mike and Rita for each other, a marriage in the ascendant, one of purity untouched by the march of time (although, as we watch over the series, this too inevitably changes over the years). Change is seen as both the driving spirit and the source of extinction for love. Rita is of the generation that welcomes change, and does not recognise any of the values and totems by which her father abides, and her new husband is a deadly enemy to Ramsey because he sees himself as the architect of such change, even though in reality he reflects values and totems just as vacuous and fatuous as his father-in-law's. Indeed, superficially Mike is the embodiment of everything Ramsey despises – swinging '60s values, tolerance, socialist politics. It is bad enough for Ramsey that Mike has married his daughter, but even worse, the younger man is living under his roof, as trapped in this environment as he is himself …

Thus, much of Alf's background and context are taken from Speight's upbringing, and much of his rage reflects the inner passion of his creator, if not his own beliefs. Similarly, Alf's character is derived from Speight's own experience, while also reflecting the tool of thematic reversal that was perhaps the most revolutionary aspect of *Till Death Us Do Part* – the idea that whatever Alf says, the real message is the reverse. Speight was resentful of *all* authority – political, religious or moral – but gave birth to a character who bows to it unquestioningly. Speight the committed socialist gave birth to a committed Conservative. Speight the atheist created a creature who is (at least in his own mind) a fervent Christian. Speight the autodidact demonstrated a fascination with all politics, social and ethical as well as moral and electoral. *Till Death Us Do Part* was to be about, as Frank Kermode observed in 1974, 'politics in a multiple sense – about the impoverished attitudes to political issues that are all the system allows to most of us; about the relations of husband, wife and children. It was a funny programme, but it had its roots in a sort of political desperation.'

Politics, to Speight, was all-encompassing: 'I thought I could put all the idiot Tory ideas into a working class man's mouth. Because I could never understand how people of that level could ever vote Tory. But that is the tragedy of the Labour Party. As soon as they improve people's lots, [those people] turn Tory. I mean, they get their big, 24-inch television and one car. And they get their house and call it *Mon Repos* or *Dunroamin'* or *Dunvotin' Socialist'*.

Later, Speight was to relate where he got his ideas for Alf's opinions: 'He was a composite of all the people I detested most in my life … I can hear absurd things in the BBC staff club and remember them when I come to write. I go to football matches every Saturday to see Fulham, West Ham or Liverpool. I get a lot of material there and in pubs.'

Speight had a blissfully happy marriage to Connie, whom he had wed in 1956, yet depicted the opposite in the lives of his characters. Fraught marriages were otherwise unknown in '60s television sitcoms. Series such *Marriage Lines* (BBC One, 1961-1966) and *Meet the Wife* (BBC One, 1963-1966) presented archetypal depictions of marital happiness between couples – often one of them middle class and the other working class – who may have encountered problems *en route* but had finished up in connubial bliss. The Garnetts' relationship was more like those depicted in the works of Pinter or Shaw or in Edward Albee's coruscating *Who's Afraid Of Virginia Woolf*, which received its London stage premieres in 1964. But Speight had deployed the downtrodden, mindless wife character type before, in the Arthur Haynes shows, and had witnessed it in *The Glums*; blueprints more conducive to his worldview of the working class than the industrious, cheerful Mrs Huggett of the '40s and '50s. It was a gender-based outlook as well as one founded on class:

> Frank Kermode: 'Alf … has a positive attitude to national history and politics, whereas his wife has nothing of the kind. Is this specialisation of political interest characteristic of working class marriages?'

> Johnny Speight: 'Of all marriages. There's no real freedom for wives; the show of democracy stops at the front door of the mortgaged house. Children – like the Garnetts' daughter – may escape control, but again at the cost of domestic strife. And Garnett's socialist son-in-law, the Scouse git, is as stupid as Garnett. So the workers are still trapped. Their terraced houses are upended into tower blocks, but that's no help … The young have sex on their minds, discover sex, marry and still [desire] sex … It's a great satisfier, or comforter, like a baby's dummy, I suppose. And then, after they've used it up, or got so used to it that it becomes normal, they go over to television, which probably also becomes dull to them. I think they're being cheated, they cheat themselves, and I cannot at the moment see any form of society that's been practised anywhere in the world that is not a cheat … For most people, it's different. It does seem like a sick joke. I mean, you put them into a place where there's no future for them at all, like those mice in wheels that go round and round and round. There's no escape, it seems. Either we cry or we laugh, I think, and some people prefer to laugh, and others cry.'

As we have seen, Alf himself had a number of fictional antecedents: Arthur Haynes' self-confident, scheming character; the anally meticulous Fred Kite; Jimmy Edwards' self-assured but idiotic patriarch in the Dennis Norden and Frank Muir radio show *The Glums*; and also the Tony Hancock character, who is pompous, conceited, selfish, opinionated, sullen, impetuous and self-indulgent. Like the latter character, Alf has no redeeming quality. He rages at everything, but is incapable of controlling either his own impulses or the changes going on in the world outside, mainly because he cannot and has no wish to understand them. Whereas old man Steptoe, another blueprint, is likeable in a pathetic way, Alf does not even share his powers of low cunning and manipulation.

In 1968, Head of Light Entertainment Tom Sloan suggested on the *Talkback* viewer reaction show that Speight had derived his ideas for Alf Garnett from his own father. Speight was quick to dismiss this: 'It's completely untrue that I based Alf Garnett on my father … He isn't like Garnett at all … He's a nice gentle man … He told me some lovely stories that I put into Garnett's mouth. I don't think my father saw Alf Garnett much. He watches ITV most of the time. Once he said, "I hear you've got a good show on the other side."'

Speight's mother liked her son's scripts for the Arthur Haynes shows but hated Garnett because of the character's habitual use of bad language. Warren Mitchell, however, recalled that Speight had drawn inspiration from his father's once stating that he was so proud of the Conservatives that he intended to borrow some boots and walk many miles in order to vote Tory.[6] This indicated right-wing views that contrasted with his son's, but Speight never provided any further evidence of his parents' Conservative values. Speight always insisted that his ideas came from reporting conversations he had witnessed involving embryonic Alf Garnetts at work, at home and at play. His maxim was that he didn't invent Alf or society, he just grassed on them. But one memory of his father was to act as the lynchpin to introduce the then Joe Ramsey to the world:

'There was one little bit in the original *Comedy Playhouse* piece that was my [based on something said by my] father. One Christmas, he was going down to the local [pub] with my cousin, and my cousin said, "They're not open yet". My father looked at his watch and said, "They're open now". My cousin said, "Your watch is wrong. Mine's right. I set it by Big Ben". "You can't go by that," said my father. He had this thing about his watch. It was always right, and you had to live by his time.'

The watch was a metaphor for Ramsey's rigid resistance to the march of time, with its inevitable element of social and political change, with which he was so obviously out of step. And change, as we shall see, was in the air in the '60s; it was a decade all about change, whether one viewed it as 'swinging' or whether one perceived it as 'the sunset decade' as a new society arose.

As David Lazell wrote in 1991, '*Till Death Us Do Part* was not so much an attempt to clarify the issues as [an attempt to present] the raucous voice of an often frustrated public opinion. [Alf] confirmed the views of those who thought things were changing too quickly, or not at all for the better.'

---

[6] That line, Mitchell's favourite Speight sentence, perhaps originally spoken in jest by Speight Snr, was to reappear not in *Till Death Us Do Part* but in *Up the Polls*, spoken by Eric Sykes as Blenkinsopp, the factory foreman from *Curry and Chips*.

5

'Shirley Temple'

Speight now had a script and a format that would combine comedy and drama, family relations and political satire, in one package, delivered in a context of total realism for the masses. He had discussed that script with an influential BBC producer over several afternoons in the bar. Now, in that determinedly '60s manner, he needed another drink, and another conversation, to get the show on the road. And in September 1964, as the nation eagerly awaited a new General Election, the third person to become involved in our story enters, determinedly stage left, at a Labour Party rally in Wembley. His name is Anthony Booth.

Booth had experienced an upbringing even more colourful than Speight's. He was born in Crosby, Liverpool, on 9 October 1931, and his father, like Speight's, was a docker. His socialist tendencies were formed at a much younger age than Speight's, from listening to his Irish-born grandfather's lectures on the evils of royalty following the radio broadcast of Edward VIII's abdication on 11 December 1936. He was also inculcated with the dangers of organised religion, the threat of war (his grandfather was a pacifist) and the evils of 'the Norman establishment'. Naturally enough, despite all this, he had a very devout Catholic upbringing. This he loathed, and it contributed to him becoming, like Speight, an atheist, socialist and republican. After leaving school, he was luckier than Speight in finding menial office jobs rather than factory work, until he experienced National Service (which he despised) at Catterick before being stationed at the American Consulate in Paris. Here, apart from meeting a host of celebrities, the ever-sociable socialist also became involved in political demonstrations and then in the intrigues of the French Communist Party. Returning to Liverpool, he worked for Cunard at the docks and also started acting at Crosby Amateur Dramatics Society. He then went to sea, met a girl and lost all his money and his job.

In 1953, he arrived in London. This led on to some five years' work in repertory theatre in the provinces, where he met his first wife (to whom daughter Cherie Booth – one day to become wife of future Prime Minister Tony Blair – was born in 1954) and started a lifelong affair with Pat Phoenix, later to star as Elsie Tanner in *Coronation Street*. He became well known amongst the Labour faithful for his activism and individual views, beginning with his loud heckling of Party leader Hugh Gaitskell regarding his stance on nuclear weapons in 1956 and his equally loud admiration of Shadow Foreign

Secretary Nye Bevan speaking out in Trafalgar Square against Anthony Eden's intervention in Suez in the same year. He became a member of the North Kensington branch of the Labour Party in 1959 after writing directly to *The Tribune* editor Michael Foot, and then befriended prominent left-wing MP Anthony Wedgwood Benn because of their shared anti nuclear convictions. He was horrified when the Conservatives were re-elected under the leadership of Macmillan in October that year. He accompanied Foot and Benn on CND marches in 1960 and shared a prison cell with Bertrand Russell and John Osborne following a demonstration in Trafalgar Square. Soon after, he worked for Peter Plouvier, the head of the actors' union Equity, to attempt his election as MP for Marylebone in opposition to Quintin Hogg, the Tory candidate who, like Benn, had surrendered his life peerage in order to stand for election. Booth happily heckled Hogg, whose long pregnant pauses proved ideal for disruption, but Hogg nevertheless won the seat. And, to be fair to Booth, he had also heckled Gaitskell – again – in 1960, at the Labour Party conference in Scarborough …

His leftist leanings and acting career also gave him a wide variety of contacts, including in the theatrical world Albert Finney, Tom Courtenay and the Redgrave family, as well as a number of American showbiz stars taking refuge in Europe from McCarthyism. His own showbusiness career moved in fits and starts, with him winning roles in such popular TV series as , *The Saint* (ITV, 1962-1969), *No Hiding Place* (ITV, 1959-1967), *Z Cars* (BBC One, 1962-1978) and *The Avengers* (ITV, 1961-1969) and even a part in that perennial favourite war movie *Ice-Cold In Alex* – until, that is, his one line, 'Sir, I've come to collect the prisoner', was left on the cutting-room floor. Never shy, on one occasion when he had written to a television director regarding a particularly juicy role he coveted, and had received no reply, he cheekily sent him a telegram demanding an answer. The play was a Northern kitchen-sink production, *Pay Day*, that had originally been offered to Patrick McGoohan, who had turned it down; Booth saw the role as an exact mirror image of his own Northern working class upbringing and was determined to play it. His nerve paid off: the director was impressed, he got the role and received excellent reviews and more work, including a short stint on *Coronation Street* (ITV, 1960-), which disappeared when the show went off air during the 1961 Equity strike. In the meantime, he attempted to write some teleplays himself, including an original working-class sitcom set in a Liverpool second hand shop, a format accepted by ATV but then dumped when *Steptoe and Son* took off with a similar idea.

Later in 1962, angered by an army recruitment drive then being conducted through TV adverts, he sent in a satirical sketch on the same theme to Ned Sherrin for inclusion on *TW3*. Sherrin liked it and asked for more, and Booth was delighted when the sketch was criticised by the *Daily Mail*, Richard Dimbleby of the BBC's current affairs programme *Panorama* and John

Profumo, the soon-to-be-disgraced Minister For War. The following year, Booth appeared in an Ealing 'quickie', *The Hijackers*, as a gallant working-class truck driver – again a role he could play with ease – and gained some kudos for his part in an advert encouraging people to join 'the tea set' – i.e. to drink tea.

In 1964, he learned of a new BBC series in preparation. This was *Catch Hand*, which centred around two itinerant building workers whose travels got them into all sorts of ethical scrapes and moral emergencies. One of these two characters, Johnny Rich, was shy, sensitive, articulate and suspiciously middle class, and that role went to Mark Eden. The other, Finn Brodie, was brash, Northern, working class, with a heart of gold. This was the role that Booth coveted, and he used the same trick as before – a telegram, this time to then BBC Head of Drama, Elwyn Jones, simply stating 'Don't cast Brodie until you've seen me' – with the same success. The series ran for ten episodes from 1 July to 2 September 1964 and gained Booth his first regular television exposure.

Booth had just finished working on *Catch Hand* when he attended a Labour Party rally on Saturday 12 September 1964 at the Empire Pool, Wembley, as the Party geared up to fight a General Election the following month against the incumbent Conservative government led by Alec Douglas Home. (Labour, led by Harold Wilson, would be edged into power with a majority of four seats, the lowest of the century.) It was the first British General Election in which politicians had a real awareness of the power of television and the lure and lustre of celebrity; at the rally, while there were working-class archetypes such as the Grimethorpe Colliery Band in attendance, there were also thespians such as Harry H Corbett and Vanessa Redgrave. Booth was hardly in their league from a media perspective, but he was a well-known activist unafraid to speak his mind. And it was while heckling another politician, this time Deputy Party Leader George Brown, for whom the satirical magazine *Private Eye* created that wonderful euphemism 'tired and emotional', that he met Johnny Speight.

Booth had already chatted to Harold Wilson and been given the opportunity to speak on stage. Soon after, he witnessed Brown's speech, in which Brown proudly stated he had secured a job for his brother. At this, Booth shouted out, 'Nepotism; that's bloody nepotism', and caused an uproar. Then Booth heard someone giggling incessantly nearby, and Johnny Speight introduced himself, still chuckling at Booth's nerve. Over a drink or three in the bar, Speight praised Booth for his activism and his acting, and – although this has never been stated – presumably also for his naturalistic portrayal of Finn Brodie in the recently-transmitted series. He also talked about a new sitcom he was trying to get off the ground, and outlined the first draft of a show centred on an East End working class family, the Ramseys, comprising 'a bigoted father, his long suffering wife, their daughter and her left-wing husband'. He also told him that the role of the son-in-law, Mike, had originally been intended for Michael Caine, who was now no longer able to accept it since his career had taken off globally following his success in the movie *Zulu*. Would Booth be interested in playing the part? He handed Booth a script, which the actor staggered home with under his arm. The next day, despite a hangover, Booth read through the script from start to finish, and was amazed by it. 'What a groundbreaking and exciting piece of work,' he was to remark later. 'There wasn't anything like it on television at the time. It dealt with politics, sex and religion – subjects that were then not considered suitable for television comedy'.[7]

Booth could see aspects of his own upbringing mirrored in the realistic situation of the Ramseys. He later recalled in his memoirs those aspects of working-class life that always resonated with him. One example was an incident where his grandfather won some money at the races, got drunk and was thrown in jail; when he later returned home, he was hit over the head with a frying pan by his wife, who then rifled through his pockets to take what remained of his winnings. Then there was the Irish history tutor who despised English history and made up his own version. Other recollections were the constant struggle for money, resulting in part from his father having suffered a debilitating industrial accident; the constant links with petty crime; the black market bartering at the docks; the Catholic sailor who blamed any problem on the Protestants … Some of these memories Booth imparted to Speight, who would use them as the basis for elements of the first series of *Till Death Us Do Part*.

Booth and Speight met again soon after, for another liquid lunch, and Booth suggested that, to add to the conflict in the script, he should play the part of Mike (with the name unchanged) as a Scouser. 'Then there can be a conflict between the north and the south. [Alf] can support West Ham and I can support Liverpool. Then they can really detest each other.'

Speight agreed, and another partnership was born. The two shared similar upbringings and similar political affiliations, and now their respective careers as writer and actor could dovetail neatly to work on a project that would satisfy all their artistic cravings. Booth was thus to influence the early series of *Till Death Us Do Part*, at least in subject matter. We can guess that storylines for episodes such as 'From Liverpool with Love', based on Irish relatives having unthinking obsessions similar to Alf's (in their case, with Catholicism and a mythical Ireland), bits of dialogue such as those about Mike and Rita disrupting political meetings in 'Peace and Goodwill', and the frequent

---

[7] In light of Speight's propensity for the late delivery of scripts, it seems likely that the document both Wilson and Booth read was not actually the full script but merely the treatment later approved by Frank Muir.

mentions of Quintin Hogg – said to be the favourite politician of Alf's wife, Else – were all suggested by Booth. As late as the 1968 series, by which point Booth had twice threatened to leave the show, his friendship with Speight was such that he could suggest an Aldous Huxley story, which Speight would incorporate into 'Aunt Maud'; and they would still drink together during the making of the first *Till Death Us Do Part* feature film, released in 1969. Their political activism later led them to a meeting at the Adelphi Hotel in Liverpool with Harold Wilson, where Booth, characteristically, lambasted the Prime Minister about his policy regarding Vietnam, while Speight asked Wilson if he could verify the rumour that US President Lyndon Johnson would expose himself to heads of state!

Booth would continue his political activities into 1966, campaigning for Wilson to be returned to power in March of that year (a theme used in the first feature film), and then helping the Liverpool dockers who went on strike along with the rest of the National Union of Seamen two months later, upsetting Wilson's fiscal policies. It was during this dispute that Booth met union steward John Prescott – later to become MP for Hull and Deputy Leader of the Labour Party in the government headed by the actor's son-in-law, Tony Blair. He also suggested to John Lennon that the Beatles should play a benefit concert for the Liverpool dockers at Anfield.

Later, Booth became marginalised in the power-plays that brought *Till Death Us Do Part* to the screen. He recalls upsetting Speight – who often used to phone him to tell him his latest ideas and discuss them with him (as he also did with Dennis Main Wilson and star Warren Mitchell) – by saying that the last script he had written simply regurgitated the same old routine, and also veered dangerously toward the right-wing in its approach; their relationship, according to Booth, never recovered from this.[8]

Back in 1964, however, Speight had now found not only a willing producer for his project in Dennis Main Wilson but also a 'name' actor in Booth. Wilson went to the BBC Head of Comedy, Frank Muir, to tell him about the idea and suggest it for *Comedy Playhouse*. Muir was in fact shown a treatment – apparently a few pages of dialogue between Mike and Rita. 'It only ran for three minutes,' he later recalled, 'but the quality of the writing was unmistakeably brilliant.' Muir brought this to the attention of his boss, Tom Sloan, who saw its potential. A *Comedy Playhouse* slot was allocated for it early in 1965, and rehearsal and recording set for June of that year.

---

[8] It is impossible to say when and over which script this falling out took place, but it could perhaps have been the 1974 show 'Party Night', in which Booth's role as Mike is reduced for the first time to a few grunts and moans.

6
The *Comedy Playhouse* Pilot

IF THERE WASN'T ANY ALF ...

The script for the *Comedy Playhouse* episode sets the Ramsey household in 10 Percy Road, Canning Town (later to be changed to an unspecified street in Wapping). It establishes that Rita and Mike have been married for only eight weeks, and that they have only recently moved in to live with Rita's mother and father. During the episode, the young couple search for a home of their own, but because of their lack of money, the places they inspect are always too dingy or the neighbourhood too terrible. The action starts with Alf checking the chimes of Big Ben with his stopwatch, and claiming he has proof that Big Ben is inaccurate – he has even written to Prime Minister Harold Wilson about it. Discussions on politics follow, with Booth's *bête noire*, Deputy Prime Minister George Brown, being referenced in place of an earlier draft's Richard Crossman, then Minister of Housing and Local Government. To add to the verisimilitude, specific details are given regarding property prices – Mike and Rita cannot even afford to get the 20 percent down-payment on a £2,500 mortgage. In order to obtain the £500 required, Mike places an insurance policy on his father-in-law's life. That aspect of the plot soon gets overshadowed by a welter of working-class realism – false teeth in glasses, curlers, outside toilets, booze, trips to the football, a fight with a rival football fan (played by Colin Welland), more booze ... Mike, despite all superficial appearances, is as indolent, self-righteous, self-centred and unprincipled as his father in law, cheating in a card game, going over his wife's head to set up the insurance policy, and revealing himself to be as pedantic as Alf with his watch when he suspects a bank clerk of miscounting a customer's money and insists that it be recounted.

As late as in the first draft script, the head of the family was still called Joe Ramsey – a remnant of the original, left-wing, Joe Stalin-type figure that Haynes had refused, perhaps? – but, in one bright wheeze, Speight then changed this to Alf Ramsey, which resonated not just with the similarly-named new England football manager (whom Speight disliked) but also with the incumbent Archbishop Of Canterbury, who had the same surname. The episode's title, 'Till Death Us Do Part', alluded not simply to the Anglican marriage vow, but also to the life insurance policy Mike had taken out on his father-in-law.

With Tony Booth already on board to play Mike, Dennis Main Wilson and Johnny Speight now had to cast the parts of the other Ramseys – Alf, his wife Else, and his daughter Rita.

Else's part was filled by character actress Gretchen Franklin. Franklin was born into a theatrical family in Covent Garden on 7 July 1911. Her father had a song-and-dance act, and her grandfather had been a well-known music hall entertainer at the turn of the century. She began working as a £2.00-a-week chorus girl in pantomime in Bournemouth. In 1929, she took dancing lessons at the Theatre Girls Club in Soho in London's West End, and she soon became a renowned tap dancer and founder member of a quartet known as Four Brilliant Blondes. She toured with *The Gracie Fields Show*, married Caswell Garth – a writer of revue sketches – and performed with another dance group, The Three Girlies, before making a gradual switch to straight dramatic roles. Her first West End break came during the War, when she landed a part in *Sweet and Low*, the first of a series of revues at the Ambassador's Theatre. Subsequently her career as a character actress burgeoned, landing her roles in such popular TV shows as *Armchair Theatre* (ITV, 1956-1978), *Gideon's Way* (ITV, 1965) and *Danger Man* (ITV, 1960-1968) and in the B-movie series *Scales of Justice* (Merton Park, 1962-1967). Readers may know her best from her appearances between 1985 and 2000 as Ethel Skinner in the BBC soap opera *EastEnders*. Her latest appearance at the point when she was cast as Else was in the Beatles film *Help!* – in which Warren Mitchell, Leo McKern, Roy Kinnear, Patricia Hayes and her friend Dandy Nichols (all, as we will see, significant names in the *Till Death Us Do Part* story) also had roles.[9]

Una Stubbs was cast as Rita. Born in 1937, the daughter of a factory worker, and brought up in Leicestershire, Stubbs had begun her career as a dancer, appearing nude at the Folies Bergère in Paris during the '50s, her 30-inch bust hidden by wafting feathers. Her aggressive style of dancing earned her the affectionate nickname 'Basher' Stubbs, and she used to show off by kicking her shoes into the audience. 'I was pathetic,' she later said. 'I just wanted to be noticed.' Early television appearances came on the ITV pop show *Cool for Cats* in 1956, when she featured as one of the Duggie Squires Dancers, then as a regular dancer on *Sunday Night at the London Palladium* (ITV, 1955-1967). She also danced at the grand opening of the BBC's Television Centre in 1960. More television appearances followed with *Rush Hour* and Anthony Newley's *The Strange World Of Gurney Slade* (ITV, 1960), and she then broke into movies with Cliff Richard in *Summer Holiday* (1963) and

---

[9] It would be nice to think that a chance viewing of *Help!* inspired the casting of most of the lead roles in *Till Death Us Do Part*, but the movie was not released until July 1965, after the *Comedy Playhouse* programme had been made. Speight had been asked to write the first Beatles movie, but had to turn it down due to prior commitments.

Wonderful Life (1964). This led on to an offer of work in Hollywood, on condition that she changed her name – 'which sounds like a fag end', as she put it – but she refused. Also in 1964, she worked on the Galton and Simpson movie *The Bargee*, alongside Eric Sykes and star Harry H Corbett. As dancing roles began to dry up on television, she sought to develop her acting career further, and *Till Death Us Do Part* provided her first significant role.

She confessed she was 'a terrible giggler' and had almost got expelled from school for it: 'It was the only thing I could do, you see. I was hopeless at everything else.' Later, when criticised by a viewer on the grounds that her on-screen giggling in *Till Death Us Do Part* was too distracting, she said that all the laughter was actually written in by Speight, and that sometimes she had to giggle through two pages of the script: 'Sometimes, I have to laugh for ages.' At the time, she lived in Hertfordshire with her husband of several years, actor Peter Gilmore, whom she had met in pantomime. Asked in a 1968 interview about her initial reaction to being cast as Rita, she said: 'I thought they wanted a big, busty blonde, yet they settled for a skinny brunette girl from Leicester, not even a Cockney. My natural inflections are contradictory, and Rita's accent was difficult for me at first. I'm much more confident now, though.' Years later, she reflected: 'I was very conscious of my lack of experience. I mean, I wasn't an actress and I wasn't a Cockney … I felt a bit of a fraud doing it, when there were probably millions of girls out there who could have done it better.' Una Stubbs was to provide the moral compass for her co-stars while recording *Till Death Us Do Part*, in the same way that Rita provided the moral compass for the Garnetts; yet another example of the show's abiding capacity to intertwine real life with on-screen art.

Casting of the most prominent role, that of Alf Ramsey, was left, for some reason, until the very last minute. Speight and Wilson had initially considered offering the part to either of two of their friends, Peter Sellers and Lionel Jefferies. Sellers was apparently keen to activate a small-screen career to match his movie stardom, but the latter took up all his available time, and indeed he was filming *What's New, Pussycat?* in Paris that summer. Speight later stated that Sellers was the first choice for many of the roles he conceived and that, owing to the actor's prodigious talent, he circled around him like 'a moth around a candle'. However, Sellers had already dropped out of any consideration for the lead role in *The Compartment* in 1961, and now his star status effectively made it impracticable for him to take on television projects. It is, in any case, difficult to envisage how a series could have been sustained with Sellers in the lead. The prospect of Sellers playing Ramsey therefore evaporated; and likewise the idea of Jeffries being cast came to nothing.

It is easy to see why both Sellers and Jeffries might have been considered suited to the role of Alf Ramsey. Sellers could easily have played him as a dour, methodical, unchanging and militant creature not dissimilar to Fred Kite in *I'm All Right Jack*; and Jeffries was an equally versatile actor who could cope well with both comic and serious material, as evidenced by his performances as the Marquis of Queensbury in *The Trials of Oscar Wilde* (1960) and as the comic gangster in *Blue Murder at St Trinian's* (1957). In truth, though, the idea that either of these established stars might take the role was simply unrealistic. As we shall see, both Speight and Wilson were later to come up with a succession of frankly wistful ideas for possible guests stars, all of them working associates or drinking partners, which were usually abandoned in the cold light of day when everyone realised that the stars in question were now either too big or too busy to commit themselves to a television series.

The other option was to secure a lesser-known character actor to fill the part, as had been done on *Steptoe and Son* with Harry H Corbett and Wilfrid Brambell, who were both excellent dramatic actors but unknown for their comic ability prior to the brilliant Galton and Simpson vehicle for their talents. Many years later, perhaps mindful of his experience with Arthur Haynes, Speight declared that he had wanted to take this approach from the beginning: 'Alf Garnett was a bigot. So bigoted, he was a figure of fun … No well-known comedian would play such a part. A comedian, to a large extent, plays himself. If he played this part, it would alter his accepted personality, it would be bad for his image. We decided to go for an actor, not a known comedian, because an actor would play the part as written and not worry about his image.'

Leo McKern was Wilson's next suggestion for the role. McKern was a fine character actor who had just completed filming his scenes for *Help!*, and Wilson had worked with him on *Sykes*. Booth recalls that McKern was pencilled in right up to the week before rehearsals in early June 1965, but threw the production team into panic when he telexed Wilson from the Azores, where he was sailing his yacht, and stated that he could not make it to London in time: 'BECALMED OFF THE AZORES. UNABLE TO BE AT THE REHEARSALS ON MONDAY. GOOD LUCK FOR THE SHOW. LEO.'[10]

Anthony Booth recalls that, having crashed out at Speight's place after another night on the tiles, he was present when Wilson phoned up on the Friday morning prior to the rehearsals to read McKern's telegram to Speight. Wilson then spent the rest of the day trying to find another candidate, which he succeeded in doing by late afternoon. There was to be a read-through the following Tuesday, 8 June 1965, some filming the next day, rehearsals between

---

[10] There have been conflicting accounts given as to exactly how close McKern came to playing Alf Ramsey. Thirty years later, McKern stated that although he knew he had been considered for the part, he had never been directly offered it. In 1997, Wilson said that Sellers was first choice, but he was busy filming in Italy at the time, and that McKern was second choice, but had just come from Hollywood 'and didn't want to know'. To add to the confusion, Warren Mitchell has stated that McKern was first choice.

14 and 17 June, and the show would then be recorded in the studio on Friday 18 June. Wilson had suddenly remembered an actor who had made quite an impression on him as a character called Pongo Wilberforce in the recent Barry Took/Marty Feldman comedy *The Walrus and the Carpenter* (BBC One, 1963-1965) …

THE FUNNY FOREIGNER

Warren Mitchell, born Warren Misell into a Russian Jewish family in Stoke Newington on 14 January 1926, had initially led a rather more privileged existence than either Speight or Booth. His father, Monty, was a china and glass merchant, very middle class, and his upbringing was very orthodox Jewish. He later said of his father: 'He was a racist of sorts. He had that "Jews only enter here" attitude, and he could see anti-Semitism everywhere. We'd go to a petrol station – we had a car, and that put us rather "above" – and if the guy spilled a bit of petrol, my father would say, "Ah, he's anti-Semitic", and I would say, "Dad, he doesn't know you're Jewish", but he'd say, "They know, they know".'

When he was a boy, his father would not allow him to bring non-Jewish friends home. Even later in life, when Mitchell met his actress wife Connie, because she was not Jewish, his father was reluctant to meet her. 'He used to ring me up and say, "Son, are you eating? Come for lunch." I'd say, "With Connie?". He'd say no, so I didn't go.' This rift was later healed when Warren and Connie had children.

Mitchell was 15 when his mother died, and this, together with the realisation that an angry Yahweh had not struck him dead when he blasphemously played football for the school team on Yom Kippur, convinced him that he could never become an orthodox Jew. He studied Physical Chemistry at University College Oxford until 1944, when he gave it up to join the RAF, training as a navigator in Canada. While in Oxford, he saw his friend Richard Burton perform on stage, and it was this that inspired him to make acting his profession. But he had been involved in entertainment all his life, aided by his father: 'When I was four, I told a dirty joke to my family (involving a pun on the French "Oui, oui" and the punchline "Not all over my new carpet"). My father laughed, clipped me round the ear and sent me to bed. I learned two things right there – that showbiz is tricky and audiences are fickle.'

Mitchell's mother had introduced him to the delights of music hall, taking him to see the great comedians of the day, including Max Miller, Vic Oliver, Ted Ray and the Crazy Gang; he said that between 1937 and 1941, he never missed a show at the London Palladium or the Holborn Theatre. He joined the Royal Academy of Dramatic Art (RADA) at around the same time he joined the Communist Party; he used to cheer whenever Stalin appeared in the Soviet films he enjoyed. ('Madness, sheer madness' was his later reflection on this, although he always classed himself as being to the left of the Labour Party.) He met Connie – actress Constance Wake – while attending a left-wing amateur dramatics group at the Unity Theatre; this was the same socialist artistic collective that Speight had attended and dismissed as 'bloody fools'. 'I had two jolly years learning posh at RADA during the day,' recalled Mitchell, 'and I was duly de-poshed at the Unity Theatre at night.'

During his early years, he also took other jobs, including as a night shift worker in a Wall's ice cream factory (the lack of sanitary arrangements in which so shocked him that he would never eat ice cream again), as a window cleaner, as a bottle factory worker and as a porter at Euston. In the latter, he initially wondered why the other porters would not allow him to get in line. He was told by another porter, 'It's yer la-di-dah accent', prompting an angry Mitchell to shout out, 'Who's next in the line, you bastards'. He claims it was here that he met his first 'know all' Alfs.

In the '40s, Mitchell understudied Alfie Bass in the theatre, was given a job singing in a band for £10 per week, and worked on Ted Willis's stage production of *The Blue Lamp* at Worthing Rep, being granted permission to use his own material in his role as a stand up comic; he later claimed that his impersonations of James Mason and Robert Newton had been not at all appreciated by the audience. He became a stooge to comedian Richard Hearne's famous Mr Pastry character, impersonating TV cook Richard Harben with fake moustache and beard and getting covered in flour and water each day, and then also to American stars Abbott and Costello on their British tour.

In 1951 he was still scraping by when he married Constance, hiring a wedding ring from a pawn shop and celebrating with a 2s 3d dinner for two at a Greek café in Kings Cross. Mitchell's career really did not take off until the mid '50s, and then much of his work was done on television. His swarthy looks and small stature helped him find a very profitable niche playing 'funny foreigners'. In 1966, he said that he was often asked to play Jewish roles that he thought were badly written; he refused to appear in one production in which the only Jewish character was a 'fence'. On the other hand, he believed that programme-makers were too sensitive to be daring in the depiction of Jews on television. (He said he had once asked Muir and Norden to write a comedy based on him as a Jew, but they had been too afraid. Ironically, in the role of Alf Garnett, he was later to spend a great deal of time *denying* that he was a Jew.) He said he had changed his real name because no-one had been able to spell it correctly when he had stood in for Pete Murray as a DJ on Radio Luxembourg, conscious that despite his British heritage he would always appear 'foreign' – a fact he was to use to his advantage in countless roles in '50s and '60s television series: 'I learned so many snippets of foreign languages that I can still go into a Greek restaurant and say in impeccable Greek, "Take your filthy hands off me. I stole the cigarettes from the hold of the ship. I'm sorry I yielded to temptation. I plead guilty". It knocks them for six … It came from a film I did with Yul Brynner.'

Apart from a funny Greek accent, he also did funny Italian (*The Saint*), funny Russian (*The Avengers*), funny Spaniard (*The Curse Of The Werewolf*) and funny Roman (*Carry On Cleo*), amongst many others. It was also this talent that enabled him to enter pure TV comedy, although he had frequently brought a comic slant to his 'straight' roles. In 1956 he auditioned for a part in *Hancock's Half Hour*: 'Just before I auditioned for the show, Sid James, whom I knew, popped out and said, "Go in and do your funny foreigner, and you'll get the job". So I did – he was right.' The role was that of a continental art/book dealer: 'It was live, and Tony came into the bookshop and said his first lines and then dried up completely. I said, "Mr Hancock, a word in your ear," and whispered the next line to him'. A grateful Hancock secured his services for more shows in the series, and even obtained for him half a page of much-needed publicity in the *Daily Mirror*, focusing on 'TV's new bearded comedian'. Mitchell's early work as theatrical understudy to Alfie Bass helped him get a part in Bass's hit comedy show *Bootsie and Snudge* (ITV, 1960-1974), with Bill Fraser. (Mitchell was later to repay both actors with roles in *Till Death Us Do Part*.) At one stage, he even attempted to return to his ambitions of being a stand-up comic himself, appearing on Benny Hill's comedy showcase: 'I was awful. It began with a song and ended with a monologue: "Her perfume was distinctive … just a touch of home-made gin … that dear old mother of mine." There was no applause. They hated me. I died a death, and I even thought I'd give up the business.'

Following on from his *Hancock's Half Hour* roles, Mitchell appeared in two Galton and Simpson *Comedy Playhouse* productions – 'Clicquot et Fils' with Eric Sykes in 1961, and 'The Channel Swimmer' with Sydney Tafler in 1962 – and also in the 1965 Arthur Haynes radio series that Speight had created. Thus Mitchell had already registered several times on the Associated London Scripts radar; but he had yet to gain 'name' status. Indeed, he later recalled that he was initially reluctant to commit himself to the *Comedy Playhouse* 'Till Death Us Do Part', because he thought he lacked that 'indefinable star quality'. Nevertheless, he decided to give it a go …

THE BIGGEST LOAD OF CRAP …

The first meeting of production team and cast, with Warren Mitchell as the latest addition to their ranks, proved to be a harbinger of things to come. Anthony Booth had again stayed the weekend at Johnny Speight's, and they arrived at the BBC rehearsal rooms in good spirits, full of excitement that at long last the show seemed about to be under way. Mitchell, arriving half an hour late, was introduced by Dennis Main Wilson to the writer, to director Douglas Argent and to the other cast members. Then, without any apology for his tardiness, Mitchell launched into a scathing attack on the script, hurling it across the table and claiming, 'That's the biggest load of crap I've read in my life!' As soon as they saw this, Booth and Speight, amused at his temerity, realised that great things were promised ...

Mitchell genuinely despised the script, according to Booth, and delivered a ten minute tirade against its inadequacies. Since he had accepted the part, and since he later became one of Speight's greatest admirers, it seems likely that his concerns related more to the structure of the script than to its incipient dialogue. The original draft starts with the family playing a card game, and with Mike winning, in response to which Else comments, in a deadpan way, that it seems very unusual that ever since Mike moved into the Ramseys' home, he has won every card game that he and Alf have played. The implication that cheating is involved is hushed up, and the conversation moves on. Later in the scene, Mike inadvertently drinks out of the mug in which Else usually places her false teeth, spraying Alf with beer when he realises his error. He offers Alf his handkerchief to mop up, and as he extracts this from his jacket pocket, the cards with which he has been cheating fall out and scatter on the floor, arousing Alf's titanic wrath. After the subsequent row, however, Mike and Alf go to a football match together, and Mike stands up for his father-in-law against an irate soccer fan. At the end of the episode, the pair stagger home blind drunk, having bonded together after a few post-match pints. Thus the episode ends on a muted and utterly uncharacteristic note with Alf praising his new son. The revised camera script, however, sees a structural alteration that provides a far superior payoff, with the cards falling out of Mike's jacket *after* the apparent bonding, thus defusing Alf's sentimental praise and ending the show on a flourish. One may suspect Mitchell's influence here; the actor would always respect Speight's dialogue, while occasionally adding his own ad libs, but would not be averse to suggesting structural changes, while insisting that these be subject to Speight's personal approval. Thus during the recording of the third series, for instance, he would insist, much to Speight's own chagrin, that the writer be dragged in to rehearsals to approve structural changes in his 'Monopoly' script; Wilson himself would have to fetch a bleary-eyed Speight from a soiree at Annabel's, the exclusive club in the basement of the Clermont Hotel in Berkeley Square.

Simultaneously, some of the business that Booth had apparently added to the draft *Comedy Playhouse* script – including a bedroom scene in which Mike walks around the room with a chamber pot on his head – seems to have been excised from the final draft. Many years later, Mitchell was to state that he sometimes got angry with Booth because the latter tended not to learn his lines and to put in unfunny ad libs. This conflict took off right from the outset, as it became obvious during rehearsals that Mitchell and Booth could not get on. Booth later attributed this partly to the fact that he was convinced *Till Death Us Do Part* would be a success, while Mitchell was equally convinced it would not be. A more likely explanation is that the very driven and puritanical Mitchell could not approve of Booth's more laid-back attitude to acting. By the Wednesday of the week of rehearsals, the two men were no longer on speaking terms. Booth saw all his early optimism evaporating. On the Thursday prior to recording, there was a rehearsal involving a new scene. Mitchell accused Booth of not learning his lines. Booth exploded and stated that he was word perfect; an assertion corroborated by the script girl. He demanded an apology, but Mitchell refused. Booth stormed out. Thoroughly depressed the next morning, Booth received a call from Wilson stating that Mitchell regretted his behaviour and would apologise to Booth that day. Booth was perfectly amenable to this, but on the set, as soon as Mitchell saw Booth, he asked everyone to stop for an announcement: 'I am sorry. Those who were there will know why I am making this apology to Tony. My director rightly insists that I apologise to my fellow actor. It was totally wrong of me to make the baseless accusation that I did.' Because not one word was directed to Booth, he could not accept Mitchell's apology at all, and this left the situation between them just as bleak …

Theatre director Peter Hall once described Mitchell as one of the most insecure actors he had ever met; Brian Rix, with whom Mitchell worked on *Men of Affairs* in 1973, suggested that he adopted an aggressive stance and refusal to suffer fools gladly as a defence mechanism for his insecurity. But Mitchell was dedicated to improving his craft, and he was already attending Stanislavski method-acting classes that summer of 1965 when he began work on the *Comedy Playhouse* programme. Here, he was to *become* the role he played, replete with obnoxious manner and abusive demeanour, and this attitude was to cause a great deal of trouble for other members of the cast in the future …

There were problems not merely amongst the actors. Wilson had a radical new idea for the opening scene of the show:

Open on close-up of Big Ben just as the clock is about to start to strike 12. Then pull away and past it and pan down river towards Mile End. Close-up on slum district, into one street and then into one house and into living room of house. A typical working-class living room with the usual collection of old furniture etc. The family, Joe [sic] Ramsey, his wife Elsie, his daughter Rita and her husband Mike. The father and son-in-law are playing cards. The son-in-law is obviously winning as there is a small pile of money by his elbow. The opening establishing shots from Big Ben into the house have been accompanied by the strikes of the clock and they are still striking as we enter the living room and the last two or three strikes of 12 are actually heard in the room coming over the radio. As the last strike dies away, Alf Ramsey pulls out his watch from waistcoat pocket and looks at it …'

This would then mix through to live action in the studio and begin the script dialogue. Wilson approached Head of Comedy Frank Muir, fresh from a two week management course on which he had been lectured on the dangers of overstepping budgets, and told him his gloriously cinematic idea, together with the necessary logistics for the hire of a helicopter, at £400 per hour. Muir was dubious; already the budget for the show would be overstretched. Gradually, however, he was won over to Wilson's view of 'Bugger the budget'; for artistic reasons, he agreed to the producer's requests and gave him the go-ahead. Then Wilson dropped a bombshell. The £400 would stretch to paying for only a one-rotor helicopter over the Thames; to shoot the East End sequence, flying over land, they would need a twin-rotor copter by law, and that would cost £850 per hour. Muir, increasingly worried, but still convinced that the idea was a brilliant one, reasoned that Michael Peacock, the new Controller of BBC One, might be sympathetic, and if asked nicely might provide contingency funds. Once again he agreed, and cautiously gave the enthusiastic producer the green light. Then Wilson dropped his other bombshell. He thanked Muir, gulped, and then nervously stated that since he had counted on Muir's support, he had already filmed the sequence. And it hadn't worked … Thankfully, when Muir approached Peacock, the latter was amenable, and agreed to make available extra funds to re-shoot the sequence, while at the same time giving Muir a lecture on financial discipline. Muir recalled the hair-raising vision of Wilson subsequently directing the helicopter pilot to fly ever lower over the cranes and derricks of Wapping, risking everyone's life and limb in the pursuit of artistic excellence.[11]

Wilson was notorious for his wild excesses of enthusiasm; later the *Till Death Us Do Part* team would become aware of his other penchant, alcohol. Barry Took recollects that Wilson never learned from experience, later spending the entire budget for Marty Feldman's series *It's Marty!* (BBC, 1969) on pre-filmed inserts well before the series was recorded. But Wilson

---

[11] Muir recounts this tale when recalling the making of the first series of *Till Death Us Do Part* rather than the introductory *Comedy Playhouse* episode. However, the aerial camera directions leading in to the opening scene in the Ramsey household appear in the *Comedy Playhouse* script, establishing the link between Big Ben and Alf in concise visual manner. Handwritten addenda mention that a helicopter, hired from Battersea Heliport for £70 an hour, can fly to a limit of 500 feet over London and will be a 'whirlwind' type with open door. Perhaps the sequence was made for the *Comedy Playhouse* pilot (to start directly after the opening *Comedy Playhouse* titles) and then reused for the subsequent series, thus saving some of the initial budget outlay. Since the *Comedy Playhouse* pilot no longer exists, it is difficult to be certain, but this hypothesis seems to fit both sides of the story.

was gold dust in the production world; although viewed as scatty and downright weird, he was invariably successful in both artistic and commercial terms, because he respected the creative vision and talents of the writer and cast.

The production had one more hurdle to overcome: winning popular approval for the show itself. Initial signs were not encouraging. Booth recalls that during technical rehearsals he heard not a single laugh from the camera crew. The actual taping of the show took place before an invited studio audience of 300 on Friday 18 June 1965, with each of the cast introducing himself or herself prior to recording. Booth remembers that for the first 15 minutes not one titter was heard from the audience. There were, after all, no indicators that this play was intended to be humorous, only straight acting from a superlative cast. Booth thought that Mitchell's pessimism might be proved correct. Then someone laughed at one of Alf's tirades, and this drove Mitchell to up the volatility, ad-libbing gestures, raising the sound of his voice, and in turn inspiring Booth to react on a heightened level. Suddenly, the audience got the message, and began to laugh. Recording overran by 20 minutes; the audience was in uproar and gave the cast an ovation. According to Booth, when the show was eventually transmitted, at 8.50 pm on Thursday 22 July, it started with five or six lines of original material, then the embarrassing silence of the early stages of recording was edited out to cut straight to last 27 minutes with hysterical audience reaction; the meaning of the title 'Till Death Us Do Part' became lost in the process. Since the BBC have wiped the show (although a two-minute extract survives courtesy of a clip shown in *Late Night Line Up* of 7 January 1966), it is hard to judge the truth of this, but by the strict timing standards of television recording, it seems unlikely either that the episode had significantly overrun or that such cuts had actually been made. Booth, who had not really been involved in sitcoms prior to this, may have simply misinterpreted an initial muted reaction from the audience while they adjusted to the show's unfamiliar scenario.

But the show still had to meet with mass approval from a television audience. Advance publicity came in the form of a *Radio Times* synopsis, written by Dennis Main Wilson, placed alongside a photograph depicting not Alf but Mike and Rita on a sofa:

Poor Else Ramsey (Gretchen Franklin) has an unnerving family to put up with. Her husband Alf (Warren Mitchell) is normal in every way except in his attitude to Big Ben. For years he has been convinced that this towering symbol of British stability and punctuality has been telling lies. In fact Alf reckons that his 30 year old watch keeps better time than the monster clock; his driving obsession is to prove his theory correct. Else's problems do not end with Alf; there is her married daughter Rita (Una Stubbs) as well. It is not so much Rita herself as her husband Mike (Anthony Booth) who is the problem. He has no job – which makes it very difficult for him and Rita to accomplish their hearts' desire, namely the placing of the down-payment on a house. Rita and Mike are living in the Ramsey household and naturally tensions arise. The atmosphere becomes really charged when Mike finds that the only way to raise the money for the deposit is for him to take out an insurance policy on Alf's life.

This synopsis highlights how Speight's unique comic slant was being placed within a framework of traditional comedy values; and it seemed to work. The audience and the critics loved it. The programme gained a Reaction Index figure of 67, second only in that season of *Comedy Playhouse* to the previous Thursday's 'Hudd', which had 68. The BBC's audience reaction report recorded some of the opinions of the carefully selected demographic sample. An electrical engineer: 'Oh how delightfully vulgar! I laughed and laughed and yet in many ways, it was all quite true to life.' A housewife: 'Hope this is a taste of things to come.' Generally the opinion was that this was 'one of the funniest shows since [the] Steptoe [episode]'. Two thirds of the sampled audience were delighted with the programme's humanity and realism, reflected in its refreshingly natural dialogue, albeit that this was seen as somewhat crude at times. They loved the uninhibited Cockney family, especially the dad, 'a real character' (so said a sheet metal worker). In the interests of balance, the report also noted the negatives: some in the sample had found the programme distasteful, 'hardly edifying'; some had found the language unnecessarily coarse; and some opined that they rarely found working-class 'slanging matches' particularly funny. There were also criticisms regarding the storyline, which some thought had petered out at the end. Overall, the show was considered well played by the cast. Warren Mitchell was said by most to be highly realistic as Alf, although Una Stubbs 'didn't seem too happy as a Cockney'. While the fight at the football ground was regarded by some as unconvincing, otherwise the production was seen as satisfactory.

If the public were happy, the critics were ecstatic: prominent *Daily Mail* writer Peter Black, soon to prove one of the programme's strongest champions, wrote: 'The most successful of this season's *Comedy Playhouse* was Johnny Speight's "Till Death Us Do Part", which took me into a solitary purple haze of laughter. The awful family he created must not die with but one performance.' Even the provinces liked the show, the *Birmingham Evening Mail* declaring: 'But fun was in the air, too – great guffaws of it in the BBC's *Comedy Playhouse* production of "Till Death Us Do Part". There was a laugh a line in this kitchen sink comedy of a young couple living in the house of the girl's parents.'

After the transmission, the jubilant cast celebrated, Speight and Wilson drinking champagne all night at the White Elephant, revelling in the early newspaper reviews that lauded the show. Their ecstatic view that they had a winner on their hands was affirmed next day when they continued drinking at the BBC bar and found their show praised by their peers. At lunchtime the following Wednesday, 28 July 1965, Speight, Wilson and Tony Booth ventured into the BBC Club again. Wednesday was the day when the BBC senior management team regularly met to review the previous week's television output and considered in the process whether or not that week's item in the *Comedy Playhouse* slot had series potential. According to Wilson, the triumvirate were eagerly awaiting the news, betting on it being a foregone conclusion, and were once again submerged in a sea of alcohol, when Tom Sloan walked in, followed by the other BBC grandees. Speight instantly approached the Head of Light Entertainment (Television), the very military-looking Tom Sloan, and stuttered, 'A-A-A-A what about that for a bloody series, mate, eh?' Sloan, who presumably was ever so slightly annoyed at being accosted by some 'tired and emotional' creative underlings who had addressed him as 'mate', said it would be over his dead body, and walked away.[12] Happily, Michael Peacock (Controller of BBC One) and a pre-gorilla-spotting David Attenborough (Controller of BBC Two) overheard this exchange, and the latter laughed and said to the former, 'If you don't want it on One, I'll have it on Two!' Peacock was later to authorise the making of the first series.

As Booth recalls, Tom Sloan was adamant that the show had no chance of becoming a series; when he, Booth, protested that it would surely win out over other *Comedy Playhouse* pilots, he was told that Sloan had already selected three other programmes as the top candidates for series development. Booth says that Sloan hated the show because it was about working class slobs who swore and ranted and insulted God, the church and the Royal Family, and because it did not constitute light entertainment as he knew it. He bet £20 that Sloan would be proved wrong. These assertions should, however, be treated with extreme caution. Sloan was certainly not the only member of the BBC hierarchy to regard the show as a hot potato, as evidenced by a memo from Wilson to Peacock just prior to a repeat screening of the pilot on 14 March 1966: 'Frank Muir rang me at home to tell me of your decision to put out the Johnny Speight *Comedy Playhouse* on Monday next. Firstly to thank you.

---

[12] The truth of this story seems to be borne out by Booth, who has stated that he and Speight got drunk after the recording of the pilot show and then bumped into Sloan; it seems likely he was actually recollecting this later incident.

Secondly, to congratulate you on a courageous and – in the long term – wise decision. PS. Just in case, I am having Props Dept bake you a special cake with a file in it.' It is also not certain that Sloan was as strongly opposed to the show as Booth has suggested. Sloan has had a bad press in certain quarters: he allegedly threatened to take Peter Sellers off the air in the 1950s, was highlighted by David Frost as one of the main opponents of *TW3* prior to its cancellation in 1964, and reportedly disliked the first episode of the groundbreaking Peter Cook and Dudley Moore series *Not Only … But Also* in 1965. He has thus been presented as the fall guy in a story of inspired individuals fighting against the hidebound BBC establishment; a Colonel Blimp-type ex-military man trying in vain to defend the Reithian principles he had been accustomed to. This seems far too simplistic a notion. Sloan, with his neat moustache, sober suit and clipped manner, was the epitome of the old, Reithian, BBC, but those who knew him admired him. Muir has described him as a rather serious, old fashioned figure who was nonetheless amenable to new ideas. According to Bill Cotton, who succeeded him as Head of Light Entertainment after his death in 1970, 'He was a good, honest, decent man, with real integrity. A very effective and conscientious manager. People liked and respected him … [He] admired creative people [even though] he found it hard sometimes to understand them.'

Sloan could be prickly at times, but he was frequently self deprecating; and, unlike the majority of the people he worked with, he was not eccentric (though one writer recalls him nibbling absent-mindedly on a tulip at a meeting in Montreux). Galton and Simpson remember that when they approached him following their *Comedy Playhouse* success with 'The Offer', which he had warmly supported, they found that he had already commissioned some audience research for it, and that he displayed the findings politely and encouragingly. It was, as we have seen, Sloan who had sanctioned that show's use of the word 'bleeding'. Sloan may have disliked *TW3*, but he had willingly entered into talks with David Frost to set up his new, admittedly more lightweight, satirical series in 1966.

In 1997, Muir stated that the only reason why Sloan was not keen on 'Till Death Us Do Part' being picked up as a series was that he thought that there were too many sitcoms featuring Cockney families around at the time. More significantly, Muir stated that the *style* of product was not important to his superior. From very early on, Sloan would repeatedly stand up for *Till Death Us Do Part* in the media, admitting that it always gave him cause for concern but at the same time praising it for all the right reasons. At the height of the show's controversy in 1968, he would appear on television to defend it concisely and elegantly. Muir dismissed the criticism of Sloan as stemming from the usual self-perpetuating myths generated by actors and writers who seek to blame others for sinking their projects. Sloan may well have been old fashioned, but only in the BBC sense that, like Voltaire, while he might not share certain views, he would always uphold the right of others to express them. As for Booth's inference of sinister reasons for the long gestation of *Till Death Us Do Part* as a series, Muir dismissed this outright, attributing the interval to the fact that it took several months to build a series in terms of script and cast and production while contracts were set up and recording dates established. This is supported by the documentary evidence, with a 26 November 1965 memo from Muir scheduling the series for April the following year; in this memo, the series is referred to as *King Dad*, a tentative title change (recalling how Galton and Simpson's 'The Offer' became *Steptoe and Son* for the series) reflecting the intended focus on Alf.

Thus by November 1965, when Speight was engaged in writing what would turn out to be his final series for Arthur Haynes, it was confirmed that 'Till Death Us Do Part' (along with two other *Comedy Playhouse* pilots, 'Hudd' and 'The Vital Spark') would indeed be accorded a complete series. However, the *King Dad* title, along with a number of other factors, was soon to change.

7
Filth and Degradation

ENTER MARY WHITEHOUSE

Between the making of the *Comedy Playhouse* pilot in 1965 and the start of production on the first full series of *Till Death Us Do Part* a year later, the debate about the growth of permissiveness on British television became more and more vitriolic, in both its social and its political context; and the arguments raised on both sides were to be integral in shaping Speight's and Wilson's vision of the new series, in terms both of style and of content. Several factions were engaged in confrontation during this period, but with regard to *Till Death Us Do Part*, these were eventually to coalesce into two powerful figures: Sir Hugh Carleton Greene, the Director General of the Corporation, who was proud to be seen as the instigator of a new and more progressive BBC, and, in the opposite corner, Mrs Mary Whitehouse, the most visible figure behind the protests that were growing against permissiveness in the media. The two grew to hate each other, and Speight's show was to march directly into their battleground and straight into their firing line.

Greene had aroused the ire of many with *TW3*, but this was nothing compared to the storm his next major shake-up was to create. This was the poaching of *wunderkind* ITV producer Sydney Newman – a down-to-earth, no-nonsense Canadian with a colourful vocabulary – to head the BBC Drama Department from the beginning of 1963. The following year, Newman introduced the seminal *The Wednesday Play*, a series of individual dramas by different writers with a contemporary edge. The subject matter was to push the debate over permissiveness to the fore, several works offending many with their subject matter. 'And Did Those Feet', which took child murder as its theme and contained the line 'God is just an idiot with a tape recorder playing back in my mind', 'Fable', a morality play in which a future Britain is ruled by ethnic minorities, and 'The Boneyard', a black comedy about Christianity, were just a few of the productions that sparked national controversy. The latter, for instance, prompted one prominent peer, Lady Laycock, to write: 'When I am invited to laugh at the fundamental agony in men's souls, I can keep silent no longer. Take care, BBC, or we may one day all be asked to split our sides at a farce called *The Goons of Buchenwald*.'

The outcry over another piece, 'For The West', led, according to the *Daily Telegraph*, to a new directive: 'BBC drama producers and directors have been told to exercise stricter control over the use of sex and bad language in their productions.' *The Wednesday Play* was to reach the zenith of notoriety in November 1965 with Nell Dunn's stunning 'Up the Junction'. This was a harrowing working-class drama of casual premarital sex and hedonistic lifestyle, shot in a documentary style and with no overall moral viewpoint, which depicted the agonies of a backstreet abortion. By that time, opposition to television permissiveness was coming to a head. It was led by Mrs Mary Whitehouse, a housewife superstar from the Midlands, a woman for whom the term 'self appointed watchdog' became a cliché.

Whitehouse is usually caricatured as a prim-and-proper figure of fun, targeted for such denigration by a liberal intelligentsia brimming over with inverted snobbery – how *dare* she, *middle-aged*, a *woman*, a *housewife*, from the *Midlands*, stand up and protest against the inevitable tide of permissiveness? In truth, she was, from the early '60s at least, the senior mistress in a girls' secondary school, Madeley Secondary Modern, and head of the art department there; she knew the impact that television could have on children, despite her enemies' assertion to the contrary. Like Speight, she came from a working class background; but unlike Speight, she still had a healthy respect for her roots. Her first brush with the media was a rather happy one, in 1953, when she was inspired to write to the BBC expressing her sympathy for the new Queen, suddenly thrust into the spotlight on the death of her father, and was then invited to make a short radio broadcast on *Woman's Hour* detailing her views. Her second contact with the BBC, ten years later, was prompted when she was approached by several girl pupils the day after the 8 March 1963 episode of the discussion show *Meeting Point* had been televised. This episode, 'What Kind of Loving?', its title inspired by that of the recent John Schlesinger film *A Kind of Loving* (1962), had discussed the new morality, and had featured a panel of self-proclaimed experts comprising a psychologist, a bishop's wife, a headmistress and a clergyman. Mention had been made of a recent pronouncement by Dr Peter Henderson, Principal Medical Officer for the Ministry of Education, that it was not unchaste to have premarital sex; and, similarly, Dr Alex Comfort had defined a chivalrous boy as 'one who takes contraceptives with him when he goes to meet his girlfriend'. The show had apparently traumatised one of the Madeley Secondary Modern pupils, who was not in any way sexually aware; and, as the teacher primarily responsible for art, Whitehouse decided to write to the Director General of the BBC to question the decision to expose such powerful ideas to such impressionable young people before the television 'watershed'. Greene was out of the country at the time, but his deputy, Harman Grisewood, agreed to see her at Broadcasting House. He was receptive, and despite his statement that surely most girls were aware of premarital sex, Whitehouse thought he sympathised with her reaction. But shortly afterwards, Grisewood resigned, allegedly because he found his boss's ideas too progressive and ultimately too offensive.

It was a seminal year in terms of social mores for the soon-to-be-swinging Britain; it was the year the British, according to Philip Larkin, discovered sex, together with the Beatles; the year when Profumo, Minister for War, was caught *in flagrante delicto*; the year when the Bishop Of Woolwich's book *Honest to God* suggested that God was dead; and of course the year when *TW3* was being broadcast. Shortly after, there would be a political crisis and shattering changes, first in the nature of the Tory government and then with the institution of the first Labour administration since 1950. Whitehouse saw *TW3* as 'the epitome of what was wrong with the BBC – anti-authority, anti-religion, anti-patriotism, pro-dirt and poorly produced, yet having the support of the Corporation and apparently impervious to discipline from within or disapproval from without'. The ongoing debate over the renewal of the BBC's Royal Charter and an approach from Jasper More MP asking her what safeguards should be applied to prevent a further slide into the morass, prompted Whitehouse and Norah Buckland, the wife of the rector of Langdon in Staffordshire, to set up a meeting for people sharing their concerns at Birmingham Town Hall on 5 May 1964. Archbishops Ramsey of Canterbury and Coggan of York expressed support, and 37 coach-loads of people attended, with minimal security, entering the hall to the cries of hecklers shouting 'We want sex!'. The scenes achieved mystical dimensions when a party of nuns stamped their feet in unison to express their support for Whitehouse and Buckland, panicking the BBC news team who were covering the event into thinking there was a riot about to happen, and they in turn caused chaos by turning off the lights. The campaign set out to gather 50,000 signatures for a manifesto, but instead received ten times that many.

With hindsight, there is a Whiggish form of historical inevitability about the growth of permissiveness during the '60s, but this was by no means a conclusive victory during the early part of that decade. It is important to realise from this distance that Whitehouse, the initiator of a pressure group (the concept of which, although familiar to us nowadays, was virtually unknown then) and stigmatised by liberals as unrepresentative, received a huge amount of public support for her views. This dissatisfaction amongst the general populace at the more superficial aspects of the social change initiated during the '60s and '70s is clearly discernible both in the BBC's own audience reaction reports on *Till Death Us Do Part* and in the general media. It must also be remembered that, at least during the mid-'60s, a lot of the criticism was aimed at the scheduling of controversial material during family viewing time, rather than at the nature of the material itself. The ITV companies were acutely aware of how their viewing figures could be adversely affected if they were to allow uncontrolled permissiveness, but the

BBC was a publicly-funded organisation that did not need to rely on ratings or commercial advertising to fund its programmes. It was not unreasonable, however, for Whitehouse to expect a moral and ethical dimension to the BBC's output, and so battle lines were drawn. The broadcasting empire soon struck back.

The meeting and formation of the 'Clean Up TV' campaign was soon to be mercilessly lampooned by a BBC Midlands series called *Swizzlewick*, a tale of corruption in a 'mythical' Midlands metropolis. It was not very subtle: the Chairman of the local Clean Up Committee was named Councillor Pepper in reference to the real-life Councillor Salt, a member of the Whitehouse taskforce, while Mrs Smallgood, the founder of a 'freedom from sex' campaign, was an obvious parody of Whitehouse herself. There was even a postman called Ernest – the same as Whitehouse's husband – whose house was given the scurrilous name 'Postman's Piece'. While Whitehouse may not have been offended by this, a projected two-and-a-half-minute sequence in a future script in which a councillor emerges from a liaison with a prostitute, zipping up his trousers, proved too much. She sent the leaked details of the forthcoming programme to the Postmaster General, then the Minister responsible for broadcasting, and the offending scene was cut from the transmission. Greene, visiting Australia, was furious when he heard of this. He saw the leak as an act of paramount disloyalty, and threatened to sack the BBC staff member responsible, when he or she was discovered. This never happened, but the incident marked the start of a long history of friction between the campaigner and the Director General. Greene consistently refused Whitehouse's requests to meet him personally and inaugurated a total communication shutout that at times involved her letters to the Corporation being redirected via newspapers and ultimately led to her BBC friends shunning her.

In June 1965, Whitehouse used the campaign's success, evidenced by the 425,000 signatories to its manifesto, to elevate it from a grass roots movement to a more empowered political lobbying fraternity. With James Dance, Conservative MP for Bromsgrove, she presented a petition that was read in Parliament by Sir Barnett Cocks. It centred on five main statements:

1. We (men and women) of Britain believe in a Christian way of life.
2. We want it for our children and for our country.
3. We deplore present day attempts to belittle or destroy it, and in particular we object to the proportion of disbelief, doubt and dirt that the BBC projects into millions of homes through the television screen.
4. Crime, violence, illegitimacy and venereal disease are steadily increasing, yet the BBC employs people whose ideas and advice pander to the lowest in human nature and accompany this with a stream of suggestive and erotic plays which present promiscuity,

infidelity and drinking as normal and inevitable.

5. We call upon the BBC for a radical change of policy and demand programmes which build character instead of destroying it, which encourage and sustain faith in God and bring Him back to the heart of our family and national life.

The campaigners promised that henceforth they would monitor and respond to perceived moral corruption on a far grander scale. This reached its apogee in November 1965 when three events combined to transform the battle into a full scale war, at the very time when Frank Muir gave the go-ahead for a *Till Death Us Do Part* series to be made in spring 1966. First, 'Up the Junction' was screened and proved to be the most controversial play so far adapted for television, attracting overwhelming expressions of disgust from Whitehouse and her group, who were eventually to succeed in preventing the BBC from repeating it. Then, on Saturday 13 November 1965, Kenneth Tynan, while being interviewed by Robert Robinson on *BBC3*, Ned Sherrin's natural successor to *TW3* in its form and content, said in a discussion about the limits of sexual content in the theatre: 'I doubt if there are any rational people to whom the word "fuck" would be particularly diabolical, revolting or totally forbidden.' This was the first time that the word in question had ever been spoken on British TV and, predictably, it provoked a furore. Brigadier Terence Clarke, Conservative MP for Portsmouth West, tried to raise an enquiry into the incident in the House of Commons, tabling a question via the new Postmaster General, Anthony Booth's cohort, Tony Wedgwood Benn. Whitehouse wrote to the Queen, asking her to use her influence with the BBC governors to prevent a repetition. Huw Wheldon, Controller of BBC Television, stated that he was surprised but 'not appalled … It was quite germane to the discussion that was taking place'. The BBC did however give an official apology on the 15 November, and sent messages down to its programme-makers that Tynan had gone too far. Sydney Newman was forced to issue directives to his staff: 'The anti-BBC hounds are baying these days even more shrilly than before … Whether all this is reaction to "Up The Junction", Kenneth Tynan's four-letter word or what, the searchlight is on us.' A memo of 22 November called for care regarding the depiction of 'violence, sexual relations and blasphemy in drama', and then another stated that 'curses like "Jesus", words like "bloody" and so on are offensive, and obscenities like "arse" etc put people off in their hundreds of thousands'.

Compounding the Director General's problems, the same month saw the announcement that he himself had prevented the transmission of Peter Watkins' visceral docudrama on nuclear war, *The War Game*, on the grounds that it was too realistic and too harrowing for public consumption. While Whitehouse may have agreed here, the liberals, already enraged by anti-permissive reaction, despised this as a major comedown.

Inspired by such recent events, on 30 November, Whitehouse and Dance announced the formation of the National Viewers' and Listeners' Association at a press conference in Fleet Street. The new organisation declared that it would strive for several safeguards: the appointment of a full-time chairman of the BBC Board of Governors, with the same wide powers as Lord Hill, Chairman of the ITA; a separate secretariat for the Board; regular reports to the nation to 'build up confidence and understanding'; and a public inquiry into the Corporation's finances, on the grounds that there was a 'developing conviction that a proportion of its revenue is being spent in ways detrimental to the public interest'. The ultimate intention was that protests regarding the BBC would be put on public record: 'We do not say that we are always right, but we have a right to be heard. If the BBC try to ridicule the views of half a million people, what else will they ridicule in the same way?'

Whitehouse went on the attack again over the latest example of alleged bad taste on the BBC, once more in *BBC3,* when in one sketch a crucifix was used as a pipe rack. Shortly afterwards, a rival pressure group, Cosmo (Freedom For TV), was set up by Mrs Avril Fox, a supporter of the (soon-to-be-cancelled) *BBC3.* Whitehouse meanwhile set out her manifesto in a book, *Cleaning Up TV,* which was published in 1966 and was to have immense consequences for Speight and his new show. Later she made what would become a famous statement: 'If anyone were to ask me who, above all, was responsible for the moral collapse that characterised the '60s and '70s, I would unhesitatingly name Sir Hugh Carleton Greene, [who] opened the doors to foul language, blasphemy, excesses of violence and sex ... [This] had the most profound effect upon the values and behavioural patterns of the day ... He had no hesitation whatsoever in shutting the doors against those like [me] who questioned both his policy and the wisdom of the new moralists. Censorship against such people was exercised most rigidly ... Why did he encourage programmes that ridiculed and denigrated our political leaders, the Church, the family, authority in all its forms, that were often anti-British, blasphemous and obscene?'

Greene, for his part, was meanwhile blithely spouting words such as these in January 1964: 'The BBC ... must not try to influence its audience in any particular direction and must mirror with the greatest possible fairness and objectivity all mainstreams of opinion without fear of favouritism.' This from the man who appeared to reschedule *Steptoe and Son* to gain Labour a few seats at the General Election later that same year. In his address to the International Catholic Association For Radio and Television in Rome in 1965, he stated: 'The actions and aspirations of those who proclaim some political and social ideas are so clearly damaging to society ... that to put at their disposal the enormous power of broadcasting would be to conspire with them against society.'

Labour MP (and future broadcaster) Brian Walden had advised Whitehouse against taking on Greene on the grounds that he *was* the establishment, and that because he had helped to put the Labour government into power, they would protect him whatever the cost. He was ultimately proved wrong, because Harold Wilson knew he could not allow unchecked criticism of his administration and grew suspicious over Greene's attempts to appear open handed.

Greene was attacked by Wilson first for the BBC's supposedly biased coverage of the Chancellor's Five Year National Plan in September 1965 and then for his insistence that the Conservative Party should in future have the right to reply to government announcements on the BBC. The increasingly paranoid Wilson government, with its majority of only four, perceived that it would have to obtain a clear mandate from the nation to instigate its socialist programme, and consequently called a new General Election for 31 March 1966. Fear of media coverage affecting the outcome of the Election, and particularly of the BBC being seen as a political arbiter, at a time when it was fast becoming apparent that the Corporation would soon be accountable for the first financial deficit in its history, meant that any mention of politics on television in the run up to the Election was subject to strict scrutiny. Even the populist ITV drama *The Power Game* had two 'political' episodes, in which its protagonist Caswell Bligh cynically aims for a position of power in the Labour Party, postponed until June 1966. The Election went ahead, and Wilson was re-elected with a majority of 98; but on the train back to London from his northern constituency, he refused to grant the BBC the first interview, hence snubbing Greene, the man who in the eyes of many had assisted his rise to power.

Thus the air in early 1966 was awash with rumours, debate and accusations about the nature of television and its influence, its content and its moral standing. This was an environment that both Speight and Wilson would have appreciated and distilled into their brand-new topical comedy series, of which Speight was busy writing the first four scripts in the spring, abetted by his drinking partner and socialist activist Tony Booth.

SWINGING TOWARDS SUNSET

If the media were preoccupied with their own judgements on morality and permissiveness, a new development seemed to encapsulate the mood of the era and seal its reputation for all time. The '60s were about to officially 'swing'. But even this was to polarise opinion in a way that *Till Death Us Do Part* would reflect so admirably and with such popularity, making it very much a product of its time ...

Attracted by the political furore that would lead to another General Election within a mere 18 months, the US news magazine *Time* reported on the new mood in Britain in its 12 April 1966 issue, declaring London the city of the decade: 'This spring, as never before in modern times, London is switched on. Ancient elegance and new opulence are all tangled in a dazzling blur of op and pop. In a once sedate world of faded splendour, everything new, uninhibited and kinky is blooming at the top of London life. London is not keeping the good news to itself. It is exporting its plays, its films, its fads, its styles, its people. The new vitality of the city amazes both its visitors and inhabitants. Britain has lost an empire and lightened a pound and in the process it has also recovered a lightness of heart lost during the weighty centuries of world leadership.'

'Swinging London' was not an invention of *Time*, as some have said; it did exist, and its existence is corroborated by numerous artistic products of varying quality far too numerous and too well known to mention here. That aspect of London in 1966 is now so famous it has become a cliché, to be cemented three months later by England's World Cup victory, now seen as the zenith of '60s exuberance, confidence and creativity. But there was another, darker side to this hedonistic swirl, and one that did not go unrecognised at the time, although it has been often overlooked since.

On the same day that *Time* characterised London and the nation in a favourable light, Anthony Lejeune proclaimed its underside in an article in the *Daily Telegraph*: 'That deep rooted changes have taken place is clear. To call them symptoms of decadence may be facile as an explanation, but has a disturbing ring of truth. They certainly deserve harder scrutiny, a more critical examination than we generally find it comfortable to give them.' He went on to deplore not only the decadent appearance of modern British youth and fashion but also the fact that the BBC could find it it acceptable to present them. Instead of seeing 'pop culture' as a sign of progress, he declared it a symptom of the British movement toward collectivism and the suppression of freedom of the individual. 'The result is plain to see; a nation which has lost its pride and its confidence, though not its complacency; which has lost the will to play a strong role in the world; a nation in which envy and mass bribery are the currency of domestic politics; a nation chronically in debt, living behind crumbling facades, which it can no longer afford to maintain.'

Two months later, as the panoply of the World Cup descended on a sceptred isle undergoing economic meltdown, the rest of the world caught up. The *New York Times* was expressing similar concerns; Anthony Lewis wrote on Thursday 9 June 1966: 'The pound trembles, the gold runs out, Britain's ships stand in the docks – but at Annabel's they come and go, talking of how short the skirts can go. The atmosphere in London today can be almost eerie in it's relentless frivolousness. There can rarely have been a greater contrast between a country's objective situation and the mood of its people.'

A brief scan of the media during that month, as attention focused on the UK, reveals the exact antithesis of the golden age aura of joy and optimism that *Time* had found and that subsequently would become embodied in the natural culture. And the British media expressed similar concerns about the collapse of the economy in a welter of industrial strife, debt and complacency, a collapse that the second Labour government in 18 months was trying – and failing – to quell.

Labour had in the event enjoyed a relatively easy General Election win at the end of March. Wilson, the consummate politician and superb orator, had continually overshadowed his Conservative opponent, the stiffly tremulous Edward Heath. 'You *know* Labour government works' was the election slogan. The public trusted Labour to tackle the economic problems facing the country. But the new government's economic strategy was blown off course almost immediately when at midnight on 16 May 1966 the National Union of Seamen went on strike in support of their demand for a cut in working time from 56 to 40 hours per week. The following week, a State of Emergency was declared, which was not to end until 29 June. The strike – which Wilson, to the astonishment of many in his party, blamed on Communist agitation – succeeded only in deepening the country's economic woes. The government now began to panic, faced with a painful choice of either sanctioning continued deflation or devaluing the pound, and this resulted in a plot by members of the Cabinet against Wilson. With a Herculean effort and great political acumen, Wilson restored his authority, and opted for continued deflation, the alternative being too horrific to contemplate (until events forced devaluation the following year). By 20 July, the government had announced swingeing cuts in the overseas budget and public investment and substantial rises in fuel and excise duties, heavy hire-purchase restrictions and a mandatory six-month freeze on wage rises, to be followed by a White Paper advocating further 'severe restraint'. At the same time, a determined attempt was made to address chronic overmanning in certain sectors of industry and general misuse of resources. But the problems continued, with lay-offs, strikes, short-time working and further industrial strife extending into the autumn.

While London was being hailed as the darling of the world's media and pop culture, the country was fast becoming bankrupt, economically, socially and spiritually, as its beautiful people partied on regardless of – or because of? – the descending economic chaos. It was into this bizarre dichotomy of a country financially and socially going down the drain while simultaneously enjoying a cultural and artistic revolution that *Till Death Us Do Part* burst onto millions of television screens in June 1966.

8
The First Series

SOMEONE ELSE

Frank Muir commissioned the first series of seven episodes of *King Dad* – as it was still being referred to at the time, with Alf still a Ramsey – on 19 January 1966, with recording scheduled to begin on 28 March. On 3 March, Warren Mitchell, sharing a train to Manchester with fellow actor John Le Mesurier and his new wife Joan, excitedly told his friend of the ideas he had for his character in the series. On 14 March, the *Comedy Playhouse* episode was repeated and encouragingly garnered a Reaction Index of 70 (higher than the original) and a slice of 17.9% of the viewing population. Anthony Booth and Una Stubbs both agreed to contracts for a series on 4 April 1966, while Warren Mitchell, who despite his enthusiasm was still cautious about committing himself to a regular television role replete with the pitfalls of typecasting, waited a further three weeks. Gretchen Franklin, however, was already contracted to a season of *Spring and Port Wine* in the West End, and had to decline to take up the part of Else, an enforced decision she was naturally to regret (as she admitted in a *This is Your Life* programme in 1995). She recommended instead her close friend Dandy Nichols, with whom she had appeared in the *Armchair Theatre* play 'The Trouble With Our Ivy' in 1961 and – both in Else-type roles – at the beginning of the Beatles movie *Help!* in 1965. For Nichols, it was to prove a fateful choice.

Nichols was born in London on 21 May 1907. Her real first name was Daisy – taken from her older sister's doll – although she kept this a secret for some years as she deemed it 'fit only for cows and barges'. She was one of five children, the daughter of an engineer. Bad at school, she failed her exams, being far too involved in playing tricks and practical jokes, and for the next 12 years she worked as a secretary, including a long spell at the Cherry Blossom polish factory. She married and later divorced a clarinettist, Stephen Wates, declaring that she was quite happy to live alone. She studied drama at night school – she had always been stage-struck, and as a child had played truant to creep into the stalls at the Old Vic, where she saw John Gielgud play his first Hamlet with Edith Evans as Rosalind. She took evening classes in diction, drama and fencing at the St Pancras People Theatre, was talent spotted performing in *Night Must Fall* at a charity show at the Scala Theatre, and was then invited to become part of a professional repertory company at the Festival Theatre, Cambridge, for the princely sum of £3 per week, a £1 drop in salary from her secretarial position. This was no problem; at the end of her first week, she told a producer, 'I couldn't possibly expect to enjoy myself so much and get paid for it too'. She enjoyed rep, which taught her, as she later recalled, 'to be punctual, self-reliant, tough as old boots'. Her six week wartime run in the Entertainments National Service Association (ENSA) was extended to 18. The war failed to dispel her spirit – she and her husband used to lay bets on where the flying bombs were going to land when the buzzing of their motors stopped. Gambling was indeed to become one of Nichols' passions, as she played poker and canasta as a regular habitué of the Browns Hotel in Dover Street. She specialised in roles as working-class mums or 'old bags' in the theatre, most memorably as a Cockney mother to Roy Hudd and Rita Tushingham in The Royal Court's production of Ann Jellicoe's *The Giveaway*. It was, said Nichols, a great comic idea, about a family who win ten years' free supply of cornflakes; but the audience did not seem to digest it. Tushingham, inexperienced at the time, didn't have a clue as to the nature of the loud noises the audience were making; Nichols said, 'Don't stop now, dear – they're booing us. Just keep on going'.

Nichols' first film role was a bit-part in *Nicholas Nickleby* in1947, but she particularly enjoyed working with Diana Dors in three early Huggett family films and then playing a mother to Dors' Ruth Ellis-type character in *Yield to the Night* (ABPC, 1956). 'She has a wonderful gift for conveying comedy, and she is a very serious dame, too', she said of Dors in 1972. Her first TV appearance came in 1946, in a live broadcast of a West End play, *The Power Without the Glory*, starring Dirk Bogarde, and the only TV drama at the time to end with the cast taking a curtain call: 'The camera panned slowly round, and one by one we solemnly took a bow.' During this production, she had a brief flirtation with star Kenneth More, one of many would-be suitors. A host of bit parts playing roles such as charlady, neighbour, or barmaid followed. Like many actors, she was superstitious, going to a clairvoyant regularly. In 1958, she was told: 'You are working, you are going to work where you live on an island, a small crowded island, and you will go out to work in a boat.' Nichols thought 'She's slipping a bit', but two months later, she was working on Richard Fleischer's classic *The Vikings*, filmed in Norway with Tony Curtis, Janet Leigh and Kirk Douglas, and staying on a yacht once owned by Barbara Hutton. But despite appearances for the BBC in such light entertainment staples as *Hudd*, *The Dick Emery Show* and *Dixon Of Dock Green*, she was most famous as a convalescent Cockney mum, Mrs Hill, speaking the opening lines in the long-running ITV soap *Emergency Ward 10*, opposite Glyn Owen as Dr O'Meara and Jill Browne as Nurse Carole Young. She spent most of the series knitting a sweater for her son in the army, only to find he had died before she had finished; 'real soap opera stuff' was her apt remark. She declared that she never did find out what she was convalescing from …

Nichols was a real character, described as 'a lady more soft-edged than stout, friendly and down to earth, happy to talk but divulging little'. She was cagey about her age and never talked about her failed marriage. She was a compulsive (and, according to Johnny Speight, noisy) eater and a smoker, but was to give up drinking alcohol in 1970 when, after becoming inebriated at a wedding, she tried to put herself to bed under a carpet. Her pastimes included playing tennis, and she relished lobster dinners. She hadn't driven a car herself since she crashed a brand new vehicle into a wall, using the accelerator instead of the brake, but she liked being driven, and was quite happy on long journeys: 'I might get out and buy a packet of crisps, but I wouldn't get restless.' Anthony Booth recalls that she invariably carried a large handbag full of a huge variety of tablets, which she would examine religiously and occasionally proffer to the cast and crew. She enjoyed life, she later said, 'in a jolly, quiet, uninspired way. Perhaps I'm a bit of a cabbage, like the character I play.' She loved the sea and loved to be alone, and was later delighted to be able to purchase a seaside flat in Frinton with the proceeds of her *Till Death Us Do Part* salary. In 1966, she lived in a luxury flat in St John's Wood.

Nichols in many ways *was* Else, albeit with considerably more intelligence, in total contrast to Warren Mitchell acting as Alf. 'Every part one plays is a conglomeration of people one has met,' she once said. 'I think it is a terrible pitfall to model a performance on one specific person. If you do, then your characterisation is liable to fail when the part calls for you to do something that is out of character for the real model'. Her own description of Else was: 'A bit of an old slag. Not dirty, but certainly not house proud! A cabbage, not very much on top, obviously. Terrible antagonism between her and her husband, not much love lost. A very satisfying part, wonderfully observed by Johnny Speight. She had got used to [Alf], like the sound of the underground at the bottom of someone's garden.' She thought that, although women enjoyed her fierce putdowns of her husband, the audience must never feel sorry for Else: 'That would be fatal.'

Dennis Main Wilson described Nichols as the perfect female clown, 'capable of maximising every comic opportunity with her perfect timing and sense of economy. Dandy can stop a show by raising a single eyebrow just one fraction of an inch'; indeed, he later stated that she was the only comic genius to rival Hancock.

Nichols signed the contract to play Else Ramsey on 21 April 1966, and the series went into production – a little later than originally planned – the following month. Muir's strategy that was that this short run of seven episodes would be merely the opening gambit to a 13 part series later in the year. Mitchell was engaged at £210 per week, Booth at £120 5s, Stubbs at £105 and Nichols at £131 5s. Wilson's idea of pitting the series directly against *Coronation Street* was picked up, and the show was scheduled to go out on Mondays at 7.30 pm. Michael Peacock had promised to spruce up BBC One's opposition to the *Street*, and Huw Wheldon recalls that he would often ask Tom Sloan to persuade stars and agents to agree to sitcoms being scheduled at this time: '[Sloane] had to get drunk night after night with those frightful agents, or write hideous letters replying to hideous letters.'

GARNETT STREET

Previous shows in the slot opposite *Coronation Street*, such as *The Frankie Howerd Show*, *Hugh and I* and *The Walrus and the Carpenter*, had gained average viewing figures of around 10 million per episode. In the days before video recorders and multiple televisions, the male head of the household would generally be in charge of making decisions about the evening's viewing, and light relief from the woman's soap on ITV could swing the ratings toward the BBC, provided the laughs were regular. Unlike the other examples, however, *Till Death Us Do Part* claimed the same thematic ground as its arch rival, as is apparent from Dennis Main Wilson's introductory description of the series in *Television Today* of 2 June 1966: 'A saga of family life … The usual token demonstration of love and warmth marred only by the horrendous crash of bigotry, greed and all the other lovely things that go to make us human beings what we are.' The new series was billed as being about a normal family with normal failings. Its working class setting – just like the *Street*'s – was miles apart from the middle class, home counties suburbia of BBC comedy big guns such as *Beggar My Neighbour* and *Marriage Lines*. Also like the *Street*, it featured ensemble acting, similar to Dennis Main Wilson's earlier hit, *The Rag Trade*.

The main focus of the BBC's attention lay elsewhere at the time, as it was about to face possibly its greatest challenge to date: televising the World Cup. It was to screen 50 hours of football over a 21 day period. On 11 occasions, a match would be transmitted live at peak evening viewing time, with a 7.00 pm start to the coverage and a 7.30 pm kick-off, with the half-time interval being used to show again all the goals and other highlights using state-of-the-art slow-motion and stop-action technology, dubbed the 'action replay'. The opening ceremony was to take place at Wembley on Monday 11 July, and the final was to be played at the same venue on Saturday 30 July. The debut series of *Till Death Us Do Part* had to be scheduled around this coverage, which meant that there would be a week's gap in transmission between the fifth and sixth episodes, and another between the sixth and seventh. Throughout the period, however, the BBC were counting on patriarchal control of the television control switch, linking comedy and football in opposition to soap opera.

One other, more lasting, consequence of the scheduling of the first series around the World Cup was that the BBC quickly realised that the name 'Alf Ramsey' was no longer a viable one for the obnoxious lead character, in view of the danger that his real life namesake, the manager of England's football team, might not approve and might even resort to litigation. Speight didn't really care about the name of his main character, and suggested that any alternative would do, but Wilson was as usual insistent on artistic freedom and urged him to select one. Speight, Booth and Wilson were out one day in Speight's Rolls Royce, driving unceremoniously around Wapping, the location for the aerial filming sequence used in the titles for the series. Wilson asked for the car to be halted in front of the archetypical East End home upon which his camera had descended. He needed to pay the occupants for their permission to retain their home in the title sequence. The address that they stopped at – 55 Garnet Street – was a typical pre-War terraced house on the corner, complete with outside lavatory. The owners were a young, working-class couple called Mahoney who had lived there for two years, ever since they were married. They were surprised to see Wilson at their door, but from then on they received £10 per series for the rights to film the roof and building, right up to 1968, when in June the houses were demolished to make way for road widening. A bit of the subsequent fame associated with the location rubbed off on Michael Mahoney, who said he was invariably called Alf when at work. And as soon as Speight saw the street name, he knew he had the ideal surname for his characters …

The first script was recorded on 17 May, having been rehearsed during the second week of that month. During these rehearsals, the characters were embellished somewhat and Speight's scripts shaped and moulded to fit them. For one thing, Mitchell decided to shave his head as much as possible when playing Alf. 'My head is a lot colder when I'm doing the show,' he told one interviewer. 'I look forward to growing enough hair to warm my neck and ears after the series. My voice is very strained, I'm shouting myself hoarse and I can't sing in the shower at present.' In some episodes, the change in the length of his hair between the shooting of pre-filmed inserts and the later studio recording was to be clearly visible. Mitchell retained a moustache, however, and almost always wore a pin-up shirt and circular, wire-framed 'granny' glasses. 'I look what I am,' he later commented. 'A Russian Jew. In those early days doing Alf, when I wasn't grey and the moustache was much darker, I looked like someone on the Præsidium on the May Day march in Red Square. So the idea of me playing a typical Englishman like Alf made me laugh.'

Alf would be a monument to an Edwardian Empire, a permanent reminder of a world on the way out, and a vivid contrast to the colourful trendiness of Mike and Rita with his staid and unchanging garb. Early episodes would play on this, with 'Hair Raising!' in particular centred on a plot concerning Alf's appearance, complete with an introductory dialogue debating fashion. But perhaps the biggest, uncredited, influence on Alf's appearance was that of the doyen of Edwardian Empire himself, Rudyard Kipling – photographs of the writer in his latter days resemble Alf to a remarkable extent. Kipling had indeed turned gung ho and jingoistic during the Boer War, according to his latest biographer, 'evoking the cartoon image of a bald dwarf with glasses and eyebrows, energetically beating some sort of drum', a description that eerily resembles a portrait of Alf. In 1964, Mitchell had appeared in the BBC anthology series *Kipling* as an Indian mystic, and some background knowledge here may have inspired him.

The essence of the series would be Speight's commitment to realism, manifested in part by Alf's language. Initially, according to Frank Muir, the writer had wished to use even stronger language, including the word 'fuck'; an idea quite anathema to the BBC at any point. Speight was adamant that he would not tone down 'bloody' to 'ruddy', on the same principle that he would never allow the use of 'frigging' as a substitute for 'fucking'. That sort of compromise, according to Speight, was using bad language; bad in an artistic sense, because it meant that the dialogue and thus the show would be rendered unreal. And Alf could not be seen to be *aware* that he was using bad language and hence causing offence – swearing was merely part of his everyday language, a demotic form that revealed his basic inarticulate fears. Muir agreed to the 'bloodies', despite this being a show scheduled for family viewing time, on such artistic grounds. He even suggested to Mitchell, who in rehearsals was initially speaking them crisply and concisely, to be freer and less uninhibited in his pronunciation, to achieve a more naturalistic style. For the first series, the number of 'bloodies' was actually relatively small, but this was soon to change.

Speight was allowed to cross the 'bloody' frontier, but further freedom was curtailed, and this led – by happy accident or design – to the invention of the series' most famous 'catchphrase'. From the first episode, Alf's insults to his wife and her ripostes were replete with references to barnyard animals – 'cow' for the bovine Else, 'pig' for the revolting Alf. Each reflected the speaker's woeful lack of imagination. 'Silly old cow' was still too strong an insult for a sitcom in 1966, and 'Silly mare', as used in the *Comedy Playhouse* pilot, too weak. Dandy Nichols in 1967 was to comment admiringly on Speight's cleverness in devising the now-famous phrase 'Silly old moo' as a perfect compromise between the over-harsh and the over-slight; an insult that went close to the edge yet never slipped over it. Yet Anthony Booth firmly places the credit at the lips of Una Stubbs; as he recalls, while the other members of the cast were loudly and vigorously debating in rehearsals the viability of using 'cow', Stubbs – as usual doing her embroidery, the serene eye of the hurricane raging around her – calmly queried the point of such heated debate when all that needed to be resolved was a question over a 'silly old moo-cow'. The ideal compromise was achieved, the insult stuck, and soon it could be heard in factories and schoolyards all over the kingdom. Its most oblique use came early on in 'Claustrophobia', the final episode of series one, when an irate Alf turns to lambaste his wife with the insult, only to direct it instead at a herd of cows that have wandered across a West Country road. In the preceding episode, 'From Liverpool With Love', Alf and Else debate the ethics of swearing, as both deny that 'moo' and 'pig' are offensive, with a frustrated Alf bellowing 'Barnyards to you!' at the climax.

Warren Mitchell himself conceived the phrase 'Scouse git' for Alf to direct at his son-in-law; an insult that would subsequently be adapted into various forms, reaching its apotheosis in 'Randy Scouse git', first used in the second series and later even borrowed as the title of a hit single by the Monkees. By the third episode, insults relating to Mike's long, peroxide-blond locks were also coined by Mitchell: 'Shirley Temple', 'Peruvian ponce' and so on. At this stage in the show's history, the swearing, including the occasional 'git', was noted in press and public reaction but did not yet give rise to marked controversy – that would come later, with the show's increasing popularity.

Alf never thought he was swearing; or, if he did, he felt that it was perfectly acceptable for him as the master of the house to do so, but not anyone else. Hence, in 'Intolerance', when Mike calls Else a 'silly old moo', Alf turns on him; and when later Rita states that her father talks 'a load of bloody rubbish', he tells her not to swear. Naturally she asks why not, when he is always 'Lord Mayoring it', and Alf's reply is, 'It's not bloody ladylike!' Both Else and Mike were to swear, but only occasionally. Muir remained worried that Alf's strong language was a little *too* strong, but Speight convinced him that it was necessary for the character, and it was retained. Muir also asked Mitchell to show at least some form of kindness to his on-screen wife, but Mitchell refused, and some time later, Muir came back to confirm that Mitchell had been correct.

With splendid temerity, Mitchell promoted the show in the tabloid *News of the World* the day before its debut transmission, predicting accurately that the Clean Up TV campaigners would have a field day with it: 'Now, there's a plot brewing to ration my ------ and my ----- in the show. I've heard I'll be allowed only one – if it's vital to the plot, or the dialogue.'

The numbers game, it seems, had begun before the show had even started; but was it paranoia on the part of the production team? Dennis Main Wilson certainly was adamant that two years earlier such a series would not even have been ventured. Mitchell went on to declare that the Garnetts would be arrested in the street if they were to trade their insults there. He also revealed that it was he who had finally quashed the idea of the series being called *King Dad*: 'I wasn't having any of that nonsense.'

Mitchell was still learning Stanislavski's method acting, with its strict guidelines on motive and character, at the time he was making the first series of *Till Death Us Do Part*. 'He used to bring back messages from his teacher saying what we should do with the show,' said Johnny Speight in 1973. 'I told him what to do with the messages.' But the dictates of Stanislavski were to cause a great deal of friction during production. Frank Muir tells a story of the early days. Midway through a Garnett rant during rehearsals, Dandy Nichols, who had been leaning against a wall by the fireplace, '… straightened up, wandered past Warren and sank into an armchair. Warren was furious. "Dandy!" he said. "What did you move for? Right in the middle of my speech, you wander vaguely right across me. You had no motivation for moving, Dandy. None. If you'd looked chilly and had seen a woolly on the chair, then, right, we'd have known what was in your noddle. But to just wander across me … You were at position A and you moved, all of your own accord, to position B. Why?"' A deadpan Nichols had a very concise reply: 'I was at position A and I farted, so I moved to position B'. Mitchell's commitment and intensity were to take an increasing toll on the oldest member of the regular cast, as were the rows between Mitchell and Booth, but at this point, Nichols was able to cope with the turmoil.

Virtually all of the show's linguistic and dramatic skeins were established in the first few episodes, most of them worked out by the cast during rehearsals. Else's habit of timely interruption of her husband's relentless monologues, forcing him to attempt to re-establish control with the keyword 'Look …' before finally angrily admitting that he had lost his thread, began in the second episode, 'Hair Raising!'. It was here too that the cast decided to leaven Speight's blocks of dialogue with comic business. Muir was to suggest to Speight that he framed his dialogues and debates in more varied settings, suggesting he incorporate for one episode ('Sex Before Marriage' in the second series) some business of decorating, which would enhance the action (and in this case actually *become* the plot). Before this, however, Mitchell himself would come up with ideas such as having Alf cutting his toenails (the clippings from which would shower spectacularly over the room) or carefully combing his virtually extinct hair as he readies himself to go out.

Perhaps the most unusual innovation came with Mitchell's decision to act as warm-up for the studio audience himself, rather than leave this to a supporting comic as was usual. In a 'brilliant one man show', as Una Stubbs recalled, he explained the series' approach of thematic reversal and, while he focused on his Alf persona, was also at pains to inform the audience that he and Alf Garnett were not the same, and that Alf's views were definitely not

Speight's. As a consequence of this, the audience settled down for the recording, and recording breaks were camouflaged by a familiar performance. Consequently, there is virtually total silence from the audience over the opening sequence of each episode, rather than the hail of applause heard on every other '60s sitcom. Mitchell's warm-up routine as carried on almost to the end of the show's life, being finally dropped at Nichols' request in the 1974 series when she found the situation too intense.

It was Dennis Main Wilson who devised the criteria for the design of the Garnetts' home, soon to be familiar across the nation: 'I called in my set designer to discuss what kind of house they lived in,' he recalled. 'And it was to be a 12 foot square front room with a scullery out the back, with an earthenware sink, a bath in the scullery with a lid on where you keep all the crockery, a copper where you heat up all the hot water to hand-bail the water into the bath and run the cold tap, and a bog out the back in a tiny garden. A front door that opened into a hall, from where the stairs go straight up, and you turn left into the front room. In the front room there's got to be a two-seater settee, two armchairs, a piano, a dining table, four chairs and a sideboard … That [would become] our trademark; that was it. That in fact was the exact floor plan and the furniture arrangement of my Mum and Dad's house, and they never spotted it. And they thought the Garnett family lived in the most dreadful circumstances!'

The living room set would remain basically the same, apart from shifts of furniture, changes of wallpaper and the occasional new photograph on the wall, for the duration of the *Till Death Us Do Part*. The aspidistra in the corner, the huge porcelain figures on the cabinet, the pictures of Churchill and the Queen (and bizarrely, in the first series, a photograph of Churchill, Stalin and Truman at Yalta), the Bakelite radio set, the silver caravels at either side of the wall, the antimacassars on the chairs – all these pieces of set dressing helped to emphasise the continuity of the Garnett household, and were to change little over the next ten years. The objects and pictures were icons, venerated by Alf as emblematic of the world he knew, or *thought* he knew; a world with values he was determined to uphold, whatever the reason. Few comedy series had ever used set design with such symbolic application before, or have done since.

MEET THE GARNETTS

'Arguments, Arguments', the very first episode of the series, was transmitted in the midst of a heat wave on the early evening of Monday 6 June 1966. It was previewed in *Radio Times* by the producer, who fleshed out the characters, all living in Wapping High Street. First, Alf Garnett: 'Narrow-minded, prejudiced, selfish, greedy, cowardly and very, very proud of himself. He is a

self-confessed expert on any subject. He is also a Tory and a Monarchist ...'
Else was described as a 'pale echo' of her husband and 'vaguely worried about
the price of eggs and the weather not being so good since Labour got in'. Mike:
'Strictly of this generation which rejects all the lovely traditional shibboleths in
which Britain has wallowed since Queen Victoria, he tears down every belief
that the older man depends on.' Mike's new bride (married eight weeks), Rita,
is 'the one beautiful flower growing in the middle of this compost heap'. The
political slant to the show's satire was emphasised in the litany of Alf's pet
hates: Charles De Gaulle, Harold Wilson, the Labour party and the Russians,
the Chinese and all foreigners, and even Edward Heath since he tried to get
Britain into the Common Market.

The episode itself cleverly reiterated all the themes displayed in the *Comedy
Playhouse* pilot. It introduced the three main tropes of the series that led to its
unique structure, nailing its manifesto to the masthead by combining political
and social satire, the interplay between the family itself, and a working class
ethos that was relentless in its detail and avoidance of sentimentality. In
essence, *Till Death Us Do Part* was a debate on the world at large that reflected
the nature of its disputants and revealed their prejudices through their lifestyle
and mannerisms.

Credit from the beginning should also be given to Dennis Main Wilson,
whose opening titles for the '60s series were indeed inspired, summing up
exactly what the show was about in a 30 second collection of images rife with
the symbolism that Speight would use to variable effect throughout its
lifetime. The opening shot – a view of the Big Ben clock tower with the bell's
sonorous tones ringing out – reminded viewers of the original basis of the
Comedy Playhouse episode: Alf's preoccupation with the time. It
simultaneously deployed the familiar BBC time tones and, even more
strikingly, by depicting the Houses of Parliament, expressed the point that
much of the series might have a political bent. The same metonym was to be
used one year later when, in July 1967, ITV began its *News at Ten*
transmissions. The depiction of the centre of power reflected the fact that the
show was focused on recognisable aspects of public life; when the camera
sweeps along the Thames and dives down on the unimposing everyman
Garnett household, it not only signifies the working class roots of the show but
also hints that the Garnetts are only one of many similar families; both integral
points in Speight's philosophy. The viewer is homing in to eavesdrop on one
family near the centre of political power yet divorced from it, commenting on
it. The title music, by Dennis Wilson (no relation to the producer), is also
distinctive. A deliberately pompous opening fanfare is followed by a brief,
nondescript banjo strum as we enter the Garnett household. At the end of the
episode, the composer ensures we leave the family's presence on an
exhilarating tune, a pastiche of Cockney favourites such as 'Colonel Bogey',
'Don't Dilly Dally', 'Any Old Iron' and 'The Laughing Policeman'.

'Arguments, Arguments' opens with Alf attempting to resole his boots one Saturday morning only a week or so after the events of the *Comedy Playhouse* pilot. He uses leather he has appropriated – illegally, of course – from the docks. Else is blithely ironing Mike's shirts, dampening the garments with water from a vinegar bottle, as son-in-law and daughter get ready to go out. To remind the viewers of the central premise of the pilot, Alf recalls that he has already written to Harold Wilson regarding Big Ben's poor timekeeping. The political debate begins almost immediately, as Else reveals her acumen by musing that the weather hadn't been too good since Labour got in again, and Mike pronounces that his father-in-law should give Labour a chance following 13 years of Tory misrule. The argument then switches from the general to the specific, as Mike refers to the family being crowded together in 'this muckhole'. In turn, Alf, provoked beyond endurance by this slight, begins a monologue stressing how he has worked hard all his life in order to put a roof over 'Mummy's' head. As he makes an expansive gesture heavenwards, he accidentally touches Else's hot iron, thus bearing out Mike's point about the house being overcrowded.

The three key themes of the series remain in evidence. There is political and social comment from Alf: 'Look, I got nothing against the working class, but what I say is, they should keep to their proper functions. An' their proper functions ain't sitting up there in Downing Street mucking about with the status quo'. There are acerbic observations on the family and her husband from Else, as Alf heads for the sanctuary of the pub: 'That's it. You've ruined their marriage – now go and ruin your liver'. And there is an utterly convincing depiction of the working class milieu: the small living room, cramped further by the four adults, with Else ironing and Alf cobbling; the shabby local hostelry, replete with its customers displaying a very working-class knee-jerk unity in the face of the landlord's attempts to bar Alf; the brief, alcohol-inspired reconciliation between Alf and Mike on the Saturday night; and finally the dull aftermath on the Sunday morning, the telly broken down, the two men with hangovers, and the arguments, arguments, beginning all over again.

Response to 'Arguments, Arguments' was decidedly mixed. The *Brighton Argus* dubbed it a winner, acclaiming it for being authentic and resolutely unsentimental and comparing Warren Mitchell to 'a matador charging at his dialogue, scoring every time and leaving blood and gore behind him'. It likened the show to *Steptoe and Son* and noted Una Stubbs as its weak point. On the other hand, the *Birmingham Mail*, apparently oblivious to the show's intended satire, found it 'a good deal of noisy, red-nosed fun ... played in knockdown manner ... yet the repeated use of bad language detracted from its entertainment. Surely the aim of a comedy is to entertain rather than to aim at realism?'

Other reviews were less charitable. Comparing the show to *Steptoe and Son* (again), the *Daily Telegraph* cited it as being too hysterical to be authentic and too out of control, and opined that Mitchell was overplaying his part. It also used for the first time what was to become a reviewer's cliché, describing Else as 'long suffering'. The *Daily Mirror* thought the episode noisy, overacted and unfunny, with Mitchell hamming things up. But the *Daily Express* went much further; 'It stinks' was its pithy headline, backed up by the opinion that 'any family viewer would become emotionally and mentally and physically sick …' Having compared the show once more to *Steptoe and Son*, this critic suggested that the prospective viewer should watch one episode and then put it on the banned list. The most measured opinion came from *The Times*, which found the episode 'sometimes nearly as funny as Mr Speight thinks it always is … The series will be noisy, honestly vulgar and at times hilarious.'

Unintentional aid for the show came from an unexpected quarter: the Conservative party, aided and abetted by what was probably some judicious leaking by the production team. The episode was said to have had Alf refer to Ted Heath as a 'Grammar school nit', and the Tories, still smarting after their second defeat in the polls in two years , were as paranoid as the Labour party regarding potential slurs from the one-eyed monster in the living room. The party officials asked the BBC for a copy of the script in order to judge its context, and thus provided the nascent series with some useful publicity. The Tory spokesperson on broadcasting, a Mr Lindsay, examined the said script at Conservative Central Office on the afternoon of Thursday 9 June 1966 and dubbed it 'highly amusing' and full of political 'throwaway gags', but said that he wanted to consider it further before making final judgement. At this point, the BBC blithely pointed out that Mr Heath had actually been referred to as a 'Grammar School twit', not 'nit', a fact backed up by Speight, who said that the second episode, yet to be shown, actually contained the offending 'nit'. (In the event, strangely enough, the word was cut: Mike interrupts Alf just as he is about to speak it, although the implication is clear.) *The Times* delightedly promised that the subsequent three programmes, already recorded, were 'rumoured to be full of similar political dynamite'. The BBC replied that the fourth episode, recorded that very week, had been cut for swearing, and that further references to Prince Philip and religion had been muffled, but would not comment further on the political references. Dennis Main Wilson noted with tongue firmly in cheek that the Garnetts were 'a rough family who are vulgar in a nice, warm way'.

HAIR RAISING!

It was arguably the second episode that really put *Till Death Us Do Part* on the map, as attested to by the peals of uncontrolled laughter that emanated from the studio audience. The storyline revolves around Alf's physical appearance, pushing him even further into the limelight and thus ensuring greater concentration on Warren Mitchell's performance. It provides a perfect example of how the external forces on which the Garnetts comment extend into the internal, familial, situation, and ultimately into the personal link between Alf and Mitchell.

'Hair Raising!' has Alf railing against the hirsute simian morons of the Labour party, on the basis that hair loss is a sure sign of 'cerebral virility'; one need to look no further than McLeod, Churchill or Douglas Home to see the proof of that ... Alf then overhears a classic working-class old wives' tale of a guaranteed cure for baldness: a hot mixture of paraffin and peppercorn to be smeared on the offending pate. Having applied this mixture to his own head – bringing the audience to a state of hysteria in the process – he dozes off, giving Mike the opportunity to daub a Kilroy face on his head using his wife's make-up. He goes upstairs to tell Rita about this, and finds to his horror that Alf has suddenly awakened in his absence and set off to the local pub, thus transforming a private joke into a public humiliation. When Alf belatedly realises that the rest of the pub has been laughing *at* him, and not *with* him, he sinks into a deep depression, only partially remedied by Mike's expiatory solution. The value of a studio audience to give context to the script and its performance is here for all to hear – they are ecstatic, their almost hysterical mirth demonstrating that Speight's show has most definitely won their approval.[13]

A HOUSE WITH LOVE IN IT

The archetypal sitcom situation follows in the third episode: that of the forgotten wedding anniversary. This may actually have been the first script that Speight wrote for the series proper, intending to smooth the Garnetts into the audience consciousness using a familiar cliché; indeed, the script bears a date of the end of March 1966, at which point the family name was still Ramsey. (The wedding anniversary was, incidentally, to prove a source of continuity problems in the future; in the televised episode, it is stated that Alf and Else are celebrating their twenty-fifth, whereas the original script specified that it was their pearl anniversary – i.e. their thirtieth – with Mike and Rita giving Else a gift made of pearls. In an episode the following year,

---

[13] The 'face painting' idea was to resurface in the 1972 series, this time with the paint applied by three lads (one played by Richard Speight), and again much later in the ITV series *Till Death ...*, when Rita's teenage son (again played by Speight junior) performs the same task; ingeniously, when chastised for it by Rita, he states that she and his father have often told him how they did the same to Granddad years before ...

Alf will state that they have been married for 32 years and 10 months.) In splendid fashion, Mike finds that his well-meaning West End restaurant treat for his in-laws is far too expensive and Alf has to assist with the finances, much to his chagrin, especially as he did not want to be there anyway. Here the old working-class social faux pas, displaced to the alien location of a posh restaurant, are paraded for the working-class audience; Else asks for jellied eels, soup and dumplings followed by tea, and fears that since foreigners tread the grapes with their feet, a bottle of wine is a bit dubious for consumption. Unlike similar scenes in other working-class series such as *Meet the Wife*, these in Speight's script transcend the clichés with their bitingly perceptive authenticity and the total lack of any implicit sentimental rapport between the family. Unlike the husband and wife characters played by Thora Hird and Freddie Frinton in *Meet the Wife*, who love each other despite their occasional friction, there is just an obvious vacuum between the Garnetts. And Speight drew on his own experience in a piece of dialogue where Else reveals that Alf first showed his desire for her by romantically throwing stones at her and her friend in Ilford: the writer stated in a 1972 interview that this was the traditional Canning Town opening gambit to an engagement. While 'A House With Love In It' is perhaps in many ways the most unrepresentative episode of the first series, and certainly the safest and most traditional, it does comment on exactly the same dichotomy that the press were concerned about: if Britain was going bankrupt, why could so many people afford to enjoy themselves …?

INTOLERANCE

The fourth episode, 'Intolerance', was important in the show's history for several reasons. First, it was the first episode to feature guest stars playing themselves – in this case, Liverpool FC footballers Willie Stevenson and Ian St John. Una Stubbs has commented that the regular cast would be grateful for such guest appearances, as it would relieve the strain of intense rehearsals and all the shouting both on and off the set; the idea was repeated in the second series and more frequently afterwards. Real-life stars would feature either in chance meetings in the pub (as in the 'Till Closing Time Do Us Part' special, which had appearances by Jimmy Tarbuck and others), on the sports field (Bobby Moore and Reg Pratt in 'Football', George Best and Roy Castle in 'Golf'), or in one of Alf's fantasies ('Up The 'Ammers!'). All of them were either golfing pals or drinking partners of Speight, who must have thought that their appeal to the audience would outweigh the potential dislocation of the very realistic framework he so desired for the show.

Secondly, and more importantly, it was this episode – its title taken from the 1916 DW Griffith film, with its notorious observations on racism and responses to it – that made clear the full extent of Johnny Speight's agenda. It is thus a seminal piece of television comedy, of which unfortunately only a fraction now survives in the archives. When Speight was writing the episode, Mitchell approached him and asked him to include anti-Semitism in Alf's catalogue of racial prejudices; Speight said he had been reluctant to do so before, as he had been afraid he might insult Mitchell's own faith. Mitchell, long since an atheist like the writer himself, told him to go ahead. He later reflected that he thought Speight had written a good script, but that, because of its controversial content, he thought no-one would laugh at it.

'Intolerance' begins with Alf and Mike in Glasgow watching a European Cup Winners' Cup match between Liverpool and Dortmund. Alf is busily insulting the Germans, particularly about the War. He shouts so much that he loses his voice and later has to visit the doctor's surgery. There he finds that his usual doctor, Dr Kelly, is unavailable, and is being covered for by his new partner, Dr Gingalla, who is – horror of horrors – black. As soon as this is revealed, everyone else in the waiting room leaves, appalled at the prospect of being treated by a black physician, but Alf remains, and remarks on their rudeness, maintaining that while everyone knows that there is a colour bar, there is no need to flaunt it so openly, stating 'We ain't all ignorant'. The warm professionalism of Gingalla is later contrasted with the humiliating treatment Alf receives from a white, upper-middle-class throat specialist, who proceeds to get his students to illustrate the problem on Alf's naked throat while dismissing the helpless patient as educationally subnormal.

Later, the Garnetts discuss in their inimitable fashion the colour problem. Else states that blacks are okay in their proper place, such as on the buses, but not when they become responsible professionals such as doctors. In her view, black men are drones, built for work; some of them, she opines, cannot control themselves when they see a white woman. Alf concedes that some 'sambos' are quite clever – they've certainly picked up all the nuances of cricket, for example. Mike points out that Gingalla is British and born in Manchester (on a very hot day, muses Alf), whereas Alf's regular doctor, Kelly, is Irish. In response to Mike's and Rita's outrage at his racism, Alf backs down and denies that he ever said blacks weren't human beings, which inspires Else to go on about other 'black human beings' such as Paul Robeson and Al Jolson …

Mike and Rita emphasise that the only difference between them and Gingalla is skin pigmentation, stressing that many British holidaymakers seek to change their skin colour by sunbathing. This gets them nowhere, as Alf and his wife start to discuss the merits of Bognor (which has a great beach, they agree, except for the tar). Mike accuses them of not listening, at which Else, uncharacteristically, berates him, stating that he prefers the blacks to his in-laws; then Mike maliciously steers the conversation towards

Alf's own racial heritage, emphasised by his Jewish characteristics. Warren Mitchell now brilliantly ignites his character with Hitler-esque rage, using his eyes to incredible effect as he screams out his denial, bellowing, then pleading, that he is *not* 'bloody Jewish'. His son-in-law states that his Semitic birth is obvious – one need only look at his hand gestures or his nose, or consider the probability that his grandfather was Solly Diamond, the 'Fish King', who set up a stall in Petticoat Lane … Alf, almost reduced to tears, disputes the rumour spread by Mike that his ancestor simply changed his name from Garnett to Diamond in order to conduct his business in the Jewish area of Whitechapel. Else is then angry at her husband, stating that he never told *her* that he was Jewish and wondering whether or not he'll want pork chops for his dinner …

In one 30-minute sitcom, the race question was brought into the open for public debate. 'Intolerance' was an astonishing breakthrough in television comedy, deploying a Jewish actor to spout racist sentiments, a clown manipulated by Speight and Mitchell to make a deep incision in the hide of racial disaffection. There is never any question as to Speight's intention, or to his moral standpoint. Symbolically, when Mike attempts to rationalise his in-laws' attitudes, Alf and Else show no wish to listen; the attitude of so many. The unthinking prejudice of the silent majority – represented by Else, with her class obsessions being used to fit her inbred racism – are displayed, while Mike's good intentions are shown as equally racist in their stereotyping. Many forms of racism are displayed – against Afro-Caribbeans, Jews, Irish, Germans and Scots. Alf never thinks about who he is addressing but merely spouts racist stereotypes, getting even these hopelessly wrong; thus Gingalla's breath is said to smell of curry, and the Glaswegians are mistaken for 'krauts' as Alf spouts clichés taken from countless war films at them.

'Intolerance' was sensational stuff, and at the time of its debut transmission was met with … almost total indifference. Only *The Times* appreciated that Alf's rages were being used to voice a host of prejudices thus 'hilariously exploding the lot' and praised Mitchell for his astonishing performance. The *Birmingham Evening Mail*, by contrast, found the episode offensive, unfunny and unconstructive. Otherwise, the show's content raised not a ripple – until its Saturday evening repeat three months later, at a time when there was a meeting of Commonwealth ministers in London and the popularity of *Till Death Us Do Part* had grown to such an extent that it was more routinely discussed in the media. Then, William Price, MP for Rugby, lashed out at the insult to 'coloured doctors', writing to the Director-General of the BBC on 12 September to demand an apology, protesting at what he saw as a blatant attempt to use 'disgraceful colour prejudice to get cheap laughs'. Speight responded by asking why he should not bring racial prejudice into the open to show people how ignorant they could be and how they could laugh at themselves and their bias at the same time. The BBC backed him up: 'The programme sought to expose colour prejudice in all its stupidity – indeed, it could almost be described as a campaign against intolerance.' The religious journal *The Inquirer* also stated in the show's defence: 'I have seen it twice and it struck me as the most effective antiracialist sermon I have ever heard preached.' The *Evening News* commented however that it was tactless of the BBC to show a programme in which a 'coloured doctor was described as a sambo and a coon' when an international conference was in progress. Price later backed down, stating with great if ominous foresight that 'people might not get the message'.

For the recording of 'Intolerance', Mitchell, unknown to the rest of the cast, invited many Orthodox Jews to join the studio audience, first entertaining them with his one man warm-up show, which was still serving as an effective preventative agent against the near embarrassment of the *Comedy Playhouse* pilot recording. Booth recounts that when the scene came where Mike turns on his father-in-law and calls him a Jew – a moment that they had fought hard to retain in the face of doubts from BBC executives – Mitchell, sensing the Jews in the audience responding positively, began to ad lib, grabbing Booth's hands and crying 'Look at those hands! Big Mick hands!' Booth in turn then asserted that Alf's typical hand gestures were Jewish in nature. As Mitchell cried 'I'm not Jewish! I'm not bloody Jewish!', the audience roared with laughter. After the recording had finished, an excited Speight rushed down and asked the audience if they had found the scene anti-Semitic, explaining that the powers-that-be had wished to cut it out. The reply vindicated Speight's ideas, and afterwards Speight and Booth went to the White Elephant to celebrate, where a tipsy Speight accosted writers Bernard Levin and Milton Schuman at a nearby table. Allegedly, he shouted, 'Did you couple of Jews miss a scene tonight! I'm telling you, it was f-f-f-fantastic! Who says you Jews don't have a sense of humour?' The silence was deafening, and an embarrassed Booth dragged his friend away, fearing the worst. But the review in Schuman's television column in the *Evening Standard* the day after the episode was broadcast was full of lavish praise, and surprise that such things could ever have been said on television and still retained their humorous context. The Campaign Against Racial Discrimination was to acclaim that the play had helped race relations with its stance. On the downside, Mitchell received racist letters labelling him a 'Jew boy' and Speight a 'Jew lover'.

The episode was important for a third reason. By putting him centre stage again, it confirmed forever that Alf Garnett, played by Warren Mitchell, was a brilliant new comic creation, and the prime focus for the series. This was to have unexpected repercussions. An early version of the script had an interesting variation on the cause of the black eye that Alf parades, and one that hinted at a more virtuous character. In this earlier version, Alf receives his black eye when he intervenes in the Glasgow pub as he sees one of the locals threatening to assault his wife. This follows on from a discourse in the doctor's waiting room when Else and another woman discuss an acquaintance called Maude Ellis and her domestic injuries inflicted by her husband. Mike thus states it is ironic that the only time his father in law intervenes on the right side for the right reasons, he suffers. Alf, it is shown, is not all bad. This was a moral side to Alf that had to be excised, in order to punish him for his bigotry; a punishment that was to grow exponentially as Speight and Wilson realised that Alf was in danger of becoming a hero rather than a villain to many of the television audience.

ALF IN EXCELSIS

Success for the Garnetts was rapid. Beginning with a ratings index of 60 and a viewing audience of 11.5% of the population, the series soon rose to even greater heights of popularity, peaking with a viewing audience of 16.0% of the population at the height of the World Cup frenzy. Its Reaction Indices were generally in the high sixties, with 'Hair Raising!' reaching a very creditable 71. The scheduling against *Coronation Street* had clearly worked, as the *Observer* reported that the show had helped to knock the latter down to tenth place in the ratings during June, while on 3 July it caused the ITV soap to drop from second to fifth place. Such announcements were grist to the mill of the Corporation's publicity machine, but it was evident that the series was an enormous success.

The *Daily Mail*'s Peter Black, the series' most consistent champion in the press, was aghast at the Garnetts' non-appearance on 11 July, when preference was given to World Cup coverage of the match between England and Uruguay: 'Their absence is only temporary. Had it not been, I would have organised a protest march on the Television Centre, for this is by a long way the best character comedy the BBC has found since *Marriage Lines*, *The Likely Lads* and *Steptoe and Son* … Warren Mitchell's Alf Garnett has grown into a creature of such dimension that he has ceased to seem just an actor's and writer's creation. For me he is a kind of English fairy, an eternal type like Puck, who somewhere quite close to us is leading for 24 hours a day the rowdy, pugnacious, boneheaded and inarticulate life from which Johnny Speight so good-naturedly cuts us off a 30-minute slice each week. I'm not sure that it isn't better than *Steptoe*, though it's entirely unsentimental centre will prevent it from being as popular. *Steptoe* never embedded itself quite so deeply into the thick of real life.'

Booth realised how popular the show was becoming due to the growth in bystanders at the camera rehearsals. Recalling the initial non-reaction to the *Comedy Playhouse* pilot, the first episodes had had only a handful of BBC staff watching the recordings; later 'People working at the BBC used to come, so they could go home and tell their friends what was happening in that week's show. There were queues for the camera rehearsals – the commissionaires, secretaries, telephone girls, actors from other shows, everybody.'

Later, Booth would be greeted with a bellow of 'Scouse git' from passers-by every time he walked down the street, much to his irritation.

Booth was still a major influence on the show at this time. It may have been he who suggested some of the plot for the sixth episode, 'From Liverpool With Love', inputting some of his memories of the Irish Catholic grandfather who created his own version of Irish history into the characterisation of Mike's father, and his own mother's Roman Catholic faith into that of Mike's mother. He also managed to get an actor friend of his, Kenneth Fortescue, a job in the final first series episode, 'Claustrophobia'. Fortescue then rewarded Booth by recommending he take his London apartment at Nell Gwyn House, soon to be dubbed 'Chavering Heights' thanks to the high-class prostitutes that frequented the premises. The balance between Mike and Alf as set out in *Comedy Playhouse* pilot was still present too, even though Warren Mitchell was getting all the plaudits. The fifth episode, 'Two Toilets … That's Posh' was the last in which the main problem that faced Mike and Rita – the inability to secure enough money to guarantee their own place – was addressed in any real depth; after that, the success of the show meant that their presence in Alf's and Else's home was guaranteed. The impact of the comedy was however still powerful – with scenes such as one where Alf rises from his tin bath to surprise his son-in-law, and one where Mike's father steals milk from a baby's bottle, the invention and humour did not flag.

The first series ended on 1 August 1966, two days after England's World Cup victory, in an episode with a situation reminiscent of that of many real-life working-class families that week: the Garnetts on holiday in Cornwall. J C Trewin, writing in *The Listener*, contrasted it unfavourably with the final episode of another BBC sitcom, *The Likely Lads*, which had gone out the week before, calling it 'all wrong … feebly scripted and acted with a kind of attacking desperation' and seeing it as patronising to country folk. But he was in the minority. Impressed with the ratings, the Reaction Index, the generally favourable critical response and the sheer publicity generated, the BBC took the exceptional step of repeating the entire series, a distinction previously unique to *Steptoe and Son*'s first series in 1962, which had cemented that show's popularity. Now the Garnetts would appear in a primetime slot, at 8.20 pm each Saturday. The repeats were launched on 20 August with a prominent feature in *Radio Times* dubbing it 'the most explosive series of the year' and depicting a montage of the rave reviews from the press. The *Observer* called it: 'The most addictive series since vintage *Steptoe and Son*. Alf Garnett – that most irrational of figures, the

Conservative working man – his placid, grumbling wife, their sexy giggling daughter and Mod son-in-law, must surely enter the pantheon of TV heroes.' The *Daily Mirror* meanwhile described it as 'alehouse comedy … rather like hearing a drunken conversation through a crack in the wall'.

The repeats built on the success achieved in the summer, attracting greater ratings, greater interest and greater controversy. By the time that the last episode, 'Claustrophobia', had its second airing, the show was being watched by 27% of the viewing population, beating ITV's Saturday night alternative, *The Mike and Bernie Winters Show*, convincingly. 'Explosive' would be an ideal description of the aims of producer and writer for the series, with Alf next primed to go off at Christmas, and Speight flushed with success waiting to press the detonator switch. Already, on 6 July, a second series was scheduled for early 1967, and this would later be extended from the initially-planned nine episodes to 13. Speight was earning £650 per script, and he sold another five-minute sketch featuring the cast to *Billy Cotton's Music Hall* for transmission on 18 September 1966. On 7 September, the *Comedy Playhouse* pilot was sold to Australia and New Zealand. BBC Enterprises advised that this market would be more fruitful if only the language in the next series could be toned down, since Antipodean standards of censorship were much stricter (*Till Death Us Do Part* was always to be rated PG there), and then totally missed the point by proposing that fewer parochial references be included amidst the political satire. Tom Sloan meanwhile told the BBC Head of Copyright that *Till Death Us Do Part* was the talk of Britain, pronouncing it to be the 'most important comedy event since *Steptoe and Son*'. BBC Scotland also reported that the series had gone down well north of the border, confirming its nationwide appeal.

9
Darlings of Wapping Wharf Launderette

THE IMPORTANCE OF BEING ALF

Tom Sloan, writing in *The Listener* on 11 August 1966, just before the repeats of the first series, saw *Till Death Us Do Part* as the logical progression of the more realistic style of comedy started by *Steptoe and Son* and then continued by *The Likely Lads*. The new show, for some people, shattered forever the earlier illusions of cosy British family life. But why was it so popular? Why was it the source of so many 'whistling kettle' moments across the nation, from Wapping to Wick, from Canning Town to Carrickfergus? What was the secret of its astonishing ratings and strong word-of-mouth reaction? As always with television success, it really came down to a combination of strong scripts, effective ideas, powerful performances and an empathic production environment. Then, of course, there was the scheduling: a working-class comedy set in opposition to a working-class popular drama series, *Coronation Street*.

This new show eschewed many of the conventions of sitcoms, for instance in its avoidance of any innate sentimentality and in its dangerous approach to language, its emphasis on political and social satire, its refusal to be hamstrung by the requirements of plot or structure. But ideas are not generated in a vacuum, and in many ways, it has to be said that without the precedent of the trailblazing *Steptoe and Son*, the show would have been a very different beast. Speight, throughout his career, always required a tried-and-trusted archetype to validate his own take on comedy or drama. First, George Bernard Shaw had acted as a catalyst for his writing, giving life, shape and context to his artistic view, supported in his 'serious' dramas by the example of dramatists such as Harold Pinter and Samuel Beckett. Then he had become acquainted with the already-established persona of Arthur Haynes, before refining and embellishing that persona and taking it as far as he could possibly go. Now, following in the footsteps of Galton and Simpson, he had devised his own situation comedy series, based on several archetypes but validated by the success of his colleagues' own creation. *Steptoe and Son*, now officially in abeyance following the completion of its 1965 series, had opened the door for *Till Death Us Do Part*; a fact that was instantly acknowledged by the viewing public in 1966, if not by Speight himself.

The parallels between Speight's creation and the tale of the two rag-and-bone men were considerable. First, there was the element of conflict between two factions. In Speight's new work, the conflict was between young, iconoclastic Mike and Rita and older, hidebound Alf and Else. In *Steptoe and Son*, it was between the young(ish), pretentious Harold and the old, traditional father figure Albert, the former always striving to achieve his ambitions in life while the latter consistently slammed him down. The weight of Harold's working-class background overwhelmed his attempts to free himself of its chains and impedimenta. The contrast between the two characters sparked off each plot, while the entrapment of the two in their working class environment, with all its stultifying poverty, provided the situation for the comedy, just as in *Till Death Us Do Part*. With the Steptoes, the bond that held the two protagonists was the filial relationship, with its awful obligations brought to the forefront; with the Garnetts, it was the life sentence of the Anglican marriage vow, not merely binding husband and wife but also son-in-law and daughter.

Galton and Simpson consistently used social comment and occasionally political satire in their comedy, the external world of change manifesting itself in the internal world of the Steptoes' relationship. The episode 'My Old Man's a Tory', for instance, sees Harold about to be selected as a Labour election candidate for his area, much to his Tory father's disgust. But Albert's perceptions change when the Labour Party itself humiliates Harold by choosing a younger, more dynamic candidate, thus bringing Albert in on his son's side. Similarly, in 'Pilgrims Progress', there are some wonderful scenes on board an aeroplane heading for France with a party of Great War veterans, erupting into a fracas thanks to Albert's nationalist comments about the French and the Americans. In both cases, political and social comment adds to the acerbity of the script, validating such ideas within a sitcom framework; an approach that Speight was to note and nurture to far more explosive effect in his own series.

Then there was the meticulous recreation of a working-class environment in the Steptoes' ramshackle house adorned with worthless bric-a-brac, forming a permanent backdrop to the situation of a family web spun by its occupants and in turn ensnaring them. The main set rarely changed over time; and *Till Death Us Do Part* was to follow the same approach throughout its run, emphasising that whatever happened in the outside world, it did not materially impinge on the situation of the prison in which the protagonists were held. For the Steptoes, the stuffed bear and life-size skeleton in their living room provided a semi-absurdist backdrop to the action, while for the Garnetts, the iconic wall-mounted pictures symbolising all the totems that Alf held dear, although subject to the occasional addition or slight rearrangement, were symbolic of the fact that only death could end this scenario.

Galton and Simpson emphasised the need for truthful language in the depiction of the traps of working-class life. *Steptoe and Son* had come in for criticism over its language since its infancy; censure later to be faced by *Till Death Us Do Part* on a much greater scale. In *Steptoe and Son*, however, despite its occasional strong language, the swearing was kept firmly in check, its carefully-applied use rendering it more acceptable to a mainstream audience. This was true even more so of the other major working-class comedy of the period, Dick Clement and Ian La Frenais' *The Likely Lads*, which commenced its final series as *Till Death Us Do Part* began its first. Dick Clement exercised enormous control over the show, not only as co-writer but also as producer and director. The central characters, Terry Collier (James Bolam) and Bob Ferris (Rodney Bewes), were inextricably linked by their class, their upbringing and their mutual wishes; if the bond was not a familial one in this case, it was almost as potent. Once again, the polarity between the two characters' temperaments was the springboard for their adventures – Bob the conscientious, self-building, ambitious and sensitive one, Terry the devil-may-care louche lad, both working-class yet both very different. The language used by the two was considerably less strong than in either *Steptoe and Son* or *Till Death Us Do Part*, more subtle and dextrous, a mannered form of pseudo-realism rather than a deliberate attempt to echo reality. And, as in *Till Death Us Do Part*, the theme of change was paramount to the comedy; change tied by tradition. For the Likely Lads in that summer of 1966, change came accidentally as the final episode had Terry sign up for the army by mistake; for the Garnetts, change would come only when, some years later, Else left the household.

But it is important to remember that although *Till Death Us Do Part* strongly paralleled some elements of *Steptoe and Son*, and owed a great debt to it for its existence, and also some elements of *The Likely Lads*, Speight used the springboard provided by his peers to develop his own concepts and ideas, refining his art now that he had seen his approach vindicated with success. He did not slavishly follow the precedents; whereas Galton and Simpson had cautiously opened the door for a realistic working-class sitcom, while keeping a firm grip on the handle, Speight slammed that door wide and then tore it off its hinges. *Steptoe and Son* may have been working-class, but not in a way many could relate to, with its eccentric premise of a father-and-son team of rag-and-bone men; it depicted a world slightly askew to that of its viewers. *Till Death Us Do Part*, with its dockhand, its housewife, its secretary and its occasional labourer, tapped more readily into the working-class zeitgeist. Whereas *Steptoe and Son*, belying signs to the contrary, had a sentimental core, as Harold could never leave his father despite all the strife between them, there was no sentiment at all on view in the Garnett household. And while *Steptoe and Son* typically had a sound structure, with clever plots and intriguing situations, *Till Death Us Do Part* always seemed to be an unauthorised snitch; a half-hour snapshot of an ordinary working-class family in the East End. Yet this is far too simplistic a view in considering Speight's achievement. While the edifice appeared simple, the elements that supported it were deeply complex. A closer look at Speight's creation reveals a breathtaking, very individual aesthetic vision, developing both intentionally from Speight's creativity itself, and from the juxtaposition of such ideas with external creative pressures that influenced and directed this grand concept into new and dangerous territory.

A ROOM FULL OF MIRRORS

Till Death Us Do Part was conceived as a political show in every sense, encompassing the politics of the family, of society and of religion as much as of government. It was a situation comedy that derived its laughs, its *raison d'être*, from political conflicts within the Garnett family. Speight, often viewed as a 'primitive' in the aesthetic sense – an artist who confined himself to simple concepts and simple constructions – actually conceived the situation with a deceptive care and attention.

The structure of the show revolved around alterity – the conjunction of two ideas that are polar opposites. The ideas generated conflict yet ensured that the song remained the same, despite subtle variations on a theme. The central conflict was between old and new; between the Garnetts, Alf and Else, in their late fifties, with their entrenched viewpoints based on empire, duty, service, and unthinking patriotism, and the Rawlinses, Mike and Rita, in their twenties, with a radically different set of values, questioning traditions rather than revering them. One pair were concerned with maintaining the status quo of their own mythologized society, the other with trying to transform the world. This resulted in a war of tradition versus change; a perfect reflection of the tumultuous battle that was transforming British society itself in the mid-'60s. It was a classically simple device to link a mere four protagonists together in a battle that in the '60s had attained a level of volcanic activity; a war of the generation gap; a war that had been long building and then suddenly exploded in the middle of that momentous decade. Then there was the conflict between the two marriages; one stale, of about 30 years' duration, of hidebound convention and sullen indifference, and one fresh, just a few weeks old, of comparative spontaneity and vigour. There was the conflict between the comfortable poor – Alf with his stable if modest income, his own home, the certainty of his employment – and the dependent poor – Mike with his casual labouring work and Rita with her poorly-paid office job that meant they had to reside with her parents. There was the conflict of political ideology

– Alf the working class Tory, right wing in all his views, self-denying of his class, versus Mike and Rita and their resurgent socialism and liberal attitudes.

Anthony Booth had added to this field the battle between North and South. Other skirmishes came between instant deference to authority and instant snubbing of it, and between ostensible Puritanism and self-aware hedonism. Individual episodes would bring out more alterity for inspection; 'Claustrophobia', for example, saw a conflict between stereotypical views of town and country. There was the conflict between hair and lack of it, between supporters of Royalty and of Republicanism, of West Ham and of Liverpool, between knee-jerk faith and knee-jerk atheism …

Such conflicts were symptomatic of a society in flux, and no character seemed to reflect the uncertain outcome of these changes more than Alf. Dennis Main Wilson on Speight in 1968: '[He] … reflects the changes in modern society's moral and social values by holding the reactionary Alf Garnett up to public ridicule – and so the radicals of this world will laugh *at* Alf Garnett. On the other hand, there are millions who prefer the old values as they were. They seem to agree with Alf and, rather than laugh at him, laugh with him.'

But there was another conflict, an internal one, within the family whose life and values were determined by the external forces that they commented upon. Thus the battles between Alf and Else, between Else and Mike, between Mike and Rita and most of all between Alf and Mike. The very nature of the situation meant that the external conflict of change versus tradition had to be mirrored by the internal one of the Rawlins' wanting to opt out of their predicament but finding themselves trapped by working-class poverty. In this we see another system of mirrors at work, as old Alf, despite Mike's protestations to the contrary, is reflected by his son-in-law, whose stereotypes and values are just as vacuous and debilitating; and one suspects that pleasant, compassionate Rita will eventually come to mirror her bovine mother after a long imprisonment within the walls of marriage.

How this system of conflicts twisted and transformed itself is in essence the story of this extraordinary series itself. The way the nature of the comedy became diluted as the system began to break down for a variety of reasons will be discussed in due course. Suffice to say at this stage that the first series showed all the art without any of the artifice of Speight's apparently simple concoction.

The third factor – a realistic context within which the war could be staged – was the necessary concomitant of all this. The working class ethos so familiar to Speight and to much of his middle-aged audience had to accommodate and nurture the conflicts; and in the mid-'60s, this ethos was supposedly changing due to what Harold Wilson famously termed the 'white heat' of technology, ushering in a greater prosperity and a greater emphasis on meritocracy and classlessness, manifested in its most superficial form in the popular culture of pop idols, film stars, designers and photographers that garnished the period. Speight however knew this to be just the tip of a large and rather ugly iceberg. He had elevated himself through his art from poverty to comfort, and now, pitched midway between tradition and change, he could observe this ferment with sincerity and comment on it with honesty. This was the nature of his comedy, and this was its appeal. The viewing of external and internal forces together through the prism of acutely-observed working-class life constituted the towering achievement of the first two series of *Till Death Us Do Part*, combining a demotic form of popular satire – a working man's response to the more rarefied intellectual sniggering of Oxbridge – with a huge amount of physical comedy. Who better to take on this responsibility than Speight, archetype of working man made good, as creator and writer, and Mitchell, insecure Jewish Londoner, and Booth, rabidly socialist Liverpudlian, as lead actors?

There was a final mirror, perhaps the most powerful of all, that needs to be understood – the form in which Speight couched his satire. To have stood away from his creation, to have exercised restraint, to have created a sense of structural distance, to have effectively told his audience that this was only a satire, as Frost or Bennett or Levin or Rushton would no doubt have done, would have been to have distanced himself from his work, to have implied censorship of his own material, to have denied the realism of his medium and thus ultimately the realism of his art. Speight's concept of art was holistic – it was indivisible, all of it contributing to the overall effect. Not for him, in Joyce's phrase, art 'refined out of existence, paring his fingernails'. Everything had to connect and everything had to be real. To have exercised too much control would have diminished the impact. Thus, rather than self-consciously explain the satire, Speight used his protagonist to convey his message in a refracted image; another example of alterity that informed this series, and one that was to transcend its historical interest and provide a great deal of concern in the future.

This manifested itself first of all in the fourth episode, 'Intolerance'. As one commentator put it, 'Thus racialism is attacked and mocked by placing into the mouth of the central character the most virulent racist notions, the established orders are attacked through a crawling, unthinking support for them, and Christianity is denigrated through grotesque support for its mythologies.' This was a stunning development in 1966, and recognised as such; but the idea was so constantly used in the series thereafter that it became devalued and ultimately led (as early as 1967) to fears that it might backfire, and that the audience might just believe everything that Alf ranted. Hence Mrs Whitehouse's objection, 'Because [Speight] was convinced that there was nothing offensive about the word "coon"' – since thematic reversal was designed to illuminate racism's inanities and absurdity – 'he could not accept that coloured people in this country could look upon its use as an insult'. This was true also of Speight's atheism. Since he was convinced that the Bible was 'bloody rubbish' anyway, he failed to see why anyone should be offended if it was mocked. Naturally, many Afro-Caribbean immigrants in the '60s found both Alf's racism and the attacks on their Christian faith hard to stomach.

It was over the issue of race that the series was eventually to encounter its greatest problems in its employment of thematic reversal; and such problems were recognised by some from the outset. Angela Barry, a teacher and race studies writer, has recalled watching 'Intolerance' as a young girl recently arrived from Bermuda and 'shedding a silent tear'. She was not unaware of racism on television, having viewed the same from America, but was totally unprepared for the vitriol with which Alf dealt out such terms as 'coon' and 'sambo'. She could not express her distaste and fear and outrage, however, because all her school friends agreed that the show was the funniest thing on TV. Thomas Baptiste, who played Dr Gingalla in the episode, was a Guyanan singer and actor who had arrived in Britain in the '50s and had appeared in John Hopkins' anti-apartheid *Wednesday Play* 'Fable' the year before; he had also had the distinction of becoming, in 1963, the first ever black actor to appear in *Coronation Street*. He felt at the time that Alf's tirades would eventually backfire, and that Speight's good intentions and brilliant method of satire would come to naught.

Just a cursory look at the press of the time reveals endemic racism. On the same day as the *Comedy Playhouse* pilot was transmitted, Don Finney of the English Rights Association in Smethwick demanded a limit on numbers of coloured people in the community, saying that, without this, 'living standards would drop' and offering to arrange, free of charge, the finding of white house-buyers for those who did not wish to sell their properties to 'coloureds'. Around the same time, news of the appointment of Britain's first black police officer was welcomed by an array of painted swastikas at the police training college in Ryton near Coventry. In the Midlands, the British version of the Klu Klux Klan was holding beacon-lit meetings and vigils. The *Daily Mail* would report in February 1967, just as the second series of *Till Death Us Do Part* was finishing, on a group of council tenants in London protesting about the arrival of an ethnic minority family with cries of 'Go home, nigger', while in West Bromwich, female factory workers went on strike when their boss employed a Jamaican girl. And it was only three years earlier that the Southall Residents Association had demanded segregated schools and house sales to whites only, while the 1964 General Election candidate for Smethwick had won his seat using the slogan 'If you want a nigger neighbour, vote Liberal or Labour'.

Warren Mitchell certainly saw that some people did not get the message. As he has often recounted, he was stopped frequently by men who loved him as Alf for 'having a go at the coons', in response to which he would turn round and state that he was actually having a go at idiots like them. Some contemporaries, though, understood the intent. John Tyndall, head of the

British National Party, would lament in 1967, 'The BBC and well-known leftist Johnny Speight had collaborated to put right-wing views in the mouth of an idiot'. In 1967, D A N Jones was to write in *The Listener*, 'While the *News Of the World* sells so well, it is natural that some people – the liberal bourgeoisie and the emancipated sons of the workers – should worry in case simple viewers take Alf's grotesque views and approve them.'[14]

For Speight, the George Bernard Shaw disciple, the most ingenious means of depicting his ideas and themes was through the monster he swore he never created but merely grassed on: in other words, through his approach of thematic reversal. Thus, the more that Alf ranted about a subject, the more the audience was meant to take the opposite view. The problem with this strategy was that it required a higher structure to indicate it, or at least a balance to stabilise it, otherwise the real message could become obscured. As Speight was an autodidact who felt he had reached his own unique views on society without any need of authority to tell him how to think, such structures, such guidelines, would have been impossible for him to bear. He provided Mike and Rita as a balance, but such was his commitment to realism that Mike, at least at first, was seen to be as big an idiot as his father-in-law. Then, very quickly, the character of Alf took over and tipped any such vague ideas of balance out of the window.

As previously noted, one method Speight adopted to indicate that Alf was wrong while still maintaining thematic reversal was to punish him for his misdemeanours, and this punishment became steadily harsher and harsher as the series progressed; yet this had the unintentional and unfortunate effect of making Alf seem in certain circumstances a pathetic or even sympathetic figure. Dennis Main Wilson had recognised this by 1972, but, perhaps inevitably given Speight's mode of working and train of thought, no attempt was ever made to change the emphasis of the series. This illustrates one of the key differences between British television, where a single scriptwriter can be left to his own devices on a series, and American television, where the dictates of higher-volume production invariably mean that numerous different writers are employed, and the series itself is given stricter parameters. Hence while *All in the Family*, the later US adaptation of *Till Death Us Do Part*, was to receive some criticism to the effect that it reinforced bigotry, this was never on the

---

[14] At the same time, concerns were being increasingly expressed about the integrity of *The Black and White Minstrel Show*; on 19 May 1967, the Campaign Against Racial Discrimination urged the BBC to stop 'this hideous impersonation' which 'is quite offensive and causes distress to most coloured people'. They also complained about a sketch featuring Leslie Crowther as a 'blacked up' Pakistani singing about the joys of living on National Assistance. These concerns that were shrugged off by the BBC, who cited the show's enormous popularity as 'good natured family entertainment'.

same scale as the opprobrium directed at its British predecessor, because *All in the Family* was not constrained to take the same uncompromising approach. While in the '60s and '70s *Till Death Us Do Part* was seen as political and social satire of a general nature, the world has changed so much that it is now remembered mainly for its treatment of just one issue, that of race – and a morally ambiguous treatment at that. All this was to come in the future, but the problems had their roots in 1966.

Another consideration here was the perennial metropolitan fixation of British culture, and in particular its focus on London. This was where the movers and shakers of the swinging '60s lived, but they were seemingly unable to grasp that, far from being typical of the rest of the nation, the capital (or at least their cosy segment of it) was very, very different. What may have been acceptable or even *de rigueur* in London did not always travel that well into the provinces, especially in a decade when the communication networks and cultural interfaces we take for granted today did not exist. While *Till Death Us Do Part* became a nationwide success, it was nevertheless the product of a handful of comfortably-off left-wing intellectuals, cocooned in their own heady metropolitan lifestyles, who were not necessarily in touch with the thoughts and beliefs of the rest of the population.

Yet the new show not only attracted plaudits from the chattering classes, it also caught the attention of the viewing public at large, winning a massive regular audience that was not only to ensure its durability but also to generate problems of its own. This brings us back to the question: why was the show so popular? Contemporary reaction to the first series suggests that, of all the factors discussed above, paramount was its realism. Una Stubbs was to say in 1968, '[The viewers] must think it's a real family on whom the cameras spy once a week'; she noted that when she and the other regular cast members repaired to the pub during breaks in rehearsals, strangers would often approach them and address them as if the Garnetts were real. An edition of BBC Two's *Late Night Line-Up* programme in February 1967 polled people about their thoughts on Speight's show, and virtually all of them said it was 'true to life'. The panel of viewers who regularly contributed their opinions to the BBC's audience reaction reports on selected programmes were also unanimous in praising its realism; it was funny, most said, because of its truth. The working-class ethos had been meticulously maintained throughout the seven episodes. This was achieved in large part by the focus of the action on the cramped confines of the Garnett home, with incidents such as Alf showering all and sundry with his toenail clippings and bumping into Else's hot iron; Mike and Rita failing to secure privacy for themselves even in their own room, as Alf shouts up and tells them to turn their radio down; and Mike's parents, Kate and Patrick Rawlins, causing disruption with their visit, forcing Mike and Rita to give up their own bed and sleep downstairs. Then there is Alf having to take his bath in the kitchen, while Else hangs up her washing there because it is raining outside. There are all the typical trappings of '60s working-class life: the habitual weekend reading of the tabloids over breakfast; the collective viewing of the telly, which invariably breaks down just when it is most required; the ritual visit to the pub, where the ritual argument breaks out, followed by the ritual drunken stagger back to the confines of home. There is the promise of a good time at a wake; the use of a tab to buy drinks on account; Dad's insistence that a certain chair is his and no-one else's. There are the blazing rows; the dinners being thrown up the wall (or, in Alf's case, out of the window, directly over the head of a passing policeman); and the air of suppressed violence, which breaks out occasionally, such as when Alf throws water or tea over his son-in-law and Mike threatens to thump him in return.

And this sense of reality is enhanced by the sheer noise levels in the home. The Garnetts are *loud*, whether engaged in their interminable arguments, or their swearing, or their comic business, or their brief but impressive acts of violence. They curse, they shout, they verbally (and sometimes physically) abuse each other on a titanic scale; in the first series, they also follow the habit of all four family members talking at once, a signature that would be dropped from the show in the future. They generate an intensity level that is at times overwhelming; a tidal wave of noise that swept out from the television set and engulfed the millions of viewers. Compared with every other situation comedy – compared with every other *programme* – *Till Death Us Do Part* was quite simply the noisiest, the most profane and the most consistently violent show on television. It could not be ignored, and some people hated it for its strident ebullience, while many more loved it.

In the '60s, when a family would have only one television set, around which up to three generations would often gather in the living room, the situation in the Garnett household was one that most viewers could recognise as truthful; a mirror image of their own lives that linked them intimately to the interminable on-screen warfare. The breadwinner father had first choice of viewing, and anyone over the age of 30, while not perhaps having to put up with a tin bath or outside toilet then, could easily recall the trials and tribulations of earlier days. Those of the same age and class as Alf, with secure skilled jobs, would relate to his lifestyle. Their older relations would empathise even more closely. Speight said that wives used to tell him that Alf was like their husbands, children that Alf resembled their father. This dynamic was to dictate the flow and direction of the show, as parents were initially bothered not so much by its content as by its language, which would embarrass them before their families. Television in the '60s was geared toward an older, more patriarchal demographic, which seems utterly alien to the target audiences of today, and the different social values of this very different world would see the father, who demanded total respect from the family he supported, anxious that the profanity used on screen might undermine that respect. The inclusion of swearing was, however, essential to Speight in the depiction of reality. 'If "bloody" is a bad word,' he noted, 'the more you say it, the more inoffensive it becomes. Alf Garnett would never say "ruddy". That, to me, is bad language. "Bloody" is good language because that is what he would normally say. I can't stand words like "frigging" … "Frigging" is bad language. "Bloody" was the worst word we ever used, though he said "Cobblers" a couple of times and "That's a load of crap".'

Speight had meticulously established a general ethos of realism for *Till Death Us Do Part*, but he went further than that; he also included many small but perfectly-formed specifics that would resonate with his target audience and add to the verisimilitude. The price of a mortgage; the cost of a slap-up meal; the need to traverse the Salisbury bypass *en route* to Cornwall; Alf's assertion that his 16 bob a month contribution is wasted on the National Health Service; the numerous references to politics and television. This approach was to be developed further in the second series, but was evident from the beginning, and the audience seemed to appreciate it. Would a writer of Speight's stature have known the price of a bottle of milk? Well, there is evidence that in the '70s, Dennis Main Wilson would regularly send Speight various demographic figures and price indices as background information for the show, and we may postulate that this had been the practice since the first series. *Till Death Us Do Part* was a social document in more ways than one. There is a great sense of location, and specifics that add to the realism. Wilson was to state: 'All good comedy is truth. *Till Death* … is the raw truth, even unpalatable at times. Everybody has known an Alf Garnett or met one. And, let's be honest, there's a bit of him in every one of us …' This was undoubtedly one of the most powerful attractions of a show that mixed the reality of fine drama with the truth of good comedy .

A realistic montage was all very well, but the script also had to be amusing and entertaining. What were the ever-increasing body of viewers of *Till Death Us Do Part* actually laughing at? Speight's writing linked social and political satire into a sitcom format to a degree that had never been seen before. This had a great deal to do with its timing, both generally and specifically. It may be hard to envisage now, but satirical tilts at politicians were a relatively new phenomenon in the mid-'60s. Society was growing more and more impatient with the lies and absurdities of governments, and the flourishing of TV had a great deal to do with this. *TW3* had started the attack on politicians in its literate, slightly smug Oxbridge way, finding a younger, more 'cultivated' audience; *Till Death Us Do Part*'s assault was a blood-spatter on the palace walls by comparison, a primal scream that the masses, feeling increasingly betrayed by the establishment, could understand and savour. When Alf declared that either George Brown or Harold Wilson was 'cooking the books', this was dangerous stuff, particularly so soon after an Election that had opened the gates to all kinds of industrial turmoil as the *sans culottes* could see victory in their grasp. And, as we have seen, in the summer of 1966, when the country was apparently on the crest of a social and artistic wave, a surge of unprecedented self-confidence and creativity, later enshrined forever in the British collective psyche, the hidden sores of economic disaster were seeping into the public arena as never before. Speight's show appeared at this precise moment, becoming for better or worse a tabloid version of the 'super electronic newspaper' that Hugh Carleton Greene so desired for the BBC.

Till Death Us Do Part set up its banner from the beginning, its opening titles linking the seat of power with the toilet seat in the Garnetts' house; the body politic, symbolised by Big Ben, connecting with the cloacal tract of its working-class bowels; mixing state and individual, pomp and poverty, democracy and demagoguery, high ideals and low life … In the first series, the audience – who had only recently been subjected to a second General Election within 18 months, and were now being told that the country was in the midst of an economic crisis – would find Alf's opinions on their leaders refreshingly simple, vicious and accurate. Choice examples included acerbic comments to the effect that Harold Wilson was enjoying an affluent lifestyle while preaching restraint to his electors; that he had rigged the 1966 Election; that the Tories could not be corrupt simply because they were too rich to need to work a scam; that Labour were intellectually subnormal ('Hair Raising!'); and that amazingly, despite the Prime Minister's exhortations for a pay freeze, some of the populace were doing extremely well, thank you very much ('A House with Love in It'). There were attacks on the National Health Service, most notably in 'Intolerance', as Alf endures three hours of waiting with only a round of 'flyblown sandwiches' to keep him company, followed by humiliation in front of the consultants. There were brief but vivid put-downs of Edward Heath and of upper-class Socialists – 'top hat and football boots' – of whom it was said that while they preached that 'all property is theft', they weren't averse to pinching some real estate of their own. Then there were criticisms of the working class themselves; they were, in Alf's estimation, bone idle, and couldn't be found at work half the time because they were in the khazi smoking; while according to Mike's father, Patrick, their bosses were equally lazy, and merciless oppressors to boot. Alf blithely accepts that hereditary peers in the House Of Lords were born to rule, repositories of classical learning from their public school education, but complains that nowadays half the Labour Lords are shop stewards and the other half 'Lord Ted Willises'. And there was confusion expressed over the new Europe: with foreigners like the 'Eyeties' and the 'Hispanioles' swarming all over Britain, and the British reciprocally settling all over Europe, how on earth would we know which side to uphold if another war broke out? How indeed.

Like the Garnetts, the viewers could recognise the changes taking place in their society, as commented on by Speight through his mouthpieces. The satire took on an especially incisive character when implanted within a sitcom, particularly one that also simultaneously satirised the opinions of the people actually watching it. With the working class portrayed as loudmouths (Alf, Mike), drones (Else) and liars (Patrick Rawlins), no wonder Mrs Whitehouse was to call this the most subversive show of the '60s. The satire was broad, cruel, frequently knee-jerk and sometimes ineffective, but always reflected the deep sense of paranoia, betrayal and insecurity of the working-class soul.

Shooting abuse at all and sundry in the spotlight was clever and appealing, but insufficient on its own to sustain the show's enormous ratings. Here the comic business came into play, much of it seemingly invented by the cast, primarily Mitchell, during rehearsals, because Speight had provided only dialogue in the script. If is clear for instance that the studio audience for 'Hair Raising!' are not being amused by satire but enjoying a good belly laugh at Alf applying his awful folk remedy, having his face painted by Mike and finally letting out an intense primal groan as he realises his humiliation. In other episodes, the audience howl at Alf's description of Mike as a 'Peruvian ponce' and Else as a Ken Dodd look-alike as the family dress for dinner; they giggle at the sight of him barely able to croak as the doctors draw a diagram on his larynx, or having a bath and almost exposing himself as he gets out with towel wrapped around him as he goes to shut the door; they snigger at Else trying to hitch up her stockings in a posh restaurant when she becomes convinced that a nearby customer is leering at her, and at Mike patronising the local yokels with his Long John Silver-isms; they guffaw at the scene where Patrick steals milk out of a baby's bottle, and at the elder Garnetts bowing and scraping to Lord Farrel ('Claustrophobia'). It was relentlessly cruel humour, with no guidelines and no sentiment, no moral superview or cosy summary, a mix of slapstick and satire, silliness and snobbery, violence and vulgarity, emanating into the living rooms of the nation.

FOR RICHER, FOR POORER ...

While the first series of *Till Death Us Do Part* had a profound effect on the British viewing public, its success inevitably also affected those most closely associated with its production. Arguably the greatest effect was on Speight. The new golden egg he had laid was to bring him a great deal of wealth and an equal helping of artistic problems. Norma Farnes, who started work as Spike Milligan's assistant at Associated London Scripts' Bayswater headquarters on Monday 22 August 1966, two days after the show received its first peak-time repeat, recalls the writer bubbling with ideas. Dressed casually in the latest fashions by Blades or Mr Fish, he would appear in the late morning, chat to Eric Sykes and then pop in to see Milligan. 'This amazing self-educated East Ender was a truly original thinker,' wrote the instantly-charmed Farnes, 'unfettered by received opinions on any subject and *so* wise. And a great observational writer.' That first day, Speight took Farnes out to the White Elephant to induct her into the ALS way of working. He drank whisky with his first course and recommended white wine for hers, ordering her the most expensive half-bottle on the menu. He then ordered a baked potato filled with caviar for himself and urged the horrified Farnes to have one too – after all, he blithely insisted, it was only a Soviet peasant's lunch …

The first series of *Till Death Us Do Part* may have been an amazing success, but it was also to exacerbate some of the problems that had always lurked behind the Garnetts' aspidistra. For Speight, the show provided the ideal framework for all the political and social comment he had always desired to unleash in emulation of his hero Shaw. In one format, all of his pet themes and frustrations – working class injustice and self-delusion, idiotic political principles based on ignorance, blind devotion to vacuous religious tenets – had been linked with a supreme, all-encompassing inner rage and then distilled, made flesh and transmitted into the nation's living-rooms, and the British populace had lapped it up. This was also a vindication of his unique style of writing, with its emphasis on dialogue rather than plot or structure. Plots were not essential to Speight's construct, because plots weren't 'real'. He dabbled with them in the first two series, notably in 'A House with Love in It' and later 'I Can Give It Up Anytime I Like', both of which revolved around comic plot clichés; but even then, he subverted the clichés to give a warped view of the traditional cosy sitcom format. As his confidence grew, so did Speight's desire to stretch and even break the constrictions of plot and structure, venturing in the second series to centre whole episodes around a single situation, such as the family eating at the dinner table or simply consulting a map as they discuss the Vietnam War. As Frank Muir commented in 1967, *Till Death Us Do Part* episodes had 'no formal construction … Most plots were either minuscule or pretty awful … because Johnny Speight knows how his characters' minds work and what they say, not what they do … A 30-minute argument alone is a whole new area'.

Ancillary characters of the kind that had provided welcome colour to the earliest episodes were largely dispensed with, and the scripts threatened at times to become unworkable, as Speight's dialogue went on and on without structural refreshment. This also led to more in-fighting during rehearsals and on set, as it meant that the cast had to work exceptionally swiftly and arduously to get each episode ready on time.

Speight's tendency toward late delivery of scripts, as when he worked on the Arthur Haynes shows, had already manifested itself on the debut series of *Till Death Us Do Part*. The dictates of a regular schedule were proving too much for the writer. He had to turn down the offer of scripting a 13-part series starring Harry H Corbett for Rediffusion. (Dick Clement and Ian La

Frenais took up the work, and it became *Mr Aitch* early in 1967.) A *Comedy Parade* radio show called 'Inner Circle', produced by Humphrey Barclay and featuring Miriam Karlin, also had to be cancelled due to lack of time. Speight had never written a complete sitcom series before, with all the strictures of a regular recording pattern, and could not – or would not – cope; a problem that was a source of increasing concern within the BBC. In a memo of 1 August 1966 praising his production assistant, Geoff Jowitt, Dennis Main Wilson commented: 'This series proved to be singularly difficult in that, as usual, scripts were either late or non-existent.'

Although the first four scripts had been delivered on time, the last three had indeed all been late. The one for 'From Liverpool with Love' had been distributed to the production crew on 23 June, only five days before recording; and the one for 'Claustrophobia' had gone out on 5 July, a mere four days ahead of the studio date. In a letter to Frank Muir in October, Wilson confessed that he was 'petrified' by the new recording dates for the second series, and joked that with Speight's track record, if the 13 episodes went ahead, he might be faced with the possibility of having to play records for half an hour each week … Furthermore, he noted, Speight left him to tidy up too much, which meant he was working seven days and seven nights a week, and 'apart from being contrary to Corporation practice, I also have a vested interest in not dying [before] the end of the series'.

The scripts that were delivered were frequently overlong and had to be edited by the cast and crew during rehearsals, or even sometimes after recording, which entailed more expense. Thus, for instance, a sequence of dialogue in 'A House with Love in It' in which Else and Alf worry that Harold Wilson might sell Buckingham Palace to 'the coloureds' was excised before recording, while some sequences in 'Intolerance' involving Frank Gatliff as the throat specialist were cut after recording. As Mitchell complained, the scripts were also full of spelling mistakes and at times virtually unreadable. Interviewed in 1991, Wilson commented: '*Till Death Us Do Part* was [made on] a weekly turnaround, and a Johnny Speight script is written in a convoluted, pre-War, old-fashioned Cockney, and it's a pig to learn … Warren Mitchell by the end of the series was exhausted, you know …'

These problems would get worse with the second series and reach crisis point with the third. As producer, Wilson had to ensure that scripts were ready and in a fit state for recording, and with a writer who not only consistently delivered at the very last minute but also presented his work as a kind of stream-of-consciousness first draft, without any revisions, rewrites or structuring of any kind, was very difficult. Muir later testified to Wilson's beyond-the-call-of-duty dedication to the series, which saw him desperately attempting to get scripts submitted on time, reshaping them during rehearsals and so forth. On at least one occasion, Wilson personally dragged

Speight out of an all-nighter at Annabel's to make him finish a script. It was also Wilson who gave each episode a title suitable for printing in *Radio Times*, for instance changing Speight's plain 'Baldhead' to the slightly more interesting 'Hair Raising!'.

Nevertheless, the always-financially-astute Speight felt that the huge success of *Till Death Us Do Part*'s first series gave him increased bargaining power, having elevated him to the position of an acclaimed and feted writer for the BBC. His work was, after all, his pension, as he was frequently heard to say at the ALS headquarters. While Dandy Nichols went on to win film parts in *Georgy Girl*, *How I Won The War* and *Carry On Doctor* and Warren Mitchell secured another role in *The Avengers*, Speight had his agent, Beryl Vertue, write to Tom Sloan and Frank Muir to request that her client receive £20,000 a year in return for delivering 20 scripts, with the added proviso that the BBC should guarantee at least seven repeats on the basis that Speight would receive half the proportionate fee again. In support of this, she cited other increased fee levels of late such as Chesney and Wolfe's £800 per script and Galton and Simpson's £1,800 for two recent TV broadcasts. The BBC, however, declined, stating that they were bound to observe the Government's recent indefinite pay freeze. Speight then asked for £800 per script, but on 17 October the BBC responded with an offer of £700 for each of 13 scripts for a series set for transmission during January to March 1967, asserting that this was a 'reasonable' offer that might be increased to £800 per script once the pay freeze was lifted. £700 per script was the amount that Speight was already due to receive under a previously-agreed contract of 19 July 1966, which had stipulated that six scripts be delivered by 9 December and a further three by 20 January 1967, the first episode being scheduled for transmission on 2 January. Negotiations continued, and early in January 1967 the BBC was to cave in to their star writer's demands. Thereafter, Speight was to return with alarming regularity with bids for higher remuneration, while at the same time continuing to prove deeply unreliable in fulfilling his commitments.

And here was another upshot: now that Speight had found the ideal vehicle to present his satire, why should he bother to look for another? In terms of its impact on his artistic ambition, the success of *Till Death Us Do Part* was arguably crippling to Speight – out, for instance, went the stage plays that had gained him such kudos in his earlier days. While he was later to be responsible for several more sitcoms – *Curry and Chips*, *Spooner's Patch*, *The 19th Hole* – and to continue to write for other shows and artists such as Marty Feldman, the spirit of Alf would dominate everything he did from this point on. Ultimately, Speight found himself following the same principle he had fought against with Lew Grade and Arthur Haynes: why change a successful format?

And why indeed? In a matter of weeks, *Till Death Us Do Part* had raised

Speight's profile immeasurably. Now he was lauded in the press, and one of the few comedy writers whose name was known to the public. The Garnetts were to be lucrative commodities both at home and abroad. Here, Speight's sales background would come in very useful, both in the financial sense and in the publicity sense, and he would push his name ever forward, bringing upon himself untold pressures as well as high fees.

Success was also to have a life-changing effect on the series' principal actor, Warren Mitchell, now a television superstar thanks to his portrayal of Alf Garnett. Having spent ten years on the margins of television as a respected and much-in-demand character actor – especially when he did a 'funny foreigner' accent – Mitchell was now the toast of the industry. On 25 November 1966, part-way through the rehearsal period for 'Peace and Goodwill', the first episode of the second series, and shortly after he had finished reprising his part of Russian Ambassador Brodny in *The Avengers*, Mitchell received the accolade of Actor of the Year from the Guild of Television Producers and Directors. He deserved all the plaudits. He had taken Speight's character and made him real, turning Alf into a colossus, a creature so angry, so overpowering, that he had become, already, a household name. His performances were truly astonishing, lighting up the television screen, smashing through it and speaking – well, shouting – directly to millions. His delivery of dialogue, his ad-libs, his comic business, much of it improvised, had brought Speight's monster to electrifying life. It was Mitchell who had habitually questioned the scripting, argued with the producer, railed against the director (at one point, Douglas Argent was to halt studio recording of the second series episode 'The Bulldog Breed' and ask, 'Ladies and Gentlemen! Who is directing this show – me or Mr Mitchell?') and howled at Anthony Booth. It was he who had advised every member of the regular cast on how they could improve their performance. ('We care, so we shout and swear,' he unapologetically told one reporter who was avidly taking in the on-set mayhem.) It was he who had created the bizarre circumstances that had helped to elevate the show to its prime position as the most talked-about on television: a group of actors arguing amongst themselves in order to depict a fictional family arguing amongst themselves, witnessed by millions of other families – who then argued amongst themselves …

Mitchell's belief in method acting saw him, and then Speight, attributing the endless conflicts in rehearsals to the spirit of Alf – creating the impression of Alf as a kind of succubus, draining the actor who played him, transforming him into the character he played. Dennis Main Wilson was later to subscribe to this view as well, feeling that the monster Garnett seemed so real as to be a human being in his own right. This is a neat aesthetic conceit, to which the response could be the same as Olivier's to Dustin Hoffman's method-acting concerns during production of the movie

Marathon Man (1976): 'Why don't you just try acting, dear boy?' In July 1966, though, Mitchell was declaring that there was a lot of Alf in him (although not the Garnett capacity for alcohol – Mitchell was a teetotaller). 'I bully. I shout. I bluster,' he said. In November of the same year, interviewed at his Highgate bungalow, surrounded by his three kids, two dogs and a host of yachting manuals, he elaborated: 'The words "Silly Moo" are not allowed in this house, though I suppose there is quite a lot of me in Alf Garnett. I'm a bit of a bully and I'm fairly dogmatic, stupid and ignorant. I said to my two eldest children once, "Your daddy is not like that awful Alf Garnett, is he?" They roared with laughter and shouted "He is, daddy, he is!" It shook me a bit, I must say …'

Speight told a story about Mitchell in the early days of *Till Death Us Do Part*: 'Warren once told his wife to wake him early with a pot of coffee and breakfast as he had to be at rehearsal. So she oversleeps, and as she's going round the house getting breakfast, he's going on at her, "Look, I told yer, didn't I, I told yer, I had to be there at ten o'clock." Finally she flung his breakfast at him and said, "You're getting more and more like Alf Garnett. The trouble is, you're not funny with it." He stormed out of the house, and halfway to rehearsal he started laughing.'

In 1986, Val Hennessy interviewed Mitchell, who was then engaged in recording the successor series *In Sickness and in Health*, and found his 'belligerence and accent so disconcertingly similar to those of Alf that I half expect him to yell "Piss off, you silly moo …"'

Mitchell found that his portrayal of the character demanded such intensity that it frequently wore him out physically; his endless quest for perfection on set in the guise of Alf was certainly to take its toll on the rest of the cast. There were other worries, too. Mitchell feared that it would be difficult for him to find the time to make further series of *Till Death Us Do Part* while also continuing to do other work, and he had an increasing concern about being typecast; a concern that in itself served as an incentive for him to seek out such other work. Could he – should he – spare the time to continue to perform as Alf? But despite this uncertainty in Mitchell's mind, he and Speight had already conceived of a life for Alf outside the confines of the show that had spawned him; and these plans would burgeon as the second series approached. Indeed, it was at about this time that Mitchell made what was probably his first solo appearance as Alf. This was at a prestigious event with ex-Tory Premier Harold Macmillan as guest of honour. At one point, 'Alf' rushed on to warn Macmillan that his fellow Tories were attempting to poison him. Totally unaware of who this crazed figure was, Mac was understandably startled; it was only later that he understood, when his daughter explained to him that Alf was a popular comedy character.

10
The Second Series

BACK FOR MORE

The official announcement of a second, 13-part series of *Till Death Us Do Part* was made by Frank Muir on 28 September 1966. Booth and Stubbs had signed contracts for the first seven episodes earlier the same month. Mitchell, with all his concerns about becoming too associated with one character, waited a few weeks longer. Fred Joachim, his agent, declared, 'Alf Garnett was by no means necessarily a wise thing to do; indeed, he feared that it could have been damaging … However, Warren Mitchell's relations with all concerned with *Till Death Us Do Part* have been so happy that he is prepared to give consideration …' Mitchell eventually signed his contract on 15 November 1966 in return for a figure of £288 15s per episode, rising to £341 5s for the final six episodes.

Dandy Nichols also agreed to return for the second series. Her casting in place of Gretchen Franklin for the first series had had a huge impact on the show. Very early on, she had realised that she would never get the same amount of dialogue that Mitchell or Booth did, but had shrewdly reasoned that less was more and acted accordingly to steal every scene she could. She developed Else's bovine look (as if she had spent her whole life watching TV, as *Guardian* critic Stuart Jeffries put it in an inspired description): the vacant, occasionally malevolent stare, the continual greed for food, the heard-it-all-before expression that would never fail to coordinate with some heartfelt barbs aimed directly at her husband. Then she began the practice of delivering monologues with such relentlessness as to render her husband's howls of protest utterly sterile; Mitchell here counterpointed with his '*Look … Listen …*' routine – which, proving totally ineffective against his wife, would usually lead to an 'I've lost my thread now' endgame. This was surely cultivated during rehearsal, and stayed with the show for its duration. Later, to wonderful comic effect, Nichols would occasionally interject a nondescript phrase of her own, 'Oo-er', into conversations, as if to register something Else thought significant. Then there was her 'Pig!' riposte to Alf's 'Silly moo!' insults, which she would employ consistently and with incredible venom, proving that Else was just as limited in her use of the English language as her husband.

It quickly became apparent that within the Garnett household, Else was always in control, despite the adjective often used to describe her, 'long-suffering'; a phrase first adopted by critics in 1966 and still used as an unwitting cliché today. But Else was no sad-eyed lady of the docklands. She may have had enough of her husband and tuned out of his belligerent behaviour years earlier, but she was never the one to suffer in the Garnett household. Else was not a character developed for the audience to sympathise with. The BBC's dossier for their 1967 entry to the Golden Rose of Montreux awards, the episode 'Peace and Goodwill', declared that Else was of 'slow mentality, unread and unintelligent'; and the *Daily Mail*'s Peter Black described her as 'an idle, comfortable old party, hopeless but not unhappy, insulated from reality by a brain that never gets out of bottom gear'.

It was generally agreed that Nichols' quiet but stunningly effective contribution was not fully appreciated by either press or public until the first series was repeated, when viewers could see beyond the explosion that was Alf and the *Sturm und Drang* interplay between Alf and Mike. As Speight said in 1971: 'People didn't realise how good Dandy Nichols was as the mum until the repeats. On the first showing, it was all Garnett, because of the words. But on the repeats, they could see how greedy Dandy was, just sitting there looking at him with marvellous eyes.'

As previously noted, Nichols arguably shared some of Else's characteristics; witness this monologue from a 1972 interview, describing her flight to New York to appear on Broadway in *Home* with John Gielgud and Ralph Richardson: 'They couldn't get me on the VC10. The jumbo was full of Americans. It was ghastly. Nothing worked, all the lights went out, the film broke down. I even got trapped in the loo. As I went in, it trapped me and got hold of me. Couldn't get out for hours, I'm telling you …' One can quite imagine Else recounting this incident in her placid monotone …

Speight had not initially given much thought as to how he might write for Nichols, but now that he knew she was adept enough to make comic bricks with the straw he provided, he could begin to tailor Else's dialogue to suit the actress's performance. Both Speight and Dennis Main Wilson now wished to emphasise Nichols' part in the show, and requested that the BBC 'recognise increased demands on her with a higher fee regardless of the pay freeze'.

On 6 October, Michael Peacock, Controller of BBC One, made an offer of an extra 50 guineas a programme to Nichols, in view of the fact that her career as a character actress might be restricted due to overexposure on the show (which then amounted to a total of 27 programmes – seven episodes in the first series, repeated, plus 13 episodes projected for the second series – to be seen by at least 11 million people). Speight and Wilson realised as well that the character had such potential that a greater concentration on her could ease the pressure on Mitchell. Nichols was thus elevated to second billing on the new series, while Booth was edged downwards, despite Mike's important role as foil to Alf and the undeniable fact that Booth had actually been the first member of the cast to sign up. Thus as Speight, Mitchell and Nichols all gained increased status on the show, Booth saw his stock falling. This would inevitably lead to further dissent within the ranks.

The personal conflicts between Booth and Mitchell that had surfaced during the making of the first series grew even worse during that of the second. Booth's lifestyle of unrestricted alcohol and womanising, which Mitchell with all his Stanislavski dourness despised, hit the media headlines. Mitchell not only fought for his own dramatic role, he also began to assume what appeared to be a proprietorial attitude toward the show itself, which did after all now effectively revolve around him. This won him respect from Speight, who, far from seeing it as a threat to his authority, was quite content for Mitchell – and Wilson – to share the burdens of responsibility. Mitchell, the Jewish, middle class, left wing-teetotaller and Speight, the atheist, working class, left-wing hard-drinker, became firm friends, which naturally Booth, Speight's fellow toper, grew increasingly to resent. Other events in Booth's life – such as his peripatetic nature, which saw him constantly moving from one flat to another – may have caused problems as well. Initially, Booth drank with Speight at the Queen's Elm on the Fulham Road or dined and drank with him at the White Elephant nearby, but a move to Hampstead by 1968 made this less convenient and may have influenced his habits. Furthermore, offers of other work did not come in for Booth as his fame skyrocketed; unlike his co-star Mitchell, he fell victim to typecasting. By March 1967, Booth would already be making noises about wanting to leave the show.

Una Stubbs' crucial and difficult role was never really appreciated during the show's lifetime. She had the unenviable task of playing the only intelligent, compassionate figure amongst all the stupidity and self-interest of the Garnett family. Rita is the lynchpin of the family in many ways, as she rounds on both her husband and her father during their conflicts. However, it would not be until the 1970s series that she would accrue greater power, when her role as a mother would enable her to let out her inner bitterness in occasional volleys of outraged anger. Stubbs' remuneration for her work on the series would never increase as spectacularly as that of her co-stars; it seems that, like Rita, she was somewhat taken for granted.

While the sharp adrenalin rush of success of the first series had swept all before it, and had caused seismic shifts within the show itself, now unsympathetic forces were beginning to coalesce outside the BBC, and to focus displeasure on some elements integral to the show. The Garnetts were now firmly on the public radar, and *Till Death Us Do Part* was quickly to become the most prominent target of attack for those who were dismayed by the increasing permissiveness in the media. As previously discussed, the first real signs of this came in September 1966, during the Saturday evening repeat season, with one MP protesting against the racial content of 'Intolerance'. Then, in late October, Bill Cotton of the BBC's Light Entertainment

Department faced a barrage of questions about the show from Church representatives during a conference of the British Council of Churches designed to debate broadcasting standards. Meanwhile, the second series was to begin with a Christmas episode, scheduled to be transmitted on Boxing Day, and to continue with 12 more episodes, closing near to Easter 1967. Perhaps predictably, things did not go entirely according to plan …

A SOUP KITCHEN FOR THE EMOTIONALLY UNSTABLE

The best drama in 1967, suggested the *Daily Mail*, was to be found in the controversy surrounding television. The occasion was a spoof set of exam questions based on *Till Death Us Do Part*, posed by the newspaper in an editorial designed as a send-up of new, trendy school curricula in English Literature. But there was a lot of truth in the statement; television *was* part of the news in 1967, and Speight's creation held centre-stage in the controversy as the show that everyone always cited in the debate over permissiveness.

The furore engendered by Hugh Carleton Greene's tenure as Director General, which had previously seen programmes such as *The Wednesday Play* attracting strong criticism, intensified toward the end of 1966 when Stanley Evans, the ex-MP for Wednesbury, sent out a 'Christmas message' on 19 December commenting on what he saw as the BBC's scandalously one-sided presentation in the *24 Hours* programme of Harold Wilson's meeting with Ian Smith of Rhodesia:

> Few developments would help this country more than a shakeup of the BBC, the advent of a new Lord Reith, and the restoration of time-honoured standards. The BBC today is a soup-kitchen for the emotionally unstable. Pet playwrights find it both fashionable and profitable to denigrate religion and authority, to pour scorn on just those customs and institutions that helped to make Britain great … It becomes clear that national pride, national awareness and pursuit of national interests is only permissible if you are African, Asian or Communist.

Greene, it was rumoured, considered suing Evans for libel. This was not the only development in the ongoing debate about media bias in the field of politics. The political climate was still such that the *Man Alive* edition 'Vote, Vote, Vote for Me' was postponed from December to 25 January 1967 in order to avoid accusations that it had influenced voting in a by-election in Nuneaton.

The power of television as a social phenomenon became *the* major talking point in the media during the first month of 1967, when the second series of

Till Death Us Do Part exploded onto the nation's screens. There were complaints about the handling of religion on TV – the Revd Ian Paisley organised a protest march in Belfast over the New Year against blasphemy in the medium. Then there were complaints about the morally corrupting influence of television – National Viewers and Listeners Association (NVLA) leading light James Dance MP appeared on *24 Hours* to protest at Jonathan Miller's dramatisation of *Alice in Wonderland*, which he perceived as attempting a deliberate erosion of traditional children's values. The NVLA also announced on 9 January 1967 a project under the leadership of the Chief Constable of Lincolnshire designed to monitor specific programmes for evidence of the depiction of promiscuity as normal, the degradation of womanhood and the misrepresentation of Christianity.

There were many other interventions that focused attention on television's ethical responsibilities, from both sides of the permissiveness debate. On 4 January 1967, Lady Snow – the writer Pamela Hansford Johnson – launched a legal action for libel against Hugh Carleton Greene, Keith Waterhouse and Willis Hall over a sketch in an edition of *The Late Show* on 19 November 1966. The sketch in question had parodied some letters she had written to Dylan Thomas in the 1930s, and had appeared to imply both that her association with the poet had been 'improper' right up until her marriage with Lord Snow in 1950 and that she had broken faith with Thomas by publishing her letters. Playwright Terence Frisby was also already in the High Court protesting about the BBC's treatment of his *Theatre 625* play 'And Some Have Greatness Thrust Upon Them ...', and specifically about their censorship of one particular phrase that he perceived as altering the entire structure of his work. On 7 February, film-maker Roy Boulting very publicly backed out of an appearance on *Midlands Today* to promote his new film *The Family Way* when the BBC refused to screen his chosen clip because it contained the word 'virgin', which they deemed unsuitable for broadcast at a family hour. Even singer and comedian Max Bygraves had walked out of a *Housewife's Choice* appearance on 5 January after objecting to some rude remarks. On the other hand, the same day that the NVLA project was announced, Hugh Cudlipp, Chairman of the Daily Mirror News Group, resigned his position on the board of ATV in protest at 'crippling restrictions on the freedom of speech' for staff wishing to comment on industrial relations or politics.

PEACE AND GOODWILL

Ingeniously, Speight was to reference this contemporary controversy over the one-eyed monster through much of the second series of *Till Death Us Do Part*. Whereas in the first series the telly had always been present in the background of the Garnett household, generally broken down, now Speight, for the first time in a television show, brought the goggle-box centre stage, switching it on and adding further to the reality of the sitcom. Everyone was talking about television – why not the Garnetts? Thus in the very first episode, 'Peace and Goodwill', we find Alf reacting to the Queen's televised Christmas message and Mike making references to David Frost's show. Later, the Garnetts talk about two bishops engaged in a debate about sex on the telly in 'Sex Before Marriage'; we see actual news footage of political figures (Wilson, Brown, Kosygin) in 'I Can Give It Up Any Time I Like' and 'State Visit'; and ultimately Speight provides a sequence in 'Alf's Dilemma' where the Garnetts have their very own symposium on television and its effect on the moral fibre of the country.

Into the media turmoil, the Garnetts bulldozed their own brand of controversy. 'Peace and Goodwill' was publicised as part of the Beeb's festive package for Christmas 1966, and the media seized on it with glee. *News of the World* reporter Weston Taylor, shortly to run a series of articles on *Till Death Us Do Part* over four weeks in January, mentioned in a piece on 18 December that he had seen the script to the Christmas show and had doubts about the wisdom of transmitting it over a religious festival. Warren Mitchell meanwhile joked that the Archbishop of Canterbury would have his 'eyebrows twitch' when he saw the show, which he asserted was totally unique for a Christmas television event. He added that he himself hated Christmas, loathing the 'siege economy', the panic over gifts and the self-indulgent over-eating. This 'bah humbug' attitude may have deceived an earlier 'exclusive' in the *Evening News* into erroneously reporting that the episode would depict Alf as Scrooge saying that a decent government would ban Christmas.

True to the show's absolute fidelity to a contemporary setting, 'Peace and Goodwill' opens at 3.10 pm on Christmas Day, with Alf standing in front of the television set and saluting Her Majesty immediately after her Christmas message to the Commonwealth. There follows a debate about the Royal Family, with Mike and Rita protesting their total superfluity and Alf and Else their essential diligence. Alf insults the Prime Minister, accusing him of fiddling the books with his Chancellor, James Callaghan. Then he and Mike launch into a heated debate about eccentric Cabinet ministers, which prompts Else to ramble on about "Ogg' (Quintin Hogg, later Lord Hailsham, Booth's nemesis in the Marylebone elections a few years before). There's talk of diplomacy and the World Cup and more from Mike on the 13 years of Tory misrule, before Alf confronts a group of carol singers whom he believes are 'on the take' just like everybody else. Inevitably, the subject of religion is broached, Alf betting Mike a ten bob note to prove that God exists. The episode ends with Alf choking on a thruppenny bit buried by Else in the now-incinerated Christmas pudding and Mike suggesting that if Alf dies and goes up to the pearly gates he should hand back the 10 bob note if he finds that God isn't there after all. Exeunt all, fighting … It was all very different from the usual cosy festive special presented by other shows.

'Surely the coarsest programme ever to have been televised at Christmas time' responded one *Daily Sketch* reader from London. 'Few people are amused by this type of humour, which hits at the very basis of Christianity' was another comment, this time from a member of the public from Birmingham referring specifically to the bet over the existence of God. Newspaper critic Shaun Usher predicted a storm over references to Minister of Transport Barbara Castle and the Queen, Alf having commented on the risibility of the former being unable to drive.[15] There were a few letters of protest, but in the event the predicted outcry did not materialise – that would come after the following week's episode. And in ratings terms, 'Peace and Goodwill' proved to be the single most popular programme of the holiday period, 39.5% of the populace (20 million viewers) having watched it.

Actor Kenneth More (soon to gain plaudits with his central role in the major BBC classic serial *The Forsyte Saga*) had a memorable Christmas because of the episode. As his partner, Angela Douglas, was in the kitchen cooking the turkey, she heard him in the lounge laughing at Dandy Nichols on the television. Knowing of More's brief flirtation with Nichols in the past, Douglas took offence at the mirth, and next minute the entire turkey flew through the air to land on More's lap. *Till Death Us Do Part* could indeed damage your health …

SEX BEFORE MARRIAGE

If 'Peace and Goodwill' represented a startling restatement of *Till Death Us Do Part*'s power to stimulate discussion and offend in equal measure, the following episode, provocatively entitled 'Sex Before Marriage' and shown on 2 January 1967, opened the floodgates to the growing debate between the new morality and the old.

One Saturday afternoon, Alf is busy attempting – and failing – to decorate the living room with a grotesque floral wallpaper chosen by his less-than-helpful wife. As always, Alf complains about everything from the state of the world to the state of the wallpaper. Rita and Mike, the latter resplendent in trendy Carnaby Street T-shirt, look on as he suffers mishap after mishap. The arguments this time centre on the working-class tradition of wetting a baby's head in the local pub, the baby in question being one Charlie Treacy's grandson, the mother of whom isn't even married. Alf

---

[15] When Radio One DJ Kenny Everett made a similar joke in 1970, he was sacked by the Corporation.

protests that even the Church of England is now promoting this scourge with its book *Sex Before Marriage*; indeed, the whole nation is becoming sex crazed, with two bishops discussing it as bold as brass on the telly the night before. Such talk, opines Alf, encourages it even more, acting as an 'aphrodaisiac' (sic). Else, too, is shocked at the thought of sex before marriage, but she turns on her husband when he, in response to Rita's accusation of being old-fashioned, remarks that he didn't touch her mother until after they were married. '*Well* after' is Else's concise response.

The conversation turns to the question of whether or not Mike and Rita had sex before marriage; Mike states that they had no chance, since Alf watched their every move, but Rita undermines this by protesting her innocence just a little too much. While Alf loudly proclaims that he trusts his beloved daughter but not Mike, Else is less certain and gets angry with Rita, who promptly backs down and denies any sex prior to her wedding. She manages to assuage the worries of her parents, who then leave, almost apologetic that they could have distrusted their daughter. As soon as they have gone, Mike and Rita collapse into giggles. Although this laughter could perhaps be interpreted as mere scorn at the parents' outdated views, the more obvious implication is that sex before marriage had indeed occurred. This left the show open to accusations that it encouraged a practice that, although common, was still regarded as anathema, at least in public circles, in the '60s. Speight of course was attacking this social hypocrisy, a notion increasingly deployed in television drama but never before in a primetime sitcom, especially one that was now fully in the nation's spotlight. The writer, producer and actors were fully aware of this, and fully expected a rapid and indeed rabid response from some sections of respectable society; they were not to be disappointed. Speight must surely have known that Mrs Mary Whitehouse had come to prominence three years before in a protest over just this issue. Sure enough, she fell for the bait almost immediately. The show was transmitted at 7.30 pm on a Monday evening, well before the family watershed of 9.00 pm, and it was this that particularly enraged Mrs Whitehouse and the NVLA.

'It was quite the worst programme I have seen during family viewing time', said Whitehouse, protesting at the 'persistent flouting of the obligation placed upon [the BBC] by Parliament' and condemning the show as 'dirty, blasphemous and full of bad language'. It should be noted that – at least at this stage – she did not call for the show to be taken off the screen altogether, but merely argued that both the message and the means by which it was conveyed were unsuitable for the timeslot. And to be fair, given her status as schoolmistress, caring for pupils who might be watching the most sensational show on television, just before the new school term began, it is difficult to see what else she could have done in the face of such apparent provocation. To Speight's satisfaction, she then proceeded to protest too much, promptly despatching a telegram containing her complaints on behalf of the Clean Up TV campaign to Prime Minister Harold Wilson. As Whitehouse probably realised, Wilson couldn't care less about satire as long as it wasn't directed against him.[16] Predictably, his office replied that he could take no action since only the Broadcasting Authority was responsible. However, Mrs Whitehouse was very conscious of the power of the media; and, following her lead, a groundswell of protests was about to build.

There were some general complaints, notably from John Cordle, 54-year-old MP for Bournemouth East and Christchurch, who sent a telegram to Hugh Carleton Greene protesting that the show was 'vulgar, obscene and blasphemous' and hinting that he would instigate legal proceedings if the tide of filth was not stemmed. When asked to comment on this, Warren Mitchell said that it was time Cordle grew up and faced facts. For the most part, however, it was the specific question of the show's transmission time of 7.30 pm that caused concern. The Revd Leslie Yorke, vicar of Christchurch in Hampshire, used his sermon on the Sunday night of 8 January to urge his 500-strong congregation to complain about the show to the BBC and their local MPs: 'The BBC must realise that they must not spend large sums of money on scriptwriters who seem to be obsessed with sex, beds, bad language and lavatories and bring into our homes the smell of the sewers. If the BBC feel they must produce such programmes, let them put them on at a declared hour when ordinary, uncomplicated people are in bed. Why should we pay for a licence in order to keep continually switching off that which should never be on?'

There were many complaints from teachers. The headmaster of Highfield Junior and Infants School in Bromley commented that all his staff agreed that a later transmission time was essential. H Buxton of Nottingham wrote, '[The show] plumbs the depths of vulgarity in its references. Since it lacks humour, it is not entertaining but a cheap way of getting the audience's attention by shocking them.' He went on to remark that 6-10 year olds now watched such filth and used the expressions 'Silly old moo' and 'You old cow' in class. Derek Belton, the head of a public school near Christchurch, banned his pupils from watching the show, telling parents in a circular letter: 'After seeing last week's edition of the programme, with its filthy bad language and blasphemous references, my faith in the BBC has been completely shattered.' He suggested that the Corporation should sack writers who were, in his eyes, guilty of 'sin of magnitude as well as an admission of their inability to produce original or intelligent material'. He said he preferred *Panorama*, Peter Scott-presented nature programmes and

---

[16] When it did directly concern him, such as when The Move promoted their single 'Flowers In The Rain' with an unflattering cartoon of him later in 1967, Wilson was ruthless in his response.

rugby coverage …

But it was not only vicars and teachers who were outraged by 'Sex Before Marriage'. Ivor Jay, television critic of the *Birmingham Evening Mail*, summed up the problem neatly, calling Auntie Beeb a 'Silly old moo' for putting the show out at 7.30 pm. While he defended its authenticity and the idea of the Garnetts generating comedy 'through ignorance violently haranguing ignorance, vulgarity vying with vulgarity', he could not support its current transmission slot, when in his estimation it set impossible double standards for parents: 'Dad guffaws at the goings on … and the youngsters join in. But let one of the youngsters refer to his sister or mum as a "silly old moo" or blithely use a swear word and Dad will clip his ear. Which is pretty confusing for a youngster. Dad, Mum and teacher may try to instil religious or moral or sexual values, then here they are on television being debased, exposed to derision – and everyone finds it funny. Consider ["Sex Before Marriage"]. Swear words and the brutish abuse apart, it mocked religion, thumbed a nose at honesty and made sex a ribaldry at farmyard level. The only moral seemed to be that anything goes so long as you are not found out. Only a joke? Don't make me laugh. The implications are too deadly serious.'

It was not only the episode's treatment of the central issue of sex before marriage to which certain people objected but also, once again, its use of swear words, which began to be religiously counted, the only way for protestors to quantify the object of their disapproval in the days before videotape. 'One word is used as often as possible,' wrote one member of the public in reference to 'bloody'. 'I have heard it said that this word is acceptable in homes. I can't believe that. It is never heard in my house, in the homes of my daughters or in the homes of my many friends. Put [the show] on later.' 'I considered [the episode] was too vulgar to be shown and was glad to use the switch on my set', opined 'Disgusted' of Kings Heath, Birmingham. In Scotland, where the show also topped the ratings, while Mrs Mary Middleton, former president of the League of Women in Glasgow, commented that the episode had been very funny, with only a few uses of 'bloody', Charles Gillies told of the shock he had felt when Alf left the room wrongly convinced that he knew the truth, and noted that he had counted 23 uses of 'bloody'. In the press, James Thomas of the *Daily Express* wrote that he had counted 18 uses of 'bloody' in 15 minutes and declared that repetition of the word belittled a series good enough to do without it. K Easthaugh, commenting in the *Daily Mirror*, agreed. He said he was not against the use of such language but was concerned at its lack of development; he deplored the repeated use of 'bloody' to get cheap laughs and remarked that the show should be less wordy and have more thought put into it, to enable it to reach the heights of *Steptoe and Son* or *The Likely Lads*.

But amidst all this criticism, there was support from an unlikely quarter. The vicar of Bothenhampton, Revd David Bailey, wrote in the *Dorset Evening Echo* on 6 February 1967: 'If you get rid of the Cockney accent, broaden the vowels and change some of the adjectives, then this could be typical of many a West Country home. And if we don't like the truth as it is depicted, then rather than criticise it, let us get on and do something about changing it'.

BBC Controller of Television Kenneth Adam commented publicly that steps were being taken to restrain the language, but that the show would definitely not be withdrawn. In a press statement, the BBC said that they had received 'a few phone calls' about the episode and noted that there was speculation in the press that a curfew would be called for the series. Johnny Speight expressed his agreement with this idea, and said that a suitable transmission time would be 9.30 pm, when no children would be watching.

Behind the scenes, Dennis Main Wilson was summoned to the office of the Head of Light Entertainment, as he later recalled:

> Can I tell you, the next morning, I was on Tom Sloan's carpet. [Sloan said,] 'You two-faced bastard, you've let me down'. I said, 'What was that?' [Sloan replied,] 'You promised me you'd never get up mixed up in sex and rude, scurrilous stuff.' I said we didn't. 'I mean,' [he went on] 'the Dandy thing last night … where the daughter laughs and says if only they knew. How dare you let me down. I've a damn good mind to take you off the show.'

However, Sloan's anger was apparently calmed. A memo he sent to the BBC's Director of Television on 5 January 1967 reveals that the Revd Patrick Lloyd, his cousin by marriage and Chaplain and Head Of Religious Knowledge at Bede College, Durham, had requested that a tape copy or script of 'Peace and Goodwill' be despatched to them since it would provide a useful basis for discussion with students regarding present-day social and moral matters. Sloan recommended Lloyd's letter as 'useful ammo' in the battle against the protesters.

A BBC Controller's meeting of 10 January 1967 heard that the Corporation had received 400 letters regarding 'Sex Before Marriage', as opposed to 130 regarding 'Peace and Goodwill'. Of these, only 34 had been appreciative; nevertheless, the meeting felt that the show should be kept in its present timeslot, but that its bad language should be scrutinised, and noted with some trepidation that even Else had sworn (once) in 'Peace and Goodwill'.

Johnny Speight viewed all this controversy with immense satisfaction and a great deal of amusement. Mischievously, he added to it by choosing this very point in time, 3 January 1967, to announce, rather prematurely, his new pay deal with the BBC, which meant that he was now the highest paid comedy writer on television. He had been contracted to write 20 shows a year from April 1967 to March 1969.[17] With repeats, this deal was worth a colossal £40,000 to him. This pronouncement was inflammatory enough for the guardians of public decency, but equally embarrassing for the BBC, not least because of the Government's ongoing clampdown on pay rises of any kind. Speight was now both the most famous writer working in television and the most highly paid; always respected within the close-knit community of the BBC's 'soup kitchen', he was now also a national figure. As that eventful January wound on, he was to find that, despite his power in the industry, fame and wealth brought with them their own responsibilities.

THE KILLERS OF CHRIST?

On Monday 16 January 1967, the day the second series' fourth episode, 'The Bulldog Breed', was transmitted, Speight guested on the Home Service daily news radio programme *The World at One*, and was asked about 'Sex Before Marriage' and the storm of controversy it had engendered. He referred contemptuously to the 'Clean Up TV People', suggested that they were 'hypocritically concealing … their fascism under the cloak of a moral campaign' and implied that such self-appointed guardians of public morality were racists and 'were like the killers of Christ'. Only a figure so cocooned in overweening self-confidence could have failed to comprehend how deeply offensive these remarks would be. His ill-advised outburst was to push the public debate onto an even more highly-charged level, particularly in terms of public relations with its intended target, Mrs Whitehouse. Listening to the broadcast while having her lunch, the main figurehead of the Clean Up TV campaign and author of the recently-published tome *Cleaning Up TV* was understandably apoplectic, and immediately telephoned the BBC to complain. She was put through to a Mr Edwards, Head of News, who was apparently equally angry at Speight's outburst, and transferred her to the BBC's Legal Department; one of the Department's solicitors, a Mr Roche, listened noncommittally and promised to investigate and ring her back. When he responded the next day, his statement shocked Mary Whitehouse: 'We do not feel there are any grounds for an apology since you, as a person, would not be associated in the minds of the listeners with the Clean Up TV Campaign … [Instead you are merely] connected with the National Viewers' And Listeners' Association.'

Whitehouse replied that while she was not asking for a legal apology herself, she had not expected the BBC to 'disassociate itself' from a libellous attack on such a group of people; furthermore, any decision by the Corporation not to issue an apology might prove damaging in the eyes of the

---

[17] These shows would not necessarily be episodes of *Till Death Us Do Part*.

public. She wrote directly to Lord Normanbrook, Chairman of the BBC, who promptly replied that since Mr Roche had explained the BBC policy, he could add nothing. Mrs Whitehouse then consulted her solicitor, who gave the opinion that Speight's remarks *could* perhaps be grounds for legal action; after consideration, she decided not to pursue the matter at that moment. Thankfully for her, only six weeks later, Speight was to hand her the ammunition she required on a plate.

While Speight was basking in the limelight, Warren Mitchell was also enjoying the benefits of his newly-acquired star status. The same week as 'Sex Before Marriage' was transmitted saw him making an appearance as a dodgy car salesman in a sketch with Tommy Cooper in an edition of the top-rated ITV comedy show *Life with Cooper* broadcast on Saturday 7 January. Of this, the *Birmingham Evening Mail* critic commented: 'The current middle-aged terrible infant of television seemed diminished, much less burly than in [*Till Death Us Do Part*]. The mammoth rage and the stroppy bellow were replaced by a refined, thinner-voiced Cockney. This was a smoothly expert and truthfully funny study in the cajoling of a conman.'

The full extent of Mitchell's incredible comic ability was revealed in the uproarious camera rehearsals for this programme, as its producer Mark Stuart told the press: 'They were both ad-libbing wildly. It was as if they bounced jokes off each other. I laughed so much I couldn't see straight and, in the end, Tommy stuffed his ears with cotton wool. It was a riot … At one point Warren pretended to drop the car bonnet down on his head, and Tommy howled and produced a great false thumb. But Warren came back – he always does … In the trade, actors say that appearing with Warren Mitchell is as risky as sharing the bill with a curly-haired toddler or a long-eared spaniel – nothing else is in the picture.'

Also on 7 January, Mitchell and Booth went to Wembley to film a segment of the match between Liverpool and West Ham for inclusion in the episode 'A Wapping Mythology (The Workers' King)'. The thousands of fans in the crowd shouted 'You silly old moo!' *en masse* as the two stars appeared on the pitch to give a spoof interview for *Grandstand*, and local policemen made the perhaps inevitable comparison that the Garnetts were now bigger than the Beatles – the benchmark of '60s popularity.

Booth relished the upgrading of his hedonistic lifestyle that his newfound star status allowed. He went on to secure another tea commercial for ITV, while his outrageous lifestyle was chronicled explicitly in one of the series of four articles that the *News of the World* ran during January on 'the show that shocks the nation'. This typically sensationalist piece presented lurid tales of the actor taking pills called 'purple flash' to boost his virility and of his unkempt Teddy Boy attire as he chatted up some girls in Piccadilly and they invited him to lunch with them in Mayfair. Finally, it told of production assistant Geoff Jowitt collecting the actor for rehearsals after a drunken night out, which would be followed by yet another night on the town until 8.00 the next morning.

Booth himself has recounted an (as usual) undated anecdote about the furore surrounding his opening of a new John Lewis store in the centre of Leeds. The entire town centre was blocked as crowds gathered; mounted police were sent in to disperse them, without success; and when Booth arrived, his jacket, shirt and sunglasses were torn off him by enthusiastic females. On another occasion, Booth responded furiously when a passer-by called him a 'Scouse git' as he walked down Lime Street in Liverpool. The man then grabbed him by the throat and asked in all innocence why the actor had insulted *him* – after all, he really *was* a Scouse git, wasn't he?

Dandy Nichols found that people would often chat to her in the street about her 'husband' Alf, as if the Garnetts were real people. Una Stubbs also frequently encountered people labouring under this misapprehension.

For Mitchell, the pressure of all this public attention sometimes became too much. Booth recalls that on one occasion, although Nichols disliked Mitchell, she responded to his complaints of fatigue by offering him a tablet from the travelling pharmacy contained in her handbag. Mitchell accepted the tablet, and Booth and Stubbs watched in awe as he suddenly became supercharged, raced through rehearsals and then dashed off home to try to get some sleep. The next morning, Mitchell was uncharacteristically late arriving for rehearsals, and slumped into an armchair. Booth initially thought that Nichols must have inadvertently mixed up the tablets, but then Nichols winked at him maliciously: it had been no accident. She gave Booth some of the same tablets – called 'black bombers' – that Friday, and he found that he was up and active all weekend. Booth classed this incident as an example of Nichols' 'brilliant and inventive retaliation against the aggravation Warren Mitchell continually inflicted on all of us'.

During the first series, Mitchell would tell his daughter Anna, upset at seeing his head painted on the television: 'Your daddy isn't Alf Garnett. Alf Garnett is famous and your daddy isn't. He's just your daddy.' Six months later, things had changed: 'At first, when I was recognised [by members of the public] it was a novelty. Then this wore off, because I found people were invading my private life, my family, my home, and nothing was my own anymore. I am not recognised [now], because I have ways of disguising myself.'

Mitchell's extracurricular activities, portraying Alf Garnett outside the confines of the television series, nevertheless continued apace. In 1968 he would tell an interviewer that he even received frequent invitations from the Young Conservatives to open fetes and give talks as Alf, despite having explained to them that his own political views were to the far left …

THE BEST LAID PLANS ...

Till Death Us Do Part continued to top the ratings during its second series as Speight explored ever more unusual territory in his very individual manner. 'The Bulldog Breed' addresses the question of the Vietnam War; a theme perhaps reflecting Booth's influence. The Garnetts are seen debating the War over a world map spread across the dinner table; a scene that continues for so long that – highly unusually for a sitcom – it takes up all but the last few minutes of the episode. The argument is brought to an end only when a lorry driver (played by Roy Kinnear, who in the 1970s would become a semi-regular on the show in a different role, that of Alf's docker workmate Sid) parks in the street just outside the Garnett front room, casting it into shadow and causing Alf to complain – and, in the process, to fall foul of the law, as he had done three times in the first series (in 'Arguments, Arguments', when he encounters a police officer while drunk, a scene cut for timing reasons when the episode was repeated; in 'Intolerance', when in a fit of pique he throws his dinner out of the window all over a passing beat officer; and in 'Claustrophobia', when he almost runs over a traffic policeman in his car).

The next episode, 'Caviar on the Dole', recalls many of the tropes featured in the *Comedy Playhouse* pilot. Mike, as devious as his father-in-law, lies to the National Assistance people regarding his unemployed status and brands Alf a Rachman-style unscrupulous landlord; and Dermot Kelly is introduced playing the same character as he had in Speight's 1963 *Comedy Playhouse* flop 'Shamrot', an Irish layabout with as great a capacity for cunning and self-delusion as any of his British working-class counterparts.

In 'A Woman's Place Is in the Home', the sixth episode, another simple idea is drawn out to comprise a 'plot', Alf becoming frustrated by a public telephone box as he attempts to order some fish and chips. (This incident will later be referred to in the third series' opening episode 'The Phone', when the Garnetts are inspired to have a telephone of their own installed.)

One of the best episodes is the eighth, 'In Sickness and in Health', when Alf is mysteriously taken ill and consigned to the tender mercies of an NHS hospital, where he is looked after by a doctor played by Mark Eden, Booth's *Catch Hand* co-star. Guest artiste Graham Stark (for whom Speight had written in 1964) plays the influenza-stricken Dr Kelly, mentioned throughout the series but seen onscreen only here, who first diagnoses Alf; and there are hilarious scenes at the hospital when the Garnetts are told by a ward sister that there should be only one visitor at each bedside, and each of them offers to leave poor Alf in response. In a clever piece of continuity, the cause of Alf's malady eventually turns out to be the same thruppenny bit that he swallowed on Christmas Day in 'Peace and Goodwill'.

'State Visit', the ninth episode, had perhaps the most politically motivated script for the show so far. Speight, prevaricating as usual as he tried to think of topical, original ideas for the show, had read the *Daily Mirror*'s front-page story of 6 February 1967, the date that Soviet Premier Kosygin arrived in London for a week of talks with Harold Wilson over the Vietnam conflict. Wilson, to his credit, was never to support the US-led initiative in Vietnam with British troops (then already overextended with the worsening situation in Aden), but this was seen as a possible option at the time, and the *Mirror* was aware of the problems such action would bring in relation to the ongoing Cold War with the USSR. Its story about Kosygin's visit was presented first in Russian, as a gimmick to inform the Russians about the paper's hopes and fears, and then in an English translation. Speight saw this, and then read that the arch Communist Kosygin was going to be staying in luxury at Claridge's Hotel, and was due to visit the Queen on 9 February. Such delicious irony – the ultimate Marxist ensconced in a top capitalist hotel, then having a state engagement with the world's most famous monarch – struck the writer as providing the basis for an ideal *Till Death Us Do Part* 'plot'. Inspired, he rang up Dennis Main Wilson and declared that he would write a new script as soon as possible to ensure its topicality. As usual, the cast received the script only just in time for the rehearsals, with the recording following a week later. Mitchell always requested a copy of a newspaper for Alf to read during recording as a convenient, and highly topical, prop. The episode thus begins with Alf reading that very edition of the *Daily Mirror* and promptly going berserk over the tabloid's headline to the effect that Britain has become merely a tiny offshore country with no global power anymore. The day after transmission of the episode, the newspaper itself reproduced the headline, proudly declaring that it was indeed this message (from a 'Bloody Labour rag … Bloody anti-British rag') that had sent Alf ballistic and prompted him to mount his own anti-Russian protest.

The script was a clever one, comparing the political ideals of older-generation armchair generals such as Alf with the irreverent shallowness of the younger generation represented by Mike and Rita, who view Mike's new retro Army tunic which so outrages Alf as just another swinging Chelsea fashion statement.   In the final scenes, an angry Alf throws a bottle of ink at his son in law, missing his target and causing the bottle to shatter against a portrait of Alf's beloved Queen. The studio audience howled with laughter, but following transmission there were a number of protests at this disgraceful slur on Her Majesty, who 'benefits this country greatly', who could not officially reply to such an insult and who in any case was extremely ill in bed at the time. (She had gastroenteritis, and the Duke of Kent had to carry out royal business on her behalf for the first time.) Mrs Whitehouse insisted that such an insult to the Queen meant that Hugh Carleton Greene had to go. The official BBC response was that the programme in no way intended to make fun of Her Majesty; a platitude for once echoed by Speight, which prompted a wry comment from the *Daily Express*: 'Let us hope that the BBC now gives us a comic series about a self-righteous scriptwriter who accepts the current list of smart, liberal beliefs (which usually turn out to be dead wrong) and who, while preaching tolerance to all mankind and getting very well paid for it, despises the opinions of the people he actually lives among.'

But Speight was having problems. 'State Visit' marked the re-emergence of an issue that had caused much concern during production of the previous series; the writer could not be relied upon to deliver a script on time, completed, structured or, as was now becoming apparent, in any form whatsoever. The production schedule for the second series allowed for a one- to two-week gap between recording and transmission of each episode, with the last of the 13 due to go out on 20 March and pencilled in to be recorded six days earlier on 14 March. By 24 January, however, it had already become obvious to Tom Sloan that to make the full series of 13 episodes to the original schedule was no longer feasible, and that the flow of weekly recordings would have to be abandoned, simply because the most famous and most highly-paid writer in British television could not fulfil his contractual obligations; a fact that Speight sought to excuse by continually complaining that the delays were due to the challenge of keeping *Till Death Us Do Part* as topical as possible. A damage limitation strategy was now hurriedly put in place. Adamant that the rescheduling should be given no publicity, Sloan waited for the arrival of script number ten, set for recording on Friday 24 February, and abandoned the idea of continuing with three further episodes as originally intended. He did however hand Speight a lifeline, conceding that a final, eleventh episode could be made at a slightly later date than originally planned, to form an Easter Monday Bank Holiday special. By 13 February, though, the scripts for the tenth and eleventh episodes still had not been received. The final episode proper of the series was eventually recorded only four days ahead of its 27 February transmission date, and was not even given a title – although it has since come to be referred to as 'Alf's Dilemma', and has also been known as 'Cleaning Up TV'. The Easter special was then not recorded until 14 March, and much of it was simply improvised by the regular and guest cast, without the benefit of scripted dialogue.

Sloan complained about this problem to the BBC's Head of Copyright at the end of March: 'Speight is notoriously bad at fulfilling deadlines and in the last series we contracted the artistes for 13 programmes but had to pay them off for two complete programmes because scripts were unavailable.' He suggested that in order to avoid this problem in future, topical lines should be added into the scripts at the last minute.

CACO ERGO SUM

'Alf's Dilemma' proved to be worth all the trouble, with a simple yet brilliant premise that merged art and real life and served as a unique platform to reflect the heated public debate about the power of television that had occurred over the past few weeks. It was also a premise that was to backfire stunningly on Speight in real life.

The episode starts for once with peace and quiet in the Garnett household, as the two men are seen reading books intently while Else is blithely chewing a Mars bar, in a world of her own as usual, and Rita is fidgeting on the sofa, evoking superbly that feeling of boredom and ennui that was such a familiar element of real life and yet so rarely depicted on television. Mike's book is *Boom at the Kop*, footballer Ian St John's record of a memorable season at Mike's beloved Liverpool FC, but Alf suggests he should instead be reading something more edifying, such as the book he himself has been muttering his agreement with for the past few moments; it is *Cleaning Up TV* by Mary Whitehouse, whom Alf praises as someone concerned about the decency and fundamental goodness so lacking in the nation. Alf explains that the author believes that television is destroying the moral fabric of the country, and this prompts a family discussion of the issue of TV filth, including 'Up the Junction', which had been prevented from being given a repeat in 1966 by an injunction from the NVLA; 'Cathy Come Home', the ground breaking Ken Loach play that had been broadcast so sensationally four months beforehand; and an unspecified documentary featuring some half-naked African dancers. Alf's vituperations are interrupted when he has to respond to a call of nature. He is suffering from diarrhoea, and is just about to rush to the outdoor bog when his wife calmly informs him that it no longer works, as it is blocked by tea leaves. Desperate, Alf decides to go next door. Else, house proud as ever, orders him to take his own toilet paper, and Alf, wanting to have some reading material with him since he might be a long time, also takes his book, which – oh, the satire! – he places in between the toilet tissue. After many toilet adventures and much railing against the horrible diseases those unclean foreigners have introduced to Britain (he cites Asian flu, the 'Paki pox' and foot and mouth as examples), Alf finds that he has to go to stay in hospital for some tests. Mike cries derisively that he must have caught the plague, and while a concerned Else considers fumigating the house, Rita decides that since Alf seems to have contracted his condition while reading Mrs Whitehouse's book, it too must be cleansed in the flames. So saying, she consigns the book to the fire (which, strangely enough, seems to have moved across the room quite a distance; a continuity error possibly attesting to the rushed nature of the entire production, which may also account for the repetition of the idea of Alf having to go hospital, as seen only a couple of weeks before in 'In Sickness and In Health'.) The episode ends with Mike and Rita intoning 'Unclean, unclean' to the hapless Alf as they celebrate their very own bonfire of the vanities …

The irony was delicious in so many ways; Alf the bigot is the upholder of the very tenets that Whitehouse holds dear, yet his tirades are the focus of her attacks. Speight must surely have been aware of the double-edged nature of Rita's book burning, itself a blatant example of bigotry; but one of the reasons that *Till Death Us Do Part* was so regularly criticised was its ambiguous lack of moral example or clear message. Whitehouse, talking of the episode later, was quite open in citing the old adage that any publicity was good publicity for her book, but she also had a serious point: 'Week after week, the silly and vulgar old man Alf is identified with all the things that have made Britain great; God, the Queen, patriotism and the Church are constantly ridiculed.' Again she challenged Lord Normanbrook to appear in a public discussion. In terms of public reaction more generally, the shit – if you'll pardon the pun – hit the fan again. A headmaster from Ewhurst complained to the BBC about the episode's low standards, anti-colour bias and undermining of integrity, protesting that the show had a diabolical influence on teenagers and ought to be consigned to the dustbin where it belonged. *The Times* meanwhile called it 'perhaps the most distasteful episode of the whole series …'

However, the show still had many supporters. On 3 March, Huw Wheldon replied to the same headmaster in a wonderfully patronising way, commenting that he thought *Till Death Us Do Part* was marvellous and provided fresh comedy that at no point intended to offend or annoy (oh, really?), adding that he nevertheless respected helpful letters such as the correspondent's (which he then no doubt proceeded to disregard). Anthony Burgess in *The Listener* was even more florid in his praise for the last episode and for the series as a whole:

> This, in masterly fashion, dealt with one of the most tragic themes in the world, totally neglected by literature – the man taken short with no lavatory available. I gather some viewers complained about this choice of subject; they should rather rejoice that the barriers Aldous Huxley railed against (as long ago as in *Eyeless in Gaza*) are at last being demolished. *Futuo ergo sum*, he reminded us; well, we've had plenty of existential futuancy, but also, he said, *caco ergo sum*. It's been left to Speight to kick open the closet door …
>
> There's your difference then, fundamentally exemplified, between the little revue tradition and the new serio-comic demotic medium. There's no doubt which is the healthier. The importance of *Till Death Us Do Part* lies in the baring of truths, which as Dr Jekyll, my grocer, put it, people are so scared to see that they cover them with laughter. [The series is] seeking out – and holding up to ridicule – bigotry, narrow mindedness and all human weaknesses …
>
> Alf Garnett is a tragic figure, a character for age-group

identification. Admittedly he goes too far; what was Harold Wilson, old twit face, doing, he asks, when Ian Smith was a Spitfire pilot?[18] The right reply – that he was concerned with statistics, an occupation at least as noble as a mess waiter's – bounces off his terrible vision of an England that has surrendered all its national values. His son-in-law and daughter offer a negative racial tolerance, a relish in exploiting the welfare state, bare thighs and sartorial puns on the term 'camp'. They're wholesale but empty, while Alf is fetid but crammed with a huge betrayed faith. His hell and punishment for excess of candour, is in this life – the 'incinderated' meal, the bug in the guts and the clogged khazi. But the hell of the children of permissiveness is perhaps too ghastly to contemplate. I look forward very much to the return of this excruciating series.

The second series of *Till Death Us Do Part* had cemented both the artistic brilliance of a simple but effective concept with massive commercial success and tremendous media coverage, and 'Alf's Dilemma' seemed to encapsulate the whole package. The show was on a (toilet) roll. But Speight, exuberant and overconfident, had gone too far. At one point in 'Alf's Dilemma', Rita helpfully explains for the audience's benefit that Mary Whitehouse is the 'Clean Up TV woman', thus publicly proving to an audience of millions that Speight himself had inextricably linked his *bête noire*'s name with the Clean Up TV campaign, and thus joining up the dots needed for Whitehouse to react to his insults on *The World at One* the previous month. She had earlier decided to let matters lie, but with a growing realisation that the 'fascist' tag had stuck, as evidenced when she faced protesters on her university speaking engagements and when she received a series of abusive telephone calls, she wrote again to Lord Normanbrook, asking for the opportunity to take part in a televised debate in the light of recent developments. This request was again refused. Then she consulted the Rt Hon Quintin Hogg QC (ironically, Else's favourite politician, gleefully insulted by Mike in 'Peace and Goodwill'), who advised her that *The World at One* broadcast had indeed been libellous, stating that although public figures could expect a certain amount of abuse, Speight's words had gone far beyond the bounds of acceptability. Thus, on 29 May 1967, Whitehouse initiated legal action in the High Court against Speight and the BBC. Neither of the defendants had a leg to stand on, and they knew it; on 27 July, Speight apologised before Mr Justice Paull, stating that he at 'no time intended those meanings [implying fascism], which they agreed were wholly inapplicable to Mrs Whitehouse and her organisation' and settled out of court, the payments going straight to the NVLA coffers. Round One to Mrs W …

---

[18] This refers to a piece of dialogue in the 'State Visit' episode.

11
Till Closing Time Do Us Part

THE TROUBLEMAKERS MEET MONGOL

The show returned a month after 'Alf's Dilemma' on Monday 27 March with the Easter Bank Holiday special, entitled 'Till Closing Time Us Do Part: A Bank Holiday Knees-Up with the Garnetts', set entirely in the local pub.[19] The title sequence was filmed on 9 March at Speight's favourite pub, The Queen's Elm in the Fulham Road, while the main recording, beautifully directed by Wilson, took place on 14 March. Perhaps indicative of Speight's scripting muse having ground to a halt, the episode was essentially devoid of plot, being filled instead by a great deal of improvisation by the regular cast and a large number of guest appearances. Nonetheless, any inherent problems were successfully transcended by the wealth of technical and acting talent that Speight could call upon to bring his sometimes unstructured ideas to fruition.

Well-known performers who agreed to guest in the special included Speight's old neighbour and close friend Kenny Lynch, one of his favourite actresses Cleo Sylvestre and new kid on the block Jimmy Tarbuck, currently a sensation at the London Palladium. (Speight had indeed been *en route* to see Tarbuck at that venue when he had learned of Arthur Haynes' sudden death on 19 November 1966.) Another guest star was Ray Barrett, lead actor from the oil-company drama series *Mogul* and its popular spin-off *The Troubleshooters* (or, as Alf malaprops, '*Mongol*' and '*The Troublemakers*'), the latter of which had followed directly on from *Till Death Us Do Part* in the BBC's schedule during the repeat season the previous year (and was to do so again in 1968). Other notable contributors included Rita Webb, who had appeared in 'Arguments, Arguments' and the Haynes shows; Dermot Kelly, who had also worked with Haynes and performed in other Speight productions including the recent *Till Death Us Do Part* episode 'Caviar on the Dole'; and comic actor Arthur Mullard.

The pub regulars from the first series, including Will Stampe, Charlie Bird and Fred McNaughton, are seen again, and a new character, Gran, a mysterious old woman who looks remarkably like the famous Giles cartoon image and is played to perfection by Joan Sims, is introduced. There is even a

---

[19] This was only the second episode in the show's history not to feature any scenes in the Garnett's living room.

non-speaking appearance by Speight himself, acting as a blind man[20] with Kelly's con artist character. The series' composer Dennis Wilson appears at the piano, and there are countless singalongs, led by Tarbuck ('Maggie May'), Lynch ('Bill Bailey') and the awful Alf. The 'silly old moo' herself gets up to sing 'You Forgot to Remember' in a stunning three different keys. There is also a mass rendition of the Beatles' 'Yellow Submarine'.

Only one political hot potato came up this time: a reference by Alf to Labour 'dropping a Pollock' in their shock by-election defeat in the Glasgow Pollock constituency on 9 March, when the Tories had taken the seat with a surprise 2,201 majority. Mrs Whitehouse, when asked, admitted that she had not understood the innuendo. Mitchell maintained that the joke was completely his own inspiration in the heat of the moment, while internally the BBC suggested to the production team that a 'device known as a "burp" be used to drown out any such future lapses'. *The Observer* reported that Alf's comment 'was still pleasing local saloon bar wits the next evening'.

While it topped the ratings for the week, the special left many *Till Death Us Do Part* fans not knowing what to make of it. Nancy Banks Smith, writing in the *Sun*, deemed it 'soft-centred, sentimental and overrun with famous faces' and said that although it had its positive points, such as Else's bawdy recollections and some good direction, the BBC should 'never again sacrifice the Garnetts so as not to offend on the British Bank Holiday'. The *Birmingham Evening Mail* was not impressed either: '[It] had nothing much to do with Alf Garnett. It was just a noisy knees-up in a London pub with Alf being predictably, half-heartedly and unfunnily offensive to Kenny Lynch, Jimmy Tarbuck and Ray Barrett. This was warm brown ale compared with the vintage Garnett.' The Revd Derek H Buckley of Hatton, Derby, lamented that the 'magnificent resources that the BBC undoubtedly has available were being utterly prostituted on such trivial drivel … the incoherencies of such a programme'. 'What a load of tripe!' wrote one viewer in a letter to the *Radio Times*. 'The landlord of any public house would have put Alf Garnett out on his ear. As a full-blooded Cockney, I strongly object to my evening's viewing being debased by such so-called comedy'.

Despite its huge ratings – it drew in 32.1% of the UK viewing population for BBC One, compared with 0.2% for BBC Two and 17.8% for ITV – the special gained a Reaction Index (RI) of only 61, compared with an average of 68 for the previous ten episodes of the second series. Many of the BBC's sample viewers considered it to have been disappointing, not as amusing as usual and padded out with too many guests. They thought that Alf Garnett had been swamped in noise, that the script had been crude, that the vocals had been raucous and that the regulars had not been given enough to do. Some,

---

[20] This is perhaps an early version of the Barmy Harry character in which guise Speight would make a number of cameo appearances in the 1970s.

however, had enjoyed it ('Just like old times in the Old Kent Road,' said one), and all had praised its direction and naturalism.

Another admirer was Kenneth Adam, Director of Television at the BBC, who referred to the special as 'a harmless evocation of a certain type of Bank Holiday fun, and cunning to boot'. Peter Black, the *Daily Mail*'s tireless champion of the show, went further: 'I can only say that [the special] was the closest television has come to catching the flavour of the English orgy, or booze-up. If you didn't like any of it, you must indeed be against the human race … It reproduced perfectly the atmosphere of a public bar during the last 40 minutes of a Saturday night.'

Looking back on it today, the special has weathered the march of time splendidly. Its boozy charm and working-class ebullience, helped by the show's usual lack of sentimentality and some superb direction, demonstrate a very welcome fresh approach to depicting the world of the Garnetts, testament to a behind-the-scenes team at the top of their creative powers.

Speight was now immune to criticism anyway. The peak of an extraordinary three months for him came when, on 10 March, he won the Best Comedy Writer award from the Screenwriters' Guild – the first of three consecutive annual triumphs in this category. Not only was the show riding high in the UK ratings, but it was soon to achieve similar success in Australia; a package of episodes was acquired by the Australian Broadcasting Corporation (ABC) on 21 March and began transmission in August, when it quickly became the most popular series the channel had ever broadcast, with 43% of the viewing population watching it in Adelaide, 47% in Melbourne and 37% in Sydney.

Till Death Us Do Part had also made the transition into another medium, with the release of two long-playing records on the Pye label. The first of these, which consisted of a number of audio selections from the show's first series, received some promotion from Dandy Nichols, who commented ominously: 'I've got an awful feeling that with me and Else, it is going to be case of "Till death … "'. The second album was specially recorded by Mitchell as Alf singing a collection of First World War songs and ballads, which he was later to use in his one man show.

Boosted by all this success, and prompted by the start of negotiations for a third series of *Till Death Us Do Part*, scheduled for the autumn of 1967, Speight now asked for a minimum of £1,000 per script from the BBC. He cited this as being what he considered the 'market value' for his talent, and warned that he could earn £2,000 per script on 'the other side'. Indeed, his Associated London Scripts colleagues and good friends Galton and Simpson had recently been granted £1,200 per script, plus £600 per repeat, for their contributions to the current Frankie Howerd show on ITV. Speight further stated that he had had to turn down four film offers in order to keep up with his *Till Death Us Do Part* commitments – an assertion that must have rankled with his long-suffering

BBC bosses, given that he most manifestly had not kept up at all. But the BBC realised that Speight had them over a barrel; 'Till Closing Time Do Us Part' had, after all, been the most watched programme in the crucial Bank Holiday schedule, and 'Peace and Goodwill' had just been entered for the Golden Rose of Montreux's *Hors Concours* – the preliminary batch of shows from which the candidates for Europe's premier TV comedy award would be selected. Clause 30 of a Government White Paper late in 1966 had attempted to peg prices and incomes except in cases of 'reasonable increases'; and this exception was what Speight now sought to rely on. He used the metaphor of selling his home and receiving its market value – now, he asserted, his market value was greater. Michael Peacock, Controller of BBC One, admitted in an internal memo of 21 April 1967, 'We must not lose Johnny Speight'. Soon after this, the decision was taken to submit to the writer's demands: 'We must pay £1,000 per script or lose this scriptwriter, which clearly would be a disaster.' A memo of 2 May shows just how quickly the Corporation gave in; on that date, Speight was contracted for eight more 30-minute shows, with an option of an extra five, for transmission from 18 December 1967 to 12 February 1968. By 11 July 1967, a commission was being mooted for a further eight episodes, to make up a fourth series for transmission between September and December 1968, together with the rights for a movie version of the show. A proviso was made by the BBC concerning the size of Speight's fee: 'Because of special circumstances … [we] do not want this to be a precedent.'

On 22 June, at a BBC management conference, Kenneth Adam suggested a 7.30 pm slot once again for the third series, since the Garnetts had proved instrumental in dislodging *Coronation Street* from its previous predominant position in the ratings, but this was vehemently opposed by Speight, who saw this as 'kiddies' time' and felt that, with its 20 million audience and RI figure of 70, the show could be put on later in the evening. The slot eventually agreed was 8.20 pm on Friday nights; a possible concession to the increasing public outcry about the dangers the show posed in its former early evening timeslot. Dennis Main Wilson, who like Adam had advocated retaining the original slot against *Coronation Street* said, in an uncharacteristic fit of depression, that he 'wished he'd never suggested [making *Till Death Us Do Part*] in the first place'.

Speight's pay packet manoeuvres led to him acquiring a reputation as a 'champagne socialist', an impression reinforced by a *Man Alive* documentary entitled *Top Class People* transmitted on Wednesday 10 May 1967. This programme was a serious examination of why working class talent – as exemplified by Speight, supermodel Twiggy, graphic artist Alan Aldridge and pop singer Sandy Shaw – was now so in demand. Speight was introduced as 'the man asked to write a new series for a vast sum of money, [having] probably amassed … more money than was ever earned by *Sons and Lovers* in Lawrence's lifetime'. It was a flattering comparison, but *The Listener* noted that although Speight was the most obviously-talented of the four people featured in the programme, he came off the worst; and this was true, not just because of unflattering editing (Speight barely appeared on screen) but also because of his nervousness, his stammer and his self-deprecating joke (used frequently in his career) about believing in his early days that George Bernard Shaw was a kind of Tommy Trinder figure, which may not have amused po-faced commentator Desmond Wilcox.

FALSE COIN! THOU ART INDEED FROM LIVERPOOL!

'Peace and Goodwill' was shown to the judging panel for the Golden Rose of Montreux on 24 April 1967, supported by a dossier of information describing the nature of the show and giving cast and crew details. Predictably, there were problems in translating the comedy into other languages. In French, 'Silly old moo' became 'Old female goat', 'You great hairy nellie' became 'You old monkey', 'nit' became 'fou' [mad] and 'coons' translated as 'negres'. The Germans meanwhile transformed 'Traitorious [sic] Scouse git' to 'False coin! Thou art indeed from Liverpool!' The Dutch and Swedish judges were very impressed, the latter expressing interest in buying the format for their own language version. The other BBC contenders were a 50-minute colour musical 'journey' around the Hebrides starring Kenneth McKellar, and David Frost's *Frost Over England*, universally criticised on its original broadcast as a stale collection of visual clichés lampooning the foreign image of Britain – Heath and Wilson doing the hokey-cokey, John Cleese karate-chopping a wedding cake, Big Ben striking as London collapses and so forth. Perhaps inevitably, Frost won the Golden Rose.

A new threat to the show emerged from another quarter at the beginning of April 1967. Anthony Booth had seen his starring role in the *Comedy Playhouse* pilot and the debut series eclipsed first by Warren Mitchell's swift rise to prominence and then by Dandy Nichols' ascent to second billing. His salary had not increased sufficiently to assuage his bruised ego, and worse still, his friendship with Speight, which had got him the job in the first place, had been superseded by Mitchell's. Booth had never managed to come to terms with Mitchell's candour, stringent work ethic and Stanislavski-dominated approach to acting. Mitchell, for his part, found Booth's easy-going attitude to life in general and acting in particular anathema to his meticulous quest for perfection, and also disapproved of the younger man's pop-star lifestyle – the taking of virility pills, the shagging of birds in Piccadilly, the excessive consumption of alcohol, and so on. This inevitably ensured confrontation over all aspects of the production. The rows that Mitchell routinely had with director Douglas Argent – prompted purely by the star's commitment to professional perfectionism, and quickly forgotten about by the two men once the immediate confrontation was over – were wearing on the nerves of both Booth and, increasingly, Nichols. There was also the ongoing nightmare of the late delivery of scripts, the frenzied attempts of the already highly-strung, alcohol-fuelled Dennis Main Wilson to make them viable for production and the associated need for ad-libs and improvised business from all the cast. Taken together, all these factors meant that the making of the show was adrenalin-fuelled but, for Booth at least, little fun. Booth was now a national star – he was even invited to the Prime Minister's birthday bash at 10 Downing Street on 16 March 1967 – and was keen to spread his wings and expand his horizons. Soon a rumour started to spread that he was intent on quitting prior to the new series, and that Una Stubbs – who, along with Geoff Jowitt, remained a confidant of his – was unwilling to work with anyone else and would thus do the same. Speight stated publicly that the show could easily carry on with a new young couple if necessary, but that he did not want them to leave. Nichols meanwhile told the *Sunday People* that she would be terribly upset if Booth went. On 6 April, the *Daily Mirror* actually reported that Booth had quit and would not be back. With characteristic flamboyance, Mitchell attempted to heal the rift. Guesting alongside Dusty Springfield on Simon Dee's *Dee Time* chat show, he shouted out: 'Come home, Anthony Booth. All is forgiven. Tony is definitely not leaving the show because of a row with myself or anybody else. In fact, he is leaving because he doesn't feel he's getting enough of the script. I feel it will be a great loss, and I really want him to stay'. The last part of this was muffled as Dee placed his hand over his guest's mouth, as they were running out of time. In the end, Booth did indeed agree to stay on, although his request for an increased salary of 300 guineas per episode was not met.

Mitchell himself had also made noises about leaving the show, for two very different reasons: first that he remained fearful of being typecast, and secondly that he was now so busy as an actor that he felt he might not have time to devote to recording a third series. He eventually signed a new contract in September 1967, but with a clause guaranteeing him sight of each script at least ten days before recording. (Even this stipulation was ultimately to be consigned to the wayside, but that was yet to come.)

Booth's new fee per episode, settled in September, was £236 5s, a £100 increase on what he had received for the second series, while Mitchell's was £500, Nichols' was £420 and Stubbs' was £157 10s.

On a lighter note, Booth was amused to learn of a complaint made to Tom Sloan on 18 May 1967 by Percy Belcher of high class tailors Richer & Co. Belcher stated that the firm had given Booth three jackets on the stipulation that he would wear them on the show as product placement. Since Booth had worn only one of the jackets, Belcher was now threatening to sue. This threat was dismissed by Sloan.

12
To Hell With It

TO LUCIFER, A SON

Invited by Mary Whitehouse to speak at the Second National Viewers' and Listeners' Association Convention in May 1967 was noted broadcaster Malcolm Muggeridge, who consented on the basis that he would be free to agree or disagree with the organisation's views. The rumour mill ground away for some weeks beforehand, as each faction wondered which way the eminent orator would lean; would the NVLA turn out to have scored an own goal by inviting him? BBC Head of Drama Sydney Newman, the man responsible for *The Wednesday Play*, could allegedly be found wandering the corridors of Television Centre muttering that Muggeridge 'would be bound to support us – wouldn't he?'. He was wrong. Muggeridge was fervently opposed to the new permissiveness, and the Garnetts were at the forefront of his anxieties as he addressed the convention: ' I am absolutely convinced that our civilisation will rush down the Gadarene slope that others have slipped down before, if we adhere to the notion that the image of life is not God but pigs in a trough. If life is pigs in a trough, if the purpose of it is to get as much as you can out of the trough, to bury your snout into it, then of course it does not matter much what you show on TV. But all that is just nothing at all. If that were life, if *Till Death Us Do Part* is life, really life, I cannot see that there would be anything to do but commit suicide. If that were life. But it is not, and what is needed on the part of people like us, is to have the voice, the inspiration, the clarity of mind, to make people see that it is not life; that all this wretched wallowing about does not even make you happy, doesn't even work ...'

Muggeridge found all the characters in the series repulsive, especially, as he wrote in a review for *The Listener* of the 5 August repeat of 'The Bulldog Breed', 'Alf with his everlasting shouted absurdities, or the young couple with their equally absurd, smugly-held leftish opinions on Vietnam, etc'. He saw the show as belonging to the same quasi-documentary genre as the other two NVLA *bête noire*s, 'Cathy Come Home' and 'Up the Junction', which he described as 'a sort of no man's land between fantasy and reality'. The result, he stated, was 'pot for the masses, to condition them for their destiny as 1984 proles. Broiler houses and factory farms … have music playing to keep the animals contented; humans, I daresay, need pictures as well. Speight started with a good comedy situation, which used to be worked very well in the old music halls, but it's been sicklied o'er with the pale cast of secondary modern thinking. I prefer *Coronation Street*.'

Muggeridge's speech to the NVLA Convention was rapturously received by the organisation as an affirmation of its stance. His mention of the invidious creation of Speight – the man who had so publicly insulted their founder member, Mrs Whitehouse, both on the radio and on television, in response to which she would imminently launch a legal assault – seemed to impel the NVLA on to greater ambitions; from now on, only the cancellation of *Till Death Us Do Part* would suffice for them.

But Speight himself was blissfully unconcerned. Early 1967 saw the addition of another string to his bow with the release of the movie *Privilege*, Peter Watkins' first major production since the controversial, and at the time still unbroadcast, *The War Game*. This was based on one of Speight's short stories, which had been submitted to producer John Heyman shortly after the writer had turned down the chance to provide the screenplay for *A Hard Day's Night* (eventually written by Norman Bogner). Set in a dystopian future where Britain is a fascist state, *Privilege* featured Paul Jones, formerly of the pop group Manfred Mann, as a pop singer whose fame becomes so powerful that various establishment elements – the government, the church, the media – use him as a means to sell their own 'commodities' to his adoring fans.

In total contrast to this, released at around the same time was *The Plank*, written and directed by Eric Sykes – Speight's one-time boss – and featuring a cast of great British comics, including Speight himself in a cameo role. The producer was Jon Pennington, with whom Speight would later bring the Garnetts to the big screen in 1968.

Capping a busy period for Speight, early May 1967 saw him being commissioned for a fee of £900 to write the script for another *Comedy Playhouse* pilot. This was originally entitled 'To Hell With It', and was intended as a sitcom vehicle for Speight's friend Jimmy Tarbuck. Produced by Dennis Main Wilson, rehearsed between 22 and 27 May and recorded on 28 May, it was tentatively slotted in for broadcast on 23 June. Such was the interest in Speight's work that Otto Leisner, Senior Producer of Light Entertainment for Radio Denmark, arranged to view the recording. It was a decision he must have regretted, because this, as with everything concerned with the production, seemed to bear out the title and suffer from a diabolical curse. Haldane Duncan, the floor manager, later called it 'the biggest no-no in the careers of everyone associated with it'. The full script was so late that a complete version arrived only on the day of recording. Duncan continues: 'The poor designer spent her days at the end of a phone in the workshops where the set was being built waiting for news; we couldn't cast anyone and we could only rehearse bits; everything was a shambles; and it was all down to Johnny not providing us with a decent script on time.' Somehow, things got worse... 'Most of the set was built on scaffolding – but guess what? The scaffolders didn't turn up, so camera rehearsals that were meant to start at 10.30 didn't get going until after 3.00. Dress rehearsal? Forget it. The show itself was the dress rehearsal. We had so many stops at this recording that, to this day, I still have a certain admiration for Jimmy Tarbuck. Every time there was a technical cock-up, he launched into his act, but his material got eaten up after an hour or so. However, his audience found those bits far more entertaining than the show, and reserved all their laughter for the recording breaks. When I had to interrupt Jimmy and say, "All right, we've sorted ourselves out and are ready to record", I could just feel the irritation of the audience, as they had to put up with another bit of boredom before they could get back to Jimmy telling jokes. 'Cos there sure weren't any in the script.'

The show itself began with a blank screen, over which was broadcast an announcement, spoken by Arthur English: 'There now follows a Party Political Broadcast on behalf of the Devil'. Tarbuck appeared as the very sharply-dressed Little Nick, son of the Devil, and wore two plastic horns on his head to signify his diabolical descent. John Le Mesurier brought his typical care-worn suaveness to the part of the Devil, anxious to retire and pass on the mantle of evil to his son. Dermot Kelly played St Patrick, telling Little Nick that 'Big G' – God – has banned alcohol from heaven, and so he wants to transfer to Hell with its bingo halls, discos, girls in mini-skirts and 24 hour pubs. A stellar cast also included Cleo Sylvestre, Rita Webb, Pat Coombs and Tommy Godfrey. There were references to a gold watch, as in the 'Till Death Us Do Part' pilot (and later in the 1974 series), to golf (a mutual pastime of Speight and Tarbuck, later also to feature in *Till Death Us Do Part*) , and to a decidedly Gadarene Malcolm Muggeridge – another example of Speight attacking someone he disliked by holding him up to ridicule in a script. The piece ended with a montage of film depicting anti-war demonstrations, hinting that it was intended to meld the theatre-of-the-absurd leanings of Speight's dramatic pieces into a light entertainment framework.

Symptomatic of the sensationalism now surrounding everything Speight touched, rumours of problems with the production began to spread on 7 June 1967, when the programme was renamed *To Lucifer, a Son*. A story was leaked that it had been postponed from its original transmission date by one week and also given a later time slot because it was considered 'too controversial' for early evening viewing in the normal *Comedy Playhouse* slot of 7.30 pm. The BBC denied this, saying that the time change was merely due to its length; at 23 minutes, it was simply too short for the slot originally intended and had to be moved to a later time when the schedule could be more easily rearranged to accommodate it. A perusal of internal BBC correspondence shows this to be the truth. Frank Muir viewed the show on 30 May; one of his last functions as the Head of Comedy at the BBC prior to his transfer to the nascent London Weekend Television the following month. His damning verdict, contained in a memo of 2 June, was phrased with characteristic tact: 'I think this programme hasn't quite come off. To [transmit it] in the *Comedy Playhouse* series would be to put it at a disadvantage. It is basically a marvellous idea, full of interesting comments and undertones and very original, but as produced it has emerged as more mystifying than funny, more unusual than effective. Jimmy Tarbuck's performance is excellent. His personality comes right through the screen; he is confident, flexible and thoroughly professional. Rather than waste his first appearance for us in a sitcom on this interesting, experimental, but, on the whole, unsuccessful programme, I think we should try to set up another vehicle for Tarbuck and remake *To Lucifer, a Son* later on. Johnny Speight can look upon this production as a dummy run of his idea, and perhaps next time we can iron out the faults, i.e. the length of the programme, the sets, the heaven sequence ... An interesting exercise, but I don't think it is quite funny enough, nor quite effective enough, nor long enough to put out in *Comedy Playhouse* ... [It has] shown Jimmy Tarbuck's value ...'

On 31 May, Terry Miller, Tarbuck's manager, had stated to the press: 'There is nothing really wrong with the play, although the subject is controversial. Jimmy would not have had anything to do with it if it had been in any way sacrilegious.'

The show eventually went out on Thursday 29 June 1967, and proved to be Speight's one and only piece of transmitted work other than *Till Death Us Do Part* under his lucrative BBC contract. In view of his status as the most famous writer in British television, it was a well-publicised event – and proved to be utterly disastrous. The press reaction was unanimously poor. Virginia Ironside, writing in the *Daily Mail*, lamented that the jokes were strictly of the 'You're a hellraiser' and 'My devil-may-care attitude' variety, while the image of Hell was childish in its unoriginality: non-stop bingo, endless war films for war criminals, lavatories covered with racks of pencils for writing rude things on the wall ... 'There was no beginning, no middle, no end,' she complained, 'just isolated incidents. It was like a *Frost Programme* on Hell – only Frost would have done it ten times better.' She finished her scathing review by calling it a 'childish flop'. Fellow critic Michael Billington was if anything even more dismissive, deeming the show 'witless, completely innocuous and astonishingly dull ... [incorporating] every old joke about Hell you could think of'. He added that any script in which 'Big G' announces he'll come down to live in Hell and is met with the response 'We'll give Him a warm welcome' could only be described as 'a load of old chestnuts'. Only Le Mesurier, thought Billington, deserved praise, Tarbuck having been his 'usual overconfident self [who] made only the most cursory attempt to assume a character.' The great public interest in Speight's work ensured that the programme achieved a high rating of 16.3% of the viewing population, yet the intense disappointment that greeted it resulted in an appalling RI of just 38. Audience reaction was summed up in one line in the *Radio Times* of 13 July 1967: 'Rotten / sick / sickening / decadent / profane / revolting / atrocious / tasteless / disgusting'.

On paper, the basic idea underlying *To Lucifer, a Son* seems to be an interesting one; but unfortunately it is impossible to give a second opinion on the finished production today, free of the expectations that Speight's notoriety forced on it in 1967, as no video copy of it has survived. At any rate, it signified the end of Speight's interest in surreal theatre, and delayed him coming up with any further sitcom ideas for another two years – until *Curry and Chips* was commissioned by, ironically, Frank Muir for London Weekend Television.

At the time, though, Speight took the programme's lack of success in his stride as ever more lucrative deals came his way. The aforementioned *Dee Time* appearance of Warren Mitchell and Dusty Springfield in April, coupled with Springfield's friendship with Speight's mate Spike Milligan, resulted in an invitation from the singer's producer Stanley Dorfman for him to write a sketch featuring Alf Garnett alone for the first of her new series of BBC One summer shows. Dorfman's assistant, Haldane Duncan, who had witnessed the production of the diabolical *To Lucifer, A Son*, advised the producer of the ever present-problem of Speight's late delivery of scripts. Consequently Dorfman told Speight that he must deliver a script for Mitchell within a week; and, for once, the writer obliged, simply rewriting an old Arthur Haynes sketch in which the comic had disrupted a magician's act. Speight was offered £150 for the nine-minute sketch on 15 June, but held out for, and managed to get, £200. The programme was recorded on 18 June and transmitted at 21.05 pm on Tuesday 15 August. Mitchell received an enormous fee of £314 5s for his pains.

The prototype for many of Alf's later solo TV appearances, the *Dusty* sketch begins with him as a heckler who is invited up from the audience when he protests that a conjuror, played by Mitchell's old mate and understudy Ken Campbell, is a fake. Alf exposes the fraud and, after the conjuror walks off, launches into a duet with Dusty on a selection of old music hall standards, similar to his own solo renditions of First World War songs recently released on long playing record. The singing then degenerates into a politico-social argument, with the host taking Rita's liberal viewpoint.

It was strikingly unusual and effective as a guest spot, but Alf's star was so much in the ascendant that any appearance was guaranteed to cause some furore; his solitary 'git' and handful of 'bloodies' sent some *Radio Times* readers into a frenzy. 'What is the BBC thinking of to allow Warren Mitchell in the first of the Dusty Springfield shows to give such a performance?' asked Mrs G Stephens of Poole. 'I have never heard so many swear words spoken in a few seconds. In fact I had to leave the room when it seemed the whole act was continuing that way. The shame of it is that Warren Mitchell could be funny if only ...' The BBC's Audience Reaction Report of 27 September on the show stated: 'It was clear that a large number of viewers took exception to Warren Mitchell's appearance as Alf Garnett of *Till Death Us Do Part*. Some remarked that although they found Alf Garnett extremely funny in his own environment, in this programme he seemed utterly out of place and embarrassingly coarse, while others thought it monstrous that this "despicable character" should be allowed to contaminate other programmes. True, the appearance of Alf Garnett "made" the show for some – "Alf Garnett was a real scream and made a good show super" – but most would clearly have preferred Warren Mitchell as himself instead of as the "revolting" Alf Garnett.'

At a meeting between Wilson and Speight in September it was agreed that while solo appearances by Mitchell as Alf were okay for his personal publicity and his bank balance, too much of this might undermine the reality of the character. They thus determined that Alf should not appear onscreen again until the next series of *Till Death Us Do Part*, although 'obviously, we have no objection to Warren Mitchell appearing in any other way he chooses'. This injunction against solo TV spots for Alf was to be maintained for the next few years. However, he continued to appear in other media. 15 and 16 June 1967 saw two more celebrations of the show, in book and audio form respectively. First came the publication of John Burke's book on *Till Death Us Do Part*[21], the third piece of tie-in merchandise to be issued within three months. It contained treatments of many of the first and early second series scripts, mainly using original versions, framed with specially-written quotes from Alf on politics, sport and so on, and came with a picture of a very serene-looking Alf on the front cover and one of a scene from 'Peace and Goodwill' on the back. Secondly, the following day, the show received further publicity from a totally unexpected quarter, when current pop sensations the Monkees released their latest single, 'Alternate Title'. This song had originally been called 'Randy Scouse Git', which Mickey Dolenz of the group has always credited as having been inspired by his viewing of an episode of *Till Death*

---

[21] The same day also saw publication of a book on *The Likely Lads*.

Us Do Part on a visit to London earlier that year.

Identification of the particular edition of the show that Dolenz saw was aided by the recovery of a complete episode of *Till Death Us Do Part* in 2009. Dolenz arrived in the UK on Monday 6 February 1967 (the same day as Kosygin) and stayed at the Grosvenor House Hotel. He was introduced to the Beatles soon afterwards, and hung out with Paul McCartney at his home and at the Speakeasy club. On 9 February he appeared with fellow Monkee Mike Nesmith on *Top of the Pops* to promote their number one hit 'I'm a Believer', followed by more weekend antics with members of the Fab Four. It is reasonable to surmise that he watched an episode of *Till Death Us Do Part* the following Monday, 13 February, with the infamous 'randy Scouse git' phrase present, and that episode was 'In Sickness And In Health'. Following Dolenz's recollections, he must have composed the song the next day:

'[I wrote the song on] the morning after the Beatles had thrown us a party at some club,' he later recalled. 'I had some girl with me … I was literally just making it up as I went along … It was just about my experiences. It was like word association, really … There was a social comment about having long hair … and being abused … by the establishment.'

The single does not specifically mention the show, being a psychedelic collage of the initial impressions Dolenz received of Swinging London, referencing the Beatles ('The four kings of EMI'), the novel idea (to an American) of girls being called 'birds' and a hotel servant dressed in tails transforming into a penguin, (an image combining the Monkees' staying at a posh hotel morphing into one of the animals they had seen when engaged on a publicity trip to London Zoo on 8 February). Dolenz liked the title of 'Randy Scouse Git', which he was told equated to 'Lecherous Liverpudlian jerk'; and, already a committed Anglophile, he suggested it for the band's next single. The single 'Randy Scouse Git' was then recorded on Thursday 2 March 1967 and released three months later.

At this point, however, the BBC, with amazing hypocrisy, stated that they would not play the disc with such an offensive title and suggested that Dolenz use an 'alternate title' – which he did, taking the suggestion quite literally, for the UK at least, and 'Alternate Title' was to reach number two in the charts the following month. The excellent single has very little to do with the Garnetts, apart from the title, the music hall-style tinkling piano and the spirit of Alf, who can be heard in the background, as voiced by Dolenz, crying out 'Why don't you cut your hair!' and 'Why don't you hate who I hate and kill who I kill to be free!', although its wonderfully raucous, chaotic chorus does seem to encapsulate the spirit of the show. As it transpired, the Monkees were the first of several pop acts to be associated with or inspired by the sitcom over the next five years …

LORD ABOVE

Aside from the brief dip of *To Lucifer, a Son*, the summer of 1967 saw Johnny Speight on a high, both critically and commercially, with his status as a household name in Britain seemingly unassailable. During July and August, his bank account benefited further from a repeat run of six episodes from *Till Death Us Do Part*'s second series at peak time on Saturday nights, for which he received £500 per episode. Strangely enough, the run included the now decidedly unseasonal Christmas episode 'Peace and Goodwill', although this had admittedly been considered at Montreux in the spring. There was some intelligence in the scheduling, however, since the last of the repeats was 'In Sickness and in Health', when the cause of Alf's medical problems is found to be the thruppenny bit he swallowed from Else's Christmas pudding in the earlier episode. There were admittedly some clouds on the horizon for the writer – the threatened departure of his friend and confidante Booth, the hesitation of Mitchell, and the defection of one of his strongest and most sympathetic associates, Frank Muir, from the blissful pastures of the BBC for the industrial conglomerate that was the soon-to-be-launched London Weekend Television (LWT) – but otherwise the skies seemed sunny, with at least two more series of *Till Death Us Do Part* in prospect and the possibility of a movie version to follow. With hindsight, however, one date that summer was to mark an unexpected change in the trajectory of Speight's career.

The date in question was Thursday 27 July 1967, when three notable events occurred simultaneously. First, Mary Whitehouse won her *The World at One* libel case against Speight, and he was forced to pay the NVLA undisclosed damages. This was less significant to Speight at the time than for the winner, whose fight against the moral malaise she believed was threatening the nation seemed vindicated. Emboldened, she was to step up her struggle with her opponent over the next few months. Then, on the same day, at the High Court, Lady Snow received apologies and substantial compensation in her libel action against Hugh Carleton Greene, Keith Waterhouse and Willis Hall over a sketch on *The Late Show* of 19 November 1966 (see Chapter Ten). Thus twice in one day Whitehouse had seen the 'moral majority' vindicated in their dealings with Greene and the BBC. But the biggest media news story of that day was the public announcement that Lord Hill of Luton was to become the new Chairman of the BBC on 1 September 1967.

Charles Hill, aged 63, of working-class stock from Islington, had studied medicine at Cambridge and gone on to an impressive career in that field, rising to become Secretary of the British Medical Association from 1944 to 1950. Even in the late 1960s he was still known to the general populace as the 'radio doctor', owing to his regular presentation of health messages in the

Ministry of Food's daily BBC radio programme *Kitchen Front* during the Second World War; he is indeed referred to by Else in the second series episode 'I Can Give It Up Any Time I Like' as the man who miraculously cured her lumbago. A change of career had then seen him turning to politics. He had become Tory MP for Luton in 1950 and had served as Minister for Housing and Local Government in the Macmillan government until 1962, when Mac had sacked him. His broadcasting experience had then stood him in good stead, and after being granted a peerage, he had been appointed Chairman of the Independent Television Authority (ITA) by Alec Douglas Home in 1963.

Hill knew a lot about broadcasting, was a forceful, no-nonsense character and a top administrator (he was also Chairman of Laporte Chemicals) and possessed an incisive intellect with regard to finance and logistics. In the past few weeks, he had gained notoriety with his draconian settlement of the ITA contract renewal for the independent franchises, which had resulted in the elimination of Television West and Wales and forced the amalgamation of Associated Rediffusion and ABC Television. This restructuring of 'the other side' had caused problems for the BBC, who had always viewed Hill's strong-arm tactics as the antithesis of their free-thinking doctrine. They had angrily commented on 13 June that high ITV salaries – always a lure for their staff, and even more so following the Government's wage freeze – were now being supplemented by huge interest-free loans offered in return for taking equity shares in the new franchisees such as LWT and Yorkshire, which they feared would prove an irresistible inducement to defect. Michael Peacock and, more crucially for Speight, Frank Muir, had indeed already defected, Muir wryly remarking: 'I feel rather like the curate of a prosperous parish in Kensington who's going to open a hut in the dock area … and I suppose I'm going for very much the same reasons.' It was a decision both Muir and Peacock were later to regret.

The BBC had at least had the comfort of knowing that such interventionist policies were limited to their commercial rivals. But then, on 15 June 1967, BBC Chairman Lord Normanbrook had died suddenly. Normanbrook had allegedly been appointed by the Tories to keep a watchful eye on Greene, but he had attained a good reputation at the Corporation with his *laissez faire* policies, the only great deviation from which had been the famous incident when he had barred Rhodesian premier Ian Smith from appearing on *Panorama* in October 1965, a decision branded by critics as editorial interference of the highest order.

Speculation had been rife throughout June and July 1967 as to who would be Normanbrook's replacement. On 26 June, Mary Whitehouse had written to the Prime Minister, urging him to consider giving the new Chairman, on his appointment, a salary in excess of the Director General's, 'to leave no doubt who holds the senior position, and on whom rests the responsibility for the standards and future of broadcasting'. Her relationship with Normanbrook had been more cordial than that with Greene. At least Normanbrook had consented to meet NVLA mainstay James Dance MP at a private luncheon just before Christmas, on which occasion Normanbrook had allegedly lamented Greene's uncontrollability. Greene himself, of course, had consistently refused to meet the 'clean up TV people' in any capacity, and was proud of the *persona non exista* status he had bestowed on Whitehouse within the BBC.

For Greene, who had apparently been tipped off by telephone the day before the public announcement, Hill's appointment to the Chairmanship came as a total bombshell. Hill's experience as Postmaster General and Chancellor of the Duchy of Lancaster under the Tories had given him a reputation for political interventionism, while his recent manoeuvres at the ITA had convinced the BBC that he was utterly ruthless. In terms of personality, whereas Normanbrook had been quiet and polite, Hill was remote and abrupt. Then there came rumours that Hill's appointment had been decided upon by the Wilson government specifically in order to control the wayward Aunty Beeb. Edward Short, the current Postmaster General, had allegedly recommended this course of action to Wilson in the light of the government's recent disastrous relationship with the Corporation. Short was later to deny this, although he would concede, 'Everybody believed Hill to be a disciplinarian who would put the BBC in its place and make the producers do as they were told, and not do their own thing as they had always done at the BBC'. Wilson had apparently remarked, 'Charlie Hill has already cleaned up ITV, and he'll do the same for the BBC'.

It later transpired that Wilson had met Hill at a Commons lunch the previous year and had told him that the job of BBC Chairman was his when Normanbrook retired. The allegation that he had selected Hill specifically in order to curb the perceived excesses of Greene has since been disputed many times – Hill himself denied that his appointment had any such strings attached – but is supported by evidence from the subsequently-published diaries of the then Leader of the House of Commons Richard Crossman, who recorded on 26 July 1967 that Wilson intended the move to supplant Greene. At any rate, its plausibility in 1967 was evident.

Till Death Us Do Part was frequently cited in the media as being emblematic of the type of controversial programming that the new broom would sweep away. 'Just how tough will Lord Hill get with Alf Garnett?' was one headline. Peter Black of the *Daily Mail* wrote that he believed Mary Whitehouse would rejoice, but cautioned that things would probably not change too much: political programmes might become duller and there might be some concessions to clean up *The Wednesday Play* and Alf Garnett … A Franklin cartoon in the *Daily Express* depicted Hill as Alf in his armchair and Greene as Else leaving him in a welter of smashed crockery, with one of those homely sayings on the living room wall altering *Till Death Us Do Part* to a scrawled 'Till NOW Us Do Part'. The caption read 'Well, they're different, ain't they?'

Hill had strengthened the role of the ITA members against their Director General, and Greene feared that he would do the same for the BBC governors. Greene believed the BBC was not a sacred institution in the Reithian tradition but a kind of 'super electronic newspaper', which had not only to be free of political influence but also to be *seen* to be free. Hill, he thought, would destroy all that. He had the 'utmost contempt' for the new Chairman. BBC executive Robert Lusty declared, 'It was the end of the BBC as I knew it, and the end of Hugh Greene too.' David Attenborough, Controller of BBC Two, told Hill to his face that his appointment was perceived by many at the BBC to be akin to giving Rommel command over the Eighth Army.

Once Hill moved into his BBC office in September, bringing with him his own ITA colour telly, skirmishes between him and Greene were not long in coming. These included disputes over cigarette advertising in the *Radio Times* and rows about a John Wells satire on Harold Wilson's motives regarding Nigeria. Within three months, Mrs Whitehouse, elated by the new appointment, was campaigning against the Beatles' *Magical Mystery Tour* TV film and specifically two lines from 'I Am the Walrus' – 'Crabalocker, fishwife, pornographic priestess; Boy you've been a naughty girl, you let your knickers down' – demanding that Greene either drop the song or cancel the Boxing Day show. Greene refused to do either.

Thus while Speight was busy writing – or rather, as we shall see, trying to write – the third series of the most controversial and most successful show on British television, he would effectively see the dangers of censorship everywhere in much the same way that Whitehouse saw the dangers of moral decay. 1967 had been the year of this great debate over the influence of television, and Speight had been heavily involved in all its aspects. He had even used Mike as a mouthpiece to criticise Lord Hill in one episode of the second series of *Till Death Us Do Part*. [22] The press were expecting a titanic clash between the forces of artistic freedom and those of artistic responsibility, and Speight and Whitehouse would not disappoint them.

As the third series was being set up, all the elements necessary for another explosion were reaching critical point. Booth, his influence over the show marginalised, still wanted to leave, and Speight was unsure how to deal with this. Speight himself had consistently failed to fulfil his BBC contract, yet still he seemed inclined to crow about his status as best paid

---

[22] 'I Can Give It Up Any Time I Like' featured, in addition to Else's comment about Hill's cure for her lumbago, a very negative observation from Mike about his broadcasting changes at the ITA.

writer on British television. At the same time, he was besieged by morality campaigners, lawsuits and court cases affecting media freedoms, and was experiencing a sense of paranoia exacerbated by the appointment of Lord Hill, whom he and many others perceived as an arch reactionary against permissiveness in the media. Familiar faces such as Frank Muir and Michael Peacock had departed for more profitable pastures on the commercial side, leaving him feeling isolated. Nevertheless, Speight was to plough on, barging his way through the unspoken conventions that bounded British television and in the process going right over the edge

13
The Third Series

THE MASK OF THE PEOPLE

No other television show of the late 1960s, or arguably of any other era, attracted as much controversy as the third series of *Till Death Us Do Part*, which (dis)graced the BBC's Friday night schedules for seven weeks from 5 January 1968. The forces opposed to the show had now begun to coalesce, while the creative elements behind it had begun to falter. The result was an unprecedented and unparalleled media bombardment that eventually saw the series ending amid a welter of public threats and recrimination, leading to a gap of almost five years in production. The hiatus came suddenly and apparently unexpectedly, but the causes of it were deep-rooted ones that in retrospect made it inevitable, considering the volatility of the people involved, the unique production environment within the BBC at that time and the problems caused by the show's overwhelming critical and commercial success – the very thing that had sustained it over the previous 18 months.

The show had been the BBC's hottest property in 1967; the only credible opposition they could mount to their old enemy *Coronation Street*. It had attracted audiences of over 16 million, a third of the British population; figures that had been equalled only by *Steptoe and Son* between 1962 and 1965. Its lead actor and writer had both won awards, and the American networks had started to express interest in making a version of their own. And no other comedy series had aroused as much interest and generated as many newspaper headlines as Speight's monster.

The time certainly seemed ripe for some new political satire in the closing months of 1967, considering the tumultuous events of the period. In November, in response to a monetary crisis, the Wilson government devalued the pound by 14.3%. The Prime Minister decided to explain this action (which was to lead to the resignation of the Chancellor, James Callaghan, at the end of the month) in a TV broadcast in which he told the people: 'It does not mean, of course, that the pound in your pocket or purse or in your bank has been devalued'. It was a statement so contemptuous of the public's intelligence, and so economical with the truth, that soon after, a late night satirical show, *The Eleventh Hour*, brutally extended the infamous joke about then US President Lyndon Johnson – 'You can tell when he's

152

lying because his lips move' – to 'darlin' 'Arold', resulting in legal proceedings in 1968. Then French premier Charles De Gaulle embarrassed the government by vetoing Britain's proposed entry into the Common Market. 1967 had also seen war between Israel and neighbouring Arab states, a ferocious outbreak of foot and mouth disease, the *Torrey Canyon* ecological disaster, a media outcry about hallucinogenic drugs, and more and more industrial strife …

What would Alf and Mike make of all this? *Till Death Us Do Part* had gained a reputation as a political and social satire, happy to take potshots at both sacred cows and contemporary figureheads. The current government seemed to be heading downhill, hapless in the face of the economic woes that were racking the nation. But those who keenly anticipated that the third series would offer an incisive demotic commentary on the national situation were to be sorely disappointed. Speight declared that if he were to write about such political events he would be repeating himself to little artistic reward; he had other, more general, developments in his sights.

In 1985, Speight was to assert that this drift away from political satire had been perfectly natural; Warren Mitchell had intriguingly suggested that he was not a 'political' writer, and he agreed: 'The Italians have a word for what Alf is, and it means the "mask of the people". You speak all their inhibitions and all their fears, all their false pride and false bravado, through one voice. But you can't be greedy. You can't impose topics wilfully. That would look like propaganda, and propaganda is what it would be. You just have to put him in a situation and see what happens.'

But the perception of Alf in the show was rather different. Here, perhaps, we can see the first signs of Speight experiencing artistic frustration with the realisation that his Frankenstein's monster had brought him constriction as well as freedom. He did not necessarily wish to write political satire simply because he was expected to; fame, he was now finding, brought with it a lot of baggage he did not desire.

The way *Till Death Us Do Part* developed over its first three series is an interesting testament to the peculiar combination of growing self-confidence and increasing paranoia that fuelled Speight at the time. The first series had shattered the boundaries of television comedy both in subject matter and in style – the merging of high-concept satire and low-brow belly-laughs, the recurrent violence, the abundant profanity in the Garnett household – and had been greeted by huge popular and critical acclaim. The second series had oozed with confidence – Speight doing away with any semblance of plot in certain episodes and daring to challenge the constraints of contemporary morality – and had been met with equal popularity but also a barrage of media opposition to its subject matter, language and scheduling. This opposition, coupled with huge changes at the BBC, had brought Speight to a pinnacle of sensitivity as he saw his artistic freedom coming under threat not just from outside, or even within, the media, but also from the expectations created by the very essence of his own creation. The third series saw the show being given a new, later time slot that should have rendered it less susceptible to controversy. But Speight was to push the envelope even further, changing the show's content and exaggerating its style to ridiculous lengths, until there was nowhere left to go …

BBC One previewed the forthcoming series with a nine-minute clip from 'Peace and Goodwill'. This excerpt – in which Alf, having railed against seasonal scroungers, attempts to pour a vase of water over some carol singers, only to be confronted by the vicar – was included in the 1967 edition of the traditional seasonal showcase *Christmas Night with the Stars*, in which various sketches based on BBC hits, including *Steptoe and Son* and *Beggar My Neighbour*, were introduced by a genial compère, in this case Rolf Harris. Speight was paid £500 for the repeat of the repeat of a part of a show exactly 12 months old – an indication of the faith the BBC still had in *Till Death Us Do Part* at that time. Indeed, the BBC promoted the start of the third series by giving the show its very first *Radio Times* cover, with a full colour photograph depicting an inebriated Alf wearing a fez and wishing good cheer to the readers, with a short preview inside that was ultimately to prove hopelessly out of synch with what transpired.

CUTTING THE CRAP

The script written by Speight as the opener to the intended eight episode series was entitled 'Monopoly' and pinned its protagonists in one easily-relatable situation, playing a board game on New Year's Eve and reminiscing about the events of the previous 12 months. This would serve to reintroduce the Garnetts to the audience, while their moves in the Monopoly game would act as a metaphor for the arguments they unleashed about Britain, the world and so on. To further enhance the realism, the episode would actually be recorded on New Year's Day, which meant that although it would be the first of the series to be transmitted, it would be the second to go before the cameras.

Problems arose from the start. On 24 November 1967, having read the script, Michael Mills, the new Head of Comedy, wrote to Dennis Main Wilson, who was not only producing but also directing this series, complaining that it was overlong and noting: 'If we could lose the word "crap" and also the last line but one on page 24, I myself would be grateful'. He also felt that 43 'bloodies' was a bit much. This was never going to go down well with Speight, for whom 'bloody' was a near-sacred word because of its use in Shaw's most famous play *Pygmalion*, where Eliza Doolittle uses it offhandedly and thus inadvertently commits a social *faux pas*. Speight's worship of Shaw meant that he would never relinquish the right to use the word in his scripts. The cuts were reluctantly actioned, the final tally of 'bloodies' being reduced to 20 (with one 'git', one 'bitch' and one 'bleeding' left intact), and other edits made to bring down the running time. Even then, further changes were called for, very late in rehearsals, when Warren Mitchell felt unhappy with some of the lines involving a dice throwing sequence. On Sunday 31 December 1967, a bleary and irritable Speight was summoned from his post-Saturday-night lie-in to the church hall where the final rehearsal sessions were taking place, in order for him to sanction the alterations. Resplendent in a camelhair coat resembling the garment that he had so admired on Eric Sykes, he finally agreed to his principal actor's suggestions, and the recording went ahead at 8.00 pm the next evening. Mitchell recounts: 'Alf began to get delusions of grandeur because he owned Mayfair. It was a very funny script, but Johnny had written it in a slapdash way – having me throwing the dice and then, two lines later, throwing the dice again – so I re-wrote the lines to make sense of the game. Johnny … used to enjoy a big night out on Saturdays, with the Fulham football team, at the Queen's Elm. We were rehearsing on the Sunday morning, and the run-through was seven minutes too long … [Speight was summoned by Wilson and] he arrived at the freezing cold Sulgrave Boys' Hall, Shepherds Bush, wearing his camelhair coat, smoking a Gauloise, and asked for a coffee. We started the run-through [again] and Johnny, who never whispered, said loudly, in his broad Cockney accent, "I never wrote that. What's he putting lines in for? You drag me out of bed on a Sunday to cut the show! Just take the lines out!" "I put the lines in, Johnny, because you didn't write the Monopoly game in properly!" "It don't matter, it's dramatic licence." "I don't believe that word, dramatic licence." Suddenly up piped Dennis, "Great! That's what I like! My wonderful star and my writer arguing! That's what makes the show so great – passion!"' Mitchell's lines were kept in.

The problem of over-writing was not unique to 'Monopoly', either. All of the first three scripts that Speight delivered for the new series were overlong, and a number of scenes involving Fred the barman (played by Will Stampe) had to be excised just before recording, meaning that although the actor was not used, he still had to be paid his usual 60-guinea-per-episode fee – a fact that cannot have failed to displease Michael Mills. Once again, the BBC was having to pay out fees to actors who were not being used, thanks to Speight's inability to structure his scripts properly or to deliver them in sufficiently good time for edits to be judged prior to the guest cast being contracted.

On viewing rough edits of both 'Monopoly' and 'The Phone', recorded the previous week, Mills was still less than happy with the former, and thought that the latter would prove a far more dynamic series opener in any case. He therefore decided to change the running order, and wrote to the

Head of Publicity warning him of the last-minute development: 'In particular, Mr Johnny Speight has been shouting the odds over the telephone to me and protesting against this alteration in the running order … [Speight] intends to protest to the BBC, and knowing his propensity for issuing stories to the newspapers making himself out to be martyred by the BBC, I imagine that it will be along such lines …'

Speight was understandably angry that the New Year theme of 'Monopoly' would be undercut by it being pushed further back in the schedule. (It would eventually be shown as third in the series.) Mills' assertion that there were few references to New Year and that the ethos would be unchanged is patently absurd considering that the plot involves the Garnetts being invited to their friend Mrs Moore's New Year's Eve party without Alf, that they all chorus 'Auld Lang Syne' at the end and that both Alf and Mike say 'Happy New Year' during the course of the episode. Furthermore, the change in running order made a nonsense of the pre-publicity for the series in the *Radio Times*, which indicated that the opening episode was set on New Year's Eve and presented the following preview by Dennis Main Wilson himself:

[Alf Garnett] returns to defend the nation once more against the inexorable tide of modern history … The pound has been devalued behind his back – De Gaulle won't have us in the Common Market – Liverpool are doing better in the First Division than West Ham – more defence cuts have left the last few red bits on the map even more defenceless – the Beatles have taken up transcendental meditation – and the Labour Party are still in power …

All these issues were to be discussed in 'Monopoly', which was not now going to be seen for another fortnight. It must be conceded that if only Speight had delivered his script in sufficient time to allow for proper consideration and adjustment before recording, all this rancour could possibly have been avoided. Mills believed that Speight's habitual tardiness was a quite deliberate ploy to enable him to sneak controversial material past the powers-that-be. Speight, on the other hand, maintained that he wanted the show to be as topical as possible and hence waited until the last possible minute before signing each script off for production. He may perhaps have been irritated that, for the first time, his script was being criticised not because of any potentially controversial content but simply because, in the eyes of Mills, it wasn't particularly funny. He was certainly angry that Mills was telling him to restrict the strong language.

Tony Booth tells an anecdote to illustrate the continual battle the series' makers faced over this issue. According to him, on the morning of camera rehearsals for one particular episode that opened with Mike telling Alf, 'You don't half talk a load of crap, you do!', and Alf responding characteristically, 'I talk a load of crap? You talk a load of crap!', Mary Whitehouse attacked the show in the press over its swearing, and particularly over its use of the word 'crap'. The word was judged too strong for an early evening timeslot, and Speight was asked to withdraw it. Then Wilson announced that the camera rehearsals would take place on a closed set and that all the BBC bigwigs, from Tom Sloan to Hugh Carleton Greene, would view them. Wilson went on to inform the cast that since the show faced cancellation over its language, the offending word would have to be replaced by 'nonsense', and the 'bloodies' and 'bleedings' by 'blimeys'. Mitchell 'went berserk' at this censorship and launched into a verbal attack on the producer, who eventually directed him that this was now the state of play and he had no option but to obey. Mitchell went back to his dressing room. Later, as Booth was standing near the set, Speight came up to him, also complaining about the censorship and the offence to his artistic integrity. The writer suggested that Booth and Mitchell should go completely counter to Wilson's instructions and supplant 'crap' with 'bollocks'. Booth, fearing disaster, demanded that this be written into the script, to which Speight reluctantly agreed.

When Greene arrived to watch the proceedings, Mitchell told Booth that Stubbs and Nichols were unaware of the coming storm. Thus the camera rehearsals began, and Booth declared 'You don't half talk a load of fucking bollocks, you do!' Mitchell replied in kind and then, to the absolute horror of Wilson, who almost collapsed in the control box, proceeded to ad-lib a four letter word into virtually every other line, inspiring Booth to equal villainy. In the midst of this hubbub, with the crew straining to view the Director-General's reaction, Nichols apparently shouted 'Bollocks to the pair of you!', to which Mitchell responded, 'You wash your fucking mouth out! I'm not having a wife of mine fucking talking to me like that!'. Mitchell then began another round of abuse, this time with Nichols in full flight as well. Finally, as Alf and Mike depart for the pub, Mike asks his wife for a quid, and Stubbs, who had so far remained aloof from the swearing, complied, crying: 'Stick it up your fucking arse!'

As the recording ended, the four waited in trepidation, sure that their BBC careers had ended, as Greene came across to speak to them. After a moment's silence, he beamed, 'Great! Don't change a fucking word!' The astonished cast applauded him as he left the studio. After that, says Booth, there was no objection to the word 'crap', and it stayed in.[23]

---

[23] Mitchell was later to say that Greene would sometimes telephone the production team to let them know that Mary Whitehouse was complaining about the show, and would then joyfully cry out that this would mean another half a million viewers.

While Stubbs has no recollection of these events, this sounds too richly detailed an anecdote to be entirely a figment of Booth's imagination. The opening lines to which he refers actually appear in the original script for the first series episode 'Two Toilets – That's Posh', the subject of discussion being Alf's assertion that Stalin was an American spy when he lived down the Mile End Road; but there would have been little reason in July 1966 for such a heavyweight executive intervention in a series that had only recently begun transmission; and on recording, the word 'crap' – which had not drawn criticism when used in the earlier episode 'A House With Love in It' – was in fact replaced by 'cobblers'. It seems likely that Booth is mixing up this earlier incident of censorship with Mills's later demands to reduce the strong language in 'Monopoly' and other third series episodes, at a time when the battle between Greene and Whitehouse was in full swing. Nevertheless, whatever the derivation of the story, the word 'crap' was cut from 'Monopoly' and the episode relegated to third place in the running order.

One amusing organisational cock-up resulted in inadvertent embarrassment for the BBC and necessitated a last minute salvage operation by the production team. Ten year old Caroline Nolte from Tunbridge Wells had asked her parents for tickets to the taping of a live television show as a New Year treat. She wanted to be in the audience for an edition of the children's series *Crackerjack*, but somehow her parents obtained four tickets to the New Year's Day recording of 'Monopoly' instead. Desperate to forestall headlines such as 'Angry of Tunbridge Wells', Warren Mitchell performed a damage limitation exercise by personally greeting the girl with a kiss, a gift, an apology and four tickets for the show of her dreams. Caroline admitted that she knew of the phrase 'Silly old moo' from her friends at school, and Mitchell gently calmed any worries from her parents by telling her, 'You are going to hear a lot of words you may not have heard before – but there is nothing very terrible about our show. I'm sure you've heard the word "bloody" at school before'. He went on to state that his own family and friends were also in the audience. The PR worked: Caroline and her parents emerged to comment that the show had been a 'marvellous treat'.

GETTING AT GARNETT?

If Speight was becoming increasingly paranoid, so were the BBC. Fully aware of the danger of controversy and that the show was under unprecedented scrutiny, they scheduled the new series in a later, post-8.00 pm[24] time slot on Friday nights, when young children were supposed to be

---

[24] The exact time varied from week to week.

in bed. The new choice of opener, 'The Phone', was previewed to the press on Thursday 4 January 1968; a rare event for a television programme in the '60s and symptomatic of the Corporation's considerable trepidation. The *Radio Times*'s printing of an incorrect synopsis due to the late change of running order had caused confusion, not least to the *Daily Mail*'s Peter Black, perhaps the show's most vociferous champion; under the banner 'Can This Be The Alf Garnett We All Know And Hate?' he wrote:

> Has somebody been getting at Alf Garnett? The script is very funny but not in the way that Alf has made so specially his own. What one misses is the social and political comment, perhaps because we have looked forward to it so much. I was struck over Christmas TV by the extent to which our political leaders have become pantomime butts. I don't remember any Prime Minister since the war being treated with such apparently sincere contempt as the comics hand Harold. What they could do would not Johnny Speight, Alf and Mike do tenfold? Well, not in this script they don't. Wilson only earns one reference, a quite inoffensive one ... [Lord Hill's] alleged concern for not offending politicians was a byword during his time at the ITA ...

Although Black found the episode very amusing nonetheless, it must have been particularly galling to Speight that he concluded his piece by stating that 'The Phone' was 'an ill-judged choice if, as I understand, other recordings were available'.

Peter Knight of the *Daily Telegraph* wrote that 'The Phone' would open 'this year's Mary Whitehouse baiting season', with its 'irreverence, raw vulgarity and earthy language'. He too noticed a lack of references to royalty, religion or Wilson, yet commented, 'It is in these ordinary, mundane situations that Johnny Speight ... often strikes his richest vein of comedy'. Scenes in which Mike asks his father-in-law to whistle down the phone to test it out and in which Else happily reads the directory were singled out in particular as 'moments that raised the level above almost any other comedy available on the box today'. Knight compared Stubbs and Booth to 'sadistic picadors teasing an outraged bull' and gave credit to Dandy Nichols as Else, although he somewhat missed the point in the process: 'It is her needling, perceptive common sense that sparks off much of the fun'. Else? Common sense? I'm sorry?

Audience research indicates that a mighty 38% of the viewing population viewed 'The Phone' on its debut transmission, and that most were pleased with it. A few echoed Black in feeling that it lacked bite in certain areas, such as race, religion and politics; one stated, '[It was] pretty mild stuff for the Garnetts and might as well have been written for Harry Worth, *Beggar Your Neighbour*, *Meet the Wife* or any one of a dozen similar shows'. Nevertheless many identified not only with the situation but also with the Garnetts themselves; either with Alf as an archetype for frustrated rage or with the working-class family as a whole. 'Funny and down to earth,' said one. 'I see a tiny bit of everyone in this. I love it'.

THE HEART THAT KNOWS NO COLOUR BAR

During December 1967 and January 1968, South African surgeon Dr Christiaan Barnard's pioneering achievement in carrying out the world's first heart transplants was the subject of immense controversy. Barnard himself was to encounter hostility from religious groups upon his arrival in London for a visit, and current affairs programmes on all three TV channels reflected the strong public concern, featuring discussions of the ethics involved in such a matter of life and death. This was all of supreme interest to Speight, still influenced by his Catholic upbringing and his Communist leanings. The morality of a doctor – and a white South African one at that – playing god seemed an irresistible subject for debate in *Till Death Us Do Part*. The writer's response was to incorporate it into his third script for the new series, in a plot deliberately reminiscent of that of the *Hancock* episode 'The Blood Donor', televised nearly a decade before and still commonly regarded at the end of the '60s as the epitome of brilliant television comedy. Speight wrote the script over the Christmas period, shortly after the death of the first heart transplant recipient, Louis Washkansky, on 21 December 1967 and around the time of the announcement of the second recipient, Philip Blaiberg, who would undergo the operation on 2 January 1968.

The episode is structured in three segments. The first of these is set in the Garnett's living room. Alf is seen holding up the *Daily Mirror* of 8 January 1968 – the date of the episode's recording – with the front page headline 'The Heart That Knows No Colour Bar', focusing on the fact that Blaiberg, a white man, has received a black man's heart. Mike dares his father-in-law to give blood, dismissing Alf's doubts about its morality. The conversation moves onto Barnard's work. Alf views the transplant in religious terms, whereas Mike and Rita hail it as a triumph of science over superstition. Referring to Washkansky's death, Alf declares it was inevitable that a normal Christian body would reject a Jewish heart. Blaiberg's predicament is, he says, even more appalling, and particularly so in South Africa with its strict apartheid – after all, which toilet should Blaiberg use? Else, blissfully off course as usual, muses that the placing of a woman's heart in a man's body might create a similar dilemma ... The second segment sees Mike, having talked his father-in-law into donating blood, accompanying him to the clinic. Alf sees a black man in the waiting room and, in his uniquely ignorant way, fears contamination from the latter's blood. He nevertheless goes ahead, and is initially surprised at the efficiency and painlessness of the exsanguinations. However, he promptly faints when the nurse shows him a pint of the actual fluid. Finally, the third segment has Alf as a self-pitying convalescent lying on the sofa at home. Here, he fantasises that he encounters Her Majesty at Buckingham Palace. As a token of respect to a wonderful lady who supports West Ham just like he does, our hero offers his own blood to her as an act of patriotism, seeking no reward except a life season ticket near the directors' box at the team's Upton Park stadium. Rudely awakened by the family's muted laughter, Alf is brought back to reality by a telephone call not from Her Majesty but from his despised sister-in-law, Maud; Else, meanwhile, comments that he had better not give any more blood, since it seems to have damaged his brain …

The timing of its transmission as the series' second episode on 12 January 1968, right at the height of public debate over Barnard's work, coupled with its inclusion of references to race, religion and royalty, guaranteed that 'The Blood Donor' would prove sensational; but even the BBC, who had anticipated the storm by allocating it half of the latest edition of the viewer reaction programme *Talkback* two days later, were taken aback by the backlash it provoked, which was to reverberate for weeks. Michael Mills, Dennis Main Wilson and Johnny Speight had however been engaged in yet more behind-the-scenes warfare, right up to the last minute. The day before the episode was broadcast, Mills was furious to discover that Wilson had failed to comply with his express instructions to excise certain things from the script. The first of these was a line where, when Alf compares God to the Queen, Mike says 'And just about as useless'. Mills had even threatened to edit this line out of the finished programme and introduce a jump cut if Wilson failed to remove it before recording. In the event, however, Wilson had simply changed the word 'useless' to 'useful', hoping that the slight shift of emphasis would avoid any trouble. The second, more substantial change that Mills had demanded was an increased emphasis on the fantasy nature of the encounter between Alf and the Queen; he had wanted Elgar-style music to be used over cloud-edged images. However, because of a lack of time, the best Wilson had been able to do was to include the sound of Alf's snores on the soundtrack and to give a slight fuzziness to the images in the initial introductory shots of Buckingham Palace.

Speight's script had, once again, been too long for the 30-minute slot and so, as before, Will Stampe's role as Fred the barman had to be excised and the actor paid off without appearing on screen. Also, a sequence where Alf witnesses the Queen – represented by a pair of female legs with some corgis on a leash – wandering in the grounds of Buckingham Palace, had to be deleted at the last minute. The frantic race to get the episode ready for transmission was further strained by the issuing of a directive on the day of transmission that if Blaiberg was to die during the day, then the programme should not be transmitted under any circumstances – in which event, 'Monopoly' should take its place, with an appropriate apology: 'The episode that you will see tonight is not that advertised in the *Radio Times*'. This necessitated not only edge-of-the-seat liaison with the News Department but also another hurried attempt to finish post-production on 'Monopoly'. As it transpired, Blaiberg survived for another 18 months with his new heart, but *Till Death Us Do Part* did not, and 'The Blood Donor' played a major role in its apparent demise. Its transmission was met by protests unmatched by any other provoked by a situation comedy show either before or since.

The least of the BBC's worries were the usual complaints regarding 'obscenities'. The Revd Eric Roberts wrote in on 13 January denouncing the show as 'depraved in mind' and 'lowdown comedy'. Huw Wheldon replied in its defence, with the ominous rider that he did not enjoy it nearly as much as he had previously. H G Leyshon of Monmouth was disgusted by the 'so-called comedy' and informed Wheldon that the Welsh didn't like that sort of thing …

More serious were the ethical, monarchist, racial and religious objections. The NVLA sent a wire to the Attorney General and a letter to Lord Hill, stating: 'Laughter is not an excuse for offending the deepest convictions held by the public on matters of Christian and Jewish beliefs, the Monarchy, racial attitudes and medical ethical issues'. They went on to point out the 'nationwide affront' of the 'insult to Her Majesty and the effect on racial problems' and declared that 'another meaningless apology' was not acceptable. Finally, they stressed that they found the programme 'a flagrant breach of the spirit of the BBC's charter'. Lorna Thompson of the NVLA also stated, 'It must have offended all Christians as well as all those who strive to end the racial problem'.

The *Daily Mail* revealed that the BBC had received some complaints regarding the treatment of 'coons' (which they obligingly translated as 'coloured people'). Ray Swire, a black actor and Equity shop steward went much further, threatening to call for an all-out BBC strike unless the Corporation apologised about the episode's racism and the offence it had caused by the jokes about heart transplants. The *Daily Telegraph* reported that BBC switchboard had been flooded with complaints regarding the remarks on Christian and Jewish hearts, while the *Sun* commented that the protests had centred on Alf's cheek in giving the Queen his telephone number (Stepney Green 1098) and offering his blood to Her Majesty. The Norfolk and Norwich Ypres Association also complained to the Prime Minister and the BBC about the tasteless affront to the Queen, stating that they were 'hurt deeply to hear the Crown and the Country debased'.

An overjoyed Speight responded that he may have 'offended the odd person, but I think the majority like the show as it is'. He believed that the ones who protested actually enjoyed being offended, and felt – with some justification – that the references to the Queen were not at all offensive.

A *Daily Mirror* editorial supported the writer and their star reader Alf:

> For be clear on this: what was being mocked on Friday night some three weeks after the death of heart-transplant patient Louis Washkansky, was not courage, pain, bereavement. It was the insensate bigotry of the Alf Garnetts of this world. That is the target on which writer and actor have their sights constantly fixed. It is not the world's coloured population, the Jews, the Tory party or Harold Wilson. It is the ignorance, the intolerance and the obstinacy which all too often distort human attitudes. And it is these shortcomings which the head of the Garnett household personifies on screen. To laugh *at* Alf Garnett is to recognise the stupidity of prejudice. It is a cleansing process that comedy can sometimes bring about. To laugh *with* Alf Garnett is to share his bigoted views. It is a monument to muddle-headedness, a reminder of deeply ingrained human folly.

The *Talkback* edition shown late on the Sunday evening two days after the broadcast did not feature any of the *Till Death Us Do Part* production team or cast, who were busy with rehearsals for the next episode, 'The Funeral', but fielded Tom Sloan to defend the show. It opened with a clip of the scene where Mike talks about Alf's 'bloody God', and proceeded to show further clips to illustrate the heart and blood debate. Then a panel of four members of the public who objected to the show were allowed their say. Florence McConnell, a mental health social worker, declared that she was 'sickened' by the references to surgery and despised the show as being 'in the worst possible taste, because it attempted to make comedy out of something that was a most sacred and serious subject'. Riad el-Droubie complained of racism, arguing that the show made fun of immigrants such as him and added to the 'colour problem'. At this point, Sloan came to the defence of Speight, assuring the audience, 'He has as much concern for the human race as anyone has. It is because he has this concern, this uneasiness – which I believe is shared by a great number of people – that he wished to make this protest about this type of surgery at this particular time.' He went on to state that Professor Barnard still hadn't proved conclusively that heart transplants were viable. As for the accusations of racism, he stated that no-one should accept any of the drivel emanating from Alf Garnett, who should be seen only as a figure of total ridicule and complete disrepute. Nancy Shrigley, a schoolteacher, said that the show was not funny because its themes of blood transfusions, heart transplants and religion were too tragic and too serious, offending many because of the emotions involved in such subjects. Comedy should not be allowed to touch such themes, she stated. Sloan replied that *Till Death Us Do Part* reflected real life, and that real life should be shown unadorned and unadulterated: 'I don't sit in my job to put out 16 times a week a sort of pink cloud marzipan view of life. Life is with us, and in comedy as in every other sort of output we do, it should be reflected.' He admitted though that *Till Death Us Do Part* was the one programme over which he was most heavily concerned, because it frequently teetered on the 'razor's edge' of what was acceptable on television.

Supporting Sloan's defence of the programme was Donald Holmes, a college tutor, who stated that he had actually telephoned the BBC to praise the show in a deliberate attempt to balance the protests. By subjecting such issues to laughter, he said, the show acted as a catalyst to purge the public's anxieties and afford some relief. He emphasised that comedy had always been a vehicle for people to discharge strong feelings, and cited *Lysistrata* and *The Frogs* by Aristophanes as examples. The treatment of serious subjects in a comic manner could only be therapeutic, he emphasised. Echoing Sloan, he declared that Alf Garnett was 'surely a figure of ridicule', which meant that his actions could not be taken seriously. Sloan went on to remind the audience that all the Garnetts were monsters: 'Alf Garnett is a coward, a braggart, an ignorant, prejudiced, despicable person; … Else is a living cabbage; the son is a worthless layabout with *Reader's Digest* knowledge; and the daughter is a doll child who has not developed since she was 14, except sexually.' He stated that *Steptoe and Son* had created the first breach with the old type of television sitcom, transforming a genre that had relied on presenting what were little more than music hall sketches with no basis in fact into a much deeper, more aesthetic creation imbued with a much greater degree of reality, and this had been subsequently been carried through into all types of social strata by such shows as *All Gas and Gaiters*, *Beggar My Neighbour* and *Not In Front of the Children*, as well as *Till Death Us Do Part*. The real success of a sitcom, he continued, could be judged by its roots in a genuine situation to which viewers could relate.

A doctor at the back of the audience interrupted at this point and was asked by presenter David Coleman to come down to the front. So doing, he stated that although he was very broadminded and appreciated that Alf Garnett [sic] was a very fine actor, as a physician he felt 'grossly insulted' by the reprehensible attacks on the medical profession (at this point shouts of 'rubbish, rubbish' could be heard from the audience), and that this made him sorry he had taken up medicine as a profession. Sloan replied that it was not his intention to ridicule any members of the medical profession. Holmes then added that Alf Garnett was 'childlike, irrational and a rather ill-informed being', but that he was not restricted to one social class – each and every one of us, he said, was afraid of our 'inner Alf' …

Each of the four panel members, making a closing comment, naturally disagreed, stressing that comedy should not deal with serious subjects; that such levity would provoke alarm and disgust in South Africa; and that the show was insulting to religion and reflected badly on the British people. But an on-screen poll of the studio audience seemed to back up the defence: only 3% found Alf's remarks on the Queen offensive; only 10% were affronted by the heart transplant debate; a mere 7% thought that the show increased colour prejudice; and 45% approved of the comedy dealing with a serious subject. Despite the overwhelming public support suggested by this poll, some of the questions were arguably rather leading (Alf's comments regarding the Queen were always in her favour, for instance, so it was hardly viable for them to be considered disgraceful), and overall the *Talkback* programme seemed only to fuel the controversy. The Head of Light Entertainment's comments were seen in many quarters as having been a weak and hypocritical whitewash of current BBC trendy thinking. One letter-writer stated that when Sloan had talked of the razor's edge, 'he would have been wiser if he had admitted that the razor had slipped more than once … He should mop up the gore and put away the razor before he does himself an injury.' Canon Norman Power, writing in to the BBC on 7 February 1968, was more penetrating, synthesising all the elements that made *Till Death Us Do Part* controversial:

> The reason we have been given for Alf's licence is this. He and his family are, we are told, so horrible, so prejudiced and so despicable that any opinion they express is expected and dispelled in derision. Fair enough. But please notice this; when accused of criticising the heart transplant, the Head of the BBC department responsible (i.e. Tom Sloan) actually stated that millions of people were disturbed at the heart transplant, believing the operation premature and that Alf was only giving voice to what many were saying. Exactly! But you can't have it both ways.
>
> Neither do I believe that in all homes viewers laugh *at* Alf rather than *with* him. Many viewers do not see Alf as a prejudiced horror, but as a jovial, lovable character who shares their views and puts them well. Many coloured people certainly see Alf as a sinister, frightening person, the mouthpiece of opinions they hear all too often. Public opinion has no chance against the more polished, more experienced and more professionally charming representatives of the BBC.

Canon Power went on to state that the poll had been full of loaded questions, and that the final hypocrisy had come when Sloan had said (incorrectly, as 'Intolerance' and 'In Sickness and in Health' had abundantly shown):

> We never ridicule the medical profession and we never have ridiculed the medical profession. So they have one sacred cow!

Humorous references to Christ, the Church, life after death and the Queen are in order, it seems, as long as nobody knocks a medical man ... When ... there is no chance of a reply, this is a form of censorship. There is no 'talkback'.

On the other hand, the *Talkback* programme had brought out some support. One viewer lambasted the continued failure by *Till Death Us Do Part*'s opponents to appreciate Speight's ironies and his demonstration of prejudice using Alf as a catalyst: 'Religion and royalty earn his comments. We must realise that this is 1968 and such questions are open to discussion ... This is a democratic country and people can say what they like within reason. No issue is sacred.' The same weekend, critic Barry Norman, in reviewing John Junkin's new ITV comedy *Sam and Janet*, being shown at the same time as *Till Death Us Do Part*, remarked: 'ITV thinks comedy is a soporific, the BBC thinks it should be a stimulant, and the BBC is right'.

Sloane once again defended the show to the press on 20 January 1968: '[It] tackles serious contemporary issues, but in a comedy vehicle. There is room on television for a comedy series with this type of approach – just one ... It is the one [show] that ITV producers envy most – but it is also the one show that would never be allowed on the commercial channel.' He went on to reiterate that it was the only show that he personally vetted, viewing scripts and the finished programmes prior to screening. 'Of course we make a few cuts. Last week we took out one line about the Queen, which I thought rather derogatory. But cuts are few. Surely no-one can take Alf Garnett seriously? Or agree with him? Alf's support for any cause is the kiss of death. He hasn't any other way of expressing himself. Naturally he distorts everything ... Speight is a primitive. He writes as he talks. He has something to say. And as long as he goes on having something to say, we'll go on with Alf Garnett.'

Less than a month later, Speight and the BBC would part company ...

SEX, MONEY AND THE GARNETTS

After all this, 'Monopoly' finally went on screen without incident on 19 January. But yet another crisis was brewing; on the day of its transmission, Booth announced his definite departure from the show. The remaining episodes of the third series would, he said, be his last. He cited his antipathy to Mitchell as one reason for his decision: 'We only speak when we have to. I can't wait to say goodbye. I find it too much of a strain working with someone I don't get on with.' In response, Mitchell himself put out a statement saying that he never discussed his working relationships with other actors: 'I do not think what happens at rehearsals is important to the public. We all have our different ways of working. All I wish to be judged on is the product people see in their homes.' Speight meanwhile publicly retorted that Booth's decision was his own, and maintained that the show could easily do without him; 'Warren is a 100% nice man. I do have my barnies with him – I do with all the cast. It's a hard show to do and we get our irritations. The people we can't do without are Warren and Dandy Nichols. Una Stubbs is also marvellous.'

Speight's blithe insouciance was merely a front however; Booth's persona was integral to the show, and both the writer and the BBC knew it. A confidential note from Speight to Sloan reveals that this time the programme-makers were taking Booth's threat very seriously indeed. Speight detailed the problems it posed. How could they explain Mike's departure from the Garnett family, for instance? Could he be said to have gone back to work at sea? If so, then Rita could not have any other lovers to act as foils for Alf's diatribes, because that would make her seem immoral. In any case, if there were to be a different boyfriend each episode, the show would have to undergo a radical rethink; it would mean dispensing the same joke each week, with the added burden of requiring at least five minutes' screen time to establish a new character. Speight admitted that Mitchell could not 'stand the sight of Tony Booth either as a man or as an actor', but noted that paradoxically the star found this antipathy invaluable in his craft, as it helped him to achieve the emotional heights required for their arguments: 'Mitchell feels strongly that he could not give the same performance with another actor because he hates Booth so much'. Furthermore, if Mike were to be recast – the only other option available – this would impact negatively on the 'reality' of the Garnett family. The whole atmosphere of the show depended upon the 'peculiar brand of horrible family togetherness', which would be disrupted by the introduction of a new actor. Booth, argued Speight, must be persuaded to stay for the fourth series scheduled for the autumn, if only by 'blackmailing' him by pointing that whoever did the series would also appear in the planned spin-off movie, already being set up for consideration during the summer.

Booth, whose departure notice was given extra bite by his involvement in a car crash immediately afterwards, was candid about his wishes. All of Fleet Street were after him, he said, but all they ever wanted to talk about was 'sex, money and the Garnetts': 'I talk to journalists about everything – war, Vietnam, God, religion – but all that ever appears is a bit about my relationship with Alf Garnett … If as an artist you are playing a part and you are good at it, you become that person, that part.' To escape from this trap, he said, he wanted to play Shakespeare or Chekhov. In the event, his next role was to be in Kenneth Tynan's nude revue *Oh Calcutta* …

In the meantime, it was business as usual with the third series: the transmitted episodes continued to top the ratings charts, and Speight continued to be late with the delivery of his scripts. 'The Funeral', episode four, featured the second appearance of Gran, played by Joan Sims. Bernard

Cribbins had originally been asked to take the role of Mr Williams the grocer, but had declined, so Bill Fraser had been cast instead. The episode was praised by Anthony Burgess in *The Listener*: 'In drama and comedy, any writer must compete with scripts as good as Johnny Speight's look at a dockland funeral in *Till Death Us Do Part*'.

Trouble with the NVLA flared again over the fifth episode, imaginatively dubbed 'Football' – a working title that the production team just did not have time to change – and transmitted on 2 February 1968. The action starts with Alf already at boiling point regarding the pranks of two boys from whom he has confiscated a football. The old misery trips over a hidden tripwire at his front door, then minutes later is assailed with cries of 'Baldy!' over the telephone. He is beside himself with rage, railing at a welfare state that grants family allowance to unprincipled mothers who in turn have children only to sponge off the state … The episode was superbly scripted, and featured guest appearances by real-life stars such as footballer Bobby Moore in a non-speaking, obscenely-gesturing part, and West Ham chairman Reg Pratt, replete with genuine World Cup paraphernalia. It gave Speight the opportunity to extract the maximum amount of bile from his creation and simultaneously to mine the maximum amount of pathos, stretching the dramatic tricks he had incorporated into the show to the limit. The recent attempts by the BBC to restrict his profanities merely inspired him to add more. Michael Mills had not only cut the 'crap' from 'Monopoly', he had also suggested that Speight limit his 'bloodies'. Speight was later to claim that he had in fact been given a quota of 25 'bloodies' per episode, indicating the pettiness of the censorship. Mills, for his part, was to acknowledge that there had indeed been such a quota, but to maintain that it had been valid, if only for artistic reasons: 'Of course, Johnny Speight's ration of 20 "bloodies" a script[25] was absurd, but what we were doing at the time was rescuing him from himself, because the word "bloody" just went on and on and became rather boring.'

Some critics had already voiced the same opinion. In 1997, Wilson stated that it was Sloan who had told him to instruct Speight that he should limit himself to six 'bloodies' an episode, but that the writer had then retaliated by including 'about 90' instead. At least 'Football' presented a bloody good reason for Alf to utter so many of them – he was bloody angry.[26]

---

[25] The actual number varies with each telling.

[26] Later, Speight was to complain about the horse trading he had had to engage in with the BBC over the profanities he was allowed for each script. He recalled that at one point he offered to trade four bloodies for two 'tits' – originally, it had only been one 'tit', but he had regarded that as a deformity … Here, he seems to have been telescoping his own experience with the Peter Cook and Dudley Moore spoof on his situation transmitted in 1970 (see later).

This surfeit of swearing was bound to attract complaints, and Mrs Whitehouse duly obliged. A friend of hers, who was a schoolteacher's wife, brought the matter to her attention that very evening. She had lost the picture on the television set when tuning in, but the sound of Alf's swearing had come out loud and clear, and she had stopped counting after 44 'bloodies'. She had already conceived of a jokey letter to Lord Hill about the show, and Whitehouse convinced her to send it immediately, together with a serious covering missive. It read as follows:

Dear Lord Hill,

Will you please spare a few bloody minutes to read these two bloody letters?

Last Friday, my bloody husband and I counted the bloody number of times the bloody word 'bloody' was used in bloody *Till Death Us Do Part*. You may be bloody well surprised to know the bloody number – 44 times – 16 in the first few bloody minutes. As a bloody result of this I found myself bloody well obsessed by the bloody word and bloody well tossed and turned the whole bloody night long.

I thought 'If it can have this bloody effect on me, what must it bloody well do to bloody children and young people'. Surely it is a bloody form of bloody brainwashing and must be bloody well stopped.

I feel I should be bloody well failing in my bloody duty as a Christian if I didn't raise my bloody voice, small though it bloody well be, and ask you as a bloody man in authority to raise your bloody voice and protest against such bloody programmes.

I may say I do not bloody well watch this bloody awful programme, nor many others like it, which I consider a bloody disgrace to the bloody BBC and a bloody waste of time, but I have bloody well seen the last bloody three and I thought the first bloody one [sic] referring to the bloody heart transplant, Jews, coloured blood donors, Lord Snowdon – referred to as a mongrel – was to say the bloody least of it, bloody well nauseating, degrading and a bloody disgrace to anyone or anything bearing the bloody name British.

I hope this will weigh as heavily on your bloody mind as it has bloody well weighed on mine and that you will do all you bloody well can to end such bloody programmes.

The reply from Lord Hill on 6 February wryly admitted that the correspondent had made her point effectively, but pointed out that Garnett suffered from 'his passionate desire to get his ideas across to his family, despite the handicap of a somewhat limited vocabulary. In his frustration, he was constantly driven to resort to bad language and in particular to one favourite swear word. This, as you will know, is not untypical of a certain type of basically inarticulate person and it added, we believe, a dimension to the character which a more socially acceptable form of speech would not have provided. We know that the bad language offended many viewers, but we believe that it may also have done something to show up the essential futility of the swearing habit.'

If only Speight had been aware of this measured reply from his perceived nemesis, it might have allayed his fears, but by this time things had gone too far. Mrs Whitehouse's friend had actually, perhaps understandably, miscounted – there were only 40 'bloodies' in all in 'Football', plus one 'swine' – but her point was clearly well made. On a lighter note, the 14 February edition of the viewer comment programme *Points of View*, headed by the inimitable Robert Robinson, blotted out the 'bloodies' in one clip, to show how Alf would sound if censored. Booth meanwhile, in an interview in *Reveille*, defended the show's language, recalling a time when a station porter had stopped him to complain about the 'bloodies'. 'It's blooming disgusting,' the porter had said. 'I've never heard such blooming language in all my blooming life.' Only, Booth noted, he hadn't used 'blooming' …

So far, the BBC had defended its star writer through thick and thin, despite Speight's surging paranoia. However, a perennial problem in their working relationship with him resurfaced on 30 January, when it became evident to the increasingly harassed Sloan and Mills that he had once again failed to fulfil his contractual quota of scripts. The session set for recording on 5 February had to be scrapped, Sloan revealing, in a letter to the Head of Copyright, 'As we feared, the worst has happened and Johnny Speight has dried up …' Speight had been contracted to write eight scripts for the third series but had delivered only seven. Sloan was adamant that because he had consistently failed to meet script deadlines, he should not be paid for the nonexistent script; however, they should not contact his agent Beryl Vertue about this, because of the 'rather tricky atmosphere' between the writer and the Corporation at the time. Better, he thought, to let the dust settle first. Unfortunately, this was not going to happen.

GOD IN A GLASS

12 February 1968 was established as the final recording date of the third series, and for this storyline Speight had conceived of the idea of an old lover of Else who, having spent 36 years abroad, would now reappear at the Garnett household to open up old wounds. He would be gentle, cultivated, dignified and well-travelled, the exact antithesis of her current spouse, and Else, not for the first time, would wonder if she had married the wrong man all those loveless years ago. Unfortunately, fate stepped in and Dandy

Nichols fell ill with bronchitis early in February, thus necessitating a frantic rethink, as she could now appear only briefly in the episode. As usual, a crisis brought out the best in Speight, and he simply decided to incorporate the star's misfortune in the narrative, reasoning that since Else was ill, her sister Maud from Southend would have to stay and look after her; an arrival that would act as a red rag to the bullish Alf. Nichols was sufficiently recovered to appear, bedridden, in four short scenes, and the others rehearsed for the final episode, now dubbed 'Aunt Maud', from 8 February. And here, things came to a head.

The script, as usual, was late. It arrived on Michael Mills' desk the day rehearsals began, and he immediately had concerns about it. Mindful of the fact that this was to be the last episode for some time, although a fourth series was mooted for the autumn of the same year, Mills read the riot act to Speight and Wilson. They came to his office for a meeting, and Mills recorded the outcome in a note dated 9 February, despatching copies to both the Head of Copyright and the BBC's Legal Adviser:

> The script (as is very usual) was late in delivery and reached my desk only on Thursday, 8 February. I perused it and became worried chiefly about the religious references ... [The BBC Legal Adviser and Mills] marked the passages on pages 16, 24, 25 and 27 which should be reduced or amended as shown on the enclosed scripts ... [Head of Legal Affairs, Television] and I objected to the reference on page 8 and requested that the theme of the wife being a virgin prior to marriage, which dominates the last scene, should be toned down very considerably. In addition, [Head Of Religious Programming, Television] suggested an additional line on page 24, in connection with speech 4, suggesting that it was the religious people Mike is referring to as snobs rather than God Himself. These requests were communicated to the producer, who came to the office with the writer, Johnny Speight, the message being that Mr Speight could not tolerate any of these excisions and that, if they were insisted upon, the script would be 'withdrawn'.
>
> This meeting took place in the fortuitous presence of Mr Marshall of the Legal Department, who happened to be in the area. Some considerable discussion took place and it was finally agreed that the reference on page 8 should stay in, that the Bible extract on Page 16 should be largely reduced, that the reference to God being in the house and the catching of God in the glass on page 25 should be suppressed and that the reference to God being worse than Hitler on page 27 should be removed. I was particularly insistent on the items on pages 25 and 27. This was agreed to.
>
> During the course of the discussion, the question of the

withdrawal of the script by Speight was discussed in detail, and the nature of 'structure' and minor alterations, as laid down in the agreement was explained to him. He was of the opinion that the excision of the God in the glass passage on page 25 would, in fact, be structural. However, the suggestion that this and the reference on page 27 might well lead to the BBC's being sued for blasphemy had some effect, and the happy result noted above was reached.

This is not to say that there will not be considerable turmoil as the result of the transmission of the script. The items referred to above are merely the peaks of possible offence. Speight has been left considerable latitude in the remainder of the script, as you will see from a quick glance. My own personal view is that this particular clause cannot be altered too soon. It does put any BBC producer or executive in an impossible position, namely that the smallest censorship can be construed by the writer as structural and the producer or executive has the unenviable choice of enforcing what he believes to be right, while facing the possible blackmail of having the script withdrawn from use on the spot. This is a particularly dangerous situation with writers like Johnny Speight, who deliver their material so late that the Corporation is already committed to considerable expense at the very moment when the production executive is making his decision.

All those involved in the meeting were no doubt aware of a highly publicised court case the previous year. This had arisen when (as mentioned in Chapter Ten) playwright Terence Frisby, of *There's a Girl in My Soup* fame, had sought a High Court injunction against the BBC to prevent them from screening the *Theatre 625* production of his piece 'And Some Have Greatness Thrust Upon Them ...' He had written the 90-minute play in 1965, originally entitling it 'The Trouble With Mary', for a fee of £825. Ted Willis, the incumbent Head of Plays, had approved the script, which was a satire on the mass media's exploitation of a mum-to-be whom they initially fail to realise is unmarried, but his incoming successor, Gerald Savory, had objected to one line and insisted that it be excised. In the scene in question, a television interview with the mother is disrupted when the girl says that she innocently became pregnant because: 'My friend Sylv told me it was safe standing up.' Frisby had objected to Savory's intention to cut this line, asserting that it must be included verbatim or else the play could not be screened at all. The upshot had been that when the play came to be recorded in August 1966, for a budget of £9,000, two versions of that scene were taped, one with and one without the line. In the ensuing legal action, which attracted much press attention, the judge was reportedly very impressed by Frisby's reference to Shaw's *Pygmalion* as an example of a famous work in which the loss of a single line could alter the entire structure. The argument that no such alteration should be made without the artist's permission was persuasive. Frisby felt that Savory's change would alter the climax of his play, and according to the Writers' Guild, the BBC as licensees were not entitled to go against his wishes; Clause 10 of the Guild's standard agreement specified that the licensing body 'shall not without the prior consent of the [playwright] or his agent (which consent shall not be unreasonably withheld) make any structural alterations as opposed to minor alterations to the transmission script.' Frisby maintained that since the script had been accepted and alterations made, but not to that line, 12 months earlier, the BBC had no right to force a cut through at the last minute. Savory's response was that he had not read the script until July 1966 and that he had two reasons for wanting to excise the disputed words: first, that the phrase would shock the viewer out of involvement in the story that he or she was enjoying; secondly, that the explicitly risqué line, while acceptable in a theatre, would offend a majority of the television audience. The judge ultimately decided in Frisby's favour, and the play was never screened.

The court references to his hero George Bernard Shaw would no doubt have caught Speight's attention and alerted him to the shivers the case had caused within the halls of the BBC; and if not, Warren Mitchell, who had appeared in another *Theatre 625* play in September 1967, might well have brought it to his notice. The BBC's trepidation over this issue had been reflected in the call out to Speight asking him to agree changes to the structure of 'Monopoly'. That time, he had approved the changes; but now, this was war!

The original script for 'Aunt Maud' has Alf reciting Old Testament references to 'Adam's rib'[27] – one of the things that Mills wanted cut. This leads to a vociferous argument between Alf and Mike about Darwin's theory of evolution. Alf's mention of heaven is greeted with disdain by Mike and Rita, the latter of whom suggests that heaven to her father is 'like Wapping, only better … with more pubs and cheaper beer'. In the next section – also objected to by Mills – Alf states that he hopes that God can hear Mike's blasphemies, to which Rita replies that He would not be in Wapping anyway, implying that God is not for the hoi polloi. Mills suggested here a one-line addition, 'Judging by the people who say they're close to God', intended to indicate that it is God's followers, or at least some of the Church hierarchy, who are being branded snobs rather than God *per se*. Mike postulates that God would be up in Chelsea or Kensington with His own class; after all, He is '*Lord* God', not a 'Harry God' or a 'Fred'. When Rita laughs at this, her father, provoked beyond measure, warns that God is

---

[27] In the Biblical story of Adam and Eve – the two humans first created by God – Eve is said to have been formed from one of Adam's ribs.

everywhere, and this leads on to the passage that Mills wanted removed completely.

Despite their differences, Anthony Booth was still frequently discussing ideas for scripts with Speight over late-night drinks at the writer's home, deciding on which sacred cow to slaughter next. Booth thought that blasphemy was the only taboo they had left to challenge, and he had told Speight an anecdote regarding Aldous Huxley. Irritated by his deeply religious father, who had insisted God was everywhere, Huxley had asked him if God was in the room with them. When his father had replied that He was, Huxley had picked up a glass, turned it over on a table and cried 'Got Him!'. Booth had mentioned that when Huxley had written about this incident, he had been condemned as blasphemous by the Catholic press. An excited Speight had immediately seized on the story and adapted it for inclusion in 'Aunt Maud'. It was this exchange that Mills knew was dynamite:

> Mike: You reckon He's in Wapping then, do you?
> Alf: Yes
> Mike: Is He down this street?
> Alf: Yes.
> Mike: Is He in this house, you reckon?
> Alf: Yes.
> Mike: In this room? (He finishes his drink)
> Alf: Yes.
> Mike: (Upturning his empty glass and slamming it down on the table) *Got Him!*

Later, Mike ridicules Alf's defence of God: 'The whole bloody thing is rubbish. 'Cos there ain't no God … You and your bloody God … that fire-and-brimstone monster. *You* created Him … He didn't create you … I mean, if He was true, He sounds a right charmer, doesn't He? I mean, you don't agree with Him …, you don't do things His way, and he bungs you in the fire … burns you. Blimey, he sounds worse than bloody Hitler!'

Mills and Sloan both maintained that the BBC would be liable to a blasphemy suit if these exchanges were to be broadcast. They also had concerns about non-theological aspects of the script, such as a line on page 8 where Alf venomously says of Maud as a schoolgirl, 'She'd show you her knickers for a bit of your toffee-apple in them days'.

Mills, Sloan, Speight and Wilson entered into intense negotiations over the script, with Speight conceding some points and refusing to budge on others. The reference to Maud and the toffee-apple stayed, but the God-in-a-glass exchange went. While the 'bloody God' passage survived virtually intact, the mention of Hitler was excised. References to the loss of Else's virginity were toned down in another passage where Alf demands to know if she had slept with George Pringle prior to their marriage, as Maud has spitefully suggested:

> Alf: I was a virgin on marriage …
> Else: I was too!
> Alf: If so, you were the only virgin in the bloody family!

The episode was recorded as planned on 12 February 1968 and broadcast the following Friday. Mills later recalled the compromises that had been made over the script: 'So Johnny came in and we had a little barney and argued the toss. I yielded on a couple of things and insisted on a couple of others, and eventually Johnny accepted it and everyone was happy. Then he goes round the corner and screams blue murder about being savagely censored! One of the television critics said, "Having seen the show and what was said, in God's name what did they cut out?"'

It is arguable that, even with the cuts, 'Aunt Maud' stands as the nastiest and most vicious sitcom episode of the '60s, featuring Alf in particularly obnoxious form – Mitchell's most spectacular piece of comic business having him furiously spit a chunk of fish over Rita and Mike at the dinner table – and the bedridden Else at one point giving the most evil grin imaginable, quite apart from Speight's dialogue at its saltiest and most venomous.

Booth has asserted that the God-in-a-glass scene was actually recorded, despite the objections of a deeply Catholic shop steward technician who asked, 'What would happen if God appeared and struck you dead?', to which Booth apparently replied, 'We'd make television history, with God making his first ever live appearance to deliver divine retribution against me'. However, Speight told the *Daily Telegraph* at the time that although some of the cut material had been reinstated after he and the cast head protested, this had not included the God-in-a-glass sequence, and it seems likely that Booth's recollection is actually of an incident from the making of the first *Till Death Us Do Part* movie a few months later, in which Speight pointedly included that very sequence.

The deals between the BBC and Speight over references to toffee-apples and virginity and the number of 'bloodies' per episode became the stuff of television legend (although the quota still wasn't working: 'Aunt Maud' had 33 'bloodies', one 'bleeding' and one 'bitch') and were expertly spoofed two years later in February 1970 in an edition of the hit Peter Cook and Dudley Moore comedy vehicle *Not Only … But Also*. Cook played Mills, while Moore played Speight, complete with a stutter that allowed for plenty of humour over swearing. Cook, as Mills, states: 'We've all got a bum, Johnny. I would not pretend that bums don't exist. But what I do ask you, Johnny, and I ask you this very seriously, is: does an ordinary English family sitting at home early in the evening want to have a barrage of 31 bums thrown in their faces in the privacy of their own living room? I think not. I don't think we're ready yet to break through the bum barrier'. Moore, stuttering to predictably lewd effect, asks for the use of one 'tit', to which Cook suggests euphemistic alternatives such as 'Bristols', 'St Moritz' or 'fainting fits'. An appalled Moore responds: 'This script is more than just a comedy, it's a social document.' Eventually, Cook agrees to 27 'bloodies', seven 'bums' and the crucial 'tit' – and Moore reveals that the script is actually for *The Sooty Show* ...

14
Falling on the Sword

QUALIS ARTIFEX PEREO!

Having apparently believed that their agreement over the script for 'Aunt Maud' had been an amicable one, Michael Mills seemed surprised and betrayed when, just prior to the episode's transmission on Friday 16 February 1968, the always-publicity-hungry Johnny Speight told the press of his anger over the 'savage censorship' he had been subjected to by the BBC. 'Someone is getting hold of my script and wrecking it so much that I don't want to know about TV anymore,' he complained, adding that he was fed up with 'trying to battle the script through … savage cuts and inserted passages at the request of the Religious Department [which] made Alf Garnett sound like the *Epilogue*'. Speight claimed that originally a third of the script for 'Aunt Maud' had been thrown out, but that a protest backed by a threatened cast walkout had ensured that most of it was reinstated. He told the *Daily Telegraph* that he blamed Lord Hill for this censorship resulting in 'idiotic and unreasonable' cuts and a limit on the number of 'bloodies' he could use. He stated that he was willing to continue with *Till Death Us Do Part* for as long as the public wanted Alf Garnett, but swore that he would never write for the BBC again 'as long as I am unreasonably censored'. Having dropped this bombshell, he flew to Torremolinos for a ten day working holiday devoted to writing the script for the planned movie, now set to be made by the British Lion film company.

It was arguably not only grossly unfair but also highly unprofessional for Speight to have aired his grievances in the press in this way, and this time an angry BBC were not about to allow him to get away with it. Tom Sloan, who had so eloquently defended *Till Death Us Do Part* on *Talkback* just over a month before, made a statement of his own, and one that gave vent to all the bitterness he felt regarding Speight's abuse of the leeway the BBC had granted him over the past two years: 'Having devoted a lot of my time in defending Johnny Speight, I have to say that if he is now talking in terms of savage censorship on the part of the BBC, this is absolute rubbish. If cuts were made to his scripts – and they were occasionally – they were made because, in my opinion, he went beyond the very broad tolerance given to a writer of his talents. The last *Till Death Us Do Part* goes out tomorrow. I did not intend to ask Speight to write any more *Till Death Us Do Part* scripts, because I had already come to the conclusion that this series was exhausted.'

The truthfulness of this statement is open to question, given that there had in fact been plans under discussion for a fourth series later that year. It seems clear though that, having constantly supported the problematic show against vociferous protests in the media only to have been stabbed in the back by the writer himself, the BBC's patience had finally run out..

Speight too felt betrayed, but he blamed the general changes the BBC had undergone over the past nine months since the death of Normanbrook. Under the aegis of Frank Muir, he said, there had been few problems, but once Muir had departed for LWT, the censorship had started. And he saw Lord Hill as the man responsible.

Internal forces had brought about the show's downfall, but external forces were about to subject it to another onslaught, which was ultimately to give Mary Whitehouse the mistaken impression that Alf's demise was her personal triumph. The doughty campaigner was already consulting the Department of Public Prosecutions (DPP) over the viability of taking criminal proceedings against the BBC, alleging that the description of the Bible as 'bloody rubbish' in 'Aunt Maud' was blasphemous. 'As a Christian', she said on 17 February 1968, 'I am not prepared to stand by and see God treated this way'. Staff at the DPP were meeting to discuss this three days later, and one Birmingham solicitor declared, '[Whitehouse] may well have a case for taking proceedings. It is open to any individual to apply to a judge in chambers for permission to prosecute'. Information regarding the alleged offence would have to be submitted within four days and proceedings taken within three months. Possible penalties for blasphemy were a fine and imprisonment, but the last time a conviction had been secured was a hundred years ago … Ultimately the idea of legal action came to nothing, but Whitehouse had another weapon up her sleeve. Hugh Carleton Greene was currently in Sydney promoting the sale of BBC programmes in Australasia, and she cabled the Archbishop of Sydney, asking him to disassociate his church from the blasphemy in the episode. She felt pleased that, when Greene returned, the show would be off the air in Britain at least. There were genuine public complaints to the BBC to back her up. One Birmingham 'believer' said that the show had been funny until 'the things were said about religion that should not have been allowed on the air'. Another stated, 'If God isn't sacred, then nothing is'.

The intelligentsia had a different view as to the cause of *Till Death Us Do Part*'s downfall. Never had one programme attracted so many front page columns and editorials in the press. The *Daily Telegraph* reflected the thoughts of many when it stated that the show's demise had finally brought to an end the wave of political satire on TV spearheaded by *TW3* and *Not So Much a Programme, More a Way Of Life*. Anthony Burgess, writing in *The Listener*, said that he believed the show had been terminated because it had finally reached its aesthetic limits, having transcended the acceptable frontiers of permissiveness: 'A more serious medium (... not a more solemn one) such as a genuine play or novel to fill in the narrative links between, say, Alf's obscenity and his religious fundamentalism was required, expansion which a television comedy could not sustain ... [*Till Death Us Do Part*] like [*Steptoe and Son*] had exploited a static family relationship in a set and narrow period of history ... [Both series] ... did a great service by extending the range of demotic speech available for television comic writers, but now the work had been done.'

In the same issue of *The Listener*, Karl Miller praised the show while simultaneously pointing out its shortcomings. It had given 'unprecedented pleasure, unprecedented offence', he said, as the BBC's 'crown jewel', with its 'magnificent comic realism' and fine acting; Alf's weaknesses had however been 'unduly burlesqued' and Speight had been 'too eager to punish him'. He accused the censors of being the 'real subversives, for the restrictions they propose could hardly fail to injure and diminish the Corporation'. It was indicative of the virtues of British television to undertake such a difficult programme, he concluded, yet 'these virtues are less evident in the manner of its departure'.

Perhaps strangest of all, the show earned itself an editorial in *The Times*, which praised the realism of the sour marriage between Alf and Else and of Alf's willing toadying to any authority and unbending patriotism disguising a dread of the unknown:

Johnny Speight's scripts revealed a shocking lot of people in a household where politics is a matter of mindless catch-phrases and argument means crushing by insult. Mrs Garnett emerged from stupor only to exult over her husband's misfortunes. Their comparatively inoffensive daughter existed only in a sort of mindless sexuality. Mike, her irresponsible but progressive mate, is as appalling a subject for consideration as Alf himself, and if the series had gone on much longer, Alf's racial prejudices, his coarseness, his cowardice and his combination of bullying arrogance with toadying servility would have attracted, it seems, as much critical comment and exegesis as *Hamlet*. Of course, it was all beautifully acted; who would have missed the sight of Dandy Nichols awakening from torpor to malicious derision, or the exquisite timing of her more obtuse remarks? And the greatest compliment to Warren Mitchell is to note that he has become a real nightmare, though not very long ago he was a sympathetic, sensitive actor. *Till Death Us Do Part* is a justifiably angry outcry against the poverty of mind and spirit in which vast numbers of people spend their lives. Yet so ambivalent is the irony and our response to irony that Alf Garnett's preposterous prejudices seemed also at times a welcome relief from the relentless drip of liberalism from the BBC.

The *Daily Express* described Lord Hill as 'a less indulgent Big Brother' and mourned that for the 'sake of a few censored words, Alf should have been forced to commit suicide'.

Milton Schuman, TV critic of the *Evening Standard*, referred to a poll conducted by the newspaper over the weekend, which yielded the following results from a sample of 100 people of different ages, class, sex and earning power: 80% said it was right for TV to upset and occasionally offend the nation; 95% thought that Alf Garnett did not stimulate racial prejudice; 97% thought that the references to the Queen were inoffensive; and 92% thought that there was no need for an independent viewers' council as urged by Mrs Whitehouse and the NVLA. The general consensus was that if a politician like Hill was seen to be in charge, there would always be suspicion of political censorship. More prescient than most, Warren Mitchell warned Schuman: 'But don't make your piece sound too much like an obituary notice. I've got a feeling that you haven't seen the last of Alf and the ghastly Garnetts. They don't die easily.'

Interviewed in 1997, Muir was dismissive of the idea that Hill was ultimately responsible for the show's demise, commenting that the Chairman, whether Normanbrook or Hill, was always a distant figure and rarely had any censorship veto over particular productions. Hill doesn't mention the issue in his memoirs, and neither does Tony Booth, despite being ever ready to cite politics as a spur. The entire sorry state of affairs seems to have resulted from Speight overreacting to the scare stories of the previous six months, including that cartoon caricaturing Hill and Greene as Alf and Else and the boardroom rumours that had permeated downward from the first shock of Greene's equally overheated reaction to Hill's appointment, coupled with the general '60s suspicion that politics was behind every contentious decision. The script and scheduling changes, the constant pressure on Speight to meet deadlines, the controversy surrounding 'The Blood Donor', the continual opposition of the NVLA and Mrs Whitehouse, the arrival of a new Head of Comedy and the general melee of the show's production had all no doubt contributed to the writer ultimately falling on his own sword. While the rift could perhaps have been healed had Sloan been prepared to be conciliatory, his contrary reaction seems quite understandable in the circumstances.

When Greene, still absent in Australia, was informed of the dispute, he commented, rather pompously, 'We are much less stuffy in our attitudes to all kinds of things …' Echoing the words of the late Richard Boyer, former head of the ABC, he added, 'We do not regard our function as achieved if we merely keep out of trouble. If our broadcasting is creative as well as being responsible, it is because the system of control is based on trust and confidence.' By the end of Greene's tour down under, 13 episodes of *Till Death Us Do Part* had been sold to New Zealand; all of them would be censored, and nearly all rated 'A' certificate, i.e. not to be broadcast until after 9 pm.

The only person who seemed to be celebrating the downfall of *Till Death Us Do Part* was Mrs Whitehouse, who believed that Hill had stepped in and applied pressure in her favour and sensed that she was finally winning her war with Greene. A month after the transmission of 'Aunt Maud', she sent an open letter to the Director-General on his return from the Antipodes:

> It has been a hard fight, with, apparently, all the odds on one side. You were in a position to tell the world that you were 'glad to offend' those who took exception to certain episodes of *Till Death Us Do Part* and you were able to use every technique and platform to ridicule those who would not pipe to your tune. The cheap satirists basked in the security of your approval. Only you can know how many of the 'conservatives' within the BBC have been eliminated or persuaded to change their approach, how many creative men and women have been denied the opportunity of broadcasting because they wished to present ideas about life which did not fit in with the atheist drift – or shall I say compulsion? – so apparent in the 'growing points' of television. And I must admit that I am astounded at your comment (Canberra, 17.2.68) that the communists within the BBC are 'none of my business', for they will certainly make the BBC their business.
>
> But we have weathered the storm too, and now the mood of the country is changing. The laughter is ringing hollow as we realise the cost to our children of the mass-produced giggle. As we hear the chorus of 'bloodies' from the infant playground we wonder at our credulity – wonder that we should ever have been taken in by the idea that it needed endless expensive university research to prove that children (and the rest of us) copy what they see and hear. I often ask myself, Sir Hugh, whether you would rank the establishment of the word 'bloody' as common parlance in the English language your greatest single achievement during your period as Director-General … Your professionalism is unquestioned. Your vision is. We know that you honestly feel you are leading – or rather dragging – a reluctant, even unintelligent, public into new, more enlightened ways. Your recent advice to Australian Broadcasters 'not to tag along with public opinion' underlines your own contempt of those who will not tread the Greene line.

Weary of his struggles with Hill, Greene would hand in his resignation on 16 July 1968.

Dennis Main Wilson was quoted on 17 February as saying that if he had to do another series of *Till Death Us Do Part*, 'I'd run out screaming and shoot myself'; he too blamed Hill for all the censorship. Interviewed by Joan Bakewell two years later, he took a more pragmatic view: 'I fully expect that if they brought *Till Death Us Do Part* back we would destroy Johnny Speight as a writer, because he would have to start repeating himself. There are not that many ideas in any one situation ... I don't think that Johnny Speight ever wrote a bad *Till Death Us Do Part*, but, my God, the pressure nearly killed him. You see, there comes a time when the mind boggles and can't create any more. You have to stop and rethink.' In a 1997 interview, the producer went even further, and cited quality control as the reason for the show's 1968 termination, asserting that he himself had suggested a trial separation between Garnett and Speight; but this seems more like a rationalisation after the event than a truthful recollection.

In the spring of 1968, Mitchell appeared on a TV show with Jonathan King to give his side of the story. No recording of that interview is available, but it led to the actor being sent a personal thank-you letter by Sloan: 'As you can imagine, the last few weeks have not been particularly easy and it was good of you to state the situation as I believe it to be.'

In 1968, it seemed that a mere 18 month after their traumatic birth, the Garnetts – on television, at least – were no more. Three years later, Speight was still maintaining, in an interview with David Nathan: 'I don't think they'll come back to television as a family. The series got a bit uptight; there was strife'

15
Alf Goes to the Pictures

THE LEAST WE CAN DO IS WAVE TO EACH OTHER

Having finished his working holiday in Spain writing the script for the *Till Death Us Do Part* movie, Johnny Speight was back in England in time for the Variety Club Awards in March 1968, where the show won the best script gong for the second year running.

Warren Mitchell, for his part, had undertaken publicity duties for his latest movie, Philip Saville's *The Best House in London*, and was already working on other movie projects, which would see him appearing as a German in *The Assassination Bureau* with Oliver Reed and Diana Rigg and – further evidencing his questionable choice of film roles – as the villain in the 'space western' *Moon Zero Two* (in which, according to one critic, he 'leered prettily').

Frank Muir meanwhile was busy setting up the entertainment department of LWT, and was briefly dragged into rumours about the possibility of *Till Death Us Do Part* transferring to become part of the new commercial station's winter line-up. *The Times* reported that Speight was talking to LWT about writing the show with two main actors (presumably Mitchell and Nichols). The writer's agent, Beryl Vertue, was also alleged to have expressed some interest in this idea during an interview in *The Stage*. Tom Sloan questioned Muir about the rumours on 27 February, stating that Speight still owed the BBC further scripts, having agreed to supply 20 a year – not necessarily involving the Garnetts – between April 1967 and March 1969 and having so far delivered only eight (the seven episodes of *Till Death Us Do Part*'s third series plus *To Lucifer a Son*). Surely, Sloan argued, Speight would be precluded from doing any work for LWT until this had been sorted out? Muir replied that such questions could be resolved only between Vertue and Sloan, and left it there. The rumours may in fact have stemmed from plans by LWT to produce an adaptation of Speight's 1965 play *If There Weren't Any Blacks, You'd Have to Invent Them*, which was ultimately broadcast in August 1968. In response to Sloan's concerns, Vertue merely stated: 'He is going to be involved in the film for quite a long time. We simply don't know [if] he will do more for television.'

The movie began shooting in June 1968 at Shepperton Studios with all four lead actors from the TV series reprising their roles. It was produced by

Jon Pennington and directed by Norman Cohen, the latter of whom was described by Tony Booth as 'a gentle, amiable Irish guy', and featured an excellent supporting cast, including Brian Blessed (whose voice was subsequently redubbed for the US release, retitled *Alf 'n' Family*), Bob Grant and Michael Robbins, later of *On the Buses* fame, along with Speight favourites Cleo Sylvestre, Edward Evans, Ann Lancaster and Leslie Noyes. Bill Maynard played the prominent role of the Garnetts' neighbour Bert, and received £1,000 for eight weeks' work. He had Speight himself to thank for the role. When he had gone to audition at Shepperton, he had been initially told that he was too tall for the part, on the basis that Bert needed to be a smaller man for Alf to dominate (a requirement that, considering Mitchell's diminutive stature, would have been rather difficult to fulfil). Disheartened, Maynard had been just about to leave when Speight had walked in and immediately approved his casting – Speight had written material for Maynard in the '50s for ten bob a time.

The budget was tight, and very quickly Mitchell began making demands that threatened to jeopardise the production, culminating in a battle one morning that Booth recalls with apparent glee in his book, *Stroll On*. Mitchell felt that the set built for the pub scenes in the movie was far too expansive, 'a Victorian gin palace that must have covered an acre', and had been filled with a coterie of extras portraying cheerful Cockney stereotypes. Mitchell exploded and told Cohen and the designer that the set was ludicrous. Cohen declared that Mitchell had seen and approved the designs in advance and reminded him that time was of the essence, but the work ground to a halt as Mitchell demanded that the director bring out the designs and prove his assertion. Cohen reluctantly agreed, and while the designs were being perused by Mitchell, Booth calmly read his copy of *The Sporting Life*, Una Stubbs clicked away at her embroidery and Dandy Nichols repeatedly inspected her bag full of pills. Mitchell again denounced the set as unsuitable and then loudly requested a meeting with the producer. When Pennington arrived, Mitchell demanded that the set be struck and replaced with a smaller one, similar to that used on the TV show. Both producer and director refused, stating that the costs in time and wages would be prohibitive. Mitchell stood his ground, even when both Booth and Nichols tried to plead the cause of common sense, and said that he would rather not do the film than use the inadequate set. He then attempted to go over the heads of Cohen and Pennington and appeal to studio boss John Boulting. On his arrival at 10.00 am, however, Boulting furiously asked Mitchell whether he was intending to play the scene or not. Taken aback, Mitchell hesitated. Boulting then ordered him to get back to work immediately, pointing out that they had already lost two hours of filming due to his recalcitrance. Mitchell saw that he had gone too far and promptly went on to film the scene, much to Booth's quiet satisfaction.[28]

While the movie was in production, Mitchell and Booth were requested by producer Ted Kotcheff, luminary of classic ITV drama anthology *Armchair Theatre* (and later Hollywood director and producer of the hit series *Law and Order*) to perform in a benefit show, *Come Back Africa*, at the Royal Albert Hall. This was an anti-apartheid event in support of the International Defence and Aid Fund to commemorate Human Rights Year and South Africa Freedom Day. It was organised by Canon John Collins, currently campaigning against Nelson Mandela's imprisonment, and the United Nations Committee on Apartheid, and stars such as Marlon Brando, Sammy Davis Jnr, Cleo Laine and Johnny Dankworth were billed, alongside rock group the Nice, dominated by the keyboard extravagances of Keith Emerson, later to form supergroup ELP. The Nice had previously used explosive theatrical devices in order to comment on the tumultuous events currently occurring in America, including firing shots from a starting pistol on stage to represent the assassinations of the Kennedys and Martin Luther King. They also regularly burned the Stars and Stripes onstage as they performed a psychedelic cover of Leonard Bernstein's 'America' from *West Side Story* in order to protest at the war in Vietnam. In the light of this, Royal Albert Hall manager Frank Munday asked Kotcheff to make every effort to ensure that such pyrotechnics did not lower the tone of the venue, and Kotcheff agreed. Mitchell had been asked to host the event and lapsed into his Garnett persona before calmly sitting down in a chair on the side of the stage and announcing, 'And now I'm going to tell you a Nice story …' The Nice came on stage, and Emerson, having impressed the audience by playing the Hall's massive pipe organ as an introduction, promptly proceeded to spray a huge Stars and Stripes flag set up on stage with aerosol paint. At the climactic moment, he went to set fire to the flag, despite (or indeed because of) the warnings, only to find to his shock that he had lost the matches, having accidentally dropped them on stage. Seeing his predicament, Mitchell graciously gave him the matches, and urged him on as he ignited the flag: 'Go on, boy, yeah, that's great'. Also from this event, Booth remembers the sight of Russian violin virtuoso David Oistrakh, constantly spied on by the KGB, jamming backstage with Johnny Dankworth.

During the filming of the movie, Booth regularly drank with Speight at the end of a day's work before returning to his home. One day he received word that his father had been rushed to hospital in Liverpool, and Boulting rearranged the film schedule to allow the actor to drive up to see him before returning to London the following night

The film was first screened in an extended run in London in December 1968. *The Times* reported that it had received an 'A' certificate (meaning that

---

[28] Over 30 years later, Mitchell's intransigence in his quest for perfection was to result in his sacking from the production of Britflick *The Mean Machine*.

children could see it only if accompanied by an adult) after mild censorship by the British Board of Film Censors, who had found two phrases too offensive. Speight, asked to comment, said 'I can't understand how they can cut the words they have and still leave in some other things'.

The Times's John Russell Taylor reviewed the film on 12 December 1968, deeming it 'not a masterpiece of cinematic art' but adding that as a phenomenon he found it fascinating:

> If he was initially the man you love to hate on television, he is now the man you love and laugh along with. Certainly he was accepted as such much less unequivocally by audiences than Liberal idealists might think and hope. After all, to begin with we cannot escape the fact that what he was actually saying – about the blacks, the bureaucrats, the good old bad new days – was however unavowably what a lot of spectators were thinking.
>
> [This] mirrored from the start Mr Speight's own deeply ambiguous attitudes … Alf at heart is not a fascist or anything else definably political, but the sheer bloody-minded, obstructive, contrary, awkward cuss who has always been (and may be even still, in these servile days) the backbone of Britain. He can and does change his mind constantly, on the principle that whatever they say, he's against it. He's cowardly, devious, surprisingly adaptable to whatever situations present themselves. He is not so much an attitude as a tone of voice and that tone of voice has found a response all over Britain.
>
> In the television series the result was latterly a playing to the gallery; the Garnetts did not so much say offensive things anymore as say fairly ordinary things offensively. The film is not so offensive, verbally or idealogically; it is probably not offensive enough.
>
> Curiously enough, the Garnett prehistory is much the most interesting part; back in the present the film becomes merely a series of snippets from the television cutting room floor. The film as a whole centres more on Alf than the television series did and he emerges, whether by accident or by design, as a disreputable Everyman, a sort of Schweik[29] of the class war. And why not; it is, after all, as Alf constantly says and seldom actually believes, a free country, isn't it?

Roger Greenspun, writing in the *New York Times* over three years later when, as *Alf 'n' Family*, the movie finally obtained a Stateside release – thanks largely to the success of the American TV adaptation *All in the Family* – was kinder, and presented an interesting viewpoint, given that the Americans

---

[29] This is a reference to the central character of Jarosalv Hasek's 1923 novel *The Good Soldier Schweik*.

had no preconceptions about the Garnetts:

> Neither an artist, nor even-quite a thinker, Alf is a man whose
> opinions are his truest memorial. Of these he has a plentiful supply …
> The film picks Alf up in 1939 and drops him in the 1970s, during
> which time the world changes – though he doesn't. A working-class
> Tory; a patriot; a coward; scorning Hitler, the Pope, 'Lili Marleen'; he
> begins as a loud-mouth fool and, by simply staying himself, ends as
> something of a loud-mouth hero. Along the way he begets a daughter,
> gains a son-in-law, loses a house, hangs onto his prejudices and (the
> film is cagy about this) keeps his principles intact. There are problems
> inherent in presenting a lovable, laughable old chauvinistic racial
> bigot; and *Alf 'n' Family* mainly solves them by looking the other way.

Greenspun also remarked that the film was a collection of strung-together
comic situations, yet he found the scene where Alf and Else wonder how on
earth their child could have been conceived, to be heart warming – a
sentiment one would not normally associate with the Garnetts.

The storyline of the movie is divided into two segments: the first depicts
the adventures of Alf and Else during the war, from September 1939 to
August 1945; then the second jumps forward to the period from Harold
Wilson's election on 31 March 1966 to the present day, June 1968. The
Garnett home is the linking factor, surviving the Blitz but later succumbing
to the developers, eventually resulting in the family's removal to the tower-
block dystopia of a sink estate (actually Denmead House on Highcliffe
Drive, Roehampton) – a scenario that would surely have resonated with the
film's target audience, as millions of Britons had been subject, for better or
worse, to much the same thing. Another link between the two segments is
the self-referential approach of having the movie both open and close in a
cinema, starting with a scene in which Alf loudly comments on a newsreel
sequence depicting Hitler's military might, which he is sublimely confident
will not result in war, and ending with one in which he is left making a one
man stand in salute to the national anthem played over the cinema's PA
system as Mike, Rita, Else and the other patrons hurriedly head for the exit.

During the course of the action we see Alf avoiding conscription, Alf
standing up naked in his bathtub as the national anthem plays over the
radio (foreshadowing the closing cinema scene), Alf trying to sneak extra
rations, Alf being evacuated to the tube and railing against the other
refugees singing 'Lili Marleen', and Alf getting soaked in an Anderson
shelter. Again, all this would have struck a chord with the film's target
audience, for whom the War was a not at all distant memory. Around 1944,
Rita is born, and we see Alf suffering from the unwanted effects of
fatherhood. Then, in the second segment, we get to witness the first

meetings with the Scouse git, complete with the God-in-a-glass incident cut from the 'Aunt Maud' TV episode – although robbed of any real impact by its inclusion in a kaleidoscopic trawl through Alf-versus-son-in-law encounters – and later the raucous wedding and reception where Alf meets Mike's parents (this time played by Liam Redmond and Shelagh Fraser) and Aunt Maud (played as on TV by Ann Lancaster). The earlier wartime scenes are recalled when Alf and Mike are spectators at another conflict between England and Germany, in the World Cup Final of 30 July 1966, when Alf sees his beloved Bobby Moore, captain of West Ham, suitably rewarded. Finally, bringing things right up to date, we see the Grosvenor Square riots of March 1968 and the destruction of the Garnetts' home in July of that year. The whole package is rounded off with a title song written by the king of sepia-tinted music hall melody, Ray Davies. A scripted ending in which, at the Garnetts' new flat, Alf discovers that his neighbour, played by Lionel Jeffries, is an ultra-left-wing mirror image of himself, was not filmed.

Many jokes from the TV show are reused in the movie, including the theft of milk from a baby's bottle from 'From Liverpool with Love' and the bathtub scenes from 'Two Toilets – That's Posh'. Some other familiar characters from the TV episodes also appear, although played by different actors – Fred the barman is played by Michael Robbins rather than Will Stampe, for example. The movie is well produced, with a professional veneer to it that many future big-screen adaptations of British sitcoms would lack, but it arguably suffers from having a scenario suitable for a half-hour TV episode overextended into a 100-minute movie, and also from the lack of the TV show's studio audience to bring direction and clarity to the proceedings. It also, as the review above suggests, concentrates too much on Alf at the expense of the other family members; and the '60s segment resembles a greatest hits package rather than a coherent screenplay. Also, because more is made of Alf's life and it is placed in its context of national suffering – food rationing, evacuation, endless bombing, for which Alf is later rewarded by having his home demolished – the character finally attains glorification as a national hero rather than a national bigot. Consequently, the movie, even more than the TV show itself, becomes a period piece, interesting for its social detail rather than its innate humour; a snapshot of its time, but not a great piece of work. While it may never have been intended to be the latter, surely something more ambitious than a very profitable cash-in could have been expected from a writer whose associates all stressed his unique muse, his incredible gift, his tortured artist status?

Following its extended pre-Christmas engagement in London, the film moved on to the provincial circuit in January 1969, and it proved to be a huge success, not only at home but also abroad – although Speight expressed anger at its restricted showings to whites only in South Africa – and took Australia by storm when it premiered there in April 1970.

Although not quite the first film adaptation of a British sitcom (versions of both *Whacko!* and *The Army Game* had been made in the late '50s), it was instrumental in kick-starting *the* British film trend of the '70s of transforming small-screen sitcom favourites into big-screen box office hits, such as the *On the Buses* movies, *Dad's Army*, *Steptoe and Son*, *Love Thy Neighbour*, *Bless This House*, *Please Sir!*, *Never Mind the Quality, Feel the Width* et al, and even in 1972 a second *Till Death Us Do Part* film (see Chapter Nineteen).

Meanwhile, at the BBC, Colin Shaw, BBC One Planning Manager, decided in July 1968 to arrange a repeat season of *Till Death Us Do Part* on Saturday evenings. This began in November 1968 and was originally intended to last for only six episodes, up until Christmas, but proved so popular that it was extended into the New Year. Indeed, the repeats hit the number one spot in the ratings, making them the most successful TV repeats ever at that point – a fact that would no doubt have been noted with delight by Speight and Dennis Main Wilson when they both attended a symposium on comedy at Birmingham University. As the repeat season coincided with the movie's release nationwide, the two effectively cross-promoted each other. Ultimately, 11 episodes were screened in the run, with 'Peace and Goodwill' and 'I Can Give It Up Any Time I Like' each receiving a third airing and the whole of the third series bar 'The Blood Donor' being included – even the extraordinarily controversial 'Aunt Maud'. There was a talk of a Garnett New Year poster being produced for the *Radio Times*, but this did not come to fruition.

Also being repeated by the BBC at this time were some of Tony Hancock's TV shows, the comic having died earlier in 1968, and this inspired a revisionist analysis in some quarters. *The Times'* reviewer Henry Raynor compared Hancock to Garnett: 'The Hancock personality and its encounters with others remains important and immediate and the skill with which Hancock played the part of his alter-ego, the exactitude of his inflection and timing, means that the programme can be watched even a third time with pleasure … [*Till Death Us Do Part* has a] far less exciting effect. So much of the scripts depended on the therapy of shock that the admirable playing … the series was given – and the drowsy alertness of Dandy Nichols for instance, is an unfailing joy – has less depth of character in which to work than Hancock or the equally memorable Steptoes'.

16
A Spate of Speight

LILLICRAP

Of *Till Death Us Do Part*'s four lead actors, Warren Mitchell remained the busiest now that the show was off the air. In 1969, he secured a long-coveted engagement to appear as Alf in cabaret in Australia (of which, more below). The same year, possibly inspired by the constant references to fish and chips in the recently-repeated 'Aunt Maud', the Findus frozen food company approached him to appear with Una Stubbs in some TV adverts for their fish fingers. These adverts have the two actors playing what are obviously their familiar roles of Alf and Rita, although – no doubt for copyright reasons – they are never named as such. They are also notable for featuring the earliest example – or, at any rate, the earliest surviving example – of Rita blowing kisses to her dad *a la* Bugs Bunny, a piece of business that Stubbs was to develop in the later *Till Death Us Do Part* shows. In March, Mitchell and Speight again walked off with awards for the show from the Variety Club of Great Britain, winning the TV Personality of the Year and Best Comedy Script categories respectively for the third time each. Then, at the end of the same month, Mitchell went back to the stage in Peter Hall's production of *My Dutch Uncle* at the Aldwych Theatre. He even found time to appear in yet another *Comedy Playhouse*, 'Tooth and Claw', the script for which had been written by Marty Feldman and Barry Took back in 1965. Produced by Roger Race and transmitted on 28 April, it starred Mitchell and Feldman as rival Jewish millionaires.

Speight also had to rise to the challenge of life without the Garnetts. He received an early boost when his play *If There Weren't Any Blacks, You'd Have to Invent Them*, broadcast by London Weekend Television (LWT) in 1968, won him an international award in Prague. February 1969 also saw him making a lucrative deal in the formation of the Constellation Investment stable, a conglomerate of stage and screen stars, with his old agency, Barrett Speight, now valued at the huge sum of £208,000. His next writing project was for the commercial channel Thames in the form of *A Spate of Speight*, a compendium of sketches featuring such luminaries as Eric Sykes, Alfred Marks, Kenny Lynch and Miriam Karlin, with music provided by the Scaffold, transmitted on 5 May 1969. He then went on to script what would be his second sitcom series, *Curry and Chips*, for LWT.

The idea for *Curry and Chips* came from Spike Milligan who, late in 1968, approached his friend Speight (who venerated him, and used to mimic him as a Nazi whenever Milligan became angry, which was rather often) to write the series, simply because he himself was too busy working on his BBC Two show *Q5* at the time. Milligan's idea was that he would play Kevin O'Grady, a Pakistani who was Irish on his father's side and hence had the nickname 'Paki-Paddy', working at a seaside novelty factory, Lillicraps, in the north of England. Eric Sykes would be the hapless factory foreman Arthur Blenkinsopp, the voice of sanity in a melting pot of racial issues; Speight's friend Kenny Lynch would play a racist Afro-Caribbean; and Norman Rossington and Geoffrey Hughes would appear as racist white Liverpudlians. The intention was to reflect political and social conflicts on the shop floor in the same manner as the Garnetts had in the home. One of the inspirations for this was an event that had occurred a mere two months after *Till Death Us Do Part* had self-destructed, and that Speight would no doubt have loved to have had Alf comment on: right-wing politician Enoch Powell's infamous Birmingham speech that brought 'the colour problem', as it was then euphemistically termed, screaming into the open. Powell, inveterate classicist that he was, knew that the date of his speech, 20 April, was also a mere 24 hours away from the anniversary of the traditional date of the founding of Rome by Romulus in 753 BC; he consequently chose to spice up the proceedings by incorporating a quote from Virgil about rivers running red with blood – a decision that was to have repercussions way beyond anyone's imagination. When his boss, Edward Heath, sacked Powell in response, dockers from Wapping – workers such as Alf – marched in protest. The other catalyst for the new show seemed to be the 'I'm Backing Britain' campaign of 1968 and the subsequent mantra for the currently-ailing British business community, 'Export or Die', with its emphasis on the workforce joining together to save the economy of the sceptred isle. This of course was ideal satirical material for Speight, who eagerly accepted his friend's proposition.

Speight, Milligan and Sykes met up to talk over the new project with Frank Muir, now Programme Controller for LWT, on New Year's Day 1969. During the discussions, it was agreed that Associated London Scripts would actually form a company called Lillicrap and provide scripts, actors, costumes and props for the series, while LWT would finance studios, directors and camera crew. Muir asked Milligan's personal assistant Norma Farnes to be associate producer, responsible for getting Speight to supply the scripts on time and Sykes and her own client to arrive at the studios on time for rehearsals and recordings. Unaware of the poisoned chalice she was being offered, Farnes accepted.

Lest the chaos surrounding *Till Death Us Do Part* should appear unique, Farnes has since related the nightmares that plagued the production of *Curry and Chips*: Beryl Vertue and Sykes engaging in rows; Milligan insulting Sykes' new agent; Farnes getting involved in difficult negotiations over wardrobe rights; and then Milligan descending into the depths of depression triggered by the news of his father's death in Australia. And then there were the problems created by Speight himself. As Muir had to approve each script on the Thursday before rehearsals began, Speight was supposed to deliver it by the Wednesday morning. One Wednesday afternoon he still had not turned up, so Farnes went searching for him at his usual watering holes, eventually finding him at the Queen's Elm pub smashed out of his mind with his footballing drinking buddies George Best, Ian St John and Jimmy Greaves. She approached him as he was playing the drums and reminded him of the need for a script. Speight reluctantly left the drum kit and went to a table to scribble some ideas on the backs of beer mats, which he blearily gave to her before resuming his jazz session. Back at the office, Farnes gave the beer mats to Sykes and Milligan and they worked into the small hours trying to salvage a script. After the recording of the series' last episode, there was a party at the bridal suite of the Royal Garden Hotel in Kensington, at which an intoxicated Speight was approached by a mystery girl who declared her undying love for him. When she was rebuffed, she announced that she would commit suicide by throwing herself out of a window. When the guests decided to call her bluff, she flounced off, but thankfully Milligan followed her and, sure enough, found her clinging to a window ledge; he managed to persuade her to come inside.

Curry and Chips ran to six episodes, all produced and directed by Keith Beckett, and was eventually transmitted between November and December 1969. It has since acquired considerable notoriety as media studies students everywhere have accessed copies of it and critically torn it to shreds. While opinions differ as to Speight's stance on racial issues in *Till Death Us Do Part*, there seems to be a strong consensus that his treatment of those issues in *Curry and Chips* was deeply offensive. Speight himself said of the show: 'It was taken off after just one series ... London Weekend said they were sorry but they had to drop it because there had been a lot of complaints. Yet we got some great reviews. You could certainly get away with more on the BBC in those days. On ITV, you couldn't mention black people; you almost had to treat them as if they were invisible.' But he also stated, in his book *It Stands to Reason*, that the ITA had not censored *Curry and Chips* in any way: 'They just forbade us to do anymore. They said Enoch [was] enough, and were only concerned with sweeping problems under the carpet where possible.'

Looking back on it now, *Curry and Chips* can be seen to represent Speight at his most acerbic in his view of contemporary Britain as a country where everyone is a racist or a fool or pig-ignorant. The whites despise the immigrants for the most stupid of reasons – afraid that they have come to steal their wives, or that they are latent homosexuals, or that they have a propensity for cannibalism. Blenkinsopp's landlady finds O'Grady attractive but still decides to charge him at the 'coloured rate'. Blenkinsopp himself initially wants to be rid of O'Grady, a hopeful new employee at Lillicrap, and despite claiming to be a reasonable person, gives him the dirtiest job of all. The ethnic minority characters are shown to be just as racist as the indigenous population, the Kenny Lynch and Spike Milligan characters going so far as to deny that they are 'wogs' at all.[30] Leaving aside its contentious racial content, *Curry and Chips* also stands as a testament to how shambolic a production *Till Death Us Do Part* could have been without the perfectionism of Warren Mitchell and the dedicated work ethic of Dennis Main Wilson. It is fairly chaotic, with the cast even becoming confused sometimes about the characters' names: Sykes mistakenly calls Milligan's character 'Patrick' instead of 'Kevin'; Lynch addresses Sykes' Arthur Blenkinsopp as 'Eric'; and Milligan actually calls Blenkinsopp 'Mr Sykes' at one point!

At the turn of the decade, Speight seemed to suffer a creative block for a time, perhaps content simply to surf along on the crest of his reputation and household-name status, having become perhaps the first television writer to attain such heights. He may well have been attempting to come to terms with his increasing alcoholism, which in 1972 he would claim to have conquered. One creative project he did undertake in 1970, however, was to work with Mitchell's old friend Ken Campbell on an LWT *Saturday Night Theatre* double bill coupling an adaptation of one of Campbell's stage plays, *You See The Thing Is …*, with a short piece of his own entitled *The Salesman*, starring Ian Holm. This was transmitted on 30 May 1970.

In the autumn of 1969, Speight had been contacted by the BBC for the rights to produce another adaptation of his short plays *The Compartment* and *Playmates*, scheduled as a double bill for *The Wednesday Play* and starring Marty Feldman in the Michael Caine roles as the main protagonist. Screened on 26 November 1969, it was a very powerful piece, with Feldman proving an excellent choice of lead. This saw the end of Speight's self imposed exile from the BBC; and, while the time was not yet ripe for the resuscitation of *Till Death Us Do Part* itself, it would not be long before Alf Garnett was making another appearance …

UP THE POLLS!

Speight received another accolade on 30 April 1970 when Eamonn Andrews surprised him with the big red book of *This Is Your Life* as he was attending a discussion on the forthcoming World Cup. Amongst those paying tribute on the programme, Eric Sykes praised Speight's abilities and Dandy Nichols, complete with handbag, talked about being lumbered with the 'silly moo'

---

[30] Speight was to repeat this idea in the next series of *Till Death Us Do Part*.

tag. Warren Mitchell appeared on screen in a message (delivered in funny foreigner accent) from down under, where he was again performing as Alf in cabaret and helping to promote the *Till Death Us Do Part* feature film. The final guest in a particularly chaotic programme was that eternal scene-stealer Frankie Howerd, who characteristically dithered so much that he caused Andrews to joke that they might as well leave the other 25 guests outside now they had run out of time. Throughout, Speight was so emotional he was barely coherent.

Alf Garnett returned to British TV on 18 June 1970 when he was secured by Dennis Main Wilson for an appearance in a one-off special to form part of the BBC's coverage of the latest General Election being contested between the Labour Party, headed by Prime Minister Harold Wilson, and the Conservative Party, led by 'Selsdon Man' himself, that grammar school twit/nit Edward Heath. Anxious to avoid any controversy, particularly after the furore that had surrounded the contentious political documentary *Yesterday's Men* that spring, the BBC scheduled the special in a post-10.00 pm slot, at which time voting in the Election would be closed and the first results still awaited for analysis by Cliff Michelmore and his Election '70 team. Speight conceived and wrote the show, dubbed 'Up the Polls! (The Campaign's Over)', as a pub discussion mirroring those that would be going on all over the country at that precise time – as if the TV cameras were simply looking in on Alf Garnett and his friends as they debated the state of the nation. Sykes and Milligan both reprised their *Curry and Chips* characters and Gran made an appearance again in the form of Joan Sims. The whole show – for which Speight received £1,000 and Mitchell £600 – was transmitted live. It was yet another example of Alf being used as a vehicle for political satire, but there is no indication that any consideration was given to bringing back the other members of the Garnett family for a full *Till Death Us Do Part* reunion. That would probably have been impossible in any event: Tony Booth was adamant that he would not return to the show, and Dandy Nichols was currently enjoying great success on stage with John Gielgud and Ralph Richardson in *Home*.

Race and the Common Market are the main themes of 'Up the Polls! (The Campaign's Over)'. The pace of the piece is uneven, and it threatens to grind to a halt at times; Sykes seems to be the main culprit here, being less able to improvise than the others, although he does get to deliver the line of Speight dialogue later so beloved by Mitchell, to the effect that his father once walked eight miles in borrowed boots so that he could vote Tory. Speight does his best to offend everybody, with cries of 'Piss off!' and 'Bastard!' providing a whole new frontier of bad language for him to cross, and Milligan as Paki-Paddy is particularly funny. The piece ends with a row over the England football team's recent World Cup defeat in Mexico and their theme song 'Back Home' being played over a Union Jack during the end credits, at the close of which someone (Mitchell, or Milligan?) throws an egg at the flag, to great applause from the audience. The BBC's own reaction to the special was somewhat mixed, an internal executive memo stating that it reflected 'a failure to execute properly [what was] a basically sound idea'.[31]

Boosted by thoughts of a renewed working partnership, Wilson and Speight had already discussed a new *Comedy Playhouse* tentatively entitled 'The Two Tramps' and centred on the same idea that seven years earlier had been rejected by Arthur Haynes. The first script outline had been submitted to Michael Mills on 18 May 1970, but Speight had then requested that the idea of a one-off pilot be abandoned in favour of a fully-fledged series. Mills and the BBC's new Head of Comedy David Climie agreed, and contracts were drawn up in August. A memo from Wilson declared amusingly of the scripts, 'Delivery date (I live in a world of fantasy) to be end of January 1971 …' The series was eventually retitled *Them*, and the star roles went to Cyril Cusack (who raved about Speight as being at least the equal of celebrated Irish writer Brendan Behan) as eccentric Irishman 'Coat Sleeves' and James Booth as down-to-earth 'Cockney'. Instead of the comedy stemming from clashes between the main characters *a la Till Death Us Do Part*, it derived from the adventures of the two vagrants on the road, and their clashes with society and figures of authority and convention who could see them only as the enemy – a case of us versus *them*. Apart from the two leads, the series featured the usual quota of high-class comic actors such as Rita Webb, Arthur Mullard and Frank Gatcliff, along with '60s *Till Death Us Do Part* regulars Will Stampe, Edward Evans and Fred McNaughton. It was apparently recorded during the spring of 1971, but took a long time to reach the screen. Its five episodes (an unusual number for a series, possibly indicative of doubts over Speight's ability to meet a longer commitment) were eventually transmitted in the very late time slot of 10.15 on Thursday evenings between 27 July and 24 August 1972, suggesting a lack of confidence on the BBC's part. The show was also largely overlooked by the media, although Speight can be seen enjoying a drink with its stars in a 1972 *Late Night Line-Up Special* on the writer. Possibly another reason for the BBC's loss of interest in *Them* was that during the course of 1971 they were starting to think about bringing back *Till Death Us Do Part*, due in large part to the astonishing success of its US counterpart *All In the Family* …

---

[31] Ultimately the concept at least must have been judged a success, as the final episode of *Till Death Us Do Part*'s fifth series would be televised in just such a slot on Election Night 1974.

17
From Alf to Archie

ALF DOWN UNDER

Alf's explosions, like Krakatoa's, had reverberated around the world, and his name would now be forever associated with a particular type of bigoted attitude or outlook. Even Denis Healey, the Defence Secretary, was heard to declare in a television interview on 18 December 1968 that a recent book's suggestions that all servicemen were brutal and stupid were 'rather like Alf Garnett's attitudes to our coloured friends'. Alf had also from the beginning afforded excellent raw material for impressionists; in the 15 January 1969 edition of *Will The Real Mike Yarwood Please Stand Up?*, for instance, Yarwood, assisted by Peter Goodright, imitated Mrs Thursday[32] meeting Bruce Forsyth meeting Alf Garnett meeting Harold Wilson ... Then there were the numerous other sitcoms that sought to emulate elements of *Till Death Us Do Part*, which would later lead Michael Mills to lament, 'For about two years after *Till Death Us Do Part* ... we got scripts about rude families shouting at one another. They were not very good ...' One example of this trend was *Charge!*, a five-episode series broadcast on BBC One in early 1969. This was co-written by and starred Robert Morley as an aristocratic snob railing about the loss of Empire and so forth while being kept in order by his West Indian housekeeper. The character was instantly recognised as an 'upper class Alf Garnett', yet *The Listener* remarked that the show failed to engage the viewer: 'Precisely because the character is upper class, he is not allowed any of Garnett's savagery.'

And then there was the global success of *Till Death Us Do Part* itself. Following the sale of the original *Comedy Playhouse* pilot to Australia and New Zealand in 1966, it was also marketed to such countries as Uganda and Namibia in 1967. Subsequent episodes were seen in South Africa, Nigeria, West Pakistan, Australia and New Zealand. Such was the show's success in Australia that, according to his later recollection, Mitchell once saw a sign outside a Sydney fish and chip shop that read, 'Hurry up and get your fish and chips: Alf's on at 8.00'. This success provided the ideal opportunity for the actor to fulfil an ambition about which he had spoken in an interview for

---

[32] From the hit comedy-drama *Mrs Thursday*, written by Ted Willis and transmitted in two series in 1966 and 1967.

the Christmas 1966 edition of the *Radio Times*: to bring the character of Alf to the stage in Australia. Having already made a few appearances as Alf around the UK, including at the aforementioned Conservative Party event with Harold Macmillan and at the unlikely venue of Chatham Prison, he began a two-week engagement at Chequers nightclub in Sydney on 7 January 1969. It was a huge success, and Mitchell got a standing ovation from the audience, although he also subsequently received some abusive letters, of which he remarked: 'It is a compliment to both of us – Garnett and me. We have incensed somebody. If I did not offend some people I would be worried. I agree with what they say about Alf heartily'.

Outside the sophisticated circles of central Sydney, however, things spiralled out of control. Mitchell took his act to a Returned Servicemen's League Club at Marrickville, where on 27 January his contract was terminated, another act was booked in his place and he was told not to return, 'quite a few protests' having been provoked by his material and behaviour. The press reported: 'According to Mr Mitchell, the audience hissed, booed and drowned [out] his words with loud drinking and noise from hundreds of fruit machines. He walked off stage twice on Saturday and finished his performance in dead silence only after the club manager explained to the audience that his comments were "only part of an act".' Apparently, Mitchell had demanded absolute silence while he was on stage, and had abused the club stewards when they had failed to secure this. The actor was, as usual, unrepentant: 'God, it was awful. After Saturday, I told the club I was willing to forgo pay for that night's show if they let me off Sunday's performance. Sacked? I didn't want to go on. Thursday night was pretty bad, Friday night was worse and Saturday night was unspeakable … Vulgarities? My God, they lapped them up. When the vulgarities stopped, they didn't like the act.' When Alf ranted on about Australia's background as a penal colony, 'a section of the crowd got horribly offended'. Many of those in the audience had been drunk and had yelled at Mitchell, so he had stopped the act, asked the club's manager to drop the contract and walked out.

Clearly, though, Mitchell was not put off by this experience. He returned again and again to Australia in the years that followed, making many more cabaret appearances and in 1973 filming an advert in which Alf promotes the national airline Qantas – or 'Quaint-Arse', as he puts it – and another in which he tries to smuggle fish and chips into the country. In early 1974, Mitchell met up with Johnny Speight in Sydney, where the writer had been invited to come and discuss the possibility of developing an Australian Alf Garnett, although ultimately this came to nothing, mainly because the popularity of the English original was overwhelming. Later that year, an appearance at another Returned Servicemen's Club again spelt trouble for the actor. Once more angered by the response to his act, he apparently started lecturing his audience, stating that they shouldn't sympathise with Alf because he was a monster; in response, the crowd grabbed him and dumped him in a swimming pool to a chorus of cries such as, 'We want Alf, not all that crap you've been giving us!'

Ultimately, Mitchell's love affair with the Antipodes resulted in him taking Australian citizenship shortly after filming some episodes of *In Sickness and in Health* in Sydney in the mid-1980s.

MEET THE BUNKERS

The success of *Till Death Us Do Part* attracted the attention of a number of overseas television producers who wanted to make adaptations suitable for their own national audiences. While the original BBC series could be appreciated in Australia, which had a common language and sufficient cultural connections with the UK to allow viewers to assimilate it, this was obviously not the case in some other countries, particularly non-English-speaking ones. Holland was the first nation off the starting block with its own version of *Till Death Us Do Part*, entitled *Tot De Dood Ons Scheidt*. In this, the Garnetts became the Hanekams, with husband Herman (a bearded Alf), wife Bets (an Else clone), son-in-law Ad and daughter Rie (a blonde). Two series of six episodes each were made by KRO Televisie, beginning in November 1969. Speight was not enamoured of this version, stating: 'They had trouble with the bigotry and prejudice of its central character and were [desperately] trying, ostrich like, … to turn him into an Alf Van Der Nice'. (Twenty years later, however, the writer would be pleased with another Dutch version, *In Voor- En Tegenspoed*, based on *In Sickness and in Health*.) Israel, too, developed its own version of the show, with a Semitic Alf lashing out at the Arabs. But the most successful adaptation came in America.

Russian Jewish American Norman Lear was a noted film producer heading his own Tandem Productions unit when he chanced to see a report about *Till Death Us Do Part* in the 11 January 1967 edition of the US trade magazine *Variety*. This read as follows (complete with numerous contemporary Americanisms!):

> This click comedy situationer, already discussed in terms reserved for the revered *Steptoe and Son* skein, returned to the schedules in superb form and shapes as a top ten ranker and certainly as the most inventive and yockful newcomer to its class in 1966. Johnny Speight, who contrived it … has an explosive gift for working man truculence and opinionated absurdity. Here it's concentrated on Alf Garnett, a Cockney paterfamilias who booms and blusters at wife, daughter and son-in-law. Riddled with prejudice and political non-sequiturs – Speight has

made him a bigoted Tory in outlook, thus giving a rebellious contrast to his aitch-dropping personality – he's never happier than when arguing, and this segment has him inveighing against Harold Wilson, socialism, the welfare state, and explaining with sublime idiocy the relationships between God and Lucifer and the background to the Queen's annual Christmas message. The series has previously aroused protests about its language ... and its general irreverence. But perhaps its saltiest ingredient is its vein of invective against sacred cows, and it doesn't offend because its train of thought is so bizarre ...

Lear was enthused by this report: 'If that could happen on American television! I grew up on that. My father and I fought those battles'. He began the process of acquiring the rights to adapt the show before he had even seen an episode. In February 1968, representatives from ABC television, possibly including Lear himself, viewed several examples of the show at the BBC; given that similar storylines later featured in the US series, these may well have been 'Arguments, Arguments', 'Intolerance', 'Monopoly', 'The Blood Donor', 'Aunt Maud' and 'Peace and Goodwill'. Lear then wrote a pilot script for the US version under the title *Justice*, the lead character having become the ironically-named Archie Justice. ABC were sufficiently impressed with this to put it before the cameras, by which point it had been retitled *Those Were the Days*. The lead role was taken by Carroll O'Connor after the original choice, Mickey Rooney, refused it due to the script's volatile subject matter. O'Connor, like Mitchell before him, came to the part as an established television character actor (and lauded stage performer) but not really a 'name' in the public's eyes. He liked the idea of the show but was very dubious that it would ever come to fruition on US television: 'I just didn't think the American people could stand to listen to a character who talked about "coons" and "hebes" and "spics", even though the public knows damn well that most people talk this way in their homes.' The actress chosen to play Archie's wife, Edith, was another TV veteran, Jean Stapleton, who also couldn't believe the show was viable.

Initially the stars' feelings seemed to be borne out. When the pilot was shown to ABC executives, they thought that although it was funny, it didn't work, allegedly because the young actors who played the daughter and son-in-law roles were not ideal. They asked Lear to record another pilot, and this was made in 1969, under the title *And Justice for All*, with O'Connor and Stapleton reprising their parts and Chip Oliver and Candice Azzara as 'the kids', Mike and Gloria. Oliver was an Anthony Booth lookalike and an Irish American (as O'Connor was in real life). In the episode, Archie insults Mike with the same venom as his British equivalent, calling him 'Shirley Temple' and 'red faced Mick', to an uncomfortable response from the studio audience. Despite having spent $250,000 dollars on the two unscreened pilots, ABC decided the project was too hot a potato and dropped it.

Lear then turned to CBS, where network president Robert D Wood had inaugurated a major reformation in the schedules, sweeping out cosy family shows in favour of harder hitting, more ambitious works intended to attract a younger urban audience. CBS agreed to make a third pilot, based on a rewritten script by Lear in which the Mike character became Polish. O'Connor and Stapleton were retained, but Rob Reiner and Sally Struthers were brought in to replace Oliver and Azzara respectively, and the family surname now became Bunker. This time, the pilot was approved, although research indicated that the idea of presenting a bigot on-screen was highly contentious, that consequently the character should be 'softened', and that the show should be tested out as a mid-season replacement before committal to a full run. Thirteen episodes were commissioned, and the series premiered at the adult-viewing time of 9.30 pm on Tuesday 12 January 1971, now under its final title, *All in the Family*.

Each episode opened with an American take on the original *Till Death Us Do Part* title sequence, featuring a shot sweeping over Manhattan and through suburbia to 704 Hauser Street in the then working-class district of Queens. The sequence began and ended with a view of Archie and Edith at the piano singing (delightfully out of tune) a song called 'Those Were the Days', expressing their yearning for the greatness and simplicity of the past, which served as the series' theme tune. (This sequence was subsequently spoofed in one episode of *The Simpsons*.) O'Connor's Archie is a much less volatile person than Alf. In appearance he is balding and paunchy but has the redeeming feature of baby blue eyes, making him altogether a far less demonic figure. The smell of sulphur and brimstone, frequently discernible in the '60s *Till Death Us Do Part* episodes, never translated to the US version. Alf's occasional mispronunciations (such as 'facketious' for 'facetious' and 'aphrodesirac' for 'aphrodisiac') are put in the shade by Archie's (with examples such as 'You're taking it out of contest' and 'This political percussion is over as of here and now'), all delivered in his usual broad Noo Yawk accent. Like Alf, Archie is a blue collar worker; he is employed at a factory, but earns good money. Edith, his wife, is as educationally subnormal as Else, but there the resemblance ends. Whereas Else is stout and lazy, Edith is wiry and hyperactive, moving around at high velocity to deal with her family's every need. Whereas Else dislikes her husband and uses every opportunity to display this in a vindictive manner, Edith *loves* her husband – loves *everyone* – unconditionally, devoid of any hint of malice. Edith has a brain, somewhere, but it needs to be picked up and carried, so she takes a long time to get to the point, as best illustrated in a truly brilliant sequence in one episode where she rambles away and Archie, impatient as ever, uses his fingers to mimic blowing his head off with a revolver in despair. One critic noted that although Edith might think that Plato was a dog, Karl Marx a great comedian and Aristotle a shipping magnate, she possessed a philosophy with a great depth of human spirit and goodwill.

The dictates of US television, with its much longer runs of episodes and its standard practice of having a group of scriptwriters on a series rather than just one, meant that *All in the Family* could – indeed had to – have a more structured format than *Till Death Us Do Part*. One consequence of this was that Edith, Mike and Gloria benefited from more well-developed characters and tended to take a bigger share of the limelight than their UK equivalents. Vindication of this approach came when, at the end of 1971, Stapleton won the Best Actress Emmy for her role as Edith – one of the first of many awards the show would garner. *All in the Family*'s Mike Stivic, unlike the original Mike, is a genuine intellectual, a sociology student who has to work part time to fund his studies; he resembles the Scouse git however in his unthinking subscription to particular tenets and repetition of certain mannerisms, which his wife occasionally points out to him. Rob Reiner, scion of a noted comic family, was to become an excellent director in his own right on his eventual departure from *All in the Family* in 1978, with such movies as *Spinal Tap* to his credit. Archie's *little goil* Gloria was similar to Rita in that she shared her husband's liberal views, but was far less vitriolic in her conflicts with her father. Sally Struthers would became famous for her charity appeals on American TV after her departure from the show – as ruthlessly caricatured in *South Park*.

From the start, the Bunkers are supported by ancillary characters too, including their black neighbours, the Jefferson family. While old man Jefferson is cut from the same cloth as Archie, his son Lionel is bright and smart and always manages to insult Archie without the bigot really realising. Here, the racial balance that had been absent in *Till Death Us Do Part* was found – an essential requirement in a nation that was experiencing violent racial strife throughout the '60s and into the '70s.

Although CBS had agreed to transmit the series, there were still concerns within the network. Some executives wanted the first and second episodes to be swapped in the running order, because the latter seemed much milder than the former. In the end, this was not done, but a decision was taken to have the opening episode preceded by an introductory voiceover, reminiscent of the *Radio Times*'s defence of the Cockney original: 'The programme you are about to see is *All in the Family*. It seeks to throw a humorous spotlight on our frailties, prejudices and concerns. By making them a source of laughter, we hope to show – in a mature fashion – just how absurd they are'. Prior to each studio recording for the show – this was one of the first American sitcoms to be made before a live audience – Norman Lear and the cast came on stage to assure those present of the same good intentions, just as Warren Mitchell had done at the BBC.

When the series premiered, it initially fared poorly in the Neilson ratings. It proved to be a slow burner, attracting, as its archetype had, critical brickbats and plaudits in equal measure, while cementing its reputation with the audience at home. The number of viewers gradually grew, enough to make a full season viable. That season went on to win two Emmys: the one for Stapleton as Best Actress and, even more significantly, the one for Outstanding Comedy Series. By the time the second season aired, over 50 million people were regularly tuning in. Lear noted with pleasure that in New York City 70% of the viewing population watched the show. In 1972, the series won no fewer than six Emmys, a quota it was to match and sometimes exceed over the following years. 704 Hauser Street became one of the most famous addresses in America; and Archie's armchair, reserved for his own use alone, just as Alf's had been, was ultimately donated to the Smithsonian museum, where it still resides today, complete with Archie's customary can of beer on a table alongside it.

Lear has said of *Till Death Us Do Part*, '[It was comprised of] stick figures. The characters simply fought, and the shows were about nothing more than the argument'. This, though, overlooks the differences between US and UK television. Not only did *All in the Family* have a coterie of different writers and directors, whereas *Till Death Us Do Part* had just Speight and faithful producer Wilson, but the number of episodes in a typical season of the former was equivalent to the entire output of *Till Death Us Do Part* in the '60s. This meant that *All in the Family* by necessity had more plots, more characters, more well-developed structures than the BBC original. Its many and varied story ideas included Edith being far too honest for Archie when she accidentally damages someone's car with a tin of peaches; the family discussing the merits of Rodin's 'The Kiss'; Edith winning a lottery ticket; Edith writing a song about the meaning of love; and the Bunkers having a full-scale encounter with terrorists. Extraordinarily, in one 1977 episode, Edith is actually raped on her birthday. As in Speight's original, the macrocosm of politics and social change is meticulously reflected in the microcosm of the Bunker household; every aspect of this world can be found *All in the Family*, the scripts seemed to be saying – a much more optimistic message than that of *Till Death Us Do Part*.

Some of Speight's original ideas were incorporated into the early episodes, mainly in the first season. The introductory 'Meet the Bunkers' has Mike and Gloria trying to celebrate the twenty-second wedding anniversary of Archie and Edith, reminiscent of the plot of 'A House With Love In It'. In later episodes, a disagreement about whether the family are arguing or debating, and an incident where Archie burns himself (here on a coffee pot rather than an iron) while gesticulating, are based on aspects of 'Arguments, Arguments'; Archie's vehement denial of assertions by Mike and Lionel that he is Jewish echo Alf's lines in 'Intolerance'; and an 'Al Jolson' reference by Edith in 'Writing the President' repeats a line of Else's, also from 'Intolerance'. The episode 'Archie Gives Blood' is heavily based on 'The Blood Donor', although here Lionel delivers many of what were originally Mike's lines. 'Christmas with the Bunkers', transmitted at the end of 1971, uses ideas from 'Peace and Goodwill'. And then there's the character of Aunt Maude, played by Beatrice Arthur (later to go on to even greater fame in *The Golden Girls*), who is introduced to the show when she comes to stay to help Edith look after her sick family, a reversal of the situation in Speight's 'Aunt Maud'. Not only is Maude's name spelt differently than in the British original, but she is also a stronger character; a four-times-divorced ultra-Democrat and activist who detests Archie and his overwhelmingly Republican stance, in contrast to the original Maud, a virtual clone of her bovine sister Else. The character proved so popular that she was soon given her own spin-off show, *Maude* (1972-1978). (Indeed, there would later be no fewer than six other spin-offs: *Good Times* (1974-1979), featuring characters from *Maude*; *The Jeffersons* (1975-1985), centring on the Bunkers' neighbours; *Archie Bunker's Place* (1979-1983), more a continuation than a spin-off; *Checking In* (1981), about the Jeffersons' maid, Florence Johnston; *Gloria* (1982-1983), following the life of Archie's daughter after she divorces Mike; and *704 Hauser* (1994), about a new family moving in to the Bunkers' old home.)

But while *All in the Family* may have reused some of Speight's material, it cast its net far wider than its British archetype in terms of subject matter. Gay and female liberation; Edith undertaking jury duty; Archie worrying about unemployment; Gloria having a miscarriage: all these topics were tackled in the first season alone. Unlike *Till Death Us Do Part*, the show rarely faced criticism over its language, Archie's insults being much less objectionable than Alf's and avoiding any realistic swearing, which none of the US networks would have accepted in the early '70s. Mike is invariably referred to as 'Meathead', while Edith usually attracts the epithet 'Dingbat' – no 'bloodies', 'gits', or 'bitches' here … Unlike Alf, Archie does not suffer embarrassing punishments for his iniquities and rarely launches into the stratosphere with his anger. The standard '*Look …Look*' interjection of the hapless Alf when subjected to one of Else's monologues becomes a more assertive 'Stifle it, Edith' in the mouth of Archie Bunker.

Behind the scenes, though, *All in the Family* did go through its stormy patches, just like the original. O'Connor grew into the character of Archie so well that he inserted his own lines whenever he deemed them necessary, and argued with Lear and various directors for the right to portray the character as he saw fit. In July 1974, irritated that Lear refused to accommodate his suggestions for a particular scene involving Archie kissing Edith under the mistletoe, he walked off set. For three episodes, Archie had to be written out of the action, allegedly going missing while *en route* to a convention outside of New York. Lear got a banning order on O'Connor working elsewhere in TV until the dispute between them was resolved. He also introduced some new characters – most notably Stretch Cunningham played by James Cromwell, who would go on to have a highly successful TV and film career – just in case

Archie had to be killed off. He and the audience then waited with tense expectation to see if O'Connor would ever return. In true Hollywood style, the star orchestrated his re-entry onto the soundstage perfectly, just in time to deliver a closing line at the end of the third episode from which Archie had been missing. Nevertheless, when several weeks later there was a strike by technicians, the militant O'Connor refused to cross a picket line until that too was resolved.

O'Connor's three-week walk-out had actually been inspired by a similar action taken by Red Foxx, one of the stars of *Sanford and Son*, the US adaptation of Galton and Simpson's *Steptoe and Son*, the rights to which Lear had purchased following the success of *All in the Family*. In fact, just as *Till Death Us Do Part* had started a craze of popular British sitcoms being made into movie versions, so *All in the Family* sparked a trend of those same sitcoms being snapped up for US adaptation, examples including *On the Buses* (which became *Lotsa Luck* (1973-1974)) and *Man About the House* (retitled *Three's Company* (1977-1984)). There were many in the British TV industry who had reason to be grateful to Johnny Speight.

Speight himself had a credit in the closing titles of every *All in the Family* episode, and for a while it seemed his Stateside success might expand further. The first *Till Death Us Do Part* movie was screened in New York in 1972 and the fourth BBC series received a US transmission in 1973. Speight himself recalls an adventure he had in Hollywood when he flew out there to discuss a new project.[33] Being English, he decided to leave the Beverley Hills Hotel, where he was staying, and go for a stroll. He was staring in amazement at the opulence of the homes and the affluence of the area when, not surprisingly, he was stopped by two patrolling police officers who asked him, none too politely, what he the hell he thought he was doing. After a while, Speight told them he was the writer of *Till Death Us Do Part*, which he helpfully explained was called *All in the Family* over in America. Starstruck at the man 'who wrote Archie Bunker', the officers took him back to their precinct, where they treated him like royalty, getting him blind drunk in the process …

Speight enjoyed *All in the Family*, saying '[It is] the best American comedy show I've ever seen. The writers have gone as far as they can in the time spot.' The BBC actually screened some episodes of the show in 1971 and 1972 (see appendix), but it proved not particularly popular with British viewers, being generally seen as a lukewarm version of the original (which in essence it was, and indeed had to be in order to achieve longevity on US TV). *The Listener*'s review was fairly typical: 'Compared with Mr Speight's series, *All in the Family* trod softly round the sore points. No-one is rude to chummy black Lionel, and he gets a big hand when he goes out.' In the '70s, while US cop shows were

---

[33] This may have been in February 1974, *en route* to Australia, where he would have the aforementioned meeting with Mitchell.

popular on British TV, US sitcoms were rarely seen here, so their different style and approach were generally unfamiliar to the viewing public, and they were not appreciated to the extent that they would be in later years. Looked at today, *All in the Family* is a wonderful show, inventive, funny, brilliantly played and challenging, although, in common with its British counterpart, it has lost some of its impact due to the passage of time, Archie's rants about Spiro Agnew and Richard Nixon now seeming as remote as Alf's moans about Harold Wilson and Edward Heath. Like *Till Death Us Do Part*, it is now recalled mainly for its stance on race, as it too was criticised at the time for reinforcing racial bigotry rather than ridiculing it. However, *All in the Family* had the balance of *The Jeffersons* to counter such complaints, whereas *Till Death Us Do Part* had no equivalent.

An amusing encounter between the stars of the two shows occurred in 1979 when Thames TV was granted a two week time slot to showcase its programmes on Channel 9 WOR in New York. Producer Malcolm Morris, originator of the British version of *This Is Your Life*, was in charge of a nightly talk show hosted by Dick Cavett in London and Eamonn Andrews in New York. He decided on a three way link-up between film star Debbie Reynolds in the Big Apple, Warren Mitchell in London and Carroll O'Connor (promoting the *Archie Bunker's Place* spin-off) in Los Angeles. As Morris later recalled: 'Carroll O'Connor … did not take kindly to Warren sliding into his Alf Garnett persona and calling the American version [of *Till Death Us Do Part*] "a lot of bloody rubbish". Debbie Reynolds was incensed by Warrens' language and threatened to walk off the programme, while Carroll pretended his earpiece had failed and he couldn't hear anything. Eamonn in New York and Dick in London were having great difficulty controlling things, and the effect was exciting but chaotic'. In 1983, Una Stubbs and Sally Struthers got on a lot better when they met at the St James Club in London to talk about their memories of playing the daughters in their respective shows; the *Daily Mail* reported that there was lots of giggling as the two stars compared notes.

ONE HEART AND ONE SOUL

The success of *All in the Family* in turn fuelled two more foreign adaptations: a Brazilian version, *A Grande Família* (which translates as *The Big Family*), and a German version, *Ein Herz und eine Seele* (*One Heart and One Soul*).

The Portuguese-language *A Grande Família* ran from 26 October 1972 to 27 March 1975 on the Rede Globo channel and, like *All in the Family*, had an expanded cast of regular characters compared with *Till Death Us Do Part*. An impressive total of 112 episodes were made, almost all in black and white, with only the last few from March 1975 being in colour. Like its progenitors, it relied on social satire for much of its comedy, although the family here was more middle-class than working-class. A one-off reunion special was transmitted on 22 December 1987, but received a lukewarm reaction from the Brazilian public. Undaunted, Rede Globo launched a remake of the series with a new cast in 2001, which ran until 2006 and even spawned a spin-off movie, *A Grande Família – O Filme* (*The Big Family – The Movie*), which premiered on 10 January 2007.

Ein Herz und eine Seele was written by Wolfgang Menge and featured actors from the Brecht Ensemble. The first (irregular) series, beginning in January 1973, consisted of 21 episodes, the first 11 of which were broadcast in black and white on the regional third channel of the North Rhine-Westphalia area and the remainder, from New Year's Eve 1973 onwards, in colour on West Germany's first channel, ARD (with three of the colour episodes being remakes of black and white ones). Alf became 'Ekel' Alfred Tetzlaff, played by Heinz Schubert in make-up that caused him to resemble Adolf Hitler, while the other three family members retained their original names, Else, Michael (not abbreviated in this case) and Rita. Alfred is just as objectionable as his British counterpart, frequently calling Else 'dusselige Kuh', literally 'silly cow', and making acerbic reference to his country's troubled '70s politics. The series proved to be a big hit, drawing up to 15.7 million viewers each week. Two episodes in particular, 'Sylvesterpunsch', about the family's New Year's Eve party, and 'Rosenmontagszug', set during the winter carnival season, gained such popularity that they are still traditionally repeated on German TV on New Year's Eve and Mardi Gras respectively. Rumour has it that the show's discontinuation in 1974 was due to pressure from Willy Brandt, the German Chancellor. A second series was eventually mounted in 1976, but was cancelled after only four episodes, probably due to public disapproval of two changes in the lead cast: Elisabeth Wiedemann, who had been extremely popular in the role of Else Tetzlaff, had been replaced by Helga Feddersen, and Diether Krebs, who had portrayed Michael, had been succeeded by Klaus Dahlen. Nevertheless, a 2002 survey found that *Ein Herz und eine Seele* was Germany's most popular sitcom of all time.

Despite this success in Brazil and Germany, it was unquestionably in the USA that Speight's creation had thundered most effectively, in the form of *All in the Family*; and this was to be, ironically, a major contributory factor leading to the return of *Till Death Us Do Part* to BBC One.

18
The Return of the Native

A RECONCILIATION

Aware of *All in the Family's* success Stateside, the BBC arranged to screen some episodes of it at the end of May 1971. On learning of this, the ever-loyal Dennis Main Wilson wrote to Duncan Wood, then acting Head of Light Entertainment, suggesting that there should be some further repeats of *Till Death Us Do Part* as well, perhaps accompanied by a major documentary on Johnny Speight, to act as an extensive trailer. Wood replied a month later that the BBC One Controller was very interested. Although the idea ultimately came to nothing – a memo of 28 May records that a rescheduling of the *All in the Family* transmissions, which eventually began on 8 July 1971, meant that a repeat of *Till Death Us Do Part* would no longer be needed (and it is unclear, in any event, how many episodes from the first three series still existed in the BBC's archives at that point) – this gradually led on to discussions about the possibility of producing a new *Till Death Us Do Part* series.

It is quite probable that the BBC had already considered the idea of resurrecting the show. At the end of the '60s, the Corporation had seen their comedy output decline in popularity as ITV launched a barrage of massive working-class sitcom hits – *Please Sir!*, *On the Buses*, *The Dustbinmen*, *The Lovers*, *For the Love of Ada*, *Never Mind the Quality, Feel the Width*, and so on. In terms of originality, the Beeb were by 1970 lagging well behind, and from this point on, they decided to revive a number of their '60s triumphs, beginning with *Steptoe and Son* in 1970, followed by *Sykes*, a sequel to *The Likely Lads* in the form of *Whatever Happened to the Likely Lads?*, and the biggest success of all, *Till Death Us Do Part*. By September 1971, knowing that Speight had already been commissioned by Ned Sherrin to write a second Garnett film, they carefully suggested that they might be interested in a new series. At first, a nervous Michael Mills offered a contract for only one script, which, if approved, might lead to the commissioning of five more. ALS agent Beryl Vertue dismissed this overture as insulting, but the BBC were prepared to be flexible, and agreed to the possibility of a short series.

Wilson wrote to Mills and Wood in October emphasising that Speight was very excited and already working on the first script, and that they would be meeting the following week to discuss episodes two and three. He proffered an April 1972 target for delivery of the scripts, but also suggested that they keep this to themselves, because if Speight found out about the target date and learned that the BBC had started to book actors for the show, he would 'become disheartened'. Mills, mindful of the events of almost four years before, responded by declaring that nothing would be considered viable until at least three scripts were in their hands, this time sending copies of his missive to the Head of Copyright and to Beryl Vertue. In December 1971, it was agreed that Speight would supply six scripts at £1,000 each, with a view to production in April and May 1972, with the last three scripts to be in the BBC's hands by 16 April. Predictably, this was to prove rather too hopeful.

Meanwhile, for a fee of £350, Speight provided a script for a short *Till Death Us Do Part* sketch to be included in the 1971 *Christmas Night With the Stars* extravaganza, this time to be produced by Duncan Wood since Dennis Main Wilson was too busy on other projects. This was just one of a number of sketches from top BBC sitcoms planned for inclusion in the programme, although illness on Wilfrid Brambell's part forced cancellation of the *Steptoe and Son* one due to be recorded on 12 December. The unavailability of both Tony Booth – who was currently appearing on the London stage in Kenneth Tynan's *Oh! Calcutta!* at the Roundhouse – and Una Stubbs – who was pregnant – meant that only Warren Mitchell and Dandy Nichols were engaged to appear, for a fee of £100 each. The sketch – the first *Till Death Us Do Part* to be made in colour (leaving aside the movies) – proved to be a splendid one, focusing on the elder Garnetts waiting to hear from their lovely daughter about the forthcoming birth of her child, with Alf anxious for it to be born on Christmas Day so that he can receive a telegram from the Queen.

Duncan Wood was very pleased with this, writing to Speight on 6 January to suggest a revised June 1972 date for the start of recording for the six episodes of series four, and stating it was essential they had three scripts by the end of February: 'You proved quite conclusively on Christmas Night just how good the show can still be and just how much mileage there is to come from it. The BBC will make every effort to transmit shows as close as possible to the recording date (5 days at moment) … [and you can] insert topical material in the last three [scripts] later on …'

Speight was indeed very enthused by the prospect of the new series, ringing up Wilson and swapping ideas. A memo from Wilson setting out just exactly what had been suggested for the series exists, dated 14 February and denoted in list form:

DMW TO JS RE PHONE, 14th February 1972:

1 .Women's Lib: Women Are Better Than Men: Dandy quotes the Queen – this inspires a dream sequence, with Dandy as Victoria and with Sean Connery or Roger Moore as gamekeeper, while Alf appears as Prince Garnett whom she treats like dirt.

2. 10 Commandments. Garnett proves modern younger generation are breaking each and every one, e.g. adultery, 'They can't cos they're all poofs'; this would give the show 10 strong gags.

3. Royal Family and Prince Charles who watches West Ham every Saturday just as his uncle, the Duke Of Windsor, had done, as a season ticket holder; Princess Anne, notes Garnett, was 'Born to rule, like her brother', and there is a discussion equating show jumper Harvey Smith's famous 'V' signs to Churchill's.

4. New baby's face, 'Like all new born babies, it looks like wrinkled Yiddisher prune' – more doubts about Alf's ancestry are roused; milkman gag line – Yiddisher nose – grow into it; Garnett thinks most coloured people are Jewish; Mike declares Jesus was Jewish; Garnett counters, 'Yeah, on his mom's side'.

5. re Bible? Women's Lib: Adam's rib proves women not equal to men; they discuss how sex started; Alf dislikes sex for being evil and promiscuous.

6. Semitism: ITA is mainly Jewish also; *TV Times*, Eamonn O'Cohen, Hughie Greenbaum.

7. USA does better in Olympics than we do because 'we flog them all our coons'.

8. Garnett is discovered to be of Scottish blood.

9. Christening in church ends in drunken brawl; Cyril Cusack stars as Anthony Booth's dad, Dermot Kelly as the priest; he insists all English are mongrels and that the only true original Britons were Celts. Garnett: Well, I'm a Celt aren't I? Booth: A Jewish Celt.

Wilson promised to send details on current politicians to Speight, together with national statistics on wages and unemployment, and – for a planned sequence involving John Le Mesurier[34] – details of the cost of borrowing money from a bank. He added that he would see Speight at the West Ham match on Monday (meaning 14 February 1972, when West Ham beat Hereford by three goals to one, which implies that he must have drafted his memo a short while before it was dated). He goes on to say that the notion concerning Harvey Smith and Churchill 'got nowhere' and warns that another idea, discussed in an earlier conversation, concerning the flamboyant, luxuriously-moustachioed MP Gerald Nabarro and his recent conviction for dangerous driving (for which he was fined the enormous sum of £1,000) might be controversial, since some MP could bring it up. He suggested instead using his own proposed theme regarding Alf and Else watching *Upstairs,*

---

[34] It may have been the intention that Le Mesurier should reprise his bank manager role from the then forthcoming, but already shot, second movie, *The Alf Garnett Saga*.

Downstairs and being nostalgic because:

a. everyone knew their place in those days
b. I am sure people feel more secure when they know their place in society, wrong though that may be
c. community feeling downstairs – security
d. set up/fits in with their ingrained inverted snobbery
e. life in those days uncomplicated, uncluttered and so [everyone earned] 'a fair day's work for a fair day's pay'
f. everyone had to believe in God
g. everyone had opportunity to learn good manners from their betters.

In other words there is some gorgeous material with which to lampoon that plodding Victorian liberalism that has held this country back for the last 70 years.

Some of these ideas were to resurface in the show, although the Nabarro gag was dropped, and Connery and Moore were mysteriously unavailable for the Victorian spoof, which was also discarded. Notably, at no point in Wilson's memo is the possibility that Booth might not want to return to the show even considered, and nor is any mention made of Stubbs' role.

Speight fell ill during March 1972 and this led to more negotiations, Wood suggesting in a memo of 9 March that the writer's failure to deliver one script by the end of February meant that the BBC would consider giving him no fees until he resumed progress. On 18 April, Wood noted 'Casting of the [Una Stubbs and Tony Booth] parts to be immediately discussed by [Dennis Main Wilson] and [Johnny Speight]', as he presumed that both Mitchell and Nichols had agreed to reprise their roles. The Head of Copyright wrote to Vertue two days later to confirm that the series of six episodes would be ready for production between 27 July and 31 August. A Christmas special was also mentioned.

But it was not all plain sailing as yet. At the end of May, the question of Booth's participation was again raised by Wood in a memo to Wilson. It had by this point been confirmed that Stubbs was available to appear, but Booth had been unswayed by Wilson's attempts to persuade him to return to the fold.[35] Mitchell believed that for the show to work, Booth's participation was essential, so in June 1972 he attended a performance of *Oh! Calcutta!* and sent his old enemy a handwritten note: 'Enjoying the show. Like to see you for a

---

[35] It is tempting to wonder if any consideration was given to asking Paul Angelis, who had played Mike in the recently-completed movie, *The Alf Garnett Saga*, to take over the role in the series as well, but there is no indication to this effect in the surviving documentation.

drink or possibly a meal afterwards. Then we can talk. Warren Mitchell.' Mitchell came backstage at the end of the performance, shook hands with the cast and then took Booth out to dinner. Knowing he had at least six more months to run in *Oh! Calcutta!*, and fortified by a supply of brandies provided by his host, Booth prepared to tell Mitchell why he would never return to *Till Death Us Do Part*. When Mitchell broached the subject, Booth, according to his later recollection (and there may be a *soupcon* of tailored hindsight here), said, 'We can't work together, Warren, I'm sorry; and I don't like my part, because I feel that Johnny has no sympathy for the young or for women. At first I thought the show was attacking the bigoted ideas of Alf Garnett, but now it has become a vehicle for expressing those ideas. Even I was fooled at the beginning, but what seemed to be a revolutionary left-wing show is really subversive right-wing propaganda.' Mitchell indicated that the BBC might be prepared to offer more money, but Booth said he didn't need it; he was working and didn't want any of the hassle. Then Mitchell said he would plead for him to return to the show, and – to Booth's complete surprise – suddenly went straight into Alf Garnett mode, crying out so that the entire restaurant could hear him: 'Because you are the only fucker in the world that I've just got to look at and I lose my mind, don't I? You drive me crazy. I hate everything about you. I hate everything you stand for. I hate your ideas. I hate what you say. I hate the way you look. That's why you've got to be in the show. Without you, I can't play the part. As soon as I walk in and see you, I'm there, aren't I?' Flattered and amused, Booth finally accepted.

It was now June 1972 and all the pieces were in place: the production dates had been set, the four original leads had all agreed to return – Mitchell for £913 per episode, Nichols for £779, Booth for £337 and Stubbs for £315 – and Speight had written the scripts – although a sarcastic note from Dennis Main Wilson's assistant reveals that there had been the usual problems with late delivery: 'As it is expected that the script will not be ready for printing until lunchtime on Saturday, the day before recording, I should be obliged if you could let me know if arrangements can be made for overtime on these days in order that the script may be run off.'

The Garnetts were now ready to face the world again – but could the world face the Garnetts?

IF YOU WANT A DEMOCRACY …

Pre-filming for the fourth series of *Till Death Us Do Part* took place in Northwood, Euston, Bournemouth and Liverpool in mid-July 1972, and studio recordings began at the end of that month. As before, Wilson found his multiple responsibilities of producing, directing and perfecting the scripts a source of anxiety and frustration. David Croft recalls that he was with Billy Cotton, Head of Light Entertainment, when Wilson phoned to inform his boss of his troubles, which prompted Cotton to give the go-ahead to Croft's proposed new comedy series, *Are You Being Served?*. Production assistant Geoff Jowitt proved so invaluable that Wilson wanted to give him a credit of 'Assistant to the Producer', but the BBC refused.

The intended second episode, 'Up The 'Ammers', encountered unknown production difficulties and was postponed to become the fifth, while Wilson's attempts to refurbish the series' 1968 title sequence by electronically tinting it sepia proved so expensive that ultimately new opening and closing titles were created instead; these were filmed on 30 August at a multi-storey block of flats, 79 Bow Sprit, West Ferry Road, London E14, a camera crew capturing shots of the Thames, St Paul's and Tower Bridge from the balcony of a flat belonging to a Mrs Hazell, who received the BBC's flat fee of £10 in recompense.[36] On 20 September, Wilson complained that he found editing the titles on the BBC's new computer system extremely problematic. 'The Bird Fancier' now moved up to second in the running order to give it extra topicality – so important to Speight – as it would be transmitted the day after the end of the pigeon racing season!

While the series was in production, Colin Strong directed a documentary on Speight, featuring Wilson and other luminaries, to form a *Late Night Line-Up* special. This was transmitted on 15 September 1972, two days after the series' first episode, and proved most illuminating. The 45-minute special centred around a very effective, characteristically honest interview with Speight talking about his early life as well as his ideas on society, interspersed with contributions from Eric Sykes, Wilson and longstanding Garnett champion George Melly, together with well-chosen clips from 'Peace and Goodwill', 'Sex Before Marriage', 'A Wapping Mythology', 'The Blood Donor' and 'Aunt Maud'. Wilson subsequently praised Strong's work in a memo to Duncan Wood and Bill Cotton, describing it as an 'excellent documentary, extremely well conceived and superbly directed and … one of the best entertainment documentaries I have seen … The clips of *Till Death Us Do Part* [have] stood the test of time.' Indeed, so impressed was Wilson that he would later ask Strong to direct the final two series of *Till Death Us Do Part* in 1974/75.

The Controller of BBC One himself, Paul Fox, viewed two of the fourth series episodes before they were transmitted. He noted that the first, 'To Garnett a Grandson', was 'very funny and that everything concerned with the programme was well up to standard'. Nonetheless, he ordered a 50% cut in a breastfeeding sequence in a hospital ward, and ordered that a line

---

[36] The sepia-tinted version of the original title sequence appears on some copies of 'The Bird Fancier', including the one still extant in the BBC archives, which also contains extra studio footage.

referring to David Frost living with the American actress and singer Diahann Carroll be taken out. 'Up The 'Ammers!' he saw as 'not as strong', but 'funny and well done', although he asked Wilson to cut by 50% a sequence of Rita having histrionics outside a supermarket when she finds that her baby has vanished. 'The only reason for asking for this cut,' he explained, 'is that [Stubbs'] performance is so good that it becomes extremely harrowing and it will take people some time to readjust themselves to comedy after this experience'. And of the episode's tagline, he commented: 'We are going to take a chance on [this] … We [will be] lucky to get away with "Piss off" said flat out like this. However it is a belter and we will keep it'. He congratulated Wilson on keeping up the standard, but warned him not to over record so much that major VT editing became necessary; this he said was not so apparent in the second programme but marred the first, which 'lacked a flow which was obviously due to the amount of cutting involved'.

Wilson was to suffer further problems during production of the fourth series, right up to the close, including studio overruns and various disasters recording the final episode. These disasters he attributed, in a 12 September reply to his boss, to the '… ever-increasing complexity of Johnny Speight's scripts. In the olden days, it was comparatively straightforward to work his dialogue in a living room or a pub – make a couple of dress run-throughs, do the show and be out of the studio with half an hour to spare. Now, however, his dialogue has become increasingly complex and his construction ditto.' As an example he cited the episode recorded on 27 August – 'Women's Lib and Bournemouth' – as having 12 separate scenes, with six recording breaks for set and wardrobe changes. He continued: 'Johnny Speight and I envy shows that get two days in the studio with less than half the complications.'

Pre-empting the Garnetts' small-screen return by a few weeks, however, was their second cinematic feature …

19
Alfie Takes a Trip

IS THIS CONCRETE ALL AROUND OR IS IT IN MY HEAD?

'He's Back!' promised the posters for the second Garnett film. *The Alf Garnett Saga* – originally billed in the UK as simply *The Garnett Saga* – premiered in cinemas at the end of August 1972 and went on general release on 2 September, the Saturday prior to the launch of the first television series in almost five years. Produced by Ned Sherrin, directed by Bob Kellett and scripted – naturally – by Johnny Speight, it had been filmed in October 1971 at Wapping, Plaistow, West Ham, Leytonstone and Elstree. The lengthy delay between production and presentation to the public may indicate a deliberate policy of synchronising its release with the much-trumpeted small-screen comeback.

Till Death Us Do Part had previously pioneered that peculiar surge in British film of transforming hit TV shows into movies for the home market (see Chapter Fifteen), as capitalised on by the tremendously successful *On the Buses* from Hammer, as well as *Dad's Army*, *Steptoe and Son*, *Please Sir!* and a host of others. In general, these were coarsened treatments of the originals, using the freer approach to sex and swearing in cinemas to exaggerate the less intellectual elements of the shows. *Till Death Us Do Part*, perhaps because it had been the progenitor, had not adopted this tactic quite so much, and had proved a polished and worthy addition to the canon of sitcoms adapted for the big screen. It had gained favourable reviews and excellent box office takings, and had been an entertaining, if flawed, attempt at preserving Alf on celluloid. *The Alf Garnett Saga* was another kettle of fish entirely.

The story sees the Garnetts still ensconced at the summit of the residential tower block to which they relocated at the close of the first movie. Whereas the latter had evoked nostalgia for a world lost, this time Speight chose to focus on the new and challenging era of the 1970s. Thus we see life in that decade in all its plastic tawdriness, with issues raised including the diffusion of communities due to resettlement and rebuilding, the dire political situation, even the physical problems of transport. Now Alf has to take the bus and train to work, whereas once he lived close enough to walk; now 'going down the pub' means going down many flights of stairs and traipsing half a mile to a hostelry devoid of character; now life consists of power cuts, sex, drugs and rock and roll for the young, and more power cuts and a world of endless dreariness for the older generation.

The freedom on celluloid to use whatever swear words he liked allowed Speight to include a sequence in which Alf and his docker friend Wally (played by Roy Kinnear, also to feature in the new TV series as the semi-regular character Sid) simply shout 'Bollocks!' at each other for several minutes for no apparent reason. Speight's old Arthur Haynes story of a tramp getting into his Rolls Royce and treating it as if it were his own is recalled in a scene in which Alf and his bank manager neighbour, played by the always-dependable John Le Mesurier, are invited into a Rolls belonging to Rita's wealthy pop star 'friend', played by Kenny Lynch. At one point, Alf even has an LSD trip.

Paul Madden, writing in *Films and Filming*, began his review by remarking that this movie was 'equally unsuccessful' as its 1968 predecessor in effectively emulating the triumphs of the original TV series. While conceding that Alf Garnett was a marvellous, larger-than-life comic creation, he commented that *The Alf Garnett Saga*'s 'varied locations ... do not prevent [it] from seeming one long repetitive and unfunny diatribe, occasionally broken up by some irrelevant scenes apparently tacked on as an afterthought'; as examples, he cites a sequence set at a West Ham match; Alf's LSD trip, the presentation of which he describes as 'gauche'; and the closing scenes involving a bedroom fire. He concludes: 'Johnny Speight's script only occasionally rises above the crudity of its protagonist.'

Apart from the snapshot it offers of life in a sink estate circa 1971 – take the flares and groovy music away and it could be the present day – the movie is an unpalatable mess. For one thing, it is laugh-free – even a typical Else monologue and the sight of Alf on a psychedelic trip fail to evoke a titter. Then, two integral cast members are notable by their absence – Rita is played here by Speight's Northwood neighbour Adrienne Posta because Una Stubbs was having a baby at the time, while Mike is played by Paul Angelis because of Anthony Booth's stage commitments and inability to get on with Warren Mitchell. Posta and Angelis both give good performances, but their characters are so different from those of their TV counterparts and so badly thought-out – Mike is a racist, immoral, hypocritical womaniser, and Rita shows more of the characteristics of Milly, the prostitute later played by Posta in the 'Party Night' episode of the fifth series of *Till Death Us Do Part*, than the delightful Stubbs prototype – that they add none of the distinctive humour of the originals. Speight's script takes his disregard of structure to the *n*th degree; the narrative staggers along without any thought for development, and interesting ideas such as the bank manager's rather kinky domestic control-freakery with his eager-to-please wife are introduced, only to fall by the wayside. Gran appears for a repeat of a gin-soaked-sandwich routine previously used in 'Up The Polls! (The

Campaign's Over)' and then vanishes. The production is little better. There are some obvious continuity lapses – the headline on Alf's copy of the *Daily Mirror* changes between shots – and the film ends abruptly, as if the money had simply run out.

Perhaps one should not have expected anything else: after all, if someone like Ned Sherrin had offered you the chance to write a film in which you could include guest appearances by all your mates (which in Speight's case included showbiz stalwarts Arthur Askey, Max Bygraves, Kenny Lynch, Bobby Moore and George Best), and in which you could even make a cameo yourself (Speight features as Barmy Harry, complete with the same beard he was to be seen sporting in drunken conversations with Dennis Main Wilson and actor James Booth in the *Late Night Line-Up* special), wouldn't you end up with a tenth-rate home movie like *The Alf Garnett Saga*? As it is, the movie is nasty, brutish and (thankfully) short, the polar opposite of its cinematic predecessor, and adds nothing to Speight's reputation as a writer.

20
Series Four

TAKING THE MICHAEL

The disastrous lapse in quality that had characterised the second movie was thankfully not apparent when the fourth series of *Till Death Us Do Part* began on Wednesday 13 September 1972, at the decidedly adult-viewing time of 9.20 pm. As Wednesday was the traditional midweek slot for *Sportsnight*, the BBC's round-up of the latest sporting events, which tended to concentrate heavily on football, this recalled the idea of linking Speight's working-class sitcom with coverage of 'the beautiful game', as in the run-up to the World Cup in 1966; it was to remain the show's regular transmission slot, with a few exceptions, for the rest of its life. The start of the new series was heralded by a full colour *Radio Times* cover depicting a christening scene inspired by (but not actually featured in) the opening episode, 'To Garnett, a Grandson', supported by an article on Garnett's creator and the first of a series of excellent little comic strips to advertise the show in its new place in the schedules. For the article, Speight was interviewed at his Northwood home with his wife Connie and children Samantha, Richard and Francis, and shown in colour photographs posing with his parents John and Joanna, both aged 81, and his Rolls Royce, bearing the number plate 'MOO 16'. Again, he denied that Alf Garnett was ever based on his father.

The new series resonated with several of the elements and ideas that had helped to propel *Till Death Us Do Part* to success in the '60s. Apart from the four returning leads, there were references made to previous episodes, both specifically – as when Mike and Rita remember that Alf thought Stalin was an American spy, an incident in 'Two Toilets – That's Posh' – and more generally, with the inclusion of a holiday escapade, recalling 'Claustrophobia', and, in the closing episode, a reprise of the memorable face-painting scenes from 'Hair Raising!' and the equally popular depiction of Alf as a helpless patient as in 'In Sickness and in Health'. There were some obvious differences, too. While all the key features of the Garnett living room (flying ducks, aspidistra, silver caravels) were still in place, the house looked less shabby in colour than it had in glorious black and white. Now, too, there was an extra Garnett for the family to look after; and not only did the stories depict the exhausting effect that baby Michael had on his mother Rita, but there were also some frantic 'squealing baby' sounds added over the closing titles.

The four stars were as superb as ever, with some joyous Else moments from Dandy Nichols, the usual towering performance from Warren Mitchell and some juicy lines expertly delivered by Tony Booth. Most pleasing of all, for the excellent, always underrated Una Stubbs, there was more to do for Rita, with some wonderful material including a harrowing sequence in 'Up the 'Ammers' where she finds her baby has been abducted. Rita takes on a real sense of maternal weariness as she finds that she now has to cope with not one but two infantile Michaels; and her marriage to Mike is cleverly shown to be heading toward the same combination of ennui, lassitude and subdued anger to which her parents' has long since descended.

There were some changes amongst the supporting cast for this series. While Will Stampe returned as Fred the landlord, Bert was now played (as in the first film) by Bill Maynard and given a much bigger role, while Roy Kinnear (who appeared as an abusive lorry driver in one episode of the second series and as Wally the dockhand in the second film) became the semi-regular Sid, Alf's colleague at the docks. Gran, played by Joan Sims, returned, and was a far more prominent presence than in her two initial appearances in the '60s. George, played by George Tovey, was another new occasional character, and would appear sporadically for the remainder of the series' lifetime. Speight found two acting spots for his son Richard, and one for his friend Spike Milligan; and Mitchell's old associate Arnold Diamond made another brief appearance, as did Cleo Sylvestre.

Of course, the broadcasting environment had also changed since the 1960s. Swearing, sex and violence were now more commonplace on TV. Nevertheless, Mrs Whitehouse was still around and ready to monitor the 'bloodies', which, despite statements to the contrary, had if anything increased.

Finally, the political situation in Britain had been transformed as well, with the surprise election of Ted Heath's Conservative government in June 1970. The political and social strife that had originated in those heady days of the '60s was now threatening to bring the country to a halt; the public were becoming increasingly politicised, too, and this had to be reflected in *Till Death Us Do Part*. In January 1972, there was a miners' strike; in February a state of emergency was declared because of the power cuts necessitated by the strike, which amongst other things meant that the use of football ground floodlights was banned, as was all neon advertising, causing the distinctive hoardings of Piccadilly Circus to be switched off for the first time since the War; and in April there was a work-to-rule on British Rail. The government's new Industrial Relations Act fanned the flames, provoking hostility from the railwaymen in June and leading to the arrest and imprisonment of five dockers who refused to stop 'blacking' lorries crossing picket lines at Hackney container depots. Less than a week later, the dockers were released as the House of Lords declared that the Transport and General Workers Union should be responsible for the actions of its members and fined it £55,000. Because such a fine had already been quashed by the Appeal Court in June, the move by the Lords was seen as provocative, and the day after, a national dockers' strike was called, which did not end until 20 August. On the international scene, the biggest story was the murderous Idi Amin's expulsion from Uganda of 20,000 British Asians, the first of whom arrived at London's Stansted Airport on 8 September 1972. All these events were used by Speight as a steady supply of fuel for the Garnetts' family arguments, restoring the image of *Till Death Us Do Part* as a satirical piece, loaded with social and political comment.

The BBC had heavily publicised the return of its golden-egg-laying goose, not only with the aforementioned *Radio Times* cover feature but also with the *Late Night Line-Up* special devoted to Speight. The results were spectacular: the show instantly became the most watched in Britain, with typical audiences of 16 million, boosting the BBC's standing in the rating's war and contributing to the second-worst autumn season in ITV's history, with *Coronation Street* again plunging down the league table. Even ITV's own JICTAR ratings[37] suggested that eight million homes, equating to 17.5 million people, had tuned in for the third episode, 'Women's Lib and Bournemouth'. *Till Death Us Do Part* had become the most-watched BBC comedy programme in two years, eclipsing other contemporaries such as *Sykes* (11 million viewers), *The Two Ronnies* (11.5 million) and new shows such as *My Wife Next Door*. At one point, Dennis Main Wilson was claiming that its audience actually exceeded 24 million people.

As emphasised by *Late Night Line-Up*'s Speight profile, the show remained not only a popular success but also a critical one, although it soon became apparent that its more trenchant supporters were less visible than previously. One journalist welcomed the return: 'As foul-mouthed and racist, ignorant and intolerant as ever, Alf Garnett re-erupted on BBC One like some eternal Colonel Bogeyman. Doubts whether the parting had been too long proved as groundless as Alf's own arguments on royalty, and politicians, West Ham and Ireland. The years might never have passed.' Others, however, begged to differ: 'Even Alf Garnett is back in a din of invective and crude language. His return is akin to a derisive gesture to NVLA's handwringing. Frankly, although he has been back but a week, I find Alf a grotesque bore … He has said it all, and there comes a time when mindless bigotry personified as a figure of fun merely gets on your nerves …

---

[37] JICTAR – standing for Joint Industry Committee for Television Advertising Research – was the system used by ITV to estimate numbers of homes viewing a particular programme; it often gave different results from the BBC's essentially competing system.

In short, ignorance is no longer bliss.'

After the studio recording of the second episode, Warren Mitchell brought a visitor, the wife of a famous rock star, to Anthony Booth's dressing room. The lady invited them both to return to her place for dinner, explaining that she was a big fan of the show. Booth declined, but Mitchell accepted. For the next few weeks, the lady appeared at each recording, and on the fifth week, when Mitchell accompanied her back to her place in Fulham, he wore his costume from the show: he had finally agreed to indulge her repeatedly-expressed wish to dine with yer actual Alf Garnett. Then came the payoff: she asked him to make love to her in her lounge. While he was momentarily speechless, she kissed him and then asked him to move to one side, explaining that she had videotaped the dinner and now wanted to record herself making love to her dream date, Alf Garnett ... Mitchell ran out of the pad as fast as he could ...

JOHNNY AND MARY

BBC Controller Paul Fox had not reviewed 'The Pigeon Fancier' – the episode hurriedly slotted in in place of 'Up The 'Ammers!' as the second in the series' running order – prior to its transmission, and this reduction in editorial scrutiny may well have contributed to another very public burst of controversy. From out of the blue, this episode saw the show becoming embroiled in a media frenzy on a scale approaching those it had sparked in the '60s. Indeed, it seems that Mrs Mary Whitehouse, who last featured in our story threatening to sue Speight and the BBC for blasphemy four-and-a-half years earlier, had merely suspended her threat like the sword of Damocles only to unleash it again when Speight played right into her hands.

The trouble derived from a few lines early in the episode when the family discuss how Jesus was conceived and Mike suggests that the Virgin Mary might subsequently have been 'on the pill'. Whitehouse wrote immediately to Sir John Eden, Minister of Post and Telecommunications:

> During the course of Wednesday night's episode of *Till Death Us Do Part* there was a conversation between the characters about the birth of Jesus Christ. The general trend was as follows: Mary could not have been a virgin as God was the father of her son, and the characters wondered how 'they (up there) did it'. Did they 'do it' like we do? And why had Mary conceived only one child? Was it because she was 'on the pill'? I hope you will agree that such talk was not only obscenely blasphemous, but a calculated offence to a great many viewers. It is abundantly obvious that the present Governors are unable, or unwilling, to effectively fulfil their role as 'trustees' of the

public interest, and the need for someone capable of dealing with recalcitrant writers and producers becomes ever more urgent.

Similar letters were despatched to Archbishop Ramsey of Canterbury (himself lampooned in the show when Else confuses him with Alf Ramsey, manager of the England football team – whose name Speight had originally used for his show's lead character), to Cardinal Heenan (whom Speight's mother knew from her church activities and who said he admired Speight) and, inevitably, to Lord Hill, still Chairman of the BBC.

Dennis Main Wilson was ordered to make strategic cuts in 'The Pigeon Fancier' in case of repeats or overseas sales, although it is uncertain whether or not he actually did so; certainly the lines in question are still present in the BBC's master tape. On 26 September 1972, he sent the following memo to Head of Light Entertainment Bill Cotton, Duncan Wood and the Head of Legal Affairs, Television:

> To please 16 million people is an extremely difficult task. To please every one of the 16 million people with a programme that sets out to reflect accurately the bigotry, the prejudices, the illiberalism and the violence that pervade the world today must surely be an impossibility. Nevertheless, we try – very hard. It is most certainly not the intention of Johnny Speight to offend for the sake of offence, nor to be outrageous purely for the sake of it.

Hill then replied to Whitehouse on 2 October:

> As I am sure you will recognise, this programme draws its humour from the dreadful behaviour of its central character, Alf Garnett, and the extreme way in which he expresses his extraordinary views. The writer and producer believe that in allowing such a character to express his opinions, they are ridiculing them both, and that laughter provoked in this way can be as powerful an influence as a sermon. Certainly there is no question but that immense numbers of people of all kinds and opinions find this character hugely funny. Although Garnett dominates the programme, his son-in-law is also in many ways a similar figure, expressing equally absurd views, although this time characterising the thoughtless attitudes of trendy, feckless youth. The audience at large, I am sure, recognises the basis of this comedy. Furthermore, the programme is so well known that it is difficult to suppose that many, if any, will turn it on without a clear idea of the kind of language and opinion that they will hear. I am sure you will have seen that according to the JICTAR figures, quite apart from our own, the programme was the most popular of any last week. The

nature of this programme, of course, means that it must be operating on the very edge of what is acceptable. As we all know, different people will make different decisions in this area. You will know, I am sure, that these programmes are looked at with care and cuts are made in them. In this particular instance, I sympathise very much with what you write. Senior people in the Television Service believe that the inclusion of this short passage was a mistake. I am particularly sorry that in the event it offended a number of viewers who have written to us since.

The 'senior people' were believed to be such luminaries as Bill Cotton; Huw Wheldon, Managing Director of BBC TV; David Attenborough, Director of Programmes; and Paul Fox, Controller for BBC One.

This reply from Hill, which came just prior to Whitehouse receiving news from the Director of Public Prosecutions that she was entitled to take private proceedings against the Corporation for blasphemy if she wished, generated enormous interest in the media, evoking such front page headlines as 'Lord Hill says sorry to Mary' and 'BBC sorry for Garnett's blasphemy'. The cartoonist Giles drew a scene of Hill genuflecting before Whitehouse, who was seated on a throne, broomstick in hand and wire halo over her head, with the caption: 'I, Lord Hill, do promise Mary, never to allow the pornographic Old Testament to be heard on BBC religious programmes.'

As usual, the fracas must be seen in context. Whitehouse's struggle with the BBC had been at a high pitch throughout 1972. There had already been criticism of the radio broadcast of the Rolling Stones' scurrilous *Exile on Main Street* numbers in July – although in that case Hill had replied: 'Could it be that, believing offending words to be there and zealous to discover them, you imagined that you heard what you did not hear?' Then there was the BBC's decision to transmit Chuck Berry's cheeky single 'My Ding-a-Ling' on Radio 1, after which it soon reached the top of the charts. In November, Whitehouse would write again to Sir John Eden, demanding that he 'decide whether [or not] it is, as we believe, a gross violation of the public duty of the BBC to include [Berry's song] on *Top of the Pops*.' In August, the Beeb had even pulled the transmission of an episode of sci-fi drama *Doomwatch*, delightfully entitled 'Sex and Violence', ostensibly for its inclusion of real news footage of a firing squad in action, but possibly because June Brown had portrayed such a blatantly obvious caricature of Whitehouse that they had feared action for libel. And it was not only Whitehouse who had been behind the recent resurgence in the battle against permissiveness. There had also been the Lord Longford Report on Pornography, which had recommended the establishment of a viewers' council to screen any naughty programmes before they hit the airwaves (a proposal that the BBC had rejected, having announced that they had already set one up themselves), and criticism from another monitoring group that sitcoms such as *Steptoe and Son* and *Up Pompeii!* were 'full of smut, vulgarity and double meaning'.

Satisfied with Lord Hill's public apology over 'The Pigeon Fancier', Whitehouse stated that she would intervene again only if such blasphemies continued through the whole series, adding in the *Guardian* that if Speight couldn't write without giving calculated offence, he should stop writing …

Lord Hill's very prominent and public apology was viewed by many as a massive climb-down by the BBC in their stance over permissiveness, as well as an abrogation of their freedom and independence to broadcast programmes with whatever content they wished. Speight, predictably, was apoplectic, and refuse to write any further scripts. 'If I'm going to have Mary Whitehouse looking over my shoulder … For a long time she was a joke, but she's not a joke any more. My suggestion is that she should go into church when the show starts, light a candle and pray for me, the cast and the BBC'. Equally characteristically, during a 7 October interview, he gleefully promised further shocks to come in the series, including Garnett ruminating on God being a Tory rather than a socialist, Mike challenging God to strike him dead within ten seconds and Alf's insistence that the Duke of Windsor was a West Ham supporter who would have sold the Crown Jewels for his team … 'It will be interesting to see what the BBC does,' noted the writer. 'By Mrs Whitehouse standards, these bits are either blasphemous or in disgustingly bad taste.'

Warren Mitchell was similarly angry: 'I think that the people who find the programme offensive are themselves offensive people and regard themselves as better people. I find it terribly offensive that we are expected to take religion seriously …'

Later, on 25 October, Mitchell and Speight met Whitehouse for an *in camera* debate on the subject, during which Mitchell apparently said to her: 'Part of Johnny's brilliance is that he can ally a bigot like Alf with a bigot like you. You're both the same'. The actor also dismissed Lord Hill's reply: 'If Lord Hill were to take the trouble to canvas the views of his audience, he would find that the majority would disagree with his apology – in fact, they would be incensed by it.' Even Dandy Nichols was drawn into the controversy, saying that Whitehouse represented a minority and that, while she herself might have been offended if she had been religious, she would have simply turned the television off. Speight received some hate mail, warning him that he would 'get his teeth kicked in' and would 'die very soon', and that God was waiting to inflict punishment on him. He was quoted by Aldo Nicolotti in the *Evening News* on 12 October as saying: 'Whoever wrote that one seemed to be a personal friend of the Lord. He didn't make God seem a very nice bloke'. He added however that such anonymous abuse worried his secretary more than it did him. Another consequence of the affair was the cancellation of a charity event in Coventry.

Mitchell had been going to accept a cheque for a muscular dystrophy charity at the Methodist Central Hall there, but the Revd John Tudor cancelled his appearance at the last minute, because of the actor's association with a programme offering blasphemy and bad language. David Duckworth did the job instead, presumably being the world's first non-cursing, non-blaspheming rugby star … Finally, Cotton and Speight appeared on the 1 November edition of BBC One's *Talkback* – the second time this viewer reaction programme had featured the Garnetts – and discussed the ethical limits of humour and satire.

With such unsought publicity, it is perhaps no surprise that the show achieved such astronomical ratings. Speight got a dig in at Whitehouse later in the year by having Alf turn off the radio when 'My Ding-a-Ling' came on the air[38], and in the 1974 series by again having Mike and Alf discuss Jesus, Mary and Joseph, and even having Mike appeal to heaven, facetiously blessing 'Mary' – a brilliant double meaning that left the viewer in no doubt as to the writer's intention.

Speight had his supporters, as well. A spokeswoman for the National Secular Society told the 7 October edition of the *Guardian*, regarding Whitehouse: 'Her insistent complaints reverberate even louder through the corridors of power. The character of the BBC is now seen acting like a naughty little boy in front of a heavy handed school mum … No-one denies a middle-aged woman her prudery and religious fantasies, but why does Lord Hill have to humour her?' A letter in the same paper complained about Whitehouse's '… Christian pressure group. I can understand Christians being upset, but what gives them a right to be free from ridicule?' A letter in the *Birmingham Evening Mail* stated: 'I should have thought any sincerely-held and deeply-felt Christian belief ought to be capable of withstanding all the blustering blather of yer actual Alf.' Another in the *Birmingham Post* declared: 'The atheist viewpoint had been suppressed for too long.'

But the *Sunday People*'s editorial of 8 October 1972 perhaps expressed the situation best: 'There is a limit to realism on the screen as in print. And the boundary is crossed when the deepest feelings of the audience are violently offended. Neither Mr Speight nor the BBC producer can dodge responsibility for what reaches the screen, they are responsible to the public, not just themselves.' Whitehouse was later to comment: 'Because [Speight] himself had no religious faith, he did not understand that to talk about the Bible as "bloody rubbish" was blasphemous in the extreme for countless people.'

The furore was somewhat dampened on 17 November when the Director of Public Prosecutions wrote again to Whitehouse, who had wanted him to

---

[38] This is omitted from the 2004 Network DVD release of the series, owing to music clearance issues.

prosecute the BBC for blasphemy although she was not willing to do so herself, and noted: 'The prospects of a prosecution for blasphemy succeeding are not sufficient to warrant my instituting proceedings … It would seem now that in order to constitute blasphemy at common law there must be such an element of vilification, ridicule or irreverence as would be likely to exasperate the feelings of others and so lead to a breach of the peace, or to deprave public morality generally, or to shake the fabric of society; or to be a cause of civil strife'. What this meant, in essence, was that a prosecution for blasphemy would be deemed viable only if a vast number of the public expressed serious offence. Lord Hill's apology had nipped any such major protest in the bud and thus – intentionally? – ensured that there was no likelihood of a recurrence of such a complaint.

A final comment on this latest championship bout between Johnny and Mary came from an unlikely source. Ian Gillan, lead singer of rock group Deep Purple, read about the confrontation while ensconced in Frankfurt recording the band's *Who Do We Think We Are!* album. Ensnared in an atmosphere every bit as fraught as that surrounding *Till Death Us Do Part*, he contributed a lyric denouncing both Whitehouse and Lord Longford (then engaged in a campaign against the British porn industry), resulting in 'Mary Long', the second song by a rock band to reference the wacky world of Speight's creation, incorporating lines such as 'Mary told Johnny not to write such trash, she said it was a waste of public money,' and questioning when 'Mary Long' had lost her virginity, and when she would lose her stupidity.

The ongoing ratings success of the series must have given the BBC no cause to doubt that their decision to revive the show had been a sound one. Nevertheless, Whitehouse was still subjecting the episodes to scrutiny, and she soon resumed her complaints, stating that it was irresponsible to show Alf looking after Rita's baby and questioning the morality of having the baby 'kidnap' itself in 'Up The 'Ammers'. Wilson, however, was quoted in the 22 October edition of the *Sunday People* as responding that a doll was used in place of the real baby in recording done after 4.00 pm, and that the script was adjusted to the baby's needs for any work before that curfew time.

THE ROYAL FAMILY

The fourth series featured some of *Till Death Us Do Part*'s best ever moments. These included a monologue in which Else moans about prices going up … and up … and up … in 'Up the 'Ammers!'; a brilliant scene in 'If We Want a Democracy We've Got to Start Shooting a Few People' where Alf meticulously prepares to eat his packed lunch only to find that Else has forgotten to pack it for him; a sequence of Alf and Else on the beach at

Bournemouth, musing on the origin of the sea; Gran's scary litany of terrible things that may have happened to baby Michael; a hilarious incident in 'Euthanasia' where Alf is manoeuvred down some stairs in a wheelchair; and many more. The episodes combined some strong plots, political and social satire, bravura acting and wonderful humour, and proved conclusively that Speight, after four years in the artistic wilderness, was still a force to be reckoned with. The BBC's own audience research report cited many respondents' pleasure at being reacquainted with the Garnetts, whom they described as 'crude and earthy perhaps, but topical and very amusing' – although 'quite a number' said that they were fed up with the endless profanity, its vulgarity and its repetition. Asked if a further series of *Till Death Us Do Part* would be welcome, 57% responded that it would, 37% indicated that they would not be particularly overjoyed and only 6% said that they found the idea repugnant. The show was a huge success because it retained the central features that appealed to a mass audience – a sense of realism, an excellent cast and very funny scripts.

For some critics, though, *Till Death Us Do Part* – or at least their perception of it – had changed. The *Daily Mail's* Peter Black, hitherto the show's greatest champion in the press, commented on 26 October that the series had featured too much raving Tory Alf and not enough half-baked socialist Mike; the arrival of Rita's baby had brought the younger couple closer together and upset the balance, so that while there were still 'loony' debates, and while much of the darkly comic material (such as Rita's despair at discovering her baby had vanished) was still effective and in character, other funny business was too knockabout and not so well distributed as before. All in all, Black felt, the show was not as good as when it had been 'a caricatured symposium of received opinions and prejudices'. Nevertheless, he summed up, it still towered over the television landscape, and Speight, like Galton and Simpson, was a 'serious writer with a strongly personal view who happens to use the comedic form'.

Amidst all this, Mitchell, like Speight before him, was elevated to the dizzy heights of *This Is Your Life*. The surprise was sprung on him on the evening of 25 October – the same day he and Speight had met Mary Whitehouse – as he played the clarinet in his local jazz group. He did not look at all pleased at the intrusion, and reportedly said, in true Garnett style, 'Bloody hell, I would tell you to sod off, but I know my mother will love it' – an exclamation that was not surprisingly edited out on transmission. He seemed uncomfortable throughout the programme as presenter Eamonn Andrews paraded such old associates as his superior from his old job as a Euston porter, colleagues from his National Service days and showbiz friends such as Arnold Diamond. At one point, Mitchell commented, Garnett-like, that there seemed to be more Jews on the stage than Christians. None of the other *Till Death Us Do Part* cast members turned up, and although Speight and Wilson were present, they were only in the audience, not on stage. To cap it all, there was a one-and-a-half hour breakdown in a live transmission link with Munich, where Mitchell's old Oxford acquaintance Richard Burton was filming a programme for HTV and wanted to pay tribute to his friend 'Mick'. During the delay, Burton became increasingly tired and emotional. The producer later recalled, 'Warren was surprised, and then looked more closely at the incoming television feed. "You're pissed", he said to Richard. [Burton replied,] "So would you be, you old fart, if you had been stuck for an hour-and-a-half waiting for this damned show".' His speech slurred and clutching his pet Shih Tzu, Burton gave a tribute that was different, to say the least. As the credits rolled, Mitchell got up and left the stage, visibly fed up with the spotlight.

A week later, the Garnetts appeared on stage in a sketch forming part of that year's Royal Variety Performance, on a bill including Jack Jones, Mike Yarwood, Elton John, Liberace and the Jackson 5. Ironically, Booth, Speight and Mitchell, all atheist republicans, now found themselves entertaining the Queen Mother and other members of the Royal Family, responsible for upholding the Church of England. Promoter Bernard Delfont, fully aware of the recent rows with Mrs Whitehouse, took extra care in the run-up to the event: 'My postbag was full of protest letters. How could I possibly think of exposing the Queen Mother to such profanity? I spoke to Johnny Speight … who evidently felt that I was fussing about nothing. I went over his script so many times, looking for double meanings, he must have thought I had taken training with the Lord's Day Observance Society. The inevitable compromise was just about all right. I let through a couple of "bloodies".'

Booth was currently signing on as unemployed at the Social Services office in Lisson Grove – a traditional place for actors to register when 'resting'. Because the Royal Variety Performance was a charity event and he would not be paid, he asked for, and received, permission still to collect his dole money, which happened to be due the same day as the recording of the show, Monday 30 October. The night before, a *Daily Mirror* journalist phoned Booth to talk to him about the forthcoming performance, just happening to mention that Liberace was staying at the Savoy and would be arriving at the London Palladium by Rolls and asking how Booth would get there. Booth replied that he would catch a bus to St John's Wood, walk to Lisson Grove to sign on, then go to Marylebone station and take the tube before strolling to the Palladium in time for midday … He told the reporter that he would be signing on at 11.00 am, and amazingly enough, the next day, a gang of paparazzi were waiting for him at the dole office, where they took some pictures, and then again outside the theatre, completely ignoring Liberace alighting from his Rolls …

Mitchell and Booth crammed into a dressing room full of other acts, including Arthur Askey, Dickie Henderson, Ken Dodd, Mike Yarwood and

Rod Hull (and Emu). Liberace watched Booth rehearsing, said he liked the show, and welcomed him into his boudoir when Booth asked for an autograph for his mother. Booth has another anecdote about the Royal Variety Performance. As he tells it, Mitchell obtained a copy of a newspaper – that day's edition of the *Evening Standard* – to use as a prop on stage, as he so often did when recording the TV series. During their performance of the sketch, as Booth looked on, Mitchell pretended to read the back page of the paper, oblivious to the fact that on the front page there was a photograph of Booth himself signing on at Lisson Grove. Then, as Dandy Nichols and Una Stubbs delivered some more dialogue, Mitchell turned over to the front page, saw the photograph and, according to Booth, 'gripped [the newspaper] tight and almost fell out of the chair. Then he started to read the article. Suddenly, up came his cue, and there was silence on stage. He looked up and stared around in panic'. As Mitchell had apparently been 'impossible' at rehearsals, Booth was tempted for a vengeful second to let him stew in his own juices. Feeling that would be against actors' protocol, however, he prompted his co-star: 'You've lost your thread, haven't you?' 'Yes I 'ave,' replied Mitchell as Alf. 'I 'ave lost my thread.' 'Was it something you read in the paper?' asked Booth. Mitchell ad-libbed for a bit until he regained the sense of the script, then the sketch continued on course. Although this is a nice story, it doesn't correspond with what really happened on stage during the Royal Variety Performance: the sketch was recorded in its entirety and still exists, and it is clear that Mitchell is holding a copy of the *Radio Times*, not the *Evening Standard*, and that he makes no slip-up in his performance. Perhaps the incident actually occurred during a dress rehearsal earlier that day.

The sketch was another excellent one, which managed to poke fun at the show's notoriety for bad language while still avoiding high treason. All four stars trooped off bowing to the Queen Mother at the end, to a good round of applause from the audience. The only person who wasn't entirely happy was Mike Yarwood: because the sketch had contained a joke where Alf mixed up the American singer Jack Jones with the British trade union leader of the same name, he was forbidden to make any further references to either Jones, forcing him to curtail a gag. Later, all the stars queued up to meet Her Majesty, led by Mitchell, looking thoroughly fed up. Booth stood next to the Jackson 5, having consumed six half-bottles of champagne in the meantime. When he met the Queen Mother, he surprised everyone by congratulating her on her horse winning at the Grand National that Saturday, before saying that he hoped she would not be worried by *Till Death Us Do Part*'s detractors. Astonishingly, the Queen Mom responded, 'Don't worry, they're only cranks.' Speight meanwhile was dragged up in front of Prince Philip by Peter Sellers, and Phil the Greek turned to Princess Anne and stated, 'This is the gentleman who writes your mother's favourite show'. Apparently, Lord

Mountbatten also liked *Till Death Us Do Part*, as Prince Charles told Una Stubbs that his uncle never went out when it was being broadcast. The final word goes to Lord Delfont: 'Afterwards the Queen Mother said to me, "Well that wasn't too bad, was it?" I think she was a bit relieved.'

The year ended with a Christmas special episode of *Till Death Us Do Part*, transmitted on Boxing Night on BBC One. This had the Garnetts meeting the cast of current West End sensation *Jesus Christ Superstar*, headed by Paul Nicholas and Dana Gillespie. It drew a lukewarm reaction from one critic, who felt that it 'laboured for long stretches. It seemed stricken by the somnolence of too much Christmas. Still it had some very funny moments.'

It had been a good year for Speight, who had been paid £1,500 for this latest script. He had had two BBC television series – one a forgotten flop, one a massive hit – and a reasonably successful movie, not to mention a very high media profile. Stateside, *All in the Family*, with its credit for Speight at the end of every episode, was enjoying unprecedented critical and commercial success and changing the face of American television. The Brazilian version, *A Grande Família*, had also launched to great acclaim, and the German one, *Ein Herz und eine Seele*, was in preparation. The immense audiences won by the fourth series of *Till Death Us Do Part* – the highest ratings the show had ever attracted – effectively guaranteed that there would be a fifth. But the usual warfare that was both a major inspiration for the show and the bane of some of its cast carried on regardless. Booth, apparently without thinking, told a reporter from the *Evening Standard* about the habitual rows in rehearsals, his dislike of Mitchell and his increasing frustration with Speight. Later that evening, after rehearsals, Mitchell gave Booth a lift to Chalk Farm tube station, where Booth saw an *Evening Standard* billboard advertising their scoop on the behind-the-scenes truth about *Till Death Us Do Part*. Horrified, Booth got out of the car and stood in front of the notice so that Mitchell could not see it. When he arrived at rehearsals the next day, however, he found Mitchell ranting about the feature to Dennis Main Wilson and threatening to sue his co-star. Booth crept in and tapped Mitchell on the shoulder, saying a polite good morning. Mitchell almost choked, and declared that he wasn't going to speak to him. He was true to his word, keeping a sullen silence apart from when he had to deliver his lines. When the rehearsals finished early, Dandy Nichols remarked, '[Booth] should give more interviews like that every day. Then we'd all have some decent peace and quiet!'

21
Series Five

A FIFTH OF GARNETT

Early in 1973, Dennis Main Wilson began negotiations for *Till Death Us Do Part*'s fifth series. Johnny Speight's agent, Beryl Vertue, was informed that pre-filming for the planned seven-episode run was pencilled in to begin on 30 July, with studio recordings to take place on seven consecutive Sundays from 19 August. Shortly after this, Duncan Wood wrote to Speight to suggest that production be postponed because Una Stubbs was expecting another baby; it seems that a script delivery deadline of 22 October was then offered – which was probably more realistic in any case, considering Speight's notorious lack of punctuality. Having accepted £1,000 per script for the fourth series, Speight now demanded more, confident that his worth had been proven. In a strange throwback to the days of 1967, the BBC turned down his demand for £1,250 per script on the grounds that it went against the government's current prices and incomes policy. Speight was eventually to accept £1,100 for each of his seven scripts. All this was part of the traditional chess game between BBC and scriptwriter; a game the Corporation knew from past experience that Speight was adept at playing. There was never any danger that it would derail plans for the new series; however, just such a danger then emerged from an unexpected quarter.

Dandy Nichols stated at this point that she had distinct reservations about continuing as Else. The actress was now 65, slightly deaf, dependent on a variety of prescription tablets, and becoming more and more worn out by the endless quarrels and crises that fuelled the show. As an example of this, Tony Booth recalls a fracas that occurred during rehearsals at the Hammersmith Gaelic Club, a long Nissen hut where the cast congregated to work at the far end. Warren Mitchell's concentration was soon disturbed by a man who came in and walked very loudly up to the actors, believing them to be in charge of the Club's booking office. Mitchell angrily demanded that a notice be posted stating where the booking office was, in order to prevent any recurrence. This didn't work, and soon a barricade of chairs was set up with a chalked notice denying admission to anyone not involved in the production. This didn't work either, and despite every attempt to stem the flow of people, including Wilson installing a set of roadwork lights, Mitchell kept having his concentration disturbed. At one point, he was sitting with his back to the rest of the hall and rehearsing his lines with Booth when he heard a massive crash; someone had entered the area and accidentally knocked over some chairs. Mitchell was furious, and vowed that he would tell the intruder exactly where to go, regardless of who he was. Then he saw Booth giggling and asked him why. Booth laughingly asked if Mitchell was going to keep his promise, and the reply was affirmative: 'Whoever this is, I'm going to tear his effing head off.' As the intruder's steps came nearer and nearer, Mitchell, still with his back to the entrance, bristled, about to explode. Then he turned around – and found that the intruder was a very polite Indian postman. Mitchell stifled his invective and, when the postman enquired if he was the hall manager, replied calmly, explaining that the person he required was in the office near the entrance. The postman then recognised the cast, apologised for interrupting them and asked Mitchell for his autograph, saying how much he enjoyed the show. Mitchell courteously obliged. On learning (from Booth's insistent prompting) what Mitchell had been intending to do to the next person who interrupted him, the postman laughed and walked off. Booth, barely able to contain his mirth, then accused Mitchell of being racist, thus starting off another argument. This, says Booth, was typical of the kind of aggravation that marred rehearsals. Later, when he and Nichols had lunch, she complained about the arguments, and Booth asked her how on earth she coped. 'That's easy, dear', she said. 'I take tranquillisers.'

In February 1973, Nichols made two requests of the production team: first, that a warm-up artiste be employed to entertain the studio audience prior to each recording, because she felt that Mitchell's warm-up act was detrimental to the cast and show; and secondly, that recording breaks be reduced to ease the pressure of taping the programme. After receiving assurances that these two stipulations would be met, she eventually accepted a new contract at the end of March 1973.

That same month, Wilson and Speight exchanged ideas for the new series. They discussed bringing in Derek Griffiths as a new semi-regular cast member; he had been glimpsed in *The Alf Garnett Saga* playing a drug dealer and had then had a memorable cameo in a similar role in the recent Christmas special, selling black market wristwatches ('None of that foreign rubbish – they're Swiss'). Speight's real-life neighbour Adrienne Posta, who had played Rita in the last film, was also considered for a part, the idea being that she and Griffiths would play the Garnetts' new neighbours; an interracial couple, with Griffiths as an immigrant trying very hard to be British, evoking a dubious response from Else and a predictably shocked one from Alf. For the first two episodes, according to this plan, Alf would be seen repeatedly insulting his new neighbour. Griffiths' character would then become determined to prove that his tormentor was really Jewish, and in the final episode would find and bring in Alf's Yiddisher brother, who – as

Wilson and Speight envisaged it – would be played by Peter Sellers, Lionel Jeffries or Leo McKern – the very same actors who had been considered for the role of Alf eight years earlier. Setting out this scenario in a memo to Head of Comedy Duncan Wood, Wilson assured him that it was just a plot device, and not designed to replace 'our normal established junketings'. Four days later, on 26 March 1973, Wood replied, saying that although he thought the basic premise was fine, he was worried that it might be perceived to have stolen its ideas from ITV's current smash *Love Thy Neighbour*, which he would find deeply ironic since the latter had so obviously stolen its premise from *Till Death Us Do Part* (and indeed, although he did not say so, from *All in the Family*, with its black neighbours, the Jeffersons). 'Can't we find some other way of getting Derek Griffiths into the show?' he asked. The answer apparently was no, as Griffiths was absent when the fifth series eventually went before the cameras, although Posta did have a one-off guest role in the 'Party Night' episode. It seems that Wood's reservations caused Wilson and Speight to think again, and thus denied viewers the opportunity to see a character apparently intended by Speight to be a sort of black version of Alf Garnett, illustrating the writer's view that racism is not restricted to white people – as seen in the Christmas special when Griffiths' character lambastes the natives for mixing him up with 'all that Amin rubbish' recently arrived from Uganda.

In the meantime, Mitchell made two more extra-curricular appearances as Alf Garnett. The first of these, which also featured Speight as Barmy Harry, came in a short sequence filmed in London for the *Paul Hogan Show* special 'Hogan in London'. In this, Hogan's amiable Aussie character and his mate visit the capital in order to help out 'Teddy' Heath. They enter a typical local pub and, encountering the outspoken idiot that is Alf, decide to deceive him into believing that they are good friends of Her Majesty the Queen. The second came in September in a sketch written by Speight for a fee of £110 for Lulu's *It's Lulu!* show. This had a remarkably hirsute Mitchell again appearing alongside Adrienne Posta and, for a fee of £500, delivering a performance very similar to the one he had given on Dusty Springfield's show six years earlier. It involved Alf heckling from the audience, coming on stage, doing a dance routine with the Young Generation, insulting his host, engaging in a row over the 'good old days' and finally singing a duet with Lulu on 'Every Little While' – the exact same song he had performed with Springfield. Other highlights included Garnett asking the orchestra to play 'pianopissimo' and stating 'I could have been another Max Bygraves if I'd been Jewish ...'

Also in 1973, Speight wrote a new show for Marty Feldman. *A Speight of Marty* was recorded in August and transmitted in October. One interesting side-note from this is that, as revealed in surviving documentation, producer Dennis Main Wilson lambasted the studio manager for having recruited such a poor studio audience; he recommended an audience made up of 40% good, solid London working-class, 30% students and young intellectuals and 30% 'general public' to ensure that the 'full scope of Johnny Speight's script will be appreciated'. This indicates that studio audiences – crucial to the success of *Till Death Us Do Part* – were not selected at random but with some care and attention to their composition.

SOS (SILLY OLD SOD)

Meanwhile, controversy continued to rage over public morality and broadcasting. In January 1973, right-wing activist and journalist Ross McWhirter, best known as one of the compilers of the *Guinness Book of Records*, asked the Court of Appeal to stop the Independent Broadcasting Authority (IBA) – a reconstituted ITA – from sanctioning the transmission of a proposed documentary on Andy Warhol, which promised to feature naked women and soft porn. In February, the Court decided against McWhirter, saying it was up to the IBA to act as censors and not the legal system. Lord Longford and Mary Whitehouse then stepped into the furore – an intervention that Speight would recall with glee in the first episode of the forthcoming fifth series of *Till Death Us Do Part*, having Mike call the pair 'tipsters of porn'. Also that year, novelist Anthony Burgess defended director Stanley Kubrick's transposition of his work into the film *A Clockwork Orange*, soon to be withdrawn from British cinemas at the director's behest, stating, 'Is there some essential difference between modes of art which makes some forms more immoral than others?' He was referring here to the hypocrisy that saw 'high art' such as novels or opera regarded as suitable for debating questions of morality, yet 'low art' such as films or television programmes condemned for doing the same thing. In October, Nicolas Roeg's cinematic masterpiece *Don't Look Now* was banned in the USA owing to its sex scenes and nudity. It was into this realm of heated public debate – and an increasingly volatile political and economic situation – that the Garnetts were set to return at the start of 1974.

Speight signed his contract to write the seven episodes of the new series, for the settled fee of £1,100 per script, in May 1973. The four star cast members had meanwhile agreed terms as well, Mitchell for £1,000 per episode, Nichols for £775, Booth for £300 and Stubbs for £250 – perhaps surprisingly, all lower amounts than they had received for the previous run. Joan Sims agreed to return as Gran for three episodes, at £300 per appearance. Three episodes were to be recorded on 9, 16 and 23 December respectively and then, after a Christmas break, the remaining four on 6, 13, 20 and 27 January, and the series was scheduled to begin transmission on the evening of 2 January.

At a planning meeting on 23 November, Dennis Main Wilson outlined to Duncan Wood the content of the first two episodes, 'The TV Licence' and 'The Royal Wedding', the latter of which would be about the 14 November marriage between Princess Anne and Mark Phillips: 'The first is a generally swingeing attack on everything that has happened in 1973. It is a typical no-plot all-sit-down-and-talk type Speight. Apart from the odd, emotional "bloody", I think you will be very happy with it. The final scene tag will be rewritten once I get the show into rehearsal. "The Royal Wedding" explores attitudes of two generations; I like it very much.' On 5 December, he despatched copies of the two scripts for approval, with a covering note: 'To save you from premature hardening of the arteries, I think it would help if I were to point out that these scripts are Speight's original drafts. I spend the first two days of rehearsal editing, rewriting and polishing so that the final product for the studio is seldom ... the same as the original'. Later, he described the final version as: 'A very last minute job – usually late scripts and Stanislavski-type improvisation during rehearsals.' He noted that he foresaw a possible problem with incorporating footage of the actual Royal Wedding into the second episode, anticipating objections to the intercutting of the 'House of Garnett and House of Windsor'. However, he described this as '... the kind of situation at which Speight excels. It ... also [brings out] the attitudes that our rather large viewing audience seem to adore from Alf Garnett. Say what you like, the British are still all Monarchists.'

Wilson also described the two episodes in a memo to Dandy Nichols, his 'Dear Favourite Lady', when he despatched copies of the scripts to her on 28 November:

Script 1 – no plot, lots of lovely chat.
Script 2 – good plot and storyline and even lovelier chat.
Script 1 is about 2 minutes over, other 2-4 minutes over.
Have rounded up the entire cast on the phone; everybody is sober, Tony's been off it for the last four months. Even I (regrettably) am only drinking wine and am thoroughly fed up, but it's all in a good cause!

In accordance with Nichols' earlier request, Felix Bowness was employed as a warm-up man for the studio recordings, for £25 per session.[39] Wilson noted that his was a 'notoriously difficult show for artists to rehearse' since sets and props were lent out to outside rehearsals. Also in accordance with

---

[39] Records exist only for the second, post-Christmas batch of recordings, so it is possible that a different warm-up man was used for the first batch, or even that Mitchell continued his tradition of doing the warm-up job himself for those three episodes – although this seems unlikely given Nichols' request.

Nichols' stipulation, the number of recording breaks per episode was reduced for this series. Probably due to pressure of work, Wilson would have a co-producer on 'The Royal Wedding' episode, in the person of David Croft.

As preparations for the new series continued, Britain seemed to plunge ever deeper into the most profound crisis it had faced since the Second World War. The Yom Kippur War had broken out in the Middle East in October, resulting in oil prices quadrupling overnight and acting as a catalyst to a power shortage. In November, the government faced huge opposition to the inauguration of the third phase of its incomes policy, limiting wage rises to 7% or £350 per year maximum, just as inflation was beginning to rocket. The Electrical Power Engineers' Association banned out-of-hours work, and ASLEF (the Amalgamated Society of Locomotive Engineers and Firemen) soon followed suit. On 12 November, the miners started a national overtime ban. The following day, Prime Minister Heath declared a state of emergency, using the campaign phrase 'SOS – Switch Off Something' to urge the saving of energy in the home, for example by keeping only one room heated – a suggestion seized on with glee by Speight as prime material for satire. On 13 December, Heath announced that a three day working week would be implemented from 1 January, affecting all industry; the temperature of home and office heating was to be restricted to 63° Fahrenheit, the national speed limit reduced to 50 mph, street lighting turned off at a curfew hour … In response, the electrical power workers then went on strike. Further restrictions were imposed on the sale of camping gas, on DIY shops and on hotels. Petrol coupons were set up. The entire television service was set to close down by 10.30 pm each evening due to the power crisis. At the same time, the IRA were busy murdering people on the mainland … It seemed that Britain was teetering on the brink of disaster.

Inspired by this, Speight and Wilson decided to emphasise *Till Death Us Do Part*'s reflection of real life. On 20 December, by which point the first two episodes had already been recorded, Wilson devised a style that would engender a 'real attitude'; this would involve the Garnetts watching real TV programmes such as *The Generation Game*, the BBC's coverage of the Remembrance Day service and *Songs of Praise* – and of course film of the wedding of Princess Anne and Mark Phillips, which was already planned to be inserted into 'The Royal Wedding'. It was an idea that Wilson had first used long before for the *Hancock's Half Hour* radio shows. Regular BBC announcers Andy Cartledge and Colin Ward-Lewis were asked to contribute to the realism by writing and performing continuity voiceovers to be heard on the Garnetts' TV set.

Speight stated in the *Radio Times*: 'Alf has got to be topical. It's the cross I have to bear. Well … not really a cross. But it's what his public expect of him … and his critics too. If he isn't, everyone's disappointed. I mean, the first story was about the Arab-Israeli war, and this one is about the Royal Wedding. Myself, I'm an atheist republican. But Alf isn't, he's out organising a street party with a piano, bunting and all. Trouble is, nobody else in the street wants to know.'

Mitchell, just about to embark on a family skiing holiday in France, was also quoted in the *Radio Times*, which came complete with a Christmas 'Look – it's yer actual guide to ...' poster advertising the new series: '"Aargh!" cried Mitchell, "Its that 'orrible poster again", and proceeded to make us some very charming Christmas snowflakes. We'd been warned that he was not addicted to Christmas but we found him full of good cheer ... "You get panicked into the Christmas spirit. There's a sentimental streak in all of us. I could easily be moved to tears by awful carol services."'

REALITY BITES

The fifth series began as scheduled, in the now-regular *Till Death Us Do Part* post-watershed Wednesday slot, on 2 January 1974, and was to prove in many ways the most effective of all in achieving Speight's original vision for the show: the political macrocosm of the nation's troubles reflected in the microcosm of the Garnetts' world; the hypocrisy and stupidity of racism; the clash between the social classes that, in Speight's eyes, had entrapped Britain for generations; the continuing struggle between the writer and the censors; and the generation-gap conflicts within the family itself. The penultimate episode, 'Party Night', could even be seen as a self-referential comment on the problems of being tired and emotional; a state in which one of the cast, one of the production team and the scriptwriter himself all regularly found themselves. In all, the seven episodes displayed outstanding acting from the cast, some wonderful comic scenes and a far greater sense of confidence than the 1972 series.

The series opener, with its aforementioned digs at Mary Whitehouse, provoked a predictably negative response from the campaigner, although for different reasons: she complained that she had 'counted 103 "bloodies" before giving up'. While she accepted that some people no longer found 'bloody' an offensive word, she emphasised that 'the tally of 45 uses in an earlier edition had now risen to more than 103'. Also unimpressed by 'The TV Licence' was critic Raymond Williams who, having expressed his worries about the fracturing of the nation, reviewed it as follows: 'Weakened by surprisingly poor technical production it was in any case no kind of comic relief. Who could go on laughing at Alf Garnett as the only truths he knew almost shook him to pieces while his wife pinched his breakfast and his son-in-law tossed over bits of chewed liberal newsprint?'

Such isolated negative reactions notwithstanding, Speight in many ways excelled himself with the scripts for this series, the possible exception being 'The Royal Wedding', which like the 1968 episode 'Monopoly' seems so determined to punish Alf by rendering him alone that it simply tails off and, despite including some laugh-out-loud moments (Else playing the piano badly for one), lacks real zest. The other episodes are all splendid, and contain some of the show's best work. 'The TV Licence' has a stunning row between Alf and the others; 'Party Night' recaptures all the boozy charm that made 'Till Closing Time Do Us Part' such a pleasure; and 'Strikes and Blackouts' has some wonderful comic business from all concerned, particularly Rita making bunny impressions with Alf's bandage after he gets stung by bees. Best of all are the classic 'Three Day Week' (which would be repeated as a tribute to Dandy Nichols after she died in 1986) and the closing shot, 'Paki-Paddy', which sees Spike Milligan reprising his *Curry and Chips* character and is so over the top as to almost defy belief. 'Three Day Week' especially combines all the elements that Speight had used so brilliantly in the past: the politics of the outside world filtering into the Garnetts' psyche; the rivalry between Else and her husband; the gradual reduction of Alf to helpless bystander …

Speight and Wilson now seemed to have *carte blanche* in terms of the show's subject matter, and their determination to be topical led to some swift changes in the running order of episodes, as evidenced by the following memo of 15 January 1974 from Wilson to Duncan Wood: 'Because of the rapidly changing current news situation, I have decided to transmit episode four ["Strikes and Blackouts", recorded on 6 January] on Wednesday 23 January. We shall decide the transmission order of episode three ["Party Night"] once the issue of a General Election is decided either way.'

'Party Night' – which, remarkably, barely featured Anthony Booth, and saw Adrienne Posta, the second film's Rita, making a guest appearance – was ultimately dropped back from third to sixth in the running order and transmitted on 12 February. The show also changed transmission days and times during the course of the series, veering from Wednesdays to Tuesdays and finally a Thursday, and local power cuts disturbed its screenings for some viewers.

When the National Union of Mineworkers (NUM) began an all-out strike on 7 February, the Heath government quickly caved in and called a General Election for 28 February. In light of this, the final episode of the series was held back to be transmitted on Election night, in a time slot just after the polling booths had closed, in a deliberate repeat of the scheduling of the 1970 special 'Up The Polls! (The Campaign's Over)'.

Behind the scenes, the rehearsals and recording sessions for the series had become increasingly fraught as scripts had been rewritten and reshuffled, and as the turmoil of the outside world had also impinged on the production. A train strike on 29 January had delayed Wilson's arrival at the BBC and forced him to edit the 'Three Day Week' episode – a day before its transmission – in the studio operations room rather than a proper edit suite. The problems had, if anything, been even worse than on previous series, and this cannot have failed to exacerbate Nichols' doubts over her continued involvement with the show.

On a more positive note, for the first time ever, the series attracted hardly any criticism from the NVLA, the political parties or similar organisations. Perhaps events in the real world were too troubling for people to get overly worked up about a TV sitcom; or perhaps the show had been to some extent overtaken by the march of permissiveness it had once spearheaded. One rare example of a letter of complaint in the press – which until recently had been full of them – came in the *Birmingham Evening Mail* on 28 January from a Mrs Williams, who said that she had counted '68 "bloodies" in last week's [episode and] at least 61 [in the one] before ...' and suggested that one way to help the country in crisis would be to turn that particular programme off and save electricity. A reply from another reader was printed two days later: 'Mrs Williams ... who suggested saving energy by cutting out the TV programme ... why bother to watch and count "bloody" words? If you want to save energy, try bathing with a friend.'

The fifth series ended at 10.00 pm on Thursday 28 February, with Spike Milligan's Paki-Paddy getting blown up by an IRA bomb and the Garnett residence being plunged into darkness by yet another power cut. Once the General Election votes were counted, the Labour Party were back in government. The NUM strike was called off on 11 March, the miners having been granted a 29% pay increase. The three day week also ended that month. The country's economic woes and industrial strife were still far from over, of course; but little of the political debate and satire for which *Till Death Us Do Part* had been famous up to this point would be in evidence for the remainder of its lifetime. The show was about to encounter its first major casting problem, and this was ultimately to change its direction for good

22
Series Six

THE DARK SIDE OF THE MOO

Although the fifth series had arguably represented a creative peak for *Till Death Us Do Part* and – like the previous series – had enjoyed huge ratings (at least when power cuts had not disrupted transmissions), there were signs that it had lost some of its lustre for the general viewing public. The Reaction Index (RI) figures had fallen from the show's traditional high level of the upper 60s to the mid 50s. Admittedly, certain episodes, such as 'Party Night', had fared better than others in this regard, but in general it seems that the show was less appreciated than it had been in the past. Perhaps events in the real world were just too painful to be laughed at in the form of satire. Certainly the show no longer shocked the nation or aroused the same huge press interest as it had in years gone by. The BBC's audience research reports suggest a general disillusionment not just with the endless rants of Alf but also with the equally continual use of 'bad' language.

Till Death Us Do Part was still a very hot property, however, not just for the BBC but also for Johnny Speight, who was on a roll and fulfilling all his aesthetic expectations. It was thus almost inevitable that a sixth series would be made. Beryl Vertue received a contract from the BBC Head of Copyright on 16 July 1974 for Speight to write six more episodes, for an increased amount of £1,250 per script with 50% repeat fees, intended for transmission in the autumn of that year. But the whole emphasis of the show was about to change as Dandy Nichols finally threw in her handbag and refused to return as Else.

The surviving BBC programme files are silent as regards the circumstances and timing of Nichols' decision to quit. By September 1974, however, an extra script had been commissioned from Speight, and it may be surmised that this was in direct response to the actress's refusal to continue, a decision having been made to write her out in a special episode. Speight's original idea was to kill the character off, but the BBC would not agree to this, allegedly because they believed that the audience would find it too traumatic, although it seems more likely that they were swayed by the thought that Nichols might one day be persuaded to return. Then came the brainwave of having Else go off to Australia to look after her sister Maud. It had already been mentioned in the series that Maud had departed from her original Southend home, allegedly because of immigrants moving into her street, and moved down under. The original Maud actress, Ann Lancaster, had died in 1970, but it was proposed that the character could be played instead by Gretchen Franklin, in a neat resonance with the show's past – Franklin having of course played Else in the *Comedy Playhouse* pilot. Nichols may even perhaps have suggested this herself, as a thank you to Franklin for recommending her for the series in 1966. In the end, however, while the idea of having Else journey to Australia was approved, it was decided not to feature Maud at all, but merely to indicate that she was ill and that her husband had paid for Else to come over and look after her.

In return for a one-off fee of £950, Nichols agreed to portray Else in the first episode departing for the airport, and also in a short insert for the second episode, supposedly in Sydney, taking a phone call from Rita. Even this, however, was apparently not trouble-free. The *Daily Mirror* carried a short interview with Nichols on 16 December 1974, just after she had completed her work on the episodes, and the reasons for her departure were laid bare: 'I didn't want to do any more programmes at all. I've never liked working with Warren Mitchell and it's become steadily more unpleasant. I shall be glad to get away from it all. I never want to do any more, no matter how much they try to persuade me. Personally, I couldn't care less what they do – I'm fed up with the whole thing.'

Mitchell, for his part, was quoted by the *Daily Mail*, under the headline 'Dandy Calls It Quits', as saying: '[There is] too much Alf Garnett [in me, but] I just concentrate on learning my lines. I am not interested in any tittle tattle about any rows we are supposed to have had. You'll have to talk to Dandy about that or any of the others.'

Speight, interviewed as rehearsals were in progress at Acton, admitted that the actors seldom had lunch together or socialised away from the studios. 'It is no secret we are not the happiest little band in the world. It is Garnett's fault. Not Warren Mitchell, the actor, though I have had my rows with him, but your actual Alf. He rubs off his bigotry on us all. The reality rubs off. On me and on the cast. I can understand Dandy. For years she has been locked up in those rehearsal rooms with Alf. All day long he screams abuse at her. Nothing else, just abuse. In the end, she doesn't know if it is Alf cursing her, or Warren Mitchell. What woman would stand for it? Being called "silly old moo" day in and day out. No wonder she has had enough'. The writer also spoke about the original exit he'd had in mind for Else, in a 'grand funeral': 'I had a scene with Alf sobbing his heart out, throwing himself on the grave. Then, at the booze-up later, forgetting all about her and chatting up a bird. But the BBC stopped the idea. They said it would be too upsetting for the public. There can be only one silly old moo, Dandy Nichols. She has breathed life into the character. I don't know what Alf will do without her. But one thing is sure – the old devil will never be quite the same.'

There were other factors underlying Nichols' departure. She was now 67 years old, and, as Booth's tales about her medicine bag emphasised, had never been in the best of health, a situation the frantic nature of *Till Death Us Do Part*'s recordings could only have exacerbated. According to *Play for Today* producer Irene Shubik, who had worked with her in 1972, she had been getting hard of hearing even then. Her reservations about working with Mitchell couldn't have been insurmountable – she would co-star with him again in the follow-up series *Till Death ...*, produced and directed by William G Stewart for ATV in 1981, and would even suggest the premise for her swansong, the further follow-up series *In Sickness and in Health*, in 1984, when it was quite obvious her illness was terminal. And it certainly wasn't the presence of Dennis Main Wilson that had brought about her departure; she would appear in his production of the one-off BBC comedy *Galton and Speight's Tea Ladies* in 1979. But the fearfully intense personalities of Mitchell and Wilson together, coupled with the heavy workload, fraught atmosphere and drunken arguments during rehearsals all got too much for her in the end, as Wilson himself conceded in an interview the following year: 'This punishing discipline was one of the reasons for the departure of Dandy Nichols ...'

Comfortably off following her long stint in the show, Nichols could now pick and choose the roles she took, such as a cameo in a Tommy Cooper show in 1975. To the viewing public, however, she would always be Else Garnett.

OUTBACK BOUND

The arguments involving Booth, Speight and Wilson, all still heavy drinkers, certainly did not diminish in Nichols' absence. Patricia Hayes, a new regular for the sixth series, recalls watching in awe during one session of rehearsals as Mitchell and Wilson embarked on a colossal row in which both threatened to quit. 'You are one person in the morning, and another person altogether after lunch,' Mitchell accused Wilson. 'So let us please from now on rehearse in the mornings only. We'll all come in two hours earlier if you like and rehearse through until 2.00 pm, without lunch, because when you go to the pub, or to the "bank" as you put it, another man comes back afterwards. A totally different and incompetent man! Who do you think you are kidding when you say you are going to the bank? Have they started serving whisky at the bank?' Wilson was incensed: 'How dare you speak to me like that. How dare you!' Mitchell responded, 'I dare because I have got to, Dennis. We cannot go on with a maniac telling us what to do in the afternoons. What you said to Pat just now was rubbish – absolute rubbish.' 'Very well!' stormed Wilson. 'Very well! If that's how you feel, I'll leave – I shall go!' 'No,' screamed Mitchell, not to be outdone, 'I'm going!' 'No, you are not – *I'm* going!' Una Stubbs, quietly doing her embroidery, saw Hayes' startled expression and told her not to worry, adding that these flare-ups were the reason Nichols had left: 'This is what Dandy could not bear.' 'Yes, I know – but I love it,' replied Hayes, guiltily. 'So do I,' admitted Stubbs …

To take some of the burden off Wilson's shoulders, a director was appointed to the show, for the first time since Douglas Argent had done the job in 1967. This was Colin Strong, who had so impressed Wilson with his work on the 1972 *Late Night Line-Up* special on Johnny Speight.

Else would remain a presence in the Garnett residence even after her departure for Australia, in the form of a wonderfully malevolent photo, which Alf would occasionally turn over when he got particularly angry at her memory. The familiar Garnett living room was also reconfigured for the sixth series, with furniture rearranged and camera angles chosen to emphasise the empty spaces left by the moo's departure. It was not only she who was gone from the show, either. Two previous semi-regulars, Sid (Roy Kinnear) and Fred (Will Stampe), were also absent now, and so too was Gran – although she would return in the very last episode of the seventh series – because Joan Sims was so much in demand at this time for other film and television work, including ITV's *Carry On Laughing!*.

'Outback Bound', the sixth series' opening episode, and the last to feature all four original leads together (leaving aside Nichols' brief insert in the second episode), was transmitted in a prestigious post-watershed slot on New Year's Eve 1974. Focusing on Else's departure, it was a strange, rather serious episode, with a deservedly valedictory feel and few laughs. It quickly saw *Till Death Us Do Part* back in the news, however, for reasons that had nothing to do with Else. A scene had been filmed in which Alf, spurred on by Mike, suspects that a package left at the airport may be a bomb and throws it into a cleaner's bucket, only to discover that it is actually just a parcel of sugar – recalling an earlier sequence of Else packing bags of sugar into her suitcase. This bomb scene was cut from the final programme at the last minute without the knowledge of either Speight or Mitchell, and both men were vociferous in their condemnation of the perceived censorship. Speight declared that he wanted to switch his work from the Light Entertainment Department of the BBC to the Drama Department, where 'the atmosphere is more professional and less timid'. As before, he stated that he would not write for the Beeb if the Garnetts were to face internal censorship, moaning that while it seemed quite acceptable for artists such as Lulu and Cilla Black to make lewd innuendos in their shows, he was being prevented from writing something he cared about. Mitchell meanwhile complained to the *Daily Mail* that the situation was '… intolerable. Instead of a team we have now become a tug of war – the cast and the writer pulling one way, the BBC the other'. There were, he insisted, humbly but wrongly, a hundred actors who could play Alf Garnett, but there was only one Johnny Speight. The BBC replied that the bomb scene had been cut purely because of time constraints, and that there was no directive regarding censorship of jokes about the IRA; a statement that seems deeply fatuous considering the state of the IRA mainland bombing campaign that year, which had seen 21 people being murdered in Birmingham only one month before.

Fuelling the censorship concerns, another scripted scene, in which Alf used a photograph of Harold Wilson as toilet paper, had been cut out before recording on the grounds that it was 'offensive', presumably because Wilson had just returned to power following a further General Election on 10 October 1974; nevertheless, the same joke had been used before in the first movie without causing any great outcry.

Mitchell was also dissatisfied with aspects of the episode's production, notably the fact that canned laughter had been added to the scenes filmed at the airport of Alf pursuing his wife across the terminal: 'Watching the New Year's Eve show was an embarrassment. It was just like one of those awful American comedies with canned laughter. Unknown to us they cut out some of the humour, some of the best lines, but left in the studio laughter. It looked faked and false.' The BBC, however, remained adamant that the episode had been cut only because it had been too long; a perennial problem thanks to Speight's practice of failing to edit his own work.

This was to be the last real sign of media interest in *Till Death Us Do Part* on a major scale. From this point on, with the show entering its final phase, media coverage and internal BBC data would become very thin on the ground.

LOVE THY NEIGHBOUR

How could Speight continue *Till Death Us Do Part* without one of its central characters? The challenge was to prove inspirational, and although the two post-Else series do not attract the plaudits or the attention of their illustrious predecessors, they feature some superb work, not just from the writer but from all concerned.

Distance rather than death has parted Alf and Else, yet Alf still has to live with this situation, and he reveals himself to be as helpless as ever. Marriage itself is a subject of debate in many of the episodes, with Alf and his neighbour Bert Reed discussing the subject in political terms (likening wedlock to the social contract between the government and the trade unions[40]), in culinary terms (Bert's wife Min makes a great meat pudding, and frankly that is the only reason he can conceive that they stay together) and even in canine terms (Alf says that he can keep Else on a short lead).

---

[40] The social contract was a sort of *quid pro quo* in which the government undertook to keep inflation under control while the trade unions promised to exercise restraint over wage demands.

It was a masterstroke on the part of Speight and Wilson to have Bert and Min as regular characters to help compensate for the absence of Else (although the idea may well had its roots in the abandoned proposal to bring in Derek Griffiths and Adrienne Posta to play the Garnetts' neighbours as semi-regulars in series five). Bert (surname then unknown) had been a presence off-screen since the *Comedy Playhouse* pilot (in which Alf talks to him through the toilet wall) and on-screen since the first episode of the series proper in 1966, played originally by Charlie Bird. He had been glimpsed again, with Patricia Hayes playing his wife, then named as Mrs Carey, in the second series' closing episode, 'Alf's Dilemma'. Then, with Bill Maynard in the role, he had made three further appearances: in the first movie, in the series four episode 'The Pigeon Fancier' and in the 1972 Christmas special. Hayes' character had meanwhile resurfaced in the series three opener, 'The Phone'. To confuse things further, Pat Coombs would play a Mrs Carey in series seven. For series six, however, while Hayes retained the role of Min (now named as such for the first time), Alfie Bass was cast as Bert.

Bass and Hayes were both supreme comic character actors who would bring a brilliant new dimension to the show. Bass, for whom Mitchell had understudied in the '50s, was well known to the viewing public for his starring roles in series such as *Bootsie and Snudge* (ITV, 1960-1974) and the black comedy *Black and Blue* (BBC, 1973). Hayes, for her part, had been a much in demand performer for years, having worked with Tony Hancock, Benny Hill and Arthur Haynes. Her first association with Speight had come when she acted in some of the radio shows he wrote for Vic Oliver on *Variety Playhouse* in the '50s 'They were marvellous, absolutely marvellous,' she later enthused. 'He wrote so well for women. In those days, it was difficult to get any decent material for women. Years later, when I came to be in *Till Death Us Do Part*, I got to know Johnny Speight, and I've been his greatest admirer ever since. In fact, when I'm asked to do a comedy series now, I say, "Well yes, if it's written by Johnny Speight, or someone better" – if there is anyone better! There's always scope for good actors as well as comedians in his material ... Even if I had only five lines, they would be spot on, with a wonderful character that I could get to grips with.'

The feeling was mutual. 'Working with Pat has been a real pleasure all the way through,' said Speight. 'She is like me – not very demonstrative – but you can tell when she appreciates your work. She will criticise if she has to say something that does not fit in with her character, but I cannot recall any unpleasantness. Pat has something that has always appealed to me as a writer – a streak of madness. Irene Handl had it, Peter Sellers had it, all the great ones have it.'

In 1971, Hayes had made a huge leap in public and critical perception when she played the eponymous 'Edna the Inebriate Woman' in Jeremy Sandford's stunning *Play For Today*, proving her drama acting ability was just as great as her comic timing. The performance won her a BAFTA.

Whereas Nichols had used silence and short sentences to enormous effect, Hayes was forever busy, her facial expressions as much on the move as her mouth. She played Min as an earnest, eccentric woman, existing on another mental plane, harbouring a logic of her own that totally perplexes Alf. She also developed her own comic business, having Min stare at Alf and then slowly repeat his last few words a split second after he has spoken them, thus ruining his narrative flow just as effectively as Else had previously. Min is oversexed, too, acting the siren luring Alf to his sexual doom in one episode, and giving him the kiss of life with rather too much enthusiasm when he falls off a ladder in another. She is also prone to hysteria, which Hayes plays on the knife-edge between utter seriousness and over-egged melodrama. In short, Hayes is quite blissfully funny, and even threatens to upstage Mitchell at times.

Bass, in contrast, generally underplays his character. Bert is a much sleazier, less volatile figure than Alf, although he is not afraid to tell his neighbour that he is wrong on occasion. He sometimes orders Min to be quiet in the presence of such a gifted raconteur as Alf, but generally he is strictly under his wife's thumb. He thus acts as a sublime balance to the energy of Hayes and Mitchell, in the same way Nichols had to that of Booth and Mitchell.

The new characters made an instant impression. The *Birmingham Evening Mail* commented: 'With Patricia Hayes as Min taking the bluster out of Warren Mitchell's Alf – and pretty near all the applause last week – dear old Dandy Nichols isn't going to be so sadly missed.' Similarly, critic Arthur Steele noted: 'Alf's endless shouting and swearing seems more wearing than of yore – but the introduction of Bert and Pat [sic] from next door offers a new lease of life for the series.'

Once again, as in 1966, the balance of power in the show was tilted away from Tony Booth, as he was left with little to do as Mike but lie on the sofa and interject occasionally. For the seventh and final series, he would fall down yet another rung in the billing ladder, to number four after Mitchell, Hayes and Bass. There may have been another reason for his more restricted appearances; Una Stubbs was later to state, in the documentary *When Pat Phoenix Met Tony Booth*, that his attendance at and commitment to rehearsals became unreliable when his private business problems mounted up and his personal debts began to spiral out of control. Previously, despite his heavy drinking, he had always been utterly professional on set; now, however, late in the show's history, his personal crises seemed to get the better of him.

This new line-up restored some of the show's power, even though at this stage public interest was clearly beginning to falter, perhaps because increasing familiarity bred increasing disinterest. The Reaction Index (RI) figures for the sixth series tended to be in the low 50s – more than ten points below the typical level in the show's heyday. This trend had already been evident before Nichols' departure, although undoubtedly many lamented her going; indeed, her farewell episode recorded the lowest RI figure and lowest audience percentage so far when it was screened on New Year's Eve 1974. Viewing figures picked up later in the series, but gone were the days when the Garnetts could arouse righteous indignation (except perhaps from Mrs Whitehouse); the world had changed too much for that, and they were victims of their own trailblazing success in this respect. Even the show's racial aspect was now ignored. The 17 March 1975 edition of the *Sun* quoted one BBC report, the *First Annual Review of BBC Audience Research Findings*, as saying: 'There is no evidence the series has much effect on relevant attitudes and prejudices in either direction.' The report characterised Alf's views as 'so extreme as to be just a joke' and said that he was seen as a 'loudmouthed, harmless buffoon'.

FUNNY BUSINESS

With one or two exceptions, such as the rather depressing opener featuring the departure of Else, the episodes of the sixth series see *Till Death Us Do Part*'s comic interplay going into overdrive, particularly with the introduction of Min, who is given some tremendous material involving such bizarre things as an aerosol questionnaire, tins of kosher soup and pickled onions. Then there is 'The Wake', with its superb focus on the aftermath of the death of Min's mother and her conviction that she will be reincarnated as a blackbird ... In contrast, two episodes seem to eschew *Till Death Us Do Part*'s traditional strengths. 'Christmas Club Books' is perhaps the least interesting of the show's entire history, while 'Wedgie Benn' not only dispenses with any semblance of narrative drive but also features comic business that, while still entertaining, shows signs of strain at times. Generally, however, the combination of strong scripts and fine acting that had sustained the show in the past remained in evidence. This is particularly so in the closing episode, 'The Letter', surely a candidate for the show's finest ever episode.

'The Letter' opens with Alf and Bert discussing marriage, and Alf asserting that women should be kept on a tight leash. Later, however, Alf returns home to overhear Min next door revealing that Rita and Mike have received a letter from Else in Australia, apparently asking the young couple and their baby son to emigrate and join her. Alf feels betrayed, and a glorious row detonates. Here, the boundary between comedy and tragedy is shown to be as paper-thin as the walls through which the Reeds and the Garnetts shout insults at each other. Alf reveals his utter helplessness as first he demolishes the living room searching for the letter and later cries out the wedding vows in strangled agony. It is an extraordinary, moving performance from Mitchell that transcends anything that this extraordinary show has hitherto presented. The episode ends on a perfect note as Mike and Rita sit together on Alf's armchair, exhausted by all the warfare, while next door, Min and Bert mirror their slumped poses. It is a final comment on the theme of marriage: the Reeds are inextricably bound together, despite a complete lack of sexual relations, or any children, or any other bond except perhaps Min's meat puddings.

'The Letter' proved convincingly that the show was artistically just as valid and just as powerful as it had ever been, albeit with the political and social comment now firmly eclipsed by the domestic.

23
Series Seven

DIVORCE DO US PART

The show's new, post-Else set-up seems for once to have galvanised Speight, who quickly proceeded to negotiate a seventh series in the summer of 1975, this time with Patricia Hayes and Alfie Bass elevated to star status over Tony Booth and Una Stubbs. Rumours that Dandy Nichols might reappear were scotched by Speight during an interview in the *People* on 20 July; he said again that he wanted to start the series with Else's funeral, because there was now no chance of Nichols returning. There seems to have been an unstated assumption that this would be *Till Death Us Do Part*'s last series, as would indeed prove to be the case, although there were thoughts of developing a new vehicle for Alf, as Dennis Main Wilson told *Radio Times* in November: 'One of the future ideas going round in [Speight's] head is a sort of *Alf Through the Ages*, a Garnett saga to show that the man's irresistible repulsiveness is an eternal aspect of the British character.' In the 1 November edition of the *Sun*, meanwhile, Speight spoke of a scenario that would see Alf move to a huge country house and join the aristocracy after winning the football pools, but then become disillusioned and try to return to his roots, even joining the Labour party. The writer said that hopefully Rita and Mike would accompany Alf, with Min as housekeeper, and that some of the humour would be provided by Alf having riding and elocution lessons. He added however that the BBC was responding coolly to the notion, owing to the expense. Like many of Speight's and Wilson's ideas, this project would prove to be a pipedream. Alf's future would instead consist of Mitchell playing the monster first on stage and then in a return to the original format in 1981 – but for ATV, not the BBC.

The seventh and final series of *Till Death Us Do Part* began on 5 November 1975 with the first of six episodes. It not only saw a rise in the Reaction Index figures and viewing numbers by comparison with the previous series, it also showcased some of Speight's best writing, although now almost completely shorn of the political bite that had first won the show its reputation. In these episodes, we get debates on such questions as whether or not Shakespeare wrote *A Christmas Carol*, whether or not it is the same work as *Scrooge*, and whether or not Gladstone was Jack the Ripper. A sequence in the splendid 'Window' plays like a scene from *Waiting for Godot*, as Alf finds himself trapped on a window ledge while Min and Ethel from across the road babble on about the wonders of the Isle of Wight. 'Min the Housekeeper' features a masterclass of acting from Hayes and Mitchell as Min attempts to seduce Alf, rendering him utterly confused; she inexplicably wants his body, he only wants her meat puddings … 'Drunk in Charge of a Bicycle' sees Alf and Bert making a bike journey through Wapping, starting at the Jolly Sailor pub near Garnet Street and ending in a police station run by James Ellis from *Z Cars*.

The comic business in this series is still the best of any sitcom. Highlights include Bert's interminable insistence on the word 'certificate', the ludicrous scenes of defenestration in 'Window', and a sequence where Alf almost immolates himself in a startling attempt to light a fire in the Garnett hearth. The penultimate episode, 'Golf', sees the unholy trinity of Alf, Bert and Min going to a golf club, meeting Roy Castle and George Best *en route*, and ends – for only the second time in the show's entire run – with Alf on top, as he receives a torrent of free drinks in the members' bar. The cutting of scripted lines from earlier in the same episode, making a rather pointed reference to the Royal Family's sexual shenanigans, saw the last controversial aspect of the show quietly expire.

After a week's break to make way for the *Sports Review of the Year*, the final episode of *Till Death Us Do Part* was broadcast on 16 December 1975. Alf returns home having been made redundant, only to be embarrassed when the others scare him into cowering submission before wishing him a happy birthday. In the end, having publicly revealed his cowardice yet again, he receives a crushing blow with the news that his wife will not be coming home: she wants a divorce. It is not death that parts the Garnetts after all. The episode does not work as well as it should; it has an excellent concept, but fails to follow it through properly, and the result – despite the presence of three of Britain's greatest female character actresses in Patricia Hayes, Pat Coombs and Joan Sims – is not a complete success. It is however effective in showing that every aspect of stability and routine that has supported Alf in the past has now been pulled away, cruelly and callously.

There was no fanfare about the series' cessation, even though this final episode seemed an obvious act of closure, with Alf humiliated, shamed and emotionally torn apart by his creator. There is no hard evidence as to exactly why the show finished at this point. Granted, it seems that viewers and critics alike had become overly familiar with it, and even its enemies had begun to ignore it. The *Daily Mail*'s TV critic had reviewed the second episode, 'Min the Housekeeper', and suggested that the show now consisted of 'mellow, W W Jacobs-style short stories in which Cockney men wrangled, pulled faces, drank too much and rarely stirred far from square one.' It was, he thought, 'Time worn [but] good value'. The *Evening News*, commenting on the same episode, wondered if Alf was going soft, and described the show as a damp squib; pleasantly amusing but lacking the political byplay, racialism and religious debate that had once made it compulsive.

Perhaps Speight and Wilson needed a break from it. Anthony Booth certainly seemed quite content to be finally relinquishing his role – which, unlike the other regulars, he would never reprise at a later date. Mitchell, however, was still up for playing the part of Alf. He appeared in character again on Bruce Forsyth's *The Generation Game* – Else's favourite show – at Christmas that year. ('No wonder she went to Australia,' comments Brucie as Alf performs in a pantomime as Baron Hardup. 'If I was her, I'd have gone to another planet.') Then, in 1976, he went on to enjoy record bookings in a London run of his one-man stage show *The Thoughts of Chairman Alf*, based on years of cabaret experience in Australia.

But *Till Death Us Do Part* had seen the writing on the khazi wall, and was never to disgrace our screens again in its purest form. After at least 1,436 'bloodies', 79 'silly moos', 89 'gits', eight 'bastards', six 'bitches', five 'arses' and three 'tits', the Garnett family had fractured forever.

24
Life After *Death*

THEY THINK IT'S ALL OVER …

Till Death Us Do Part may have expired, but this was not quite the end of the story. *All in the Family* was still running strong in America, and had given birth to several sequels, including *Maude*, *The Jeffersons* and *Archie Bunker's Place*. And that old monster Alf Garnett was unstoppable.

Following on from its successful London run in 1976, which earned Johnny Speight yet another award, *The Thoughts of Chairman Alf*, or at least a concise, Christmas-themed version of it, was presented as a one-off special for the small screen on 26 December 1980, made by ATV for the ITV network. By this point, according to the *Daily Mirror* of 11 July 1980, Warren Mitchell and Dandy Nichols were 'good friends again' and were intending to record a series together. That series eventually emerged the following year as *Till Death …*, again made by ATV, with scripts by Speight and direction by seasoned light entertainment producer William G Stewart. It ran for six episodes, and was shown in different slots by the different ITV companies. LWT scheduled it at 10.30 pm on Fridays from 15 May 1981; Michael Grade, Director of Programmes for LWT, stated that this slot had been chosen in the belief that the audience for stronger material – the American spoof *Soap* was cited as an example – was more discerning on a Friday night (presumably after a few drinks at the local).

The premise of the show was that Alf and Else, now back together again, had retired to Eastbourne[41] and were sharing a place with Min (again played by Patricia Hayes), whose husband Bert had recently merged with the infinite. Location filming took place in February 1980 in Pevensey Bay – leading the press to gleefully point out that the typical £25,000 cost of bungalows there was in reality well beyond Alf's budget. 52 year old Aubrey Hastie, who ran a newspaper shop, allowed the crew to film around his home. It had originally been planned that both Tony Booth and Una Stubbs would make occasional guest appearances as Mike and Rita visiting their retired parents, but ultimately only Stubbs took part. This was because Booth had sustained extensive burns in a drunken incident at his flat in 1979

---

[41] This is a rare example of an ITV company setting a series outside its own region, ATV being the franchise holder for the Midlands.

and his injuries were still so serious as to prevent him from acting on screen, or indeed from doing anything much at all for several years. Booth would later recall, with a touch of bitterness, that of all the cast and crew of *Till Death Us Do Part*, only Stubbs had contacted him in hospital during his long, slow recovery.

Till Death … is a good show, with the cast as superb as ever, and features some lovely references back to *Till Death Us Do Part* – most notably when Rita's now-teenage son Michael (played by John Fowler) paints his grandfather's face, having been inspired by his mother's oft-told anecdote of how she and his dad did the same thing years earlier. Speight's eternal battle with Mary Whitehouse is also recalled by a sequence in the opening episode where Min is excited about Alf's tales of theatrical nudity in *The Romans in Britain* – a production that had notoriously provoked an unsuccessful legal challenge from Whitehouse when staged at the Royal National Theatre in 1980. The critics' reaction to *Till Death* … was, however, decidedly mixed. The *Daily Express* said that although the Garnetts' return was welcome, there seemed little point to it, and the *Financial Times* was even more scathing: 'Where once there was shock, belly laughs and outrage, there is now pathos, sad smiles and lethargy. Dandy Nichols, whose immense strength as Elsie [sic] was always that she said so little and looked so much, now gets more lines than are good for her character.' Although these criticisms were well wide of the mark – the show was actually as raw and unsentimental as ever, Speight's scripts were excellent and Nichols' contribution was admirable – they were perhaps only to be expected, given that comparisons were bound to be drawn with memories of the illustrious forebear that had not been seen on TV for some years. This would not have mattered if the show had been a hit with the general viewing public, but unfortunately it wasn't.

Two factors in particular worked against the show succeeding. First, as previously mentioned, it was transmitted in different slots in the different ITV regions, and this meant that it was inconsistently publicised and its audience was fragmented. Secondly, and far more damagingly, the episodes were recorded without a studio audience, an approach that the *Sunday Times*'s reviewer was quick to decry: 'It was the sound of Alf Garnett appalling people that was absent. An explosive guffawing, audibly mixed with squeals of outraged sense and sensibility'. Admittedly this opinion was not universally shared – a review in *The Spectator* of 30 May 1981 stated, 'At last someone has had the courage to put on a comedy show without a lot of guffawing morons in the background' – but it is difficult to deny that the lack of any audible reaction was detrimental to the show. The silence that meets hilarious incidents such as Min reacting to Alf's pro-Whitehouse views, or Alf greeting the vicar blissfully unaware that he has been made up to look like a punk rocker, is palpable. Because Speight's scripts were not blatantly comedic, but derived their humour instead from essentially dramatic situations, the reaction of a studio audience was really essential to signal the intended response, as witnessed to telling effect in early *Till Death Us Do Part* episodes such as 'Hair Raising!'. And, unlike on American shows of the '60s, it was not canned laughter that the viewers at home heard on the soundtrack but an absolutely genuine audience reaction. The lack of any such reaction in *Till Death …* meant that there were no signals, no pointers, and the comedy seemed to fall flat.

Till Death … did not continue past its first series, and was soon forgotten. When in 1985 the BBC announced that Dandy Nichols was to return to the role that had won her fame, no mention was made of the fact that she had already done so only four years earlier. *In Sickness and in Health* was the title of the second follow-up show, which erased memories of retirement to the seaside and returned Alf and Else to Wapping to live in a small flat, where they would again receive occasional visits from their daughter Rita. Amid rumours of rows between Speight and Dennis Main Wilson, experienced BBC producer Roger Race took the helm this time.[42] Speight was later to say that Nichols had 'nagged' both him and Warren Mitchell to set up the show, but from the start it was obvious that she was too ill to undergo extensive recording. Placed in a wheelchair for Alf to push around during film scenes, and with a nurse on hand throughout rehearsals and recording sessions, a severely malnourished Nichols was now 78 and wasting away. She died in February 1986, after completion of the show's first series – which ran for six episodes from 1 September to 13 October 1985 – and a Christmas special – transmitted on 26 December 1985 – by which point she would at least have had the comfort of knowing that *In Sickness and in Heath* was a great success.

Speight said of Nichols, 'She was a lovely person, highly intelligent, a great conversationalist, and a wonderful actress with a great sense of comic timing … Una Stubbs was like a real daughter to her.' Later that year, Mitchell also praised his long-time co-star in an interview with Val Hennessy: 'Dandy was so marvellous, marvellous at those odd lines that puncture Alf's balloon …' He admitted that they had had their bust-ups, but said that their friendship had been based on mutual admiration for each other's talents, likening this to the relationship between tennis rivals Jimmy Connors and John McEnroe. John Gielgud, with whom Nichols had starred in David Hare's *Home* on Broadway in 1970, sent a bouquet to her funeral. The BBC, for its part, repeated as a tribute the 'Three Day Week' episode, which went into the top ten of the TV ratings for that week.

In Sickness and in Health continued regardless, the second series beginning with Alf returning from his wife's funeral – an idea similar to that conceived

---

[42] Ironically, back in 1972, Wilson had had cause to make an internal complaint after the BBC's in-house magazine *Ariel* erroneously cited Race as producer of *Till Death Us Do Part*.

but not executed ten years earlier. A wealth of new regular or semi-regular characters came in: Min (played as before by Patricia Hayes), her mad sister Gwenneth (Irene Handl), landlady Mrs Hollingberry (Carmel McSharry), Alf's drinking companion Arthur (Arthur English), upstairs neighbour Mr Johnson (Ken Campbell) and gay West Indian care worker Winston (Eamonn Walker), the latter providing a target both for Alf's racial prejudice and for his homophobia in one neat if increasingly unlikely package. The show eventually ran for six series in all[43] as a solid if unexceptional part of the Beeb's sitcom armoury. It reused several old situations (Alf trapped in a window, Alf versus carol singers, milkmen selling all kinds of black market products) and repeated some old jokes. It also, notably, had several episodes shot in Australia, featuring Alf meeting Mrs Hollingberry's Antipodean family in Sydney. But it lacked the bite and increasingly the realism that had anchored its spiritual forefather. As Mitchell himself mused: 'It's not such a joyous, rampaging argument as it once was.' A *Daily Telegraph* review of April 1990 neatly summed up *In Sickness and in Health* as a 'cosy folk memory and a reminder that really inspired comedy is something that reaches the screen only once or twice in a decade'.

In 1992, the show was cancelled by the BBC, allegedly because of fears that Alf's racism might be misinterpreted in the light of the then current race relations problems in London. Within the BBC, it was also stated by Jim Moir, Head of Light Entertainment, that the show 'needed a breather', and by Robin Nash, Head of Comedy, that although there would be no more series for the time being, the Corporation would not 'rule out appearances in the future'. The show ended with very respectable audiences of eight million. Warren Mitchell, speaking on BBC Radio, urged viewers to complain about the cancellation, saying 'It's a dreadful decision'. Speight meanwhile declared that he was shocked, and hinted at political pressure to get the show resurrected, recalling that Alf Garnett bore a remarkable resemblance to the irascible Conservative politician Nicholas Ridley.

In the press, however, the 'BBC kills Alf Garnett' stories soon passed, and there was no major protest. Mitchell resumed his work in the theatre and, over the years that followed, made many more stage appearances as Alf, including in a bizarre link-up on a national tour with Cockney novelty act Chas and Dave to sing old-time knees-up songs. He briefly brought Alf back

---

[43] The second series (six episodes) ran from 4 September to 9 October 1986, the third (six episodes) from 22 October to 27 November 1987, the fourth (seven episodes) from 7 September to 19 October 1989, the fifth (ten episodes) from 1 September to 3 November 1990 and the sixth (seven episodes) from 21 February to 3 April 1992, with further Christmas specials on 23 December 1986, 25 December 1987, 25 December 1989 and 30 December 1990, the latter being a little longer than usual at 35 minutes.

to the BBC in 1994 in one episode of *Noel's House Party* and again in 1996 when he hosted *The Spirit of '66*, a celebration of England's famous World Cup victory of 1966, featuring clips from 'A House with Love in It' and 'Intolerance'. He then made the excellent hour-long special *An Audience With Alf Garnett*, produced by LWT for the ITV network and transmitted on 5 April 1997. This led later the same year to *A Word With Alf*, a series of 18 sketches, each of about seven minutes' duration, featuring Alf pontificating on various subjects in the pub, with guest appearances by Mrs Hollingberry (Carmel McSharry, as before), produced by Carlton for the cable channel UK Gold and transmitted in various slots between 30 November 1997 and 12 June 2000. Lastly, LWT made a series of six *The Thoughts of Chairman Alf* programmes, with Mitchell in character as Alf entertaining a studio audience drawn from the public. These were transmitted between 23 September and 4 November 1998. All these projects were, naturally, scripted by Speight.[44]

The Garnetts received numerous mentions in the media after Tony Blair, married to Cherie, the daughter of the randy Scouse git, became Prime Minister in 1997. This even prompted a delighted Speight to propose a new series with Alf as the Prime Minister's father. This did not come to pass, however, and Speight died of cancer in 1998, a mere year after Shirley Temple's son-in-law had come to power. His demise had been preceded by that of Dennis Main Wilson, and would be followed by those of Patricia Hayes, Pat Coombs, Frank Muir … all ascending to their well-deserved places in TV heaven.

Life without the Garnetts or the Rawlins continued for the three surviving actors of the original troupe. Anthony Booth carried on acting in roles in *Holby City*, *Eastenders*, *The Bill* and *Doctors* until ill health prevented him after 2010. Una Stubbs had possibly the most interesting television career of all of the cast. After her starring role alongside Jon Pertwee in *Worzel Gummidge* and *Worzel Gummidge Down Under* during the 1980's, she appeared in varied roles in *The Worst Witch*, *Mist: Sheepdog Tales*, *Midsomer Murders* and the Benedict Cumberbatch reboot of *Sherlock*, as Mrs Hudson, which gave her some international acclaim.

Warren Mitchell continued to tread the boards both theatrically, televisually and cinematically. At the turn of the millennium, Mitchell's method-acting intensity got him into trouble on the set of the Vinnie Jones-starring movie *The Mean Machine*, his strident suggestions resulting in his premature departure from the production. This sparked several press

---

[44] There was also at this time another successful foreign remake, in the form on *Sei Hoi Yut Gar* (*All in a Family*), produced for the Hong Kong channel TVB. The first series, consisting of 11 episodes, was transmitted in 1994 and the second, of ten episodes, in 1996, each episode being of 25 minutes' duration.

headlines mourning the sacking of 'lovable Alf'.

With roles in such diverse works as *Gormenghast*, *The Price* and *Waking The Dead*, Mitchell continued as a much respected actor for as long as his health would permit, passing away aged 89 in 2015 at his home in Highgate; he had once pre-wrote his own obituary for a newspaper: "Warren Mitchell struggled in the latter part of his career to discard one particular television image. He overcame typecasting and played many parts to some critical success. He is survived by his wife, children, grandchildren – and Alf Garnett." It proved to be a perfect summation of his life and career.

Having initially been reluctant to commit himself to appearing in a series, Mitchell ended up developing a symbiotic relationship with Speight and the character he created; a relationship that was to last for over 40 years. He always gave Speight full credit for Alf's success, even though this was unquestionably due as much to his own luminous ability. Famously, on one occasion when a critic praised his performance as Willy Loman in a production of *Death of A Salesman* and simultaneously suggested that he had always hidden his dramatic talent under a bushel when he played Alf, Mitchell's response, quoted in the media, was: 'Alf was no less challenging or rewarding a character to play than Willie Loman … Alf Garnett is one of the great dramatic creations of our time. Boorish he may have been on occasion … boring he never was. I love the old bastard.'

The death of Warren Mitchell, perhaps more than the death of Speight years before, meant that a resurrection of *Till Death Us Do Part* or its offshoot was surely now impossible. However, unexpectedly, the following year the show flickered briefly into activity again. In 2016, there was a renaissance in interest in the now 50 year old TV series. First up, a complete copy of that key episode 'Intolerance' was discovered in the loft of a private collector. Whilst around 8 minutes of it had been extant for some time, now one could see this 1966 classic in all its glory, receiving its public debut at a 'Missing Believed Wiped' event in Birmingham. Then Network DVD announced the December release of a box set of the entire series, promising not just the extant video material, including 'Intolerance', but all the audio recordings made of the missing episodes. Furthermore, an unusual twist came in September 2016 when *Till Death Us Do Part* returned to British TV screens in a unique manner. It comprised one of a trio of 'The Lost Sitcoms' specially made as part of a general celebration of classic British sitcom, notionally six decades old after the genre's first foray with *Hancock's Half Hour*. Controller of BBC Comedy commissioning Shane Allen said: 'The British sitcom is a huge part of our national identity and cultural heritage. This season is about celebrating the BBC's rich legacy at a time when British comedy is as popular as ever … our audiences have deep affection and nostalgia for iconic shows.'

One of the strands in this celebration was 'The Lost Sitcoms' trilogy consisting of classics originally wiped by the BBC but now recreated by a completely different cast following the original scripts. As with the originals, they would be recorded in front of a live audience. The series' chosen were obvious – the progenitor, an episode of *Hancock's Half Hour*, a 1970 episode of *Steptoe and Son* and of course, *Till Death*. This naturally garnered the most pre-publicity because of the controversiality surrounding its protagonist, billed in one quarter as 'notoriously anti-socialist, racist and sexist'.

Unusually, the theatricality of Sixties television would also be recreated in this short series, with an opening shot of a studio theatre, deliberately stylised sets, and even a curtain call by the actors at the end. Despite this, the shows were still broadcast in colour. *Till Death Us Do Part* was the opening shot, and having made what may have seemed like a brave decision to deal with Alf directly, the BBC then commissioned 'A Woman's Place Is In The Home', one of the very few episodes that did not have any racial content, no sense of political engagement and very little in the way of social comment. This was noticed immediately by the media, and even its star, Simon Day, stated that that one could not expect the BBC to broadcast such racial expressions as used by Alf Garnett in this day and age, which simply illustrated the corner the BBC were painting themselves into. Here the emphasis was on gender politics, with cast members telling of hushed gasps from the studio audience at Alf calling the girl in the phone box a 'Saucy little bitch', and stressing the feminist liberation expressed by Else in reaction to her husband's misogyny. So, from the beginning, the production failed to grasp many of the ideas implicit in Speight's original creation. This was of course explicit in the stylised design of the production – one of the founding tenets of the original show was its anchoring in grimy realism, whereas the context of the 2016 show seemed garish, brightly apparelled and adrift in another dimension, eschewing the entire spiritual focus of the original. Such design merely emphasised the archaeological nature of the enterprise, which in many ways was of course the point – it asked its viewers to imagine a world without instant technology, populated by a dinosaur without any of our modern day values. In doing so in this fashion, however, it merely displaced many of the reasons that the show was a classic sitcom and offered nothing in return. It was no accident that the most successful enterprise of this short series was the *Hancock* recreation, because it did not have to rely on the strong sense of presence and historical context that *Till Death Us Do Part* and *Steptoe and Son* was founded upon.

Ben Fuller, an experienced comedy director, helmed the piece, and an experienced comic actor and writer, Simon Day, portrayed Alf, *sans* moustache but replete with trademark spectacles, pocket watch and waistcoat. Day rightly refused to do an all-out impersonation of Mitchell and invested his portrayal with a touch of pathos rather than of brimstone. However, this at points seemed to heighten the limitations implicit in an actor playing an actor playing a TV legend. One expected a Mitchell clone, but didn't get one, and at times this led to a lack of energy in the dynamics of the episode. To fit the show into a 25 minute slot, some of the 'business' in the original was glided over. And, to be fair, the choice of 'A Woman's Place Is n The Home' was not an example of the best script that the series could offer, one of the first to illustrate that Speight was having trouble finding his muse, one of those that relied mainly on the sheer popularity of the show to sustain its drive but without displaying many of those elements that contributed to its incipient greatness. Again, that was perhaps another sign of a self – imposed restriction in 'The Lost Sitcom' concept – it had to be a staged piece with a finite number of cast members and no film inserts, thus immediately limiting the choice of project to unearth and reboot.

Reaction to the programme was mixed, with some critics praising the idea behind it but questioning the choice of script. Others appreciated the efforts of the cast, particularly Simon Day and Lizzie Roper as Else, but noted that the entire experience merely highlighted the show as a period piece. One critic stated that *Till Death Us Do Part* should have remained lost, because of its racism, again missing the point not only of its intentions but also of the need to place it in its historical context. Transmitted on BBC Four rather than one of its main channels, 'A Woman's Place Is In the Home' could never be anything but an interesting curio (even the *Radio Times* review called it 'of curiosity value only'), and the 5-minute factual short, 'Let's Talk About Alf', broadcast immediately after, did nothing except suggest that, period piece or not, Speight's series deserved to be examined in more than a bite sized archaeological experiment. *Till Death Us Do Part*, even after this needlessly stylized production, was too replete with shibboleths that could not be expressed in our modern society. The only thing 'The Lost Sitcoms' proved was that fifty years on, Johnny Speight could still cause controversy.

THE NATIONAL ALF

The march of time means that *Till Death Us Do Part* can now be examined in a new light. Its critical reputation has not diminished; most commentators agree that it was of crucial importance, even if they disagree over some of the specifics. But in the wider world it seems to have been largely forgotten. While the name Alf Garnett is still generally recognised by the public, and can still be seen used in the media as a term to describe anyone with bigoted attitudes, feelings toward *Till Death Us Do Part* itself seem to have cooled somewhat. In recent years, it has barely scraped into various 'favourite TV show' polls: it appeared in a *Radio Times* Top 40 in 2003 and ranked at number 32 in a BBC survey to find Britain's Best Sitcom in 2004, but it did not register at all in the 2005 Comic Relief Thirty Top Comedies list. Of course, such headcounts are affected by many factors – demographics, current trends, means of registering votes and so on. During the '90s, *Till Death Us Do Part* was often criticised for its lack of plot, whereas now, in the light of the overwhelming success of 'character comedy', such criticisms seem out of touch. In the '60s it was seen as a political satire, but now it is noted only for its racial content. Times and trends change.

The windmills that Speight's creation tilted at a generation ago – politicians, the NHS, organised religion, royalty – still survive, even if the sails have shifted somewhat. In many ways, Speight's vision is as relevant today as it was in 1966. Only the furniture and the language have changed. The idea of families like the Garnetts having to live together has largely been consigned to history with our caring, sharing welfare state. Else would now simply divorce Alf, who would perhaps be viewed today as a perpetrator of domestic violence – not physical mistreatment, but verbal abuse and vilification of his wife on a continuous basis. Mike and Rita would be given a flat somewhere. The morality imbued by Speight – the idea that Mike would not cheat on his wife, for instance – seems rather quaint nowadays. The talk of class, the predominance of the manufacturing industry, the lack of a car, or of a telephone, all seem quite alien in this day and age. Speight's contention that the show was a 'social document' has been borne out in more ways than one, since it depicts a society now long gone, even though the preoccupations of that world – race, royalty, religion, government – are still felt as strongly as ever today, and in many ways are far more absurdly delineated than even Speight could have conceived. The stupid, self-serving politicians, the short-sighted facile decisions they make, the blinkered racism, the reliance on a narrow-minded faith; all are even greater concerns in our contemporary society than they were a generation ago.

The show's once-realistic visual elements – one TV set in one room, a coal fire, an outside loo, a tin bath, flying ducks on the wall, an alabaster Arab bust, pictures of heads of state, an aspidistra in the corner – are also now relics of a bygone era; so much so that they may inadvertently appear almost surreal nowadays. Even the ideal of the working class has vanished from television, except ironically in those programmes Speight thought of as 'space fillers' – soap operas such as *Coronation Street* and *EastEnders* – to which *Till Death Us Do Part* was intended as a kind of antidote over a generation ago. We now have – supposedly – classless accents on TV, these being deemed progressive in comparison to the standard BBC cut glass speech of the past. At least Speight would no longer be so self-conscious. In the '90s, the writer memorably described Britain as 'a banana republic, without the bananas' – he never lost his unique chemistry of cynicism and humanism, even as the world changed around him.

Those windmills have turned in other ways. Although by the mid-'60s the public was already becoming disillusioned with politicians, *Till Death Us Do Part* acted as a catalyst for this by generating disenchantment on a massive, proletarian scale. This was not the smug, public-school snickering initiated by *TW3* and perpetuated by everything from *Monty Python's Flying Circus* to *Have I Got News For You*. Speight's political satire was demotic and incandescent and spared no-one, fuelled by a genuine rage at the absurdities and untruths foisted on the public by its so-called democratic masters. While most people today regard politics and politicians with healthy scepticism, this *realpolitik* outlook was not so evident when *Till Death Us Do Part* was on screen. The same kind of changes have occurred in the public's attitude toward the monarchy, which in the '60s and early '70s was an institution that still had respect and awe, rather than the kind of soap opera status it has today, brought on in part by the family's own self-inflicted wounds in its mistaken attempts to modernise its public image. As for religion, even the deference paid to Christianity in the '60s, when Speight would launch broadsides at it on a weekly basis, has now vanished in the larger dimension, while at the same time other religions – Islam most of all – have stepped forward to become major talking points.

Noted critic and broadcaster Clive James has stated that *Till Death Us Do Part* provided 'the biggest single moral problem television was ever faced with – do the audience applaud [Alf's] bigotry or do they see through it?' In James's view, it is a bit of both. Dennis Main Wilson said in 1972 that Alf began as a monster and become beloved by the public. Both seem correct. *Till Death Us Do Part*'s audience enjoyed Alf getting his comeuppance, but at the same time he was a figure they could secretly admire. He was a monolith, a relic, but he embodied feelings that the radical changes transforming the country were not necessary and not wanted – at least amongst a certain generation. Alf's philippics against change were raucous, inarticulate, objectionable, but always heartfelt. He took a stand against the march of the jackboots of change, trampling underfoot the world of the ordinary man. And the more Speight punished his antihero, the more Alf attracted sympathy. He became an underdog, and the nation loves its underdogs, especially when they rail against the unstoppable progress of the state or the fracturing of society, both overriding elements of post-War Britain. Warren Mitchell said of Alf in 1986: 'He's much too big a character to knuckle under. He's a brave man, a survivor, a bigoted old idiot who will probably wind up leading a one-man revolution, waving a banner outside No 10.'

In several of the obituaries written on the character when he seemed to have made his last TV appearance in 1968 he was compared to Shakespeare's most famous metaphor for the working man, Falstaff; George Melly, T P

Worsley, even Hugh Carleton Greene made the association: 'We still recognise ourselves in Falstaff, a man who lied, drank, wenched, bragged and belched his way through the mean streets and rowdy pubs of his time. The more cowardly, bragging and dishonourable Falstaff is, the more we love him. It is the same with Alf Garnett. The more outrageous and extreme his tirades grow, the more we adore him. But make no mistake, we don't admire him, not in the least. We laugh not with him, but at him.'

Speight, Mitchell and Wilson knew 40 years ago that Alf Garnett would be a character instantly recognisable to the British in any time, in any situation, and that of course is one of Speight's greatest achievements.

In an interview in 2002, Anthony Booth stated that one third of Britain's population were appalled by *Till Death Us Do Part*, one third agreed with Alf and the final third said 'Yeah, I know, but it's bloody funny, innit?'. He was pleased to reflect that *nobody* should have been left without being offended in some way during each episode's half hour. The Garnetts offended viewers over language, over religion, over the Queen, but none of that seems to matter anymore. Alf's pronouncements on race, on the other hand, are still seen as utterly relevant.

It is of course in terms of race that the world on which *Till Death Us Do Part* commented has changed most irrevocably. The golden age of television that spawned the Garnetts was fortunate in that its movers and shakers were free to comment on society without feeling constrained by any perceived moral responsibility. In the '80s, this relationship between the media and real life was transformed. The march of that form of social engineering pejoratively called 'political correctness' has placed a barrier between the racial ideas of *Till Death Us Do Part* and its general perception today. The idea that the constant use of particular words could instil negative archetypes was anathema to Speight. The arsenal of abuse with which Alf Garnett machine-gunned the ethnic minorities – 'coon', 'sambo', 'john-john', 'four-by-two', 'nigger', 'black', 'wog' – and which Speight and Mitchell intended as a satirisation of unthinking, brainless racism is now ironically seen as contributing to such racism by its very presence. Most critics accept that Speight (in both *Till Death Us Do Part* and *Curry and Chips*) meant well, but take the view that by commenting on the issue he inadvertently opened a Pandora's box of racial demons. As we have seen, the racial aspect of *Till Death Us Do Part* was misinterpreted by some as early as 1966, but there was still a feeling back then that the underlying intention of the show, that Alf should be seen as an idiot, was generally understood – even by the likes of the National Front, who complained in 1967 that the BBC had placed the most influential opinions on race in the mouth of a bloody fool. Speight always maintained that such stupidities should not be harboured and concealed but exposed and discussed in an open forum. This is essentially the opposite of 'political correctness', the best of which forces us to think about the potentially harmful effects our words and actions may have, even if unintended, but the worst of which merely replaces old stereotypes with new ones, equally ridiculous. Speight countered the *pas devants les enfants* doctrine by pointing out that the ethnic minorities could be just as racist as the natives.

Warren Mitchell never had any doubts about the anti-racist slant of his show, frequently citing the story of the man who approached him at a football match and congratulated Alf for attacking 'the coons', to which the actor replied that in fact he was attacking idiots like *him*. The very fact that the idiot, and no doubt many others like him, could easily misinterpret the show in that way was never addressed, perhaps symptomatic of the arrogance of that generation of television artists. Writers Maurice Gran and Lawrence Marks, responsible for such popular shows as *The New Statesman*, *Birds of a Feather* and *Goodnight Sweetheart*, once called *Till Death Us Do Part* 'the bravest piece of programming the BBC ever made', but then said that they would be quite happy if the word 'coon' was never mentioned on television again. Today the media have to be *seen* to be responsible, even if this necessitates curtailing certain artistic freedoms. And, to be fair, Speight himself opined in an interview in the '60s that there were certain artistic freedoms – pro-fascist or pro-apartheid plays were cited – that should not be given a public platform. Two things have to be remembered here: Speight's scripts were *always* anti-racist but *always* realistic. He simply wrote in a different world. History teaches us that while it is quite understandable for us to project our contemporary feelings and ideas onto past societies, we should always recognise their different, frequently conflicting ideas, and never, ever project change as having been *inevitable*.

Hugh Carleton Greene opened the doors of the BBC to a new, bolder, more challenging style of programming in the '60s, and Speight and his cohorts barged their way in, gate crashing the decade's party, creating a new, less deferential, more ambiguous moral tone. *Till Death Us Do Part* thus became the most influential comedy show of all time. Apart from its tremendous popular success, which saw the name Alf Garnett entering the familiar idioms of the English language, it was also partly responsible for the transformation of British television in terms of the ideas that could be presented and the manner in which they could be expressed. The very limitations of Alf's vocabulary were to lead to the attrition of all those mores that had kept television in check; it is of course true that society itself was ultimately responsible for this, but *Till Death Us Do Part* mounted the first assault on the battlements. Its popularity inspired further sitcoms that featured self-contained groups of people locked in conflict and caught up in the social and political maelstrom that engulfed the period; *On the Buses* (with its perennial industrial problems reflected in the humour), *Love thy Neighbour* (race and the 'hood) and countless others owe their existence in part, if not to Speight, then at least to the power generated by his creation. The popularity of the first film involving the Garnetts kick-started that very '70s phenomenon, the transfer of small screen sitcom to big screen movie, with varying degrees of success. The show's domestic celebrity then led to its adaptation for the US market by Norman Lear, and *All in the Family* subsequently changed the face of American television. Its influence can still be seen decades later in such shows as *Married with Children* and *The Simpsons*. Speight's combination of drama and humour, without any overt direction to the audience as to which was which, provided a template that has since been followed by many other shows such as *The Office* and *The Royle Family*, and his marginalisation of plot in favour of 'character comedy' has likewise proved hugely influential. *The Royle Family* even focused on reflecting the ennui and lassitude of contemporary life; the same approach *Till Death Us Do Part* had pioneered in the '60s.

But then there is another view, equally valid. Hugh Carleton Greene, in his much-screened 1982 BBC interview, appears as smug, self-congratulatory and deeply patronising in his reflections on the '60s as Lord Reith had in his opinions on the decade before. He strikes the viewer as a grandee with a mandarin attitude that will brook no opposition, whatever the reason. Mitchell cites him telephoning the cast of *Till Death Us Do Part* during rehearsals to laugh at Mrs Whitehouse, gleefully anticipating the boost that her complaints would give to the audience figures, as a sign of his stalwart support. This hints at a complete lack of cultural or ethical interest on Greene's part in the face of the ratings god. Greene continually stated that the BBC should never be partisan, and yet was widely perceived as a publicist for the Labour Party. The Director General was not alone in his smugness. At no point did Mitchell ever doubt the efficacy of his satire, even when Alf's racist insults were clearly taken at face value by that legendary football supporter whose idiocy he often recounts. And there's an odour of hypocrisy about Speight's platitudinous statements that he could never understand why working men voted Conservative – as if, while he could earn what for some would be the equivalent of two years' wages for a single script, others of the working class should never be allowed to develop or change politically. Both Mitchell and Speight had flirted with Communism, an ideology that ultimately proved to be as stupid and vicious as anything Hitler or Mussolini ever came up with. As late as 1972, Speight could blithely declare that he thought Chairman Mao was getting it just about right in China; a statement that at the very least smacked of incredible naivety, even at that time. Why on earth put your trust in such men? Speight may have expressed genuine anti-racist sentiments in the '60s, but he seems to have done so without any thought as to how his mode of expression would affect those on the receiving end of racism – and, since most West Indian immigrants at least were also deeply religious, he was dealing them a double blow by attacking the tenets of Christianity at the same time. Hindsight lends a sense of inevitability to creative and cultural change, but this was never the case in reality. Mrs

Whitehouse was merely the very vocal tip of an iceberg that was forever ignored by the chattering classes of the sunset decade, as a handful of brilliant glitterati hijacked the cultural revolution that swept through the '60s.

Journalist Garry Bushell in his television programme *The National Alf* concluded that the heirs of the randy Scouse git had taken control of the media; and, as Speight recalled, Mitchell had predicted this years earlier, foreseeing that *Till Death Us Do Part* would come under attack from the liberals once the reactionaries had finished their assault. Such is the price of fame and the cost of freedom – Speight should really have known what was coming. In that alien world of 1966, in that alternate universe of the 1960s, the liberals still controlled the media, but had the opportunity to say what they wanted, within reason, and without regard for responsibility or ratings.

But ultimately the fact remains that *Till Death Us Do Part* was the most influential and most interesting situation comedy of all time, as evidenced by its extraordinary history and the extraordinary people who made it in the midst of extraordinary times. No other show could come near it. *Till Death Us Do Part*, for better or worse, changed the face of television.

THE LAST TEMPTATION OF JOHNNY

On the far wall behind the drinks cabinet, just to the left of the radio, positioned above the photo of Winston Churchill, a new picture appears in the Garnetts' living room, picked up by some blasphemous git for a bargain price in some dusty old shop on the King's Road. It's one of those pop-art prints based on da Vinci's The Last Supper, *but instead of featuring those film stars from the golden age nestled around the iconic Marilyn Monroe, it depicts 12 different figures grouped around their creator, watching the Queen's speech on the telly, just out of sight …*

From left to right:

Sid, half-eaten sarnie in his hand, slouched against the wall, thinking about developing a cough so he can extend his Christmas holiday by a few days.

Mike, feet on the table, reading the Morning Star, *glass of whisky in front of him.*

Rita, bored, tired, baby Michael wailing in her arms.

Min, a smile across her angular features, clutching a goldfish bowl containing Uncle Fred, staring at the telly and wondering whether that Mr Heath that Mike Yarwood plays is the same person as the Prime Minister.

Alf, wearing a paper crown, standing to attention, saluting Her Majesty, pint of mild on the table beside him.

Johnny Speight, in his forties, wearing his camelhair coat, glass of Scotch in one hand, a smoke in the other, watching intently but obviously thinking about something else.

Else, open mouthed, staring blankly at the screen, eating from a packet of Golden Wonder crisps.

Bert, tucking into his meat pudding, wiping his nose with his sleeve.

Gran, dozing off over her gin, made greasy by the sandwich she has just dipped into it.

Fred the barman, resplendent in scarlet waistcoat, wiping a beer glass with his towel.

Dennis Main Wilson, chatting to Fred, waiting for his drink, watching Speight with a quiet intensity.

Paki-Paddy, carrying a battered suitcase, wearing a turban, dressed in an emerald green suit and staring at Alf and thinking what a bloody white fool he is.

And who would be Judas? Lord Hill, besuited, white-haired, with his NHS glasses and calm demeanour? Or Mary Whitehouse, wearing a hat of the most pungent lilac, garbed in a multicoloured frock with matching handbag, making notes of the number of profanities spoken in the programmes that follow …?

On the wall behind the master and his disciples is a mysterious Latin description, a code worthy of Da Vinci that contains the key to eternal life for Alf and the Garnetts, the Garnett family motto:

Ego sum iens ut tabernus

I'm going down the pub …

I hope Mr Speight would have been amused.

Episode Guide

The following episode guide has been compiled from a variety of sources – audio and video recordings; BBC written archive material, such as scripts and audience research (RI = Reaction Index) reports; press cuttings; and so forth. It gives transmission dates and times, recording dates, cast lists and plot synopses. In addition, there are the following sections: *Arguments, Arguments* lists the main political, religious, racial and social topics that are debated by the family in that edition of the show; *Bloody Language* enumerates, *a la* Mrs Whitehouse, the swear words and verbal abuse handed out; *Funny Business* is a subjective run-down of the highlights of the comic business on view; and *What Else?* wraps up any other information of interest about the episode.

Following extensive repeats of the first three series in the '60s, most of these episodes were junked by the BBC[45]. Over the past few years, several episodes or parts of episodes have been recovered. For each episode prior to the fourth series (from which point on, every episode still exists in some visual form in the BBC archives), I have noted any material that survives as of 2016.

A word about episode titles: these are given in the *Radio Times* and on BBC documentation for the first two series, but not for the subsequent ones. The correct titles therefore become less obvious from 1968 onwards. I have relied on a variety of sources for these – listings of the repeats of the third series in 1968/69 (which gave basic titles such as 'Football' and 'The Puppy'), Speight's 1973 script book and the general consensus amongst television historians. Surviving BBC programme files for the show are sparse, and information occasionally conflicting or not extant.

The two spin-off movies, although obviously not episodes of the TV series, are covered in this guide for the sake of completeness, but by way of summary details rather than full entries. Included as well are details of specials such as 'Up the Polls! (The Campaign's Over)', 'Christmas Night With The Stars' and sketches such as the Royal Variety Performance show.

---

[45] See Appendix B for details of this.

COMEDY PLAYHOUSE

TILL DEATH US DO PART

Recorded 18 June 1965
First transmitted Thursday 22 July 1965 at 8.50 pm, with an RI of 67
Repeated Monday 14 March 1966 at 9.20 pm, with an RI of 70

With Robert Dorning (Bank Manager), Derek Nimmo (Estate Agent), Colin Welland (Liverpool Football Fan), Eric Dodson

As Big Ben strikes midnight over the radio, Alf Ramsey, playing – and losing – at cards with Mike, his new son-in-law, checks his pocket watch and declares that Big Ben is wrong again – it's been so ever since Labour came to power. Mike winks at his new bride Rita and suggests that Alf write to the Prime Minister about it. He is stunned when Alf replies that he has. He even sent an SAE to guarantee a reply. However, as is typical of Wilson the socialist, he hasn't even acknowledged the letter. Only the Tories have standards now – all the best people are Tories. He's proud to be Conservative himself. Mike retorts that he has nothing to conserve, and he and Rita proceed to complain about the slum they have to live in. Else says she is fed up with all the arguing and is off to bed, while Alf tries one last time to win a game of cards against Mike – unsuccessfully.

As Alf gets ready for bed, he wonders if Mike is cheating at cards; next door, Rita and Mike also prepare for bed, and Rita too is suspicious of Mike's winning streak. Mike denies cheating and starts to kiss her; Alf listens at the wall, disapprovingly noting the squealing going on next door. Inspired, he touches Else – who rolls over in bed and tells him not to be so daft …

Next morning, Alf is reading his paper in the kitchen. Else tells him that Mike and Rita have gone house-hunting again, but Mike will be back in time for the football. Alf leaves for the outside lavatory armed with his newspaper. While seated there, he hears his next door neighbour Bert engaged in similar mode and asks him if he is going to the match. The answer is affirmative – Liverpool are a great team; Alf replies that West Ham are better …

Meanwhile, an estate agent shows the young couple around a dilapidated flat, scruffy and distinctly unappealing, with no privacy. Mike and Rita are distinctly unimpressed …

Back at home, Mike plays patience with his pack of cards, a suspicious Alf having declined a game of pontoon. Mike tells his wife that he hopes to get a bank loan later that morning. Rita is dubious – they need 20% deposit to obtain a mortgage and they cannot even begin to afford that.

At the bank, the manager quickly realises that Mike hasn't a clue about finance. When he explains the need for collateral, Mike gets very uptight and accuses the

banks of lending money only to those who already have it – a typical Tory trick …

Later, Mike tells Rita that he has found another way to obtain the money for the deposit: he has taken out a life insurance policy on his father-in-law; when Alf kicks the bucket, he and Rita will receive £500. Alf and Rita furiously denounce him, but Mike is oblivious, sauntering off to football with a sullen father-in-law … At the match – they arrive late, thanks to Alf's watch – they shout for their respective teams but a Liverpool fan threatens to thump Alf. Mike comes to the defence of his father-in-law, and a fight erupts …

Once again, Big Ben strikes midnight over the radio in the Ramseys' living room, as the women await their respective husbands. The two men stagger in, arm in arm, blind drunk, Mike proudly sporting a black eye, Alf a mysterious 'broken' leg. As Else places Mike's jacket on a chair to enable her husband to sit down and rest, a misty-eyed Alf declares that he hasn't lost a daughter, he has gained a son … At that moment, Else picks up a pile of cards that have fallen out of Mike's jacket. All of them are either kings or aces. Mike loudly protests that it was only a joke, but Alf, his leg miraculously cured, strides over to threaten him … The arguments begin all over again.

ARGUMENTS, ARGUMENTS

Labour versus Conservatives.

BLOODY LANGUAGE

At least ten 'bloodies', one 'bleeding'.

FUNNY BUSINESS

The rows about Alf's Conservative bias; Alf and Mike shouting rival slogans at the football match; Else resisting her husband's amorous advances in bed; Mike interrupting the bank teller and making sure he recounts some money; the revelation about Mike's card cheating …

WHAT ELSE?

The original script differed quite markedly from the one eventually recorded. Aside from the distinctions described in the main text of this book, there was originally a much longer bedroom scene between Mike and Rita, in which the former tries to allay the latter's anger over his cheating at cards by playing the fool. He places the chamber pot on his head and says it's very John Lennon, adding that his family used to keep tadpoles in theirs, while Rita comments they this one was used for beer at her christening. When Mike learns that the chamber pot belonged to Rita's Gran, who died in the same room, he expresses a fear of death; then he canoodles with Rita while, on the other side of the wall, Alf listens in disgust. Mention of Cabinet minister Richard Crossman, then Minister of Housing and Local Government, was originally in the script, but later replaced by George Brown, Labour's Deputy Leader.

The Ramseys' address is explicitly stated by Mike to be 10 Percy Street, Canning Town. Charles Clore, the famous Jewish financier, is mentioned sarcastically by Rita. (His name would crop up again in 'Till Closing Time Us Do Part', with Jimmy Tarbuck likening Alf to him, and in the 'Three Day Week' episode in 1974.) None of the familiar pieces of invective later used in the series are deployed, and the script does not include any of what would become Alf's trademark phrases such as 'Look ...' and 'I've lost me thread'.

Robert Dorning would reappear in the second series episode 'Caviar on the Dole'; Colin Welland was well known to the viewing public from his regular role in *Z Cars*.

The BBC commissioned an audience research report for this production; the 266 questionnaire replies revealed an audience satisfaction rating as follows:

A+	A	B	C	C-
22	43	21	10	4

The equated to a Reaction Index figure of 67 – considered extremely high, although the report indicated by way of comparison that *Hudd* had received a figure of 68. There were many positive viewer comments quoted in the report: 'Oh, how delightfully vulgar! I laughed and laughed yet in many ways it was all quite true to life' (an electrical engineer); 'One of the funniest shows since *Steptoe* ... It was alive from start to finish' (a sheet metal worker). Two thirds of the sample considered the show delightfully humorous and realistic; they found the dialogue refreshingly natural (albeit somewhat crude at times) and loved the uninhibited Cockney family, especially the dad, a 'real character', the set-up being viewed as ideal for a series. Some, on the other hand, found the programme distasteful, commenting that the setting was hardly edifying and the language was unnecessarily coarse, and that they rarely found working class 'slanging matches' particularly funny. Some felt that there was not much story and that the episode petered out at the end. The performances were generally praised, except for that of Una Stubbs, who some thought 'didn't seem too happy as a Cockney'; Warren Mitchell was seen as especially good and 'highly realistic'. In technical terms, some said that the fight at the football ground was unconvincing, otherwise most found that the direction and production proved satisfactory. 'I hope this is a taste of things to come,' concluded one housewife.

Other press comments showed that the appeal of the show was not restricted to London. The *Birmingham Evening Mail*: 'But fun was in the air too – great guffaws of it in the BBC's *Comedy Playhouse* production of "Till Death Us Do Part". There was a laugh a line in this kitchen sink comedy of a young couple living in the house of the girl's parents'. Of the 1966 repeat, the same newspaper would comment: 'The original was a memorable diversion laced with some pretty fruity English. It has *Steptoe*'s potential.'

The show attracted 16.9% of the UK viewing audience (with 16% watching ITV at the same time)

The only surviving clip of this production comes from a *Late Night Line-Up* special on television humour shown on 7 January 1966; other clips featured in the programme came from such shows as *The Likely Lads*, *Woodhouse Playhouse*, *Barney is My Darling* and *Hancock*, and guests included Johnny Speight, Marty Feldman, Ian la Frenais, Richard Waring and Duncan Wood. A drunken John Antrobus made an unscheduled appearance before being thrown out, and both Speight and Feldman seemed to have overindulged in the BBC hospitality suite beforehand. It appears that an audio recording of the episode is not available.

This was, of course, Gretchen Franklin's only episode as Else, Dandy Nichols having taken over the role for the series proper.

SERIES ONE

The opening title sequence for this first series features the show's title in speech marks, with Anthony Booth's name appearing after Warren Mitchell's but before Dandy Nichols' and Una Stubbs', an order that was to change in Nichols' favour for subsequent series. Dennis Wilson's closing music is an adapted medley of 'Colonel Bogey', 'Any Old Iron', 'Don't Dilly Dally', and 'The Laughing Policeman'. Rehearsals for the show were held at Sulgrave Boys' Club on the Goldhawk Road in London W12 and later at St Nicholas Parish Hall in Bennett Street, London W4. Recordings usually took place, before a studio audience, on Tuesdays, and all episodes were directed by Douglas Argent. Several episodes featured the whole Garnett family talking at once in certain sequences, a practice that was to stop after this series. There were a mere 20 'bloodies' for the whole series … All episodes were initially transmitted at 7.30 pm on BBC One on Mondays, directly in competition with ITV's *Coronation Street*. There was no episode on 11 July 1966, due to the screening of the opening ceremony of the World Cup and the first match (England versus Uruguay), or on 25 July, because of coverage of the first semi final. Mitchell received £210 per episode, Nichols £115 5s, Booth £120 5s and Stubbs £105. The entire series was repeated, with a fanfare of ecstatic previews in the *Radio Times*, at around 8.25 pm on Saturday evenings from 20 August, ending on 1 October. Of the seven episodes, 'Arguments, Arguments' 'A House With Love in It' and 'Intolerance' exist. Complete soundtracks of the other episodes exist as off-air audio recordings.

1.1: ARGUMENTS, ARGUMENTS

Recorded 17 May 1966
First transmitted Monday 6 June 1966 at 7.30 pm, with an RI of 60
Repeated Saturday 20 August 1966 at 8.25 pm, with an RI of 69

With Rita Webb (Singer in Pub), Will Stampe (Fred the Barman), Charlie Bird (Pub Regular), Fred McNaughton (Pub Regular), Paul Lindley (Pub Regular), Tom Clegg (Policeman)[46]

Meet the Garnetts – a typical weekend of family rows, marital rows, drunken rows, political rows, arguments at home, arguments at the pub and yet more arguments …

---

[46] Clegg's sequence was edited out of the repeat for timing reasons, although he was still credited.

ARGUMENTS, ARGUMENTS

The General Election (on 31 March); the (forthcoming) World Cup; the salaries and corruption of (Labour) MPs; the 13 years of Tory misrule; the price of eggs; Wilson making a fortune betting on the last Election; the price of houses; the working class; the armed forces; the Church; the definition of the word 'argue' …

BLOODY LANGUAGE

The first appearance of 'silly moo', four 'silly mares', one 'bleeding', six 'bloodies', a 'bloomin' great pudden', a 'fat git', a 'cobblers', a 'blue-eyed virgin', a 'Geordie yobbo', a 'pig', a 'grammar school twit'.

FUNNY BUSINESS

Else commenting that even the weather has been poor since Labour got in; Alf's reaction to Mike's declaration that they live in a 'muckhole'; Alf burning his hand on Else's iron; Mike responding to Alf's taunt of 'Geordie yobbo' by saying that he's a Scouser – 'Well, they're the worst kind of Geordies,' retorts Alf; Else's parting shot at her husband's declaration that he is going to the pub – 'That's it, that's it – you've ruined their lives, now ruin your liver!'; the display of working-class unity when Fred bars a disruptive Alf; the drunken bonhomie between Alf and Mike; Alf's sentimentality repulsed by a merciless Else, mirrored by the behaviour of Mike and Rita in the next room; Mike and Alf ending up in the same bed …

WHAT ELSE?

The action is set eight weeks after Mike and Rita got married. This episode features Alf's first malapropisms – 'prerojative' for 'prerogative', 'stratus quo' for 'status quo' – and first use of the 'learn something' and 'lost my thread' tropes. Dennis Howell, Minister for Sport, is blamed for choosing a lousy England World Cup team (this having been announced to the public on 7 May 1966) and there is also a reference to the World Cup going missing. (The Jules Rimet Trophy had been stolen on 20 March 1966 from the Methodist Central Hall in Westminster. Pickles, the dog that subsequently found it, secured a deal with the same management as Spike Milligan.) There are references to stink bombs and heckling of the Tories, probably alluding to Booth's protests at the election of Quintin Hogg at Marylebone a few years before. Other politicians mentioned include Harold Wilson, Edward Heath and Alec Douglas Home. A reference to Rita Webb's character being Jewish was cut from the script. Mention is made of the Big Ben/pocket watch motif of the *Comedy Playhouse* pilot. The episode attracted 11.5% of the UK viewing audience on its initial showing, and 14.7% on its repeat. It survives intact from its repeat showing.

Birmingham Evening Mail: 'Till Death... is going to provide a good deal of noisy, red-nosed fun, played in knockdown manner.'

Daily Express: 'It stinks... [It would make] any family viewer emotionally and mentally and physically sick ... See one and then put it on the banned list.'

Brighton Evening Argus: 'A winner...Warren Mitchell charges at his dialogue like a bull at a matador, scoring every time and leaving blood and gore behind him ... working class to his last pint.'

Radio Times reader's letter: '[I enjoyed it but] the repeated use of bad language detracted from its entertainment. Surely the aim of comedy is to entertain rather than to aim at realism?'

1.2: HAIR RAISING!

Recorded 24 May 1966
First transmitted Monday 13 June 1966 at 7.30 pm, with an RI of 71
Repeated Saturday 27 August 1966 at 8.25 pm, with an RI of 70

With Will Stampe (Fred), Charlie Bird (Pub Regular), Fred McNaughton (Pub Regular), Paul Lindley (Pub Regular), Wally Patch (Hair-restorer Debater), Eddie Malin (Hair-restorer Debater), Henry Longhurst (Barber)

An argument about the social mores and decadent attire of the younger generation turns to focus on Alf's most prominent feature, his bald pate. Alf states that he lost his follicles when stationed in the hot countries during the War and declares that it's a sign of cerebral virility, a tribute to intellectual Toryism, in contrast to the hirsute stupidity of the Labour Party. And now he's in a more humid climate, he feels that his hair is growing again ... But doubts creep in after a conversation with Else, and while the youngsters are out, Alf tries on Rita's hairpieces, only to be caught out when they return earlier than planned. Next day Alf visits the barber, and starts to worry about his baldness. In the pub he overhears a conversation about a sure-fire hair-restorer involving paraffin, bay leaves and peppercorns. Inspired, he creates this concoction, and then secretly – and painfully – administers it to his head. Later he dozes off in his chair. Mike decides to play a joke on his father in law. He uses cosmetics from Rita's handbag to draw a face on Alf's bald head, and then proudly goes upstairs to inform his wife. On returning to the living room, he finds to his horror that Alf has slipped out to the pub ... Mike rushes out and finds the entire pub laughing uproariously at Alf's painted dome, while Alf is blissfully ignorant, believing that they are laughing at Mike's hair. Back home, a chance look in the mirror reveals the depths of his public humiliation …

Mike meets Fred the barman in the street and tells him that Alf is so depressed that he hasn't spoken to anyone for days. He admits that it is up to him to make restitution, and he gets the others to encourage Alf to 'secretly' place a sign saying 'Kick Me' on the back of his jacket. At the pub, the others find this mildly amusing, Alf considerably more so, but then one of the customers opines that while this jape is funny, it's nowhere near as hilarious as that night when Alf walked in with a face painted on his head …

ARGUMENTS, ARGUMENTS

Fashion; capitalism; hair (and lack of it) as evidence of intellect and virility.

BLOODY LANGUAGE

One 'bloody', three 'bleeding lavatory brushes', a 'silly mare', three 'silly gits' (two from Else), one 'silly moo' and a 'blooming great pudden'.

FUNNY BUSINESS

Alf's reaction to his daughters kinky clothing and Mike's outrageous Robin Hood get up; Mike's groovy 'Make the scene and purchase the gear, man'; Alf saying that he wouldn't let Else go out dressed like Rita and get 'oggled'; Mike calling Alf 'Ringo'; Alf's conversation with Else regarding hair as a sign of virility; Else being asked to imagine Alf with hair – after careful consideration, she says she can't, and calls him 'Silly old git with a bald head'; Alf caught by Mike and Rita trying on one of his daughter's hairpieces; Alf in agony as he administers the hot potion; Mike almost setting fire to Alf's paraffin-soaked head as he lights up his cigarette; Mike whistling 'The Red Flag' as he paints Alf; the studio audience's laughter drowning out that of the pub-goers as Mike's brush strokes are admired; Alf's primeval howl of desperation as he realises the extent of his embarrassment …

WHAT ELSE?

The working title of this episode was 'Baldhead'. Else says she has been married to Alf for 30 years. Real people mentioned include Harold Wilson, Ringo Starr, (Ian) McLeod, Rab Butler, Winston Churchill, Quintin Hogg and Prince Philip; Edward Heath is again called 'grammar school'. Else supports her husband in his critical comments on the younger generation's attire and in his plan to get his own back on his son-in-law. The face painting joke would reappear in 'Euthanasia', the final episode of series four, and in an episode of *Till Death* ...

This episode achieved the highest ever Reaction Index for the series, and the studio audience were audibly in hysterics throughout ... It attracted 13.9% of the UK viewing audience, and 20.0% on its repeat.

Birmingham Evening Mail: '... amusing and enjoyable, but too much bad language, calculated to offend ...'

1.3: A HOUSE WITH LOVE IN IT

Recorded 14 June 1966
First transmitted Monday 20 June 1966 at 7.30 pm, with an RI of 68
Repeated Saturday 3 September 1966 at 8.55 pm, with an RI of 68

With Will Stampe (Fred) Charlie Bird (Pub Regular), Fred McNaughton (Pub Regular), Paul Lindley (Pub Regular), Jack Bligh (Pub Regular), Jacques Cey (Head Waiter), John Junkin (Wally)

Alf and Else have reached their silver wedding anniversary, and are to be treated by Mike and Rita to a slap-up meal up the West End. Alf has forgotten the occasion, but Mike comes to his rescue by buying Else some pearl earrings and a card and claiming they are from Alf. He then takes his father-in-law up the pub prior to getting ready for their posh restaurant meal. Here Alf learns that old Bert has just died and there is going to be a wake in the Tinto Road, complete with free booze. He says he would love to go and pay his respects but, to his chagrin, Mike reminds him that they are going up West ... After a series of embarrassments at the French restaurant, Alf drunkenly harangues the diners regarding his pride in his 'little girl'. His sentimental reminiscences are interrupted by Mike, who asks him for some money, as he hasn't enough cash to pay the £12 6s bill. During the consequent row, in which Alf moans that he could have had a free booze-up at the Tinto Road, Rita inadvertently tells her mother that Alf had forgotten the occasion and that Mike had been forced to buy his anniversary gift. Else turns on her selfish swine of a husband, and Alf suggests that if he had remembered the anniversary he would have bought her a better gift than the crap Mike purchased, while his message for Mike is that next time he has an anniversary, his son-in-law should do him a favour ... and forget it.

ARGUMENTS, ARGUMENTS

Anniversaries; Mediterranean cuisine; the Labour Party; bankrupt Britain and the current economic climate ...

BLOODY LANGUAGE

Two 'silly great moos', three 'silly moos', one 'bloody', one 'miserable old git' (from Else), and, right at the end, one 'crap'. Mike's peroxided hair earns him what would become the long-running insult 'Peruvian ponce' from Alf.

FUNNY BUSINESS

Alf berating the 'silly great moo'; Else, fag in mouth, berating her husband; Alf's utter ingratitude to Mike and Rita; a mention of the sex life of the milkman; Wally's cameo; Else's gambling, complete with the bill for her dairy products; the doffing of hats as Bert's funeral cortege passes the pub; Fred announcing the alcohol requirements of 'the bereaved ones'; Alf denouncing Mike as a 'Peruvian ponce', and Else as 'Ken Dodd'; Else's declaration, 'Had yer penn'eth?' to the diner at the next table as he gazes at her conspicuously adjusting her stockings; Alf saying he picked up a lot of things abroad that Else doesn't know about, and Else responding that she doesn't doubt it, and it is all right as long as he didn't bring those things back; Else and Alf reflecting on their first meeting at the Ilford Palais; Else gathering the plates at the restaurant table like a good working class mum; Alf's drunken haranguing of the other diners ...

WHAT ELSE?

The script for this episode seems to have been one of the first written for the series; it is dated 28 March 1966 and still refers to the family as the Ramseys; Gretchen Franklin's name is crossed out and Dandy Nichols' pencilled in. Its use of the wedding anniversary sitcom cliché (together with the working-class dietary *faux pas*) suggests a safety-net provided by Speight, which was then pushed back until the characters were developed. This may explain some curious details in the script. In particular, the original script refers to Alf and Else celebrating their pearl anniversary of 30 years (as also mentioned later in 'Two Toilets – That's Posh') and this is still reflected in the televised episode with the emphasis on pearls in the gifts Else receives, but by this point the anniversary has been amended to silver for 25 years. The more homely and good natured atmosphere than usual in the Garnett household (Else gives one of her very few kisses to Alf in the show) also suggests that this was one of the earliest scripts, and that Johnny Speight was still finding his feet with the characterisation. The idea of Mike being more refined than the others (displaying knowledge of French food and wine) is quickly forgotten in subsequent episodes. Another difference between the original script and the eventual recording is that in the original, the Garnetts return home for their final arguments, having been forced to pay a £24 bill.

This episode has the first of Alf's oft-repeated complaints that kisses make his head all wet, the first visit of a milkman, and the first evidence of Else's love of gambling. Edward Heath is again referred to as 'grammar school' and Ken Dodd is also mentioned. At one point, Alf gazes at the bald pate of another diner and says he has a very good hair-restorer he could use, referring to the previous week's episode. Wally the milkman was played by John Junkin, another of the Associated London Scripts contributors – he was to reprise the role in 'Peace and Goodwill' and 'Sex Before Marriage' in the second series. His monologue (with variants) was to be reused in *The Alf Garnett Saga* and in an episode of *In Sickness and in Health*.

Three bottles of Ribena were used to simulate the red wine at the Garnetts' table, three copies of the *Daily Mirror* were ordered for the recording day – one for the camera rehearsal, one for the actual recording and one as a spare – and real *escargots* were obtained for the production. Self-sealing wage packets were also ordered but not used in the recording. Alf croons 'My Old Dutch' and he and Else sing 'The Honeysuckle and the Bee'.

The show attracted 13.8% of the UK viewing audience, rising to 21.9% on its repeat. This episode survives complete in the BBC archives.

The *Birmingham Evening Mail* stated that the show was popular because 'bad language and crude domestic explosions and derisions must provide the catharsis for many a well-trained, put-on husband.'

1.4: INTOLERANCE

Recorded 7 June 1966
First transmitted Monday 27 June 1966 at 7.30 pm, with an RI of 68
Repeated Saturday 10 September 1966 at 8.40 pm with an RI of 65

With Will Stampe (Fred), Thomas Baptiste (Dr Gingalla), Pat Coombs (Woman in Surgery), Frank Gatliff (Consultant), Dennis Golding (Boy in Surgery), Pam Oswald (Nurse), John Young (Scotsman), Peter Kelly (Scotsman), Theodore Wilhelm (German Supporter), Keith Goodwin (Policeman), Lionel Wheeler (Policeman), Ian St John (Himself), Willie Stevenson (Himself).

After Mike and Alf are thrown out of the European Cup Winners' Cup match between Liverpool and Dortmund in Glasgow, Alf returns home sporting black eyes – and with no voice, having lost it while shouting at the match. He refuses to tell Else how he received the shiners, and has to write his requests down in a notebook. He visits his local doctor's surgery, where everyone else in the waiting room walks out in disgust when they learn that Dr Kelly is unavailable and has been temporarily replaced by a black doctor. Alf however receives excellent treatment from Dr Gingalla, and laments the actions of the others – everyone knows there is a colour bar, but there's no need to be rude about it ... He is then sent to a throat specialist who humiliates him in front of his students by drawing a diagram of his thyroid cartilage on his throat, denouncing him as badly- educated and therefore inclined to speak too harshly from his throat rather than his diaphragm.

His voice restored, Alf recounts the tale of his NHS treatment to his family, complaining about the flyblown sandwiches, the expense of the tea, his patronising treatment at the hands of a toffee-nosed git doctor ... Mike defends the NHS, but Alf says that Labour don't use it despite the fact that they introduced it ... Alf's ignorant talk of Gingalla enrages Mike and Rita, who denounce his intolerance. Mike points out that the British love to go abroad to change their colour by obtaining a suntan, and that the only difference between Alf and Gingalla is skin pigmentation. He decides to make his point in a more personal way by insisting – much to his father-in-law's horror – that Alf is Jewish. His grandfather's name, Mike insists, was Solly Diamond ... Alf declares that this is all lies, and, in a fury, throws a cup of tea over Mike, who then recounts how Alf received his black eyes ... While in a Glasgow pub after the match, Alf insulted Liverpool's Ian St John and Willie Stevenson, and then howled invective at some locals, thinking they were German ... and they promptly floored him. Alf, says Mike, hates everyone – coloureds, Scots, Irish, Germans – but doesn't even know why or who they are ...Then Else accuses Alf of secrecy over the fact that he was Jewish – if she had known, she would not have cooked pork chops ...

ARGUMENTS, ARGUMENTS

Football; the NHS; immigration; the Labour government.

BLOODY LANGUAGE

Two 'bloodies', the first use of 'Scouse git', a 'great pudden', a 'great pillock', a 'silly old moo'.

FUNNY BUSINESS

Alf – definitely the star in this one – threatening to write to the Home Secretary when he is arrested at the match; his pathetic croaks as he is rendered helpless at the doctors; Fred's amusement at Alf having lost his voice; a ludicrous conversation in the doctor's waiting room between Else and another lady (Pat Coombs) about black people; Else's 'Oo-er' at Alf's description of the vocal chords; Alf's instruction to his daughter to stop swearing because 'It's not bleeding ladylike'; Else interrupting her husband with her tales of great black people, such as Al Jolson ('He was black in *Sonny Boy*'); Else joining her husband in defending her racial prejudice against the younger generation, generating a 'Silly old moo' from Mike; Else missing the point about Mike's tirade on suntans and pigmentation by talking about Bognor; Alf's hysterical insistence that he is 'not bloody Jewish'; Else berating her husband for not telling *her* he was Jewish; the violence always implicit in Alf's relations with his son-in-law when Mike threatens him after Alf has soaked him with tea; Alf telling the Liverpool footballers where they went wrong, trying to 'learn 'em something'; Alf's '*Kamerad*' and '*Kaput!*' taunting of the Scottish fans as he thinks that they are German.

WHAT ELSE?

This script was rewritten by Speight before recording, apparently in part to show Alf in a worse light. Originally, Else commented on neighbour Maude Ellis having a black eye from walking into a door, and Alf responded disapprovingly that she had obviously been beaten by her husband. Then, in the pub in Scotland, Alf overheard a local boasting of handing out similar treatment to his wife, and promptly tried to teach him a lesson. (The Maude Ellis story would later be grafted into 'Caviar on the Dole' in series two.) The final scene was originally to have seen Alf grab his pork chop dinner and throw it out of the window, only for it to land on a passing policeman – this was apparently edited out prior to transmission, along with some dialogue in the consultant's surgery, due to time constraints. Originally Dr Gingalla was called Dr Agawalla.

Dr Kelly is referred to as the Garnetts' local GP throughout *Till Death Us Do Part* and is seen on screen in the episode 'In Sickness and in Health' in 1967, played by Graham Stark.

This episode is unusual in having the opening credits superimposed over a stock film sequence of the football match – the European Cup Winners' Cup match at Hampden Park, Glasgow on 5 May 1966, when Borussia Dortmund beat Liverpool by two goals to one – rather than over the standard title sequence. It is the first to feature guest stars playing themselves.

Location filming with Warren Mitchell and Tony Booth was carried out at Fulham FC on the evening of 5 June 1966, continuing until 1.00 am the following morning, and required two special banners reading 'Liverpool – The Greatest in the Land'. This footage was later intercut with the film of the actual match. Rehearsals for the studio recording took place at St Nicholas Parish Hall, Bennett Street, London W4.

After completion of the episode, Dennis Main Wilson wrote a thank you note to Pat Coombs: 'Loved having you. What a delicious lady actress you are!'. He also sent an apology to Frank Gatliff for having had to excise some of his lines.

The episode attracted 16.1 % of the UK viewing audience on its initial showing and 26.7% on its repeat A photograph of the scene in the pub with Ian St John and Willie Stevenson promoted the initial transmission in the *Radio*

Times.

Birmingham Evening Mail: '[It] got tangled up in the colour prejudice business last night. It really wasn't very funny and developed into what a lot of people probably thought was a somewhat offensive programme, with most of the people concerned shouting their heads off. The revelations of stupidity as evinced in the show were neither entertaining nor informative. As a comedy situation it did little for anyone.'

The Times: 'It demanded that Mr Warren Mitchell display a ripe series of ignorant prejudices on every subject from football to coloured people, and hilariously exploded the lot. It left behind an uncomfortable feeling that Mr Mitchell had provided a portrait from life and not a flight into fantasy.'

Daily Mail: 'Speight's script wherein virtually all the jokes came out of old Garnett's blinkered and besotted racism (the Anthony Booth character taunted him for being Jewish) was like a sunburst of laughter over a dark patch.'

1.5: TWO TOILETS – THAT'S POSH

Recorded 30 May 1966
First transmitted Monday 4 July 1966 at 7.30 pm, with an RI of 65
Repeated Saturday 17 September 1966 at 8.20 pm, with an RI of 68

With Arnold Diamond (Estate Agent)

The Garnetts debate Alf's assertion that Stalin was an American spy. Alf calls the Russians 'Western Oriental Gentlemen' – much to his daughter's mirth – and suggests that foreigners should stay in the countries that the British Empire allocated to them before Labour gave it away. He complains that it will be even worse when Britain joins the Common Market, and they take our jobs ... Mike and Rita retire to their room to discuss how they can escape the crowded house – perhaps they can persuade Alf to sell this property and use the money as a deposit for a bigger one? That Saturday evening, Alf decides to forego his traditional visit to the pub and instead have a bath while listening to a boxing match on the radio. The only way he can do this is by using a tin bath in the kitchen, and Else constantly thwarts his attempts to settle down as she forces him to get out of the water and open the kitchen door and then keeps barging past to retrieve the washing from the line and hang it up near the bath. After Alf accidentally knocks the radio into the bathwater and silences it, he overhears a conversation behind the washing – Mike, thinking his in-laws are at the pub, is talking to an estate agent about their predicament: a crowded two up, two down with the added burden of their aged and possibly senile parents ... As the agent leaves, estimating the value of the property at £750, Mike is gleeful – until Alf emerges from behind the washing and furiously empties a bowl of water over him. Next morning, Alf cuts his toenails during the family breakfast and complains that Mike was trying to sell his house over his head. A damage limitation exercise by Mike and Rita almost placates him – they emphasise the possibilities of a bigger home in leafy Wanstead, with a front room, a parlour, a proper bathroom and no less than two inside toilets! Alf almost comes round to their idea of using this house as a deposit for the new £2,500 home…but Mike enrages him by suggesting that he become their lodger as he is too old to be accepted for a mortgage. Alf storms out, bumping into the estate agent and promptly destroying the 'For Sale' sign he has brought along …

ARGUMENTS, ARGUMENTS

Alf's assertion that Stalin was an American spy; the Common Market; the Labour Party's contention that all property is theft; Heath, the grammar school twit; Wilson trying (and failing) to behave like a gentleman; De Gaulle hating Wilson for his lack of gentility.

BLOODY LANGUAGE

Four 'silly moos', five 'bloodies', a 'silly great girl', the first use of 'Shirley Temple', a 'Liverpool toe rag'.

FUNNY BUSINESS

The argument about Stalin; Mike talking to his father-in-law as if he's mentally challenged; Else's priceless contention that she is not against foreigners *per se*, but they really should live in the countries they have been allocated to; Alf's worries that if there is a war while Britain is in the Common Market, the British may not know which country to fight; Else's recollections about sex and marriage; the bath business, as Else comes to and fro, threatening a wind blowing right up her husbands 'Khyber Pass'; Alf blaming the BBC for not making their radios waterproof; Alf looming out from behind the washing to confront Mike; Alf cutting his toenails, with pieces flying into the sugar bowl and all over the breakfast; Alf's economic strategies, covered by *Magna Carta*; Alf listening in silence for several minutes to the others talking before exploding at Mike.

WHAT ELSE?

The extended bath sequence was barely mentioned in the original script. Speight's original line with Mike describing Alf's opinions as 'crap' had 'cobblers' substituted on recording.

Edward Heath is again called a 'grammar school boy'; Else again eats her husband's breakfast remains; we learn that £400 is the minimum amount required as a deposit on a new house. The Garnetts' home is valued at £750; in Chelsea, suggests Mike, it would be worth £8,000. Mike and Rita have still been married for only eight weeks … Wanstead, mentioned as the area where Mike and Rita want to live, is where Speight's parents had always wanted to move to.

Guest cast member Arnold Diamond was an old friend of Mitchell's. He would reappear in the third episode of the fourth series and in the second movie, and would also pay tribute to Mitchell on *This Is Your Life* in 1972.

The episode attracted 15.2% of the UK viewing audience on its first showing and 23.0% on its repeat.

1.6: FROM LIVERPOOL WITH LOVE

Recorded 28 June 1966
First transmitted Monday 18 July 1966 at 7.30 pm, with an RI of 70
Repeated Saturday 24 September 1966 at 8.55pm, with an RI of 67

With Patrick McAlinney (Patrick Rawlings), Julia Jones (Kate Rawlings) Will Stampe (Fred), Charlie Bird (Pub Regular), Fred McNaughton (Pub Regular)

Else opens a letter addressed to a Mrs Williams and wrongly delivered to her house, looks at it and then disposes of it, much to Alf's fury. In return, Else accuses her husband of steaming open a letter addressed to Mike, informing him that his parents are coming to visit – Alf has attempted to cover up this iniquity by resealing the envelope with condensed milk. Alf says that Mike's mother is all right, although her liberal use of holy water does annoy him, but he hates her ignorant Mick husband … The couple arrive, and it is clear that Mike's father, Patrick Rawlins, is a habitual liar and rampant Socialist, while his wife Kate is a devout Roman Catholic. They instantly anger Alf when they ask if they could stay the week since there is no point going back to Liverpool because Patrick is now on strike. The arguments start immediately. Alf and Patrick row over the economy, class warfare, ghosts and leprechauns, the Tories and Irish independence, swearing … Mike tells Rita that his father once lied that his wife had died, just so he could take a collection for her from the factory where he works. His father has misty-eyed views of Mother Ireland, yet has never even been there … Finally, Mike hears that his father has been spreading the rumour in the local pub that Mike is illegitimate. Mike asks him to leave, but Patrick has the last laugh – when Alf visits the pub, Fred asks him for the £2 Patrick borrowed, with Alf as the guarantor …

ARGUMENTS, ARGUMENTS

The workers (Patrick on strike blaming the bosses, Alf saying all the workers do is sit and smoke in the bog); ghosts and fairies; the Tories and Ireland.

BLOODY LANGUAGE

One 'Shirley Temple', one 'clever dick', one 'ignorant red-faced Mick', one 'bleedin git', one 'bleeding', two 'bloodies', two 'silly moo's, one 'lying moo', one 'good-for-nothing lazy gits'; a (paraphrased) 'silly cow', and one 'silly bitch'.

FUNNY BUSINESS

Alf, on reading about a sensational murder in the tabloids, noting that although they had murders in his day, at least they kept the bodies clothed; Else steaming open a misdirected letter to see if the contents are worth the walk over to deliver it to the correct recipient; Alf accidentally biting his tongue (a judgment from heaven, says Else); Alf denouncing working men as idle, while Patrick insists that the bosses are dead drunk in their offices most of the day, only emerging to berate the hard-grafting employees; Alf and Else criticising each other for swearing – Alf denies that he is being rude by calling his wife a silly moo, she defends her right to call him pig, then when Alf calls her a silly bitch instead, she replies 'That's better'; Alf's malapropism 'phenomenonon ...'; a debate on ectoplasm, Cardinal Wolsey and the 'Little People' (who apparently forced Patrick's father to get drunk all the time, even though he was strictly teetotal); Else and Alf lying in bed and overhearing Patrick and Kate in the next room wondering why Else has put up with her pig of a husband for so long, a sentiment with which Else immediately agrees; Patrick finding that there is no milk for his tea, going outside, seeing a baby in a pram and, while the mother is distracted, stealing the baby's milk bottle; Patrick adopting airs and graces in the pub and suggesting that his own son is illegitimate, as he was born while Patrick was away in Burma winning his Military Cross; Else and Kate moaning about their respective husbands; Else's admiration at Patrick's contention that his hand was torn off during his brave fight for the Emerald Isle's freedom (and then restored by amazing plastic surgery); Alf rousing Patrick to fisticuffs with his talk about uneducated Micks and violence.

WHAT ELSE?

The milk bottle joke would be reused in the first movie, with Alf the perpetrator this time. Many of Patrick's self-deluding Irish myths were first uttered by Dermot Kelly's character in Johnny Speight's *Comedy Playhouse* flop 'Shamrot' in 1963. The fight between Alf and Patrick when the former insults the latter's country would be emulated in the very last episode of *Till Death Us Do Part* (with Scotland replacing Ireland as the subject of Alf's prejudice). Location filming was carried out on 22 June for the sequence where Mike's parents arrive by train.

The episode attracted 16.0% of the viewing audience on its initial transmission and 25.3% on its repeat.

1.7: CLAUSTROPHOBIA

Recorded 9 July 1966
First transmitted Monday 1 August 1966 at 7.30 pm, with an RI of 67
Repeated Saturday 1 October 1966 at 9.00 pm, with an RI of 65

With Ken Fortescue (Lord Farrel), Felicity Brown (Lady Moncrieff), Syd Bromley (Local Yokel), Victor Platt (Policeman), Jerold Wells (Policeman).

The Garnetts go on holiday to the West Country, Alf hiring and driving the car, badly – moving at only 18 mph in the fast lane, reversing down a motorway, almost knocking over a policeman and sinking a mere six pints of beer at a hostelry en route *... Mike learns to his horror that his father-in-law has not passed a driving test, because he learnt to drive during the war when a test wasn't necessary. When they arrive at their holiday cottage, Alf and Else are stunned by the 'claustrophobia' of its location – row after row of empty fields that make them wish they had opted for the crowded beaches of Bognor as usual. They declare that the cottage is too spartan, then find that the tap water is brackish and the plumbing terrible. Alf gets soaked as the family desperately try to stop a leaky tap, and is thus forced to use a spare Carnaby Street outfit of Mike's when he and his son-in-law venture to the local pub. At the pub they encounter the local yokels, feudal relics whom they both despise. Back at the cottage, the family argue about the House of Lords, Alf stating that the Socialist Lords wear false ermine ... Next day, the Garnetts encounter the Lord and Lady of the manor, and Alf finds to his horror that they are Socialists ... This sets off another argument, and soon, it seems just like home ...*

ARGUMENTS, ARGUMENTS

The House of Lords (not needed says Mike; essential says Alf, because they are all scholars); Socialist Lords barely able to pay their way; fox hunting.

BLOODY LANGUAGE

Various 'gits' ('toffee-nosed', 'ill-mannered', 'stupid' and 'stupid old'), three 'misbegotten Socialists', no fewer than five 'silly moos', plus a 'silly great moo' and Else referring to 'silly moo', three 'bloodies', two 'pigs', a 'Scouse pig', a 'Scouse yobbo', a 'great pillock'.

FUNNY BUSINESS

The Garnetts trying to navigate their way via Salisbury; Alf's road rage as he goes through a red light; Alf parking between two other cars so tightly that the Garnetts have to squeeze their way out, with Else showing her bloomers to the other pub patrons; a glorious scene with a herd of cows, when Alf finds his car surrounded by *real* silly moos; Rita musing that the cottage looks '*olde worlde*' and Alf sarcastically commenting that he bets the '*khazi wazi*' is a bit '*pongy wongy*'; Alf getting soaked by the water in the basin; Alf being described as Jimmy Saville without the wig; Mike doing blatant Robert-Newton-as-Long-John-Silver impressions to the local yokels; Alf ranting on about the non-viability of the Lords having to stand for election, while Else witters about the Greeks and Prince Philip; Mike revealing his ignorance of history by saying that William the Conqueror has been dead at least 300 years (when 1966 was actually the nine hundredth anniversary of the Battle of Hastings); Else rambling on about Baldwin cheating her Aunt Kate out of 30 bob; Alf and Else bowing and curtsying to the Lord and Lady, much to Mike's amusement.

WHAT ELSE?

Speight completed the script for this episode very late, and it underwent various amendments in its journey to the screen. Lord Ted Willis is mentioned on screen but not in the script. Else's rheumatism in the script becomes lumbago in the televised version (see also 'I Can Give It Up Anytime I Like'). Pythagoras (a clever, non-restaurant Greek) is mentioned in the script but not on TV.

In his book *Stroll On*, Tony Booth mentions a prominent tout called Ringo Charlie who used to cruise up and down Soho in 1966; could this have been the inspiration for Ginger Charlie, mentioned in the script?

Ken Fortescue was a friend of Booth's – Booth got him the part of Lord Farrel in return for Fortescue securing him an apartment at Nell Gwyn House, nicknamed 'Chavering Heights' because it attracted a number of high-class prostitutes. Booth was subsequently evicted following one of his all-star drinking bouts (allegedly involving Sean Connery, amongst others).

This is the only episode in which the Garnetts ever make use of a car. Real people mentioned include Quintin Hogg (who renounced his peerage for electoral office as MP for Marylebone), Alec Douglas Home (who renounced his peerage to stand for the post of Prime Minister) and Stanley Baldwin.

The studio recording of the episodes was originally scheduled for 28 June 1966 but was postponed by two weeks, probably due to the late delivery of the script. Rehearsals took place at St Nicholas Church Hall between 4 and 8 July 1966. Location filming took place on 30 June and 1 July, but there is no record of where it was done.

An Audience Research Report was commissioned for the 1 August showing. It noted that the show attracted 18.3% of the viewing audience, as opposed to the 22% watching *Coronation Street* on the other side. The response from the 308 questionnaires completed by the viewing panel enabled a Reaction Index of 67 to be compiled from the following:

A +	A	B	C	C-
25%	33%	31%	8%	3%

The report indicated that despite a small drop in appreciation for this particular episode (the minimum for the others was 68), most viewers expressed regret at the conclusion of a splendid series. The general contention that the episode 'was not as funny as some of the others' was based on an apparently disappointing climax where the family met the lord and lady of the manor, coming at the end of a very thin plot. Nevertheless, for many, it provided 'just the sort of hilarious comedy' they had enjoyed in the rest of the series. 'The Garnett family was endearing, and their behaviour, if exaggerated, very true to life.' The report cited comments that the series 'showed good understanding of human nature' and that they 'seem a very real family'. The humour was enjoyed because it was so broad – 'down to earth, good, common humour'. However, even those who enjoyed the laughs complained of 'the crude language, the eternal abuse and the overdone catchphrases' together with 'the senseless political arguments' and 'the shouting'. These objectionable aspects did not spoil respondents' enjoyment, although a sizeable minority wondered, 'Must we have such language at the time of evening when children are watching?' The report concluded that the cast 'acted with gusto' both in this episode and the rest of the series, with Warren Mitchell praised in particular. Production wise, the outdoor shots and car sequences were thought to be especially well done.

The episode attracted a huge 27.7% audience share on its repeat showing in October

J C Trewin in *The Listener*: '[It was] all wrong, a crudity about a Cornish holiday, feebly scripted and acted with a kind of attacking desperation. A local yokel was grim enough, the local country folk were worse.'

SERIES TWO

The second series was intended to consist of 13 episodes, but only ten (plus, a little later, the Bank Holiday special) were made due to Johnny Speight's failure to submit scripts. New closing theme music with syncopated raspberries courtesy of Mitchell was added, together with an alternate shot for the opening title sequence. The show's title was no longer presented in speech marks. This series saw the debut of such catchphrases as 'yer darlin 'Arold' (referring to Harold Wilson) and 'randy Scouse git' (for Mike), while the tally of 'bloodies' quadrupled to 85 in total. Again, all episodes were directed by Douglas Argent, and the show was recorded on Tuesdays. Alf and Mike were occasionally seen reading books in this series – later, only Mike would be seen doing so. The cast were given pay rises thanks to the show's success; Warren Mitchell received £288 15s for each of the first seven episodes, then 325 guineas per episode for the rest; Dandy Nichols received £160 per episode; Anthony Booth's pay increased to £136 per episode; and although Una Stubbs' wages remained the same at £105 for each of the first seven episodes, she was paid £120 15s for each of the remainder. This was the first time that Nichols' wages and status – her name now came second on the closing credits rather than third – eclipsed Booth's. All but three of these shows were repeated within the next two years. In 2016 'Peace and Goodwill', 'In Sickness and In Health' and 'State Visit' and two-thirds of 'Alf's Dilemma' still survive intact, although clips from several others remain, mostly from the 1972 *Late Night Line-Up* special on Johnny Speight. The Bank Holiday special also survives. All the other episodes survive as off-air audio recordings.

2.1 PEACE AND GOODWILL

Recorded 29 November 1966
First transmitted Monday 26 December 1966 at 7.00 pm, with an RI of 69
Repeated Saturday 8 July 1967 at 9.25 pm (no RI available); and Saturday 21 December 1968 at 10.05 pm, with an RI of 65.

With John Junkin (Wally the Milkman), Billy Milton (Vicar)

Christmas Dinner with the Garnetts, and there is very little peace and goodwill; Mike and Rita laugh at Alf standing to attention as the Queen's Speech ends on television, and an argument then ensues about the value of royalty and the stupidity and cupidity of the Labour Party. Wally the milkman interrupts proceedings and heavily hints that that he needs his seasonal tip. Alf cries that at Christmas, everyone seems to be on the take, and as if to prove his words, he hears carol singers outside. He goes to the door intending to douse them with water from a flower vase, only to discover that the vicar is present, thus forcing him to drink the water as he reluctantly hands over a contribution ... He continues to moan about the scrounging at Christmas, prompting accusations that he is a Scrooge. Having complained about the cigars and socks he has received as gifts, he goes on to say that he has always done his best for his family, and tearfully recounts the tale of how he used his win on the 'doggies' to buy his lovely daughter a dolls' house and a china dolly. Rita is visibly moved, tearfully murmuring that she does not remember; Else declares that the reason for this is that Alf got blind drunk, fell down the stairs and smashed the bloody lot ... The arguments move on to the meaning of Christmas. Mike dismisses it as Bible mythology, but Alf is so sure of another, higher, world that he bets Mike ten bob that Heaven exists ... Rita brings in the Christmas pudding, deluged in spirits, which ignite spectacularly when Mike sets light to it. As they eat, Alf feels a pain in his chest, and Else declares that he must have swallowed the thruppenny bit she hid in the pudding. Alf thinks he may be poisoned, and Mike says that if he ascends to the Pearly Gates and finds that Heaven does not exist, he should remember to send down the ten bob he owes him. At this, Alf throws his pint of beer over his son-in-law ... Exeunt all, arguing ...

ARGUMENTS, ARGUMENTS

The benefits of the monarchy; prime ministers; Ernest Marples, the bike-riding ex-Minister of Transport; the Labour government and the wage freeze; drinking; the meaning of Christmas; Christianity and mythology.

BLOODY LANGUAGE

Eight 'bloodies', a 'poor old git', a 'socialist Scouse git', an 'ignorant, misbegotten, lying, layabout, socialist Scouse git', a 'traitorous Scouse git', a 'poor old git', a 'silly pillock', a 'pillock', a 'great hairy nellie', four 'silly moos', and a 'blasphemous swine'.

FUNNY BUSINESS

Else's contention that the Queen's Christmas dinner is kept warm in the oven for her while she does her speech; accusations of Harold Wilson sleeping it off after a night out drinking, fiddling the books with James Callaghan, and putting the England footballers in red shirts to pretend Labour won the World Cup; Alf referring to foreign royalty as 'cloth cap kings riding about on bikes'; rows about bikes scraping against the Queen's passage; Alf's assertion that if the Queen did belong to a political party, it 'ain't the bloody Labour Party'; Rita's complaint that her father is so mean he wouldn't give anyone a cold; the vase scene with the carol singers; the violence (socks, vase, beer, custard, all thrown around); a meticulously-timed scene where Alf sits down and misses his chair; the hilarious dolls' house story; Alf's venomous dismissal of God's 'oppo' Lucifer; Mike's intent stare and murmurs of 'Yeah, yeah …' as if Alf is mad; Alf's 'hear no evil' stance as Mike explains that Christianity is a con trick; 'It'll burn,' says Mike regarding the whisky poured on the pudding – *'You'll* burn,' replies Alf; the final incineration of the pudding.

WHAT ELSE?

The action is set in real time between 3.10 pm and 3.40 pm on Christmas Day. Mike recalls the Rt Hon Quintin Hogg being interviewed by 'that geek David Frost' on TV recently, prompting him to cry 'Tell the truth! Tell the truth!'; this was possibly an ad lib by Tony Booth, who had assisted the Labour candidate in competition for Hogg's seat in Marylebone.

During rehearsals on 28 November, Mitchell mistimed the action of Alf missing his chair on sitting down, sustaining bruises and grazing – 'Could be a severe handicap to my career as an up-and-coming belly dancer, most disfiguring', he wrote to his agent the following week.

Dandy Nichols was interviewed about the show by Judith Chalmers on 2 December 1966 for *Welcome Christmas*, transmitted on Christmas Day.

A seven minute clip of this episode, featuring the carol singers sequence, was shown as part of the 1967 edition of the BBC's then annual *Christmas Night with the Stars* programme. The same sequence was later remade as the *Till Death Us Do Part* sketch for the 1971 edition of the same programme, this time involving a black vicar, and was also reused years later in the Christmas edition of *In Sickness and in Health*. The *All in the Family* episode 'Christmas with the Bunkers' borrows some material from Speight's script, notably the cigars reference and the dolls' house story. Talk about Alf being the only one to stand for the national anthem in the cinema would be reflected in the first *Till Death Us Do Part* film, which ends with Alf alone standing to attention while the rest of the audience moves out. The joke about the England team's red shirts would also be reused in that film.

This edition of *Till Death Us Do Part* was entered for the 1967 Golden Rose of Montreux prize, but lost out to a programme made by 'that geek' David Frost.

An Audience Research Report was conducted for this opening show of the second series, and noted that it attracted an astonishing 39.5% of the viewing population (as opposed to 12.8% for ITV and 1.8% for BBC2). It bestowed a Reaction Index of 69, based on the following response:

A +	A	B	C	C-
33%	34%	16%	10%	7%

The report stated:

> [There was] a fairly widespread feeling that on this occasion the scriptwriter, Johnny Speight, had, perhaps, gone rather too far. Politicians were evidently felt to be a legitimate enough target (although even here some thought there was too much argument and 'mickey taking') but royalty and – in particular – religion were hardly subjects for such distasteful treatment (especially at Christmas) and parts of the programme were not only embarrassing but offensive. Together with the vulgarity and swearing 'characteristic' of this programme, a sizeable proportion of viewers echoed one housewife. 'I have always thought this programme rather coarse but this was the worst of the lot. It's a pity that, to get a laugh from the riff-raff of the country, religion and royalty have to come into it.'

Despite the usual complaints about coarse language being deployed when children might be watching, most viewers seemed delighted with the show and its 'knocking down' of hallowed institutions. One viewer echoed many by saying, 'I just don't know how they get away with a lot of it, but it's very funny, even if it occasionally takes your breath away.' Again, the reality of the situation was appreciated: 'The principal feature of this show is that it portrays humanity as it is and not what many pretend or would like it to be.' Mitchell and Nichols were especially praised, and the settings, camerawork and direction approved.

The second repeat of this episode two years later attracted a 31.1% audience share.

A film print of the episode still survives in the BBC's archives. It has one small section missing, but fortunately this can be found in a clip in the *Late Night Line-Up* special on Johnny Speight from 1972.

The Revd Eric Roberts from Liverpool: 'A vulgar intrusion into a low down row between man and wife …'

Headmaster Derek Belton of Sopley Park School, Christchurch: 'After seeing last week's edition of the programme with its filth, bad language and blasphemous references, my faith in the BBC has been completely shattered.'

A letter printed in the *Birmingham Evening Mail*: '[It] … reached a new low on Boxing Day evening … when bets were placed on the existence of God. This was utterly incredible when we have just celebrated the birth on Earth of Christ, the son of God. Few people are amused by this type of humour, which hits at the very basis of Christianity.'

2.2: SEX BEFORE MARRIAGE

Recorded 6 December, 1966
Transmitted Monday 2 January 1967 at 7.30 pm, with an RI of 65

With John Junkin (Wally the Milkman), Leslie Noyes (Decorator)

Aided by his family, Alf is trying to hang some new wallpaper in the living room, and making a right pig's ear of it. As Mike and Rita kiss while pasting the paper, Alf glares and complains about the intricacy of the pattern, the lack of speed shown by his son-in-law and the fact that they are running out of time. He moans that he gave up his traditional Saturday football for this … Else suggests that he should never have gone down the pub at lunchtime, but her husband says he had to – it was the occasion of wetting the baby's head of Charlie Treacy's grandson. The parents, glowers Alf, aren't even married, symptomatic of a decadence that has even seen the church publish its own guide, Sex Before Marriage. *The whole country, he says, has gone sex mad … This prompts Mike and Rita to debate the ethics of premarital sex, arousing Alf's suspicions as to his daughter's virginal status prior to their wedding … Rita denies that any hanky panky took place, and eventually an outraged Alf and Else concede that Mike and their daughter were innocent prior to their wedding day. But when her parents leave the room, Rita and her husband burst out laughing – if only they knew … Meanwhile, Else reminds her husband that he once tried to have sex before marriage with her … Wally the milkman arrives, offering a variety of black market goods at knockdown prices, prompting Alf to denounce a welfare state that encourages such thievery. Then he asks Wally for some bottles of cheap whisky … More talk about maternity leads to a discussion on God, with Mike denying His existence. When Else's constant to-ing and fro-ing through the lounge delays Alf's wallpapering even further, Mike suggests he call God, who'd make short shrift of such a manual task. Alf is left alone when the others walk out in disgust at his constant complaints, and he muses on the miraculous way in which God created everything in seven days, whereas nowadays all the workers sit on the bog smoking fags. Then he sees to his fury that his cuts of wallpaper are too short. God has forsaken him … Later, Alf has paid a local decorator eight and a half quid to finish off the job, yet wants to pretend that he himself has just completed it. As the decorator is about to leave, Else comes in. The workman hides the money and loudly praises Alf's work. Alf asks Else what she thinks, and after a long stare, she replies that now she isn't so keen on the floral design she chose … An infuriated Alf shouts that he is going*

own the pub. But he returns only moments later – he has just realised that he has
spent all his money ...

ARGUMENTS, ARGUMENTS

Socialists and their encouragement of free love; the prospect of one million unemployed caused by Wilson's Selective Employment Tax, and of that million then breeding like rabbits, sponging off the NHS; the Tories forcing people to pay 1/6d for orange juice when it used to be free; too many religions, although there's only one true one; the Church talking about sex on the telly; the existence of God.

BLOODY LANGUAGE

Twelve 'bloodies', four varieties of 'Scouse git' ('dirty minded', 'randy', 'randy socialist' and 'blasphemious'), two 'Shirley Temples', four 'great puddens' (including 'moonstruck' and 'silly'), two 'silly moos' (including one from Rita to Alf), a 'great hairy nellie', a 'long haired pansy' and (in reference to Mike's groovy T-shirt) one 'bloomin' great street map'.

FUNNY BUSINESS

Alf's utter incompetence at wallpapering; Else agreeing with Alf about the embarrassment caused by some bishops talking about sex on telly the other night; Else siding with Alf against the idea of Mike and Rita having had premarital sex; endless scenes involving Else – who really steals the episode – disrupting Alf's wallpapering by complaining about her husband, making patterns out of off-cuts of paper, deciding to go out, and then in, going to the toilet, collecting her cardigan to go to the toilet, returning from the toilet ...; Else damning her husband when he declares that they never had sex until after they were married – 'Well after,' she says; Else's long silence before accusing Alf of wanting to have sex before marriage when they met at the Green Man in Wanstead and he tried to seduce her with egg flips; Else accusing Alf of being too drunk to have any more kids; Wally and his array of black market goods, which he says fell off the backs of lorries, a statement Else completely believes; the quiet and rather touching way Alf considers the existence of God, talking to himself; Alf launching into a series of curses, then realising that he's been communing with God – 'I'll paper this room out if it's the last thing I do – it won't be, though, God, will it?', he says nervously.

WHAT ELSE?

Virtually the whole of this episode centres on the business of decorating –

a situation suggested to Johnny Speight by Frank Muir when he thought the writer needed to frame his dialogue in a more interesting manner. This is the first episode in which Alf insults Mike using the phrase 'randy Scouse git', and the last to feature Wally the randy milkman. Leslie Noyes, cast here as the decorator, was an associate of Speight's from the Arthur Haynes shows and was to reappear in the 1975 series. Mike wears a dazzling 'Carnaby Street' T-shirt.

The episode was watched by 34.9% of the viewing population. It was never repeated and no longer exists, although one clip of the Garnetts decorating survives in the 1972 *Late Night Line-Up* special on Speight.

'Disgusted' of Kings Heath, in a letter to the *Birmingham Evening Mail*: 'I considered it too vulgar to be shown and was glad to use the switch on my set.'

Birmingham Evening Mail: '*Till Death Us Do Part* descended to offensive vulgarity. Its coarseness in the past has been more than balanced by the brilliance of its humour. It even, on occasions, pointed a moral. But last night's story was vulgar without point. Its title 'Sex Before Marriage' contained a hope that it may have been a cautionary tale. True, it had its precious moments, but as a whole it was just smoke room stuff.'

2.3: I CAN GIVE IT UP ANYTIME I LIKE

Recorded 22 December 1966
First transmitted Monday 9 January 1967 at 7.30 pm, with an RI of 67
Repeated Saturday 22 July 1967 at 9.30 pm (no RI available); and on 16 November 1968 at 9.40 pm, with an RI of 64

The Garnetts are watching the commercial channel (none of that BBC rubbish, insists Alf) through a haze of cigarette smoke from Mike, who is coughing continually because he also has a cold, and pipe fumes courtesy of Alf. When Mike's cough continues, Rita urges him to give up smoking, much to Alf's cynical merriment. Eventually, the two men make a pledge that they will both stop smoking, contributing the money saved to either Else or Rita, whoever is the first to detect that her respective spouse has broken the pledge. Alf finds his end of the bargain very difficult to keep, what with that bloody fool Wilson smoking his pipe on the telly and with Else and Rita puffing away in the living room. He even suggests that if Mike wants to call it off, he will happily agree. But Mike says he feels marvellous now he's quit … Alf is getting desperate, and even an impassioned rant about the wonders of the Royal Family in a democracy fails to quell his aching need to smoke. He attempts to smoke secretly – in the outdoor bog, and in the bedroom while his wife is downstairs – but is thwarted by Mike's suspicions and by Else's habit of returning spent matches to the matchbox. Then he has a brainwave – he lets his wife discover him smoking, and is seen by Mike and Rita proudly lighting his pipe, declaring that he is supporting the nation's shattered economy by smoking (for Queen and country). Then he goes to the cinema with Else to celebrate her winnings. For once, it is Mike and Rita who are left speechless.

ARGUMENTS, ARGUMENTS

Television programmes – not as good since Labour came to power, allegedly; Lord Hill and his work at the ITA; Labour politicians being dragged up from the slums, unlike the Royals; the Queen and Prince Phillip – they should have the power to veto the Labour government, says Alf, and Philip should be Prime Minister; the nature of democracy; MPs Michael Foot, Konni Zilliacus and Ian Mikardo ('Bloody foreigners' says Alf).

BLOODY LANGUAGE

Eight 'bloodies', five 'Scouse gits' (including 'long-haired', 'rotten' and 'nosey'), one 'silly moo', a 'great hairy nellie', two 'cobblers'.

FUNNY BUSINESS

Else interrupting Alf to talk about Lord Hill, the old radio doctor, curing her lumbago; Else's contention that everyone was healthier when Hill was the radio doctor, to which Mike replies that if he had stayed there, then the telly would have been better too; Alf opining that pipe smoking is much healthier than cigarette smoking; Else's 'Oo-er' as she listens to Mike's suggestion about her and Rita being referees; the attempts to symbolically throw cigarette pack and pipe into the fire; Rita, as Alf storms off to bed, telling her husband that her father will be impossible to live with now, and Else responding that he's been impossible to live with for the last 30 years ...; Alf roaring about Harold Wilson's deplorable dress sense – and his pipe smoking – as the television news shows the premier disembarking from an aeroplane; the observation that the Queen is never seen with a fag in her mouth ('Nor 'im, Phillip', agrees Else); the debate about Philip being Prime Minister; Alf's attempts to smoke secretly, in the outdoor toilet, and while pretending to say his prayers in the bedroom.

WHAT ELSE?

References to Lord Hill, the ex-radio doctor, 'a Tory subservient to Labour', and head of the ITA, were to rebound on Speight when Hill became BBC Chairman that summer. Else mentions *Emergency Ward 10*, in which Dandy Nichols had starred. Edward Heath is again referred to as a 'grammar school twit'. Alf again recalls his time in the burning heat of the desert during the War. Mention is made of a recent national opinion poll in which most people said that the Queen should be able to veto the government.

This episode attracted 31.7% of the viewing audience on its first transmission, and 28.0% on its 1968 repeat.

Birmingham Evening Mail: '… in the well-known ribald style, was about giving up smoking. It thus delivered a message suitable for young people in terms that are not.'

Reader's letter in *Birmingham Evening Mail*: '*Till Death Us Do Part* is surely not representative of the British theatre today. Do ordinary families behave in such a way, shouting each other down? I doubt it.'

2.4: THE BULLDOG BREED

Recorded 3 January 1967
First transmitted Monday 16 January 1967 at 7.30 pm, with an RI of 64
Repeated Saturday 5 August 1967 at 9.25 pm (RI Unknown)

With Roy Kinnear (Lorry Driver), Fred McNaughton (Policeman)

Mike attempts to persuade his father-in-law to make a contribution to the Medical Aid for Vietnam scheme, but this only prompts a debate about war – the Vietnam War, the Second World War and the First World War. Alf spreads out a world map across the table, but doesn't quite know where Russia or even Asia can be found on it. Labour is again blamed for giving away the Empire, especially all the nice bits … Else points at Eire, convinced it is the Isle of Wight, and happily recalls the latter's summertime pleasures. Mike and Rita meanwhile kiss and cuddle, much to Alf's fury. Alf is convinced that the younger generation's anti-war stance is part of a Trotskyist plot. He defends the causes of the First World War and proudly declares his service in the desert in the Second World War. His true 'bulldog breed' spirit is revealed, however, when the room is darkened by a huge lorry parking right outside the window. His angry remonstrations with an equally belligerent lorry driver almost lead to violence, avoided only by Alf making a strategic retreat. Then he goes out and starts to let the lorry's tyres down in revenge, only to find not only the driver but also a policeman staring at him. The driver hands a tyre pump to Alf; Alf refuses, so the driver hands the pump to the policeman, who now hands it to Alf, and this time Alf has to obey … So much for the bulldog breed!

ARGUMENTS, ARGUMENTS

Vietnam; Harold Wilson; Ian Smith and Rhodesia; the Bomb; Kosygin; Trotsky; the Second World War; the First World War; racial prejudice.

BLOODY LANGUAGE

Nine 'bloodies', one 'bleeding', two 'silly moos', a 'great hairy nellie', a 'Scouse git', an 'ignorant Scouse git', a 'mean old git', four 'fat gits' and a 'Shirley Temple'.

FUNNY BUSINESS

Else demanding her shilling contribution back when Alf suggests the Russians are behind the charity; Else's blissfully recalling the Isle of Wight as the others try to find Vietnam on the map; Alf's conviction that the British could resist nuclear war more effectively than the Japanese because they are a better breed; Alf's assertion that George V had, like a true gentleman, offered to settle the Great War with a boxing match against the Kaiser in the grounds of Buckingham palace; Alf and the lorry driver threatening each other in the street, wearing each other out with their challenges.

WHAT ELSE?

This episode represents the first real experiment by Johnny Speight in virtually ignoring the 'situation' (so prominent in the first three episodes of the second series) in favour of presenting a 'symposium' on a particular topic, with most of the episode devoted to the Garnetts gathered around a map of the world. The studio audience seem confused at some points, and a nervous silence greets some of the early conversations.

This marks the first appearance of Roy Kinnear in the show; he was to return (in a different role) as a semi-regular in the 1972 and 1974 series. The wonders of the Isle of Wight were to be mentioned again in the seventh series episode 'Window' in 1975, in a discussion between Min and Ethel. Fred McNaughton had appeared in the first series as a pub regular.

Mike calls his father in law 'Cassius' at one point, in reference to the boxer Cassius Clay, aka Muhammad Ali. This scene would be reworked in the last episode of the 1975 series, with Alf and (in that case) Wally coming to blows.

Warren Mitchell and Tony Booth appeared at a real anti-Vietnam war event at the Royal Albert Hall in June 1968.

The episode attracted 32.6% of the viewing audience on its initial transmission.

H Buxton, Nottingham, letter to the BBC: '[*Till Death Us Do Part*] plumbs the depth of vulgarity … lacks humour … It is not entertaining

… a cheap way of getting attention … It influences children.'

2.5: CAVIAR ON THE DOLE

Recorded 15 December 1966
First transmitted Monday 23 January 1967 at 7.30 pm, with an RI of 68
Repeated Saturday 18 January 1969 at 9.35 pm, with an RI of 66

With Will Stampe (Fred the Barman), Dermot Kelly (Irish), Robert Dorning (National Assistance Inspector), Barbara Keogh (Counter Clerk), Lewis Ward (Man at Employment Exchange)

Mike has lost his job again, but he is quite happy – Harold Wilson has just increased unemployment benefit to £11 10s a week. Alf is enraged, railing against the typical socialist ploys of champagne and caviar on the dole. Mike retires to bed, taunting his father- in-law by saying how much he will enjoy his leisure the next day after he visits the employment exchange. Else asks Alf to explain redeployment, a consequence of Labour's Selective Employment Tax, but Alf has a hard time getting through to her. Else blames Mike's unemployment on those Chinese lascars flooding into the country and sobs that she and Alf might lose Rita as well as Mike if he is redeployed away from London.

The next day, a similar conversation takes place in the labour exchange as a man with a broad Irish brogue complains that foreigners are taking all the jobs. Another man agrees, saying that the Irish are the worst, and then asking the first if he is Irish. No, replies the first man, he is English through and through. When the other has gone, Mike, who has overheard, quietly insists that the first man is Irish, isn't he? Only by birth, replies the man – he and his parents are English. He asks Mike for some coppers, but Mike insouciantly suggests that he should find a job and then get made redundant and claim benefit; meanwhile, he should ask the Pope for a subsidy … Mike walks off to chat up the female assistant and ask to see someone about his rent, while the Irishman curses him…

Later, an ecstatic Mike is having a drink and explaining to Fred the barman that he is now so much better off, with an increased benefit and £5 a week national assistance towards his rent – which, considering he pays Alf only one pound a week for his lodging, means he has made a vast profit. But when Fred replies that the government checks up on this, Mike begins to worry …

Returning home, Mike surprises everyone with his deference to Alf, arousing suspicion when he self-importantly hands over £2 10s extra rent to his father in law, just to reward him for paying his taxes all his life … Rita sees through him, and Mike confesses what he has done. Alf is furious, but Rita begs her father to play along now to avoid giving Mike away. Alf demands that Mike pay him the £5 he owes plus £2 extra. A knock on the door reveals the national assistance inspector, who stuns Alf into silence with an attack on his Rachman-like behaviour as a landlord, overcharging the young couple for their rent in such a terrible property and threatening to turn his poor pregnant daughter out onto the streets … He leaves, warning Alf against any further intimidation of the couple. Alf turns to face his tearful wife, who has believed everything the man has said, and now cries out at his cruelty to his only child. She worries that if Mike leaves on redeployment, she will be stuck here – with him …

ARGUMENTS, ARGUMENTS

The Labour government; the Selective Employment Tax; national assistance.

BLOODY LANGUAGE

Six 'bloodies', a 'great hairy nellie', a 'lazy, good-for-nothing git', a 'silly old git', a 'stupid Scouse git', a 'blooming great girl', a 'sweet Miss Liverpool' (Alf to Mike), one 'bleeding', a 'silly great pudden'.

FUNNY BUSINESS

Alf's assertion that Mike and company vote for Labour so they can be put out of work and exist on benefits; Mike whistling 'The Red Flag' to deliberately enrage Alf; Alf later realising he has been unconsciously whistling 'The Red Flag' as well, and changing the tune to 'God Save the Queen'; Else and Alf ganging up against Mike's 'effeminacy' as he brushes his long hair; Alf thumping the table in anger and accidentally impaling himself on Else's needle; Else's quite stunning lack of intelligence when an increasingly irritated Alf tries to explain redeployment to her – she asks why the government don't move factories and docks around the country rather than people, to nicer places such as Bournemouth, prompting him to suggest that she move down to the Cornish farm and stay with all the other silly moos, to which she replies that he should do the same and stays with the other dirty pigs; Dermot Kelly's denial of his Irish birth, followed by his aside of 'English pig!' to the other jobseeker and then 'Protestant pig!' to Mike; Mike's denial that he is English – he comes from Liverpool; Alf choking on his dinner when he realises Mike's deception; Alf's instant deference to the national assistance man.

WHAT ELSE?

Else tells Rita about Maude Ellis's husband Harry hitting his wife because she hadn't got his dinner ready; a line initially intended for 'Intolerance'. There is a reference to the Garnetts' rural holiday, as seen in 'Claustrophobia'.

Dermot Kelly had played the same work-shy, self-deceiving Irishman in Johnny Speight's *Comedy Playhouse* episode 'Shamrot' in 1963. Prior to that he had appeared in the stage production of Speight's *The Knackers Yard* in 1962, and then as a regular on the Arthur Haynes shows. He was also to appear in 'Till Closing Time Us Do Part'. Robert Dorning had played a similar officious role in the *Comedy Playhouse* episode that launched *Till Death Us Do Part*.

The episode attracted 32.7% of the UK audience on its first showing and 34.1% on its 1969 repeat.

Radio Times blurb for this episode in 1969: 'Mike's job becomes redundant – but he finds out how to live in idle luxury.'

2.6: A WOMAN'S PLACE IS IN THE HOME

Recorded 17 January 1967
Transmitted Monday 30 January 1967 at 7.30 pm, with an RI of 66

With Geraldine Sharman (Girl in Phone Box), Fanny Carby (Woman at Phone Box), Lewis Ward (Ted), Julie May (Angry Neighbour), David Graham (Telephone Operator)

Alf comes home late from work to find no family, no fire and no meal – Else left his dinner in the oven, where it eventually 'incinderated'. Else and Rita arrive back at 9.30, having been out to the pictures. They are now awaiting Mike, who has gone to buy the three of them some fish and chips. Else states it is not her fault that Alf's meal was burnt – he should have come home on time. Alf declares that he had to work overtime and demands a proper hot meal, not the tinned stuff in the pantry. The others suggest he phone the fish shop, where Mike is queuing, and order an extra meal. Alf goes to the call box at the corner, only to be delayed by a girl who is on the phone professing her undying love to a certain Charlie. Finally able to use the phone, Alf grows even more frustrated on getting a crossed connection and hearing a man ask to speak to his sister, Mrs Williams. He then becomes apoplectic when the operator states that he cannot give him the number for Sammy's Chip Shop (which he says is in 'High Street, Wapping'). Finally Mike innocently turns up with fish and chips – for just three … Rita volunteers to go back and get her father some. Later, Mike tells Alf that his daughter has rung the phone box to ask what kind of fish he wants. The two men go out again, only for Alf to find the same girl in the call box; a potentially tricky situation that Mike expertly defuses with his charm. Alf eventually picks up the phone, only to realise that he still doesn't know the number, and howls for Mike, prompting a neighbour to shout out and tell him to shut up. Then the phone rings – but it is Ted Williams again. Alf hangs up. It then rings once more; Alf picks it up, finds that it is Rita, but then automatically slams it down again. Another ring – it is Ted! Alf slams the phone down and turns to find that

Mrs Williams is at the call box door, asking if he has finished, because she wishes to call her brother Ted … The phone rings – this time it is Rita again, asking if Alf wants skate or rock. An exuberant Alf replies that he wants skate, then marches out, telling Mrs Williams to give her brother a message – that he is a stupid git. Back in the house, Else reproaches him for swearing, which Alf hotly denies. He smiles when Rita returns – until she declares that Sammy's had run out of fish altogether. However, she says that there is a phone message for him. Crestfallen, Alf goes into the call box, picks up the phone – and finds it is Ted Williams, who tells him that if anyone is a stupid git, it is he. Alf is speechless.

ARGUMENTS, ARGUMENTS

No political, religious or social rows, only an argument about swearing.

BLOODY LANGUAGE

Seventeen 'bloodies', two 'silly moos', a 'nosey bloody moo', a 'nosey moo', a 'bloomin' great pudden', a 'great, long-haired Scouse git', a 'randy Scouse git', a 'bald-headed old git', an 'old git face', a 'great stupid pillock', a 'silly great pillock', a 'great pillock', a 'saucy little bitch'.

FUNNY BUSINESS

Alf trying to light the fire (repeated in a 1975 episode on a more spectacular scale); Alf apologising to the Queen for knocking her picture over; Alf overplaying his hand when he tells his daughter that he wouldn't eat anything she cooked now she has insulted him, before sitting in a dead sulk; the hilarity of Else and Rita at Alf's plight; the love struck teenager talking to 'Charlie' and insulting 'baldy' Alf; the business with the telephone; Alf reading out some call box graffiti – 'The Pope's the head of the Mafia'; Mike commenting on the wonders of Sammy's fish as Alf gazes in hunger on his son-in-law's meal; Alf vehemently denying that he bloody swears; Mike telling Alf that he is inarticulate, and Alf denying that 'bloody' is swearing (possibly a message from Johnny Speight to his detractors).

WHAT ELSE?

This episode marks the second use of the famous 'randy Scouse git' insult. This situation with the phone will be referred to by Rita in the first episode of the third series the following year, 'The Phone'. The chip shop was originally referred to as 'Wally's' in the script. Is the Ted Williams at the other end of the telephone the same Williams who would appear in 1968's 'The Funeral' (played by Bill Fraser)? Mrs Williams was first mentioned in

'From Liverpool with Love'; she is 'the nosy bloody moo at number 37'. Alf sarcastically calls Mike 'Jimmy Tarbuck' at one point.

Fanny Carby had appeared in previous Speight shows and was to feature as Blenkinsopp's landlady in *Curry and Chips* in 1969. David Graham, who voiced the telephone operator, was known for his voice work on *Thunderbirds* and for his Dalek voices on *Doctor Who*.

The episode attracted 31.4% of the UK viewing population.

On September 1st 2016, a new production of this 'missing episode' was shown on BBC 4 as the opening shot of 'The Lost Sitcoms' trilogy, starring Simon Day as Alf, Lizzie Roper as Else, Sydney Rae White as Rita and Carl Au as Mike.

2.7: A WAPPING MYTHOLOGY (THE WORKERS' KING)

Recorded 24 January 1967
First transmitted Monday 6 February 1967 at 7.30 pm, with an RI of 69
Repeated Saturday 15 July 1967 at 9.20 pm (RI unknown); and Saturday 11 January 1969 at 10.00 pm, with an RI of 66

With Will Stampe (Fred)

Alf affixes a picture of Edward VIII, ex-Duke of Windsor, to the wall, claiming he was the Workers' King, the greatest monarch the country ever had. When Mike and Rita ridicule him, Alf insists that his father was great friends with the Duke of Windsor; they both supported West Ham and drank in the Royal Crown, where they were the only ones who could down a yard of ale in eight-and-a-half seconds flat. Else states that knowing the fondness of Alf's fathers for liquor, at least that part of the story is true. Mike asks how Alf senior knew that his Duke of Windsor was the real one, and Alf replies that one can recognize the implicit breeding in royalty ...

Alf opens a letter to reveal that he has won two tickets for the West Ham versus Liverpool match the following Saturday. Mike automatically thinks he will receive the other ticket, but Alf says that he might sell it on the black market and make a profit; nevertheless, Mike follows Alf to the pub, and it is not long before a drunken Alf has agreed to Mike's requests, following some strategic double whiskeys and Mike's enforced denunciation of his darlin' 'Arold ... Alf revives the earlier conversation by telling Fred that the Duke was West Ham's greatest fan ... Tearfully, Alf explains to Mike that Stanley Baldwin forced the abdication of Edward not because of Mrs Simpson but because he was jealous of the East End's veneration of their monarch ...

At the match in Liverpool, Alf and Mike get drunk; even more so when Alf's team loses. Their respective wives meanwhile watch highlights of the match on TV, waiting for their spouses to return. When Alf and Mike stagger in, Alf tries to cuddle Else, much to her disgust, while Mike falls on the sofa. Alf blames Wilson's political chicanery for West Ham's loss, claiming that the premier used his power over his Liverpool constituency to win the match. Then he gives a toast: to Bobby Moore, to Alfred Ramsey (Master of the Queen's Football) and to the Duke of Windsor, the Workers' King. After which, he collapses to the floor in a drunken stupor, to a baleful glare from his wife …

ARGUMENTS, ARGUMENTS

Royalty; football; Harold Wilson; trade unions.

BLOODY LANGUAGE

Two 'bloodies', three 'moos', a 'Mr Clever Dick', a 'bolshie peasant', a 'great hairy nellie', a 'long-haired Scouse pansy', a 'socialist twit', a 'bloomin' great pudden' and (Mike to Alf) a 'two-faced, four-eyed old git'.

FUNNY BUSINESS

Alf trying to get confirmation from Else that his father knew the Duke of Windsor – 'You knew my father …' – 'Yeah, and he was a bigger liar than you are!'; Mike pointing out to Alf that royals do breed in the same way as the rest of us, and Else telling him to be quiet as they don't want that kind of talk in their house, thank you; Else stating, to Alf's supreme indignation, that he hasn't had *her* permission to go to Liverpool yet, and complaining that while *he* can afford to go to Liverpool, *she* can never afford to see her sister Lil in Southend – when Alf shouts back that he'll pay for her to go and see her sister, she calmly replies that she doesn't want to …; Alf insulting Lil and Else's mother, referring to the latter as 'old horseface'; Alf forcing Mike to denounce Wilson; Alf's sentimental recollections of his father's chats with his mate 'Teddy'; Alf and Mike getting royally drunk; Alf's drunken attempts to cuddle his wife, followed by his complete collapse; more malapropisms – 'fackeeshus' (for facetious); 'ees-queery' (for equerry); 'It's yer honewort and yer mally partnse' (for *honi soit qui mal y pense*).

WHAT ELSE?

Warren Mitchell and Tony Booth did an interview in character for *Grandstand* on 7 January 1967 at the Upton Park ground of West Ham, who were playing Liverpool in the FA Cup. They later entered the stand to be greeted by the 48,000 supporters shouting 'Silly moo!'. The match was then filmed for *Grandstand* with shots of Alf and Mike enjoying it. Liverpool won by two goals to nil. Else's sister in Southend, referred to here as 'Lil', would by 1968 have become 'Maud'. Alf's father was either a 'haulage contractor' (according to Alf) or 'a junkman' (according to Else).

An audience research report was commissioned for this episode, which on first showing attracted 32.6% of the viewing population (with ITV winning 20.7% for *Coronation Street*; the BBC Two viewing figures were too small to be considered). Its reaction index of 69 was made up in the following way:

A+	A	B	C	C-
29%	34%	25%	7%	5%

The average RI for the series was 67, and this episode was considered well up to standard. Viewer comments included: 'Another hilarious edition of a screamingly funny comedy show'; 'As usual we had a good laugh at Alf and his family. What a joy they are, so real and so funny'; 'Alf and family reduce my family to tears of helpless laughter every week and tonight was no exception'. There were, however, misgivings over 'the crude language, the constant abuse and the eternal shouting ... It was all very well to call a spade a spade, but must it always be referred to as a bloody shovel?' Particular concern was expressed that this was being transmitted at a time when children were likely to be watching. Some wished for 'Alf's lectures' to be toned down, without losing their comic effect. A very small number were reported to be disgusted by the 'grotesque' family's amorality and vulgarity, seen as an insult to the lower working classes. Warren Mitchell was praised, although some thought he tended to drown out the rest of the excellent cast. Dandy Nichols, the report continued, 'was often said to have interpreted the character of Else with quite remarkable restraint and with the perceptive insight of a genius ... "In her own quiet way, Dandy Nichols never puts a foot wrong – every word, gesture and expression tells. Hers is always a superb performance."' There was also praise for the football match – 'Obviously the real thing – a good touch this' – and the presentation in general was seen as excellent.

The episode attracted 30.9% on its 1969 repeat. A clip of the Garnetts discussing the royal picture survives in the 1972 *Late Night Line-Up Special* on Johnny Speight.

2.8: IN SICKNESS AND IN HEALTH

Recorded 31 January 1967
First transmitted Monday 13 February 1967 at 7.30 pm, with an RI of 69
Repeated Saturday 12 August 1967 at 9.15 pm (RI unknown); and Saturday 4 January 1969 at 9.45 pm, with an RI of 67

With Graham Stark (Dr Kelly) Mark Eden (Surgeon), Anthony Sharp (Surgeon), Tommy Godfrey (Man with Broken Leg), Valerie Murray (Nurse).

Alf is lying in bed, repeating **ad** nauseam *that he is in agony with a pain in his stomach and shouting repeatedly for his wife, who is downstairs with the others, happily ignoring him and watching television. Alf staggers downstairs and demands some medication – whisky would do.*

Alf is back in bed when Dr Kelly arrives, coughing incessantly and complaining that his cold never goes away because they keep sending sick patients to his surgery. His cough improves for a moment when Else pours him some whisky ... Kelly says that as far as he can see, there is nothing wrong with Mr Garnett. Alf however notes that the last patient he told that to, poor Tom Murphy, died soon after. He is determined to get a second opinion and decides to see a specialist. Moaning about the fact that he has to go on a bus rather than in an ambulance, or even in a Rolls considering the amount of National Insurance he has paid in, Alf bids a sad farewell to his family and sets off for the hospital. There he terrifies another patient with a broken leg (grimly forecasting the pain ahead as they take his plaster off, tearing the hairs off his leg) and expresses surprise at the apparent humanity shown by the coloured nurses.

Else, Mike and Rita come to visit, bearing fruit and chocolate, which Else starts to demolish as they ignore the patient and chat about the weather. Soon after, Alf watches in mortified silence as two frightfully posh doctors blithely discuss the operation they will perform on him the following day – an envelope incision, with large flaps to provide plenty of room to muck about inside ... Alf's horror grows when they agree that they must not drink too much brandy at that night's dinner party and must hurry the operation if they are to go to their golf match at Wentworth the following afternoon ...

Visiting time again, and Mike plays on his father-in-law's fears by commenting that the hospital is nicknamed 'the butchers shop', with the Harley Street doctors practicing their horrors on the poor. Else goes on about Alf's payments into a funeral club, and Rita starts to cry as her father gives a farewell speech entrusting his beloved wife and daughter to Mike, of all people. Else says she will be all right – she will have Rita and Mike to look after her, as well as his insurance ... Alf looks suitably dismayed, as he is trundled off to surgery ...

Next day, the surgeon hands Else the cause of Alf's pains, discovered during surgery – the thruppenny bit that Else placed in the Christmas pudding and he blithely swallowed. As Alf groans, the surgeon suggests she give the coin to her husband as a souvenir, but Else refuses – it's hers, and she'll keep it for herself.

ARGUMENTS, ARGUMENTS

The NHS; bloody Harold Wilson.

BLOODY LANGUAGE

Fourteen 'bloodies', one 'Randy Scouse Git', one 'Scouse git', two 'silly moos', an 'ignorant bloody Mick'.

FUNNY BUSINESS

Alf screaming for Else at the beginning; Alf saying his family will be happy when he's gone, Mike agreeing but Else telling him not to worry, since only the good die young; Alf moaning about the NHS; Dr Kelly examining this very awkward patient; the first Garnett kiss we ever see in the show, after Else asks, 'Ain't you going to kiss me?' and Alf replies, 'Eh? Kiss *you*?'; Alf cleaning out his pipe using medical instruments; the nurse saying to Alf, 'We must go back to bed', which instantly arouses his idiot prejudices; Alf repeating 'I'm in agony' as a mantra; the others' reaction to the news that, since only two visitors are allowed near the patient, one of them must leave Alf's bedside – each of them eagerly volunteering to be the one to go; Alf's silent trepidation as the posh doctors blithely ignore his feelings, in a direct contrast to the earlier scene involving the nurse; Else chatting happily about life after her husband's death; Else's her final complaint about Alf hanging on to *her* thruppenny bit; and lots more.

WHAT ELSE?

The discovery of the thruppenny bit links this episode in to 'Peace and Goodwill'; a fact that the programme planners recognised on its second repeat, scheduling it for the week after the repeat of the Christmas episode in January 1969. Dr Gingalla (see 'Intolerance') is mentioned again.

Graham Stark was billed as guest star for this episode; Speight had previously written for his TV show. Mark Eden had been Anthony Booth's co-star in *Catch Hand* a couple of years earlier. Tommy Godfrey was to appear again in the first film the following year.

Warren Mitchell inadvertently trod on a tack during rehearsals for the scene in which Alf gets out of bed and goes downstairs.

33.2% of the UK viewing audience saw the episode on its first showing and 31.0% on the 1969 repeat.

2.9: STATE VISIT

Recorded 14 February 1967
First transmitted Monday 20 February 1967 at 7.30 pm, with an RI of 68
Repeated Saturday 29 July 1967 at 9.30 pm (RI unknown)

Alf is reading the **Daily Mirror** *heralding Russian premier Kosygin's visit to the UK. He becomes enraged by the editorial declaring that Britain is now just a tiny offshore island, crying that this is traitorous – the British will rise up and push these smelly foreigners into the sea. As Mike and Rita howl with laughter, Alf compares himself to Ian Smith, another war hero trying to protect his country against the 'wogs'. It is all Wilson's fault – he was probably a 'conchy' during the war, like Herbert Morrison, and is now inviting Kosygin to stay at Claridge's at the nation's expense. Land, he asserts, is now the most important issue, and Labour are giving it away. Else agrees, citing Alf's recent dispute with his neighbour over two inches of fence. Mike insists that Wilson is talking to Kosygin to ensure Britain is not caught up in the cold war between Russia and America – after all, if they sneeze, we catch a cold, and now there is the added danger of nuclear weapons ... Alf says that Labour have only invited the Russian over so they can enjoy a reciprocal all-expenses-paid holiday on the Black Sea, in the same way that Brown and Wilson recently stayed in Paris with De Gaulle and in Rome with the Pope. His Holiness, says Alf smugly, will not be pleased if he visits Claridge's and stays in the same room as the heathen Kosygin. (At least they will have changed the sheets by then, muses Else.) Alf is angry that Her Majesty will have to meet the godless Russian, and shows Mike a family tree that proves that the Royal Family are indeed descended from God. Mike suggests that this means the Queen must have coloured blood if she is descended from Mohammed as well.. Mike further infuriates his father-in-law by saying that Britain is a second division country in the same way that West Ham is a second rate team, having lost to third division Swindon the other week. Then pictures of the summit meeting appear on the telly, and Alf jeers at the politicians, vowing to make a personal protest the next morning at No 10 ...*

Next morning, Else isn't impressed by Downing Street's terraced houses, and prefers No 11's curtains to No 10's. Alf suggests that Callaghan, the Chancellor, has to live next door so that Wilson can keep an eye on him, and Else adds that its also a good arrangement when he wants to borrow a few bob. There is no movement around the street, and Alf thinks that Wilson is probably lying in following a skinful last night with the Russkies. He suggests that they move on to Buckingham Palace. There, however, they see only the changing of the guard (which must wake the Queen up every morning, says Else). They return home to find Mike showing off his fab new gear – a classic Victorian redcoat army tunic – which Rita remarks might look cool in Chelsea but looks daft in Wapping. Alf is outraged at Mike's treachery and orders him to take the uniform off; when Mike refuses, Alf tries to tear it off him, but fails miserably, then in his fury snatches a container of inky fluid Rita has been using and throws it towards Mike. To his horror – and much to Mike and Rita's mirth – he misses and the fluid splatters all over a portrait of Her Majesty.

ARGUMENTS, ARGUMENTS

The Russians; Wilson; President Johnson; Mohammed; the Bomb; Royalty; football; George Brown.

BLOODY LANGUAGE

Ten 'bloodies', one 'bolshie basket', a 'Shirley Temple', two 'silly moos', one 'bleeding', an 'atheistic antichrist Scouse git', an 'ignorant Scouse git', a 'hairy Scouse pillock', a 'Scouse git'.

FUNNY BUSINESS

Rita's declaration of 'Super!' as Alf defends Ian Smith's fighter pilot experience and denounces Wilson; Else going on about Alf wishing to row with everyone, unlike Kosygin and Wilson; Alf's declaration 'I ain't bloody stupid' (and Mike's response, 'No, but you do a very good imitation'); Alf's rant about the godless Soviets, and the Queen's divine right; 'Never so many has had it … and given it back … to so few' misquotes Alf; Alf's 'Did we give in?' in reference to the last War, and Else's 'You wanted to' in reply; Mike's Churchillian impressions; Alf's fury at the television pictures of Brown and Kosygin holding hands; Alf and Else discussing Downing Street.

WHAT ELSE?

The day after transmission, the *Daily Mirror* proudly described the plot and Alf's anger at the 'offshore island' headline they had displayed in Russian in their earlier edition featured in the episode. Mike refers to West Ham losing by two goals to Swindon Town on 31 January. At one point, Mitchell refers to 'Ian Smith' as 'Ian Wilson' by mistake. George Brown was still Deputy Prime Minister at the time of broadcast.

This episode attracted 33% of the UK viewing audience. Mr Niven of Chichester in a letter to BBC: 'I was horrified and disgusted at the bottle of ink thrown at the Queen's picture and the laughter [that ensued] … She benefits the country greatly, and she cannot reply …'

Birmingham Evening Mail: '*Till Death Us Do Part* ranges from being uproariously funny to being crude, rude and tasteless … and provokes a wide range of reaction. Last night's ... seemed largely in the latter categories ... It was not very funny and much of it must have been offensive to most.'

2.10: ALF'S DILEMMA

Recorded 24 February 1967
Transmitted Monday 27 February 1967 at 7.30 pm with an RI of 70

With Will Stampe (Fred), Patricia Hayes (Mrs Carey), Charlie Bird (Bert Carey), Amber Thomas (Girl), James Holbrook (Policeman)

While Mike is reading Boom at the Kop *by Liverpool's star footballer Ian St John, Alf recommends the book he is reading, Mary Whitehouse's new tome* Cleaning Up TV. *This launches the Garnetts into a discussion first of football and then of the moral standards of contemporary television, including such programmes as 'Up the Junction', 'Cathy Come Home' and that documentary featuring bare-breasted African dancers that Else accuses her husband of 'ogling' the other night. All of it is pure, unadulterated bloody BBC filth, opines Alf. He further remarks that topless coloured women are different from topless white women. Else chimes in that youngsters are so naïve now that if the fashion were to go naked, then Mike and Rita would do so. The family then debate the ethical implications of women wearing topless wedding dresses at church ceremonies ...*

   Suddenly Alf is stricken by a bout of diarrhoea, which he says he has been suffering from all day. He is about to rush to the outdoor toilet when his wife reminds him that it is blocked because she has been emptying tealeaves down it. She says that Mrs Carey next door has offered the use of her facilities, so Alf rushes round there, armed with Else's loo paper and his copy of Mrs Whitehouse's book. Unfortunately he is forced to wait and suffer Mrs Carey's interminable conversation as her grandfather has fallen asleep on the toilet and she doesn't want to wake him yet ...

   Relieved after his ordeal, Alf returns to the fray and remarks that his condition is due to the microbes carried by foreigners invading the country – yer German measles, yer Asian flu and yer Paki pox. He insists that immigrants are the germ carrier, spreading their pestilence across the nation, and that Mrs Whitehouse should clean up the whole country and not just TV. Mike and Rita dismiss his racialist ravings as idiotic. Alf then blames Harold Wilson for inviting all the foreigners in, roaring that the Prime Minister should put any immigrants in quarantine to stop the bugs they carry. Else, meanwhile, blithely carries on about Alf's parents having had bugs – bedbugs. Alf states that paper breeds disease, and that even letters posted by immigrants are dispersing bacteria. Then he suffers another attack and runs next door. On returning, he finds that Else has asked Mike to get him a drop of brandy from the pub to ease his stomach ... but it is too late. Alf rushes next door again, but finds the Carey toilet is occupied by her sleeping grandfather once more, so he then runs down to the pub, only to find that Fred is emptying it at last orders and won't allow him in. Desperately, he hails a taxi to take him to the nearest public convenience …

Next day, Alf is preparing to go the hospital for treatment – the doctor has diagnosed him as a carrier for the stomach-churning streptococci. Mike reminds his father-in-law about his earlier statements regarding immigrants being carriers, and declares that Alf is unclean. Rita says that they should burn Mrs Whitehouse's book because it may carry similar germs. As she places it into the fire, Else wonders if she should have the whole room fumigated. Her husband's protests are drowned out by cries of 'Unclean, unclean' from Mike and Rita …

ARGUMENTS, ARGUMENTS

Harold Wilson, the turncoat; football; Mrs Mary Whitehouse; television; immigration; the NHS, apparently due to cost £100 million extra.

BLOODY LANGUAGE

Thirteen 'bloodies', one 'Scouse git', one 'Scouse twit', one 'silly moo'.

FUNNY BUSINESS

The opening scene, as the household is quiet for once; Mike's invective against Mary Whitehouse, timely interrupted by Alf; Else denying that she is 'promiscuous', even though she doesn't know what it means; Alf's blank-faced shock at Rita enunciating the words 'bare-breasted'; the priceless scene where Alf stuffs Mrs Whitehouse's book between sheets of toilet paper; Else's snobbery about next door's airs and graces over her toilet paper; Mrs Carey's endless chatter and repeated tapping of a sauce bottle as Alf desperately waits to go to the toilet; Alf imparting 'What your Harold Wilson ought to do …' three times only to be interrupted by Else's monologue about his mothers bedbugs; Else's interjections about foreigners getting their false teeth on the NHS; the door knob coming off the Careys' door as Alf seizes it.

WHAT ELSE?

This episode was untitled in the *Radio Times* and on the BBC's audience research report, which simply describes it as 'Final Episode'. An alternate title sometimes used is 'Cleaning Up TV'.

The script for this episode was another very late one from Johnny Speight. The film sequences involving Alf's travails were shot on 21 February, just six days prior to transmission.

We discover that Else likes *Mrs Thursday*, Ted Willis's immensely popular series centred on a char lady (played by Kathleen Harrison, once Mrs Huggett) who inherits her grateful boss's business interests. Dandy Nicholls had in fact played another charlady, Ethel Turner, in that series. Mrs Carey muses on the possible advantages of having two toilets, like her sister living in Blackheath – which was where producer Dennis Main Wilson then lived ... She suggests that Alf could also use Mrs Salmon's toilet next door, but then realises that Alf is not speaking to her because of a row over a new fence, as mentioned in 'State Visit'.

The audience research report on this last episode in the series records that it was watched by 36.7% of the UK viewing population, with 20.0% tuning in to ITV for *Coronation Street* and 0.2% to BBC Two. The reaction index of 70 was based on the following questionnaire data:

A+	A	B	C	C-
30%	36%	24%	4%	6%

The report noted that, despite the fact that the audience could not help but laugh, many thought the subject was distasteful, a typical comment being, 'Subjects in the past have been acceptable, but reference to the function of the human bowels, when treated in this fashion, is totally unnecessary.' Several found the racial content and bad language disconcerting, particularly when children were watching, and a few thought the situation repetitive. Most viewers were enthusiastic and some could even sympathise, having recently had Alf's 'bug' themselves. It was vulgar but true to life, they said, and many enjoyed Alf's identification with Mary Whitehouse: 'If the "toffee noses" don't like it, they need not watch.' All four family members came over as 'real, and human characters'; one respondent stated, 'I have spent many years in the East End of London working among people so very like the Garnetts.' Warren Mitchell was usually considered beyond reproach, but some felt he had overplayed the part. Many praised Dandy Nichols. 'I've never heard so much expressed in an "Oo-er" as from her!' said one. Tony Booth and Una Stubbs were liked, too, although a few found the latter weak.

The opening and closing scenes of this episode survive, but the discussions about television and some film sequences depicting Alf desperate to find a toilet are missing.

A reader's letter in the *Radio Times* during the 1968 repeat season: 'Commenting on its revival, a writer in *Radio Times* describes *Till Death Us Do Part* as "lower than lowlife comedy", certainly a better description than the same writer's "provocative variation on satire". For myself, I can scarcely wait to savour again those moments of tense breathtaking drama when Alf Garnett has a stomach upset and finds the lavatory door locked against him.'

(This correspondent was to be disappointed: 'Alf's Dilemma' was never repeated.)

Viewer R W Cooper, in a letter to the BBC: '… perhaps the most distasteful episode of the entire series.'

TILL CLOSING TIME US DO PART (A BANK HOLIDAY KNEES-UP WITH THE GARNETTS)

Recorded 14 March 1967
Transmitted Monday 27 March 1967 at 8.20 pm, with an RI of 61

With Ray Barrett, Kenny Lynch, Cleo Sylvestre, Jimmy Tarbuck, Arthur Mullard, Rita Webb, Joan Sims (Gran), Charlie Bird (Pub Regular), Fred McNaughton (Pub Regular), Geoff Thompson (Musician), Sid Lucas (Musician), Dennis Wilson (Musician), Johnny Speight (Blind Man), Dermot Kelly (Thief), Will Stampe (Fred), John Caesar, Pat Gorman, Judy Gallinare (Salvation Army Woman), Maggie Stock (Salvation Amy Woman).

The Garnetts celebrate the Easter Bank Holiday in a pub, where they meet Kenny Lynch, Jimmy Tarbuck, and Ray Barrett amongst others, Gran gets her pension nicked by a couple of buskers, Alf gets very drunk, Rita and Mike get sentimental and Else gets to sing …

ARGUMENTS, ARGUMENTS

None to speak of; just some raucousness, one political comment and some talk of Princess Margaret and her husband.

BLOODY LANGUAGE

Six 'bloodies', two 'Scouse gits', a 'bleedin' lavatory brush', a 'mean old git', a 'dirty Scouse git', a 'randy Scouse git', a 'silly moo'.

FUNNY BUSINESS

Alf's malapropisms – he refers to Roy [sic] Barrett's popular series as '*The Troublemakers*' (*The Troubleshooters*) and '*Mongol*' (*Mogul*); Gran downing her milk stout in one and complaining there was no gin in it; Else's stunning vocal prowess, as she sings 'Remember' in three different keys; Gran on the point of collapse during her song; Alf suggesting that Ray Barrett's facial potholes should be fixed; Else's seagull headpiece; Else mixing up Leslie Howard (of *The Scarlet Pimpernel* fame) with Frankie

Howerd; Alf's joke about yer darlin' Harold having 'dropped a Pollock' at the recent by-election in the Glasgow Pollock constituency; Else embarrassing her husband by telling of him quaking with nerves on their wedding night.

WHAT ELSE?

This special was directed by Dennis Main Wilson, with Douglas Argent credited in documents (but not on screen) as production assistant.

The opening titles were different from the show's usual ones – no music, just the pub soundtrack over some arty photo shots of Fred, Alf, Else and the others drinking, eating or cavorting. These sequences were filmed on 9 March 1967 (with a 'no alcohol' proviso) at Speight's favourite watering hole, The Queen's Elm, Fulham Road, London SW3, courtesy of landlord Sean Treacy. The end titles featured the pub-goers spilling out onto the street, with the usual closing music. There was an almost top-capacity audience (307 tickets) for the subsequent studio recording, which lasted an hour and included two retakes.

Notable features of the special include Gran's debut, an uncredited visit from Johnny Speight (as a blind man) and Dermot Kelly's second appearance in the show, apparently playing the same character as in 'Caviar on the Dole' – his cry of 'English pigs!' was cut from the finished version. Cleo Sylvestre is seen for the first time; a joke she makes about her colour ('Watch it, it comes off') would be reused in the first movie. The numerous guest stars appearing as themselves include Kenny Lynch and Jimmy Tarbuck, the latter of whom drives a sports car on which Alf hitches a ride on the bonnet. Pianist Sid Lucas was Lynch's regular accompanist.

Alf mentions the Prospect of Whitby, a famous old pub in Wapping Wall. He also remarks on Princess Margaret's then husband Anthony Armstrong-Jones buying property in the area, another line that would be repeated in the first movie. Ken Dodd, Frankie Howerd and Alfie Hynes (the reclusive property developer most famous for building Centrepoint) all get a mention. There are many ad libs from the cast, including references to Alf as Ian Smith, a joke from Lynch about a tycoon and Warren Mitchell's 'dropped a Pollock' gag, the by-election in question having taken place just five days prior to the special being recorded. A joke about Alf having a stocking over his face is used for the first time, but certainly not the last.

Songs sung in the pub are:

- Cast: 'Lily of Laguna', 'Me and My Girl', 'Only Girl in the World', 'Yellow Submarine'
- Rita Webb: 'Nobody Loves a Fairy', 'Knees Up Mother Brown'
- Warren Mitchell: 'My Old Dutch', 'Strangers in the Night', 'We'll Gather

Lilacs'
- Joan Sims: 'Love's Old Sweet Song'
- Jimmy Tarbuck: 'Maggie Mae'
- Kenny Lynch: 'Bill Bailey', 'Easter Parade'
- Dandy Nichols: 'Remember'

Mitchell had previously sung 'My Old Dutch' in 'A House with Love in It', and would do so again in the very last episode of the show in 1975.

An audience research report was commissioned for the special, which was seen by 32.1% of the viewing population (with 17.8% watching ITV and 0.2% BBC Two). Its RI of 61 – quite a bit lower than the average series average of 68 – was based on the following scores:

A+	A	B	C	C
19%	33%	27%	15%	6%

The programme was generally seen as a disappointment; much less amusing than previous episodes, with too many guests and general noise and confusion drowning out the Garnetts. The thin script was considered crude, with too much swearing and too many personal remarks. In light of this, and the proliferation of off-key singing and bawdy tone, many stated that they expected to find such activity actually in a pub and not transmitted as holiday entertainment on television: 'Bar parlour entertainment should be confined to the pub and not brought into the living room, where children are likely to be watching a supposed family programme'. Despite this, many in the sample enjoyed the special as being true to life ('Just like old times in the Old Kent Road'), even though they thought that the Garnetts were not given enough to do. The guests seemed to enjoy themselves, it was said, although Ray Barrett looked uncomfortable. The programme may have been noisy, but it was a very vivid depiction of a night out at the local, and all concerned were to be congratulated on its natural feel. 'It all seemed quite impromptu to me,' declared one viewer.

This programme survives complete in the BBC archives.

The Revd Derek H Buckley, of Hatton, Derbyshire: 'Considering the magnificent resources which the BBC undoubtedly has available [it's regrettable to see them] being prostituted on such trivial drivel … Was that the best you could find for a holiday evening?'

Reader's letter in the *Radio Times*: 'What a load of tripe! The landlord of any public house would have put Alf Garnett out on his ear. As a full-blooded Cockney, I strongly object to my evening's viewing being debased by such so-called comedy.'

Birmingham Evening Mail: '… warm brown ale compared with the vintage Alf Garnett.'

SERIES THREE

This series was shown on Fridays at 8.20 pm, just before the national news and after *The Good Old Days* or *The Man from Uncle*. ITV programmes in the same time slot included at first *The Frank Ifield Show* and later *Sam and Janet*, a sitcom starring John Junkin and Viviene Martin. Once again, a different shot of the Houses of Parliament was used in the opening titles sequence. Will Stampe, as pub landlord Fred, was booked at 60 guineas per time for the first four episodes but not used due to cutting of Speight's overlong scripts – he was nevertheless paid off on all occasions, and mistakenly received a credit in *Radio Times* for 'The Phone'. Rehearsals were conducted at the Drill Hall in Shepherd's Bush. Plans for one episode due to be recorded on 5 February were cancelled when Speight 'dried up' and failed to deliver a script. The 'bloody' quotient increased to at least 150, double that in the (much longer) second series. More pay rises were granted for the regular cast: Mitchell received £500 per episode, Nichols £420, Booth £235 5s and Stubbs £157 10s. This time, the show was mainly recorded on Mondays, and Dennis Main Wilson, rather than Douglas Argent, was the sole director. All episodes bar 'The Blood Donor' were subsequently repeated in 1968 or 1969. In 2016 'The Phone' and 'The Blood Donor' survive virtually intact whilst most of 'Aunt Maud' was also extant. Five minutes of 'The Puppy' aka 'The Dog' survives in poor quality. All episodes survive as off-air audio recordings.

3.1: THE PHONE

Recorded 18 December 1967
First transmitted Friday 5 January 1968 at 8.20 pm, with an RI of 70
Repeated Saturday 23 November 1968 at 9.40 pm, with an RI of 66

With Patricia Hayes (Neighbour)

Saturday afternoon, and Alf is watching a horse race on television, becoming more and more excited as his horse, Vashti, sweeps home to win. Ecstatic, he reckons he has won £17 10s. Just then, however, Mike comes in, to inform him that he could not get to the phone in time to call in the bet, because Mrs Moore was calling the doctor regarding Mrs Weatherby's 'funny turn'. Alf rages at the iniquity of this, but Mike suggests that he get his own phone installed; then he can call the bets in whenever he wants. Rita adds that he can also call the fish shop and order a meal. A dubious Alf is finally convinced, although Else remains worried that a phone may attract burglars, who listen out for the ringing and, if no-one answers, realise that the house is vacant.

The phone is installed, and Alf and Else stare in wonderment at the new gadget on their coffee table, discussing how they can try it out. Else suggests they call her sister Maud in Southend, but she does not know the number, which infuriates Alf. At that point, the telephone rings, and Alf nervously picks it up. It is Mike and Rita ringing from the call box nearby, but Alf is unaware of this as Mike adopts a supercilious voice and impersonates the operator, requesting that Alf whistle a tune down the line in order to test the new installation. Alf hesitatingly obliges, and Mike and Rita can barely suppress their giggles. 'The operator' thanks Alf, who puts the phone down in bewilderment.

Back home, in the face of Alf's scepticism, Mike rings directory enquiries to get the number for Else's sister. He then hands the phone to his mother-in-law, who is overjoyed to talk to Maud – and tells Alf that he's a pig for doubting they could get the number. Alf blames Wilson for having a nationalised industry that requires the customer to test the phone out by whistling down it, but just then Mike and Rita begin to repeat the same tune Alf had whistled earlier, and Alf realises he was duped …

Alf is calmly watching a Western movie on TV when Else brings in the neighbour, who would like to telephone St Mary's Hospital and ask about her father. The neighbour rings, but the noise of the television drowns out the conversation, and Else turns it down, much to Alf's chagrin; even worse, Else has taken her husband's assertion that phone calls should now cost them only 2d a time quite literally, and refuses to accept the neighbour's proffered 6d …

During the night, Alf hears the phone ringing downstairs and glumly goes down to answer it. It is the hospital, asking to speak to the neighbour. Alf angrily dons overcoat and hat and wakes up the neighbour, who accepts the phone, fearing the worst. Daddy however is faring well, and now she can sleep soundly – unlike Alf, who slams the phone down …

Saturday afternoon again, and the Garnetts are watching the horse racing, Alf having bet on Pundit's Son. But the TV pundit now recommends Punjab Gun – has Alf misheard the hot tip? He calls the bookies to change his bet, then changes it back again when the commentator claims the horse looks sluggish. A new hot tip is forecast in the form of Amy, and Alf rings up to change his bet yet again. Then Amy is beaten at the post by Pundit's Son … Alf is disconsolate – he has lost £25! And 8d, adds Else – for four phone calls …

ARGUMENTS, ARGUMENTS

Just a rather half-hearted grumble about Wilson and nationalised industry.

BLOODY LANGUAGE

Eighteen 'bloodies', three 'silly moos', one 'bleeding', and a 'silly old git'.

FUNNY BUSINESS

Alf's uncaring comments on Mrs Weatherby's terminal illness; Alf trying to convince his doubting wife that the telephone is a good bargain; the elder Garnetts' awe and nervousness over the telephone ringing; Alf's humble reaction to the supposed telephone operator; Else settling down to read the telephone directory; Else commenting that Maud sounds just like she is in the room, Alf responding 'Thank God she ain't' and Else then agreeing with Maud's disparaging remarks about her husband; the neighbour repeating everything for Alf's benefit as if he is a dotard; Alf jangling the coins in his pocket to signify that the neighbour must pay for the call; the neighbour's melodramatic exclamations at the news regarding her father, and tightening of her dressing gown as Alf looks on ...

WHAT ELSE?

Some unspecified technical fault occurred during transmission of this episode.

The fact that there is no studio applause over the closing titles suggests that the ending as originally recorded may have been cut due to overrunning.

The Garnetts' phone number is Stepney Green 1098 (as mentioned in 'The Blood Donor' as well). Maud is revealed to be Mrs Page of 17 Westlands Drive, Southend (near the Kursaal, says Else helpfully). The neighbour's father is called Mr Shears. The terminally-ill Mrs Weatherby will shuffle off her mortal coil in 'The Funeral'.

The *Radio Times* synopsis was: 'Alf Garnett, the last of the great non-spenders, is finally persuaded to have a telephone installed.'

An audience research report was commissioned for this first programme of the third series, in a new time slot, which attracted 38.0% of the viewing population – as opposed to 13.5% for ITV and 1.1% for BBC Two – and received an RI of 70 (higher than the last series' average of 68), based on the following scores:

A +	A	B	C	C-
25%	41%	25%	8%	1%

Most respondents found this episode up to standard, although some remarked on the absence of political or religious bite: 'Pretty mild stuff for the Garnetts and might as well have been written for Harry Worth, *Beggar Your Neighbour*, *Meet the Wife* or any one of a dozen similar shows'. The situation, installing a phone, was seen by some as too tenuous to sustain the episode. A scarce few found the characters and language totally repellent. Most, though, thought that this was an amusing show, with realistic and funny dialogue. 'I must say for the first time I sympathised with Alf,' admitted one. 'We have had similar experiences with our phone, especially when the phone box on the corner is out of order. I particularly remember when we were woken up at 3.00 am only to find it was a wrong number. My husband, a very mild man, did an Alf Garnett then.' All aspects of the episode – including the situation and the personalities of the family themselves – were thought to be true to life, and although the language was felt by many to be strong, that was seen as authentic as well. Most were pleased with the new time slot. The performances were seen as excellent, especially that of Dandy Nichols, as the report noted: 'Her facial expression was a delight, they said, and her lines, although fewer [than Mitchell's], equally telling'. Costumes and setting were also praised for their 'good eye for detail'.

The repeat showing attracted 27.5% of the viewing population. This episode survives intact.

3.2: THE BLOOD DONOR

Recorded 8 January 1968
Transmitted Friday 12 January 1968 at 8.20 pm, with an RI of 59

With Carolyn Moody (Nurse)

Mike accuses his father-in-law of being too scared to give blood. Alf responds that everyone's blood is different and he does not want his to be mixed with that of someone such as Mike – a scruffy Scouse git. Mike and Rita insist that all blood is the same, and that transfusions are medical miracles, but Alf is adamant that they're wrong – royal blood, for example, can't be tainted, just like that of pedigree dogs and horses. Anyway, only God can work miracles, not doctors … Mike scoffs at Alf's religious convictions and points out the pioneering heart transplant surgery of Dr Christiaan Barnard in South Africa. Else says that she feels it is wrong to put a woman's heart in a man's body. Alf agrees: the man might get women's feelings! And what if they put a black man's heart in a white man's body? If it was in South Africa under apartheid, which toilet would he use? No, asserts Alf, prolonging life like that is against His will … and in Heaven, the donor will want his heart back. Mike questions Alf as to what his God actually looks like, and Alf replies that He's like the Queen … only Higher. Mike uses reverse psychology and bets Alf five bob that even if he offered his blood the hospital would not take it. Alf then accepts his challenge …

At the clinic, a wary Alf notices a black man waiting to give blood and worries that he might become infected and even turn black. Mike says that if that were true, the best way to get a white boxing champion would be to drain Cassius Clay of his blood and inject it into a white man … At that point, a still-outraged but nonetheless fearful Alf is told that the nurse is ready for him …

Later, Alf is sitting up, drinking tea and declaring to the nurse that giving blood never bothered him – he was a sergeant at Dunkirk and saw waves of blood on the Channel. He leers at the nurse, recalling the saucy young things the nurses were in those wartime days. The nurse is unimpressed and asks him to hold his arm out while she affixes a plaster. Grimacing, Alf heroically complies – it doesn't bother him, and he won't make a fuss, he insists. Just then, the nurse picks up his pint of blood, and when Alf sees it, he swoons to the floor…

Back home, Alf lies on the sofa, groaning, while the others eat breakfast. Soon he dozes off, and imagines himself summoned by the Queen at Buckingham Palace to honour him for donating his blood. He bows and then chats to her about the quality of royal blood. He offers any of his organs if she wants them – just call him on Stepney Green 1098. He suggests that he and Else move in to the Palace – Else can help out by washing Philip's socks, for instance. He scans the room, commenting on the Windsors' royal portraits (Edward VIII notable by his absence), and then notes that Her Majesty is a West Ham fan, having pictures of the team and its captain Bobby Moore. He claims that her Christmas message was the best thing on the telly over the festive season, and then takes his leave, declining any reward, except maybe a season ticket to West Ham. HRH makes a joke about the chairman Reg Pratt's name, and then apparently dozes off …

Alf's dreams are rudely interrupted by the telephone ringing. He thinks it's probably Her Majesty calling for him and immediately picks it up, only to slam it down equally quickly – it's Else's bloody sister Maud from Southend! As Mike and Rita laugh, Else comments that he had better not give any more blood, as it seems to have affected his brain.

ARGUMENTS, ARGUMENTS

Religion; royalty; apartheid; medical ethics.

BLOODY LANGUAGE

Ten 'bloodies', a 'silly moo', a 'scruffy Scouse git', and two 'blasphemous Scouse gits'.

FUNNY BUSINESS

Rita once again saying that her father is too mean to give anyone even a cold, prompting Else into a monologue about the fact that he always gives *her* a cold; Alf noting that not even your Harley Street doctors can walk on water, yet God can; Else's musings over the problems of heart transplants mixing up men and women and their toilets; the worries over a Jewish heart rejecting a Christian body because it is not kosher; Alf's warnings about doctors pinching body parts during surgery; Alf's nodding deference to the black man waiting to give blood; Else saying that the only thing she thinks is special in Alf's blood is the alcohol content inside it; Alf chatting to HRH …

WHAT ELSE?

Lord Snowdon gets a mention. Mike is seen reading *The Tribune*, as Alf scans the 8 January 1968 edition of the *Daily Mirror*, emblazoned with the headline 'The Heart That Knows No Colour Bar'. As originally scripted, part of the fantasy scene was to have involved the Queen being represented by two corgis, but this was not shot as the episode overran. A number of other changes to the script were requested by Head of Comedy Michael Mills, not all of which were made (see Chapter Thirteen).

Carolyn Moody would also appear as a nurse in the first episode of the fourth series in 1972.

'The Blood Donor' was watched by 38.1 % of the viewing population, but its RI of 59 was the lowest that *Till Death Us Do Part* attained in the '60s. It was the only episode from the third series not to be repeated in that decade. However, it survives intact in the BBC archives.

The Sunday after its transmission, the episode was discussed on the BBC's viewer opinion programme *Talkback*, hosted by David Coleman. The basic format of *Talkback* was that each discussion would involve a figure connected with the BBC show in question – in this case, Tom Sloan, Head of Light Entertainment – and an informed viewer who was in favour of the programme – here it was Donald Holmes, a lecturer – fielding questions and comments from a panel composed of members of the public who disliked it. In this case, half the show was devoted to *Till Death Us Do Part*, the other half to *The Wednesday Play* entry 'House of Character', a portrait of mental illness, this production being represented by its scriptwriter David Rudkin and science fiction author John Brunner.

The first season *All in the Family* episode 'Archie Gives Blood' follows much of the plot and dialogue of 'The Blood Donor'.

3.3: MONOPOLY

Recorded 1 January 1968
First transmitted Friday 19 January 1968 at 8.20 pm, with an RI of 62
Repeated Saturday 28 December 1968 at 9.35 pm, with an RI of 66

With Pat Coombs (Neighbour)

It is New Year's Eve and the Garnetts are grouped around the table playing a game of Monopoly, Alf becoming extremely irritated by his wife's dilatory behaviour. Meanwhile, they discuss transcendental meditation, Alf angry that the 'heathen' Maharishi is staying at Claridge's, his room no doubt costing a lot more than the few coppers the local church receives. Else says that Alf never goes to church anyway, and when her husband picks up a card ordering him to Go Directly to Jail, she tells him that it is a judgement from God, punishing him for his swearing. Mike sarcastically warns his father-in-law that He is everywhere and always listening and watching. The dice rolls off the table into a tray of water, which Else has placed in order to drown any incoming mice ... Alf lands on Marlborough Street, which he decides to buy, praising his own business acumen and surveying his prize properties – Piccadilly, The Strand, Pall Mall and Trafalgar Square – with their touch of class and nice rents. Then Mike reminds him he cannot buy Marlborough Street, because he is still in jail ...

The neighbour comes in to beg a cup of sugar since all the shops are shut; then she asks for a packet of tea, and in a literal response to Alf's sarcasm, takes a bottle of milk as well. Alf says that this is typical – half the country is on the 'ear'ole' now, thanks to Harold Wilson. Mike replies that the country is broke thanks to too many military commitments, and Alf rages that this was not so under Macmillan – it is so unfair that after so many conflicts, Britain still has nothing to show for its military prowess. Else suggests that Wilson could borrow off the Queen, but Alf insists that she would give money only to her own party. Mike suggests that she and Phil the Greek ought to leave the country as part of the 'brain drain', but Alf says she would never do this – it's not the horse that's at fault, its the jockey, Wilson ... It's all bad news Britain – train crashes, plane crashes, flu, foot and mouth ... It's all Labour's fault. Even the Americans won't help, having the nerve to win all the Ryder Cup golf tournaments that the British should be winning.

The others aren't listening – they're getting ready to go out. Alf asks where they are going, and Else replies that they have all been invited to Mrs Moore's party across the road – all except Alf, that is. They suggest Alf goes to the pub, but he says he is broke, and he sulkily rejects Rita's offer of ten bob to help him out. The others leave, and as the sound of joyous celebrations come from across the street, all the lights and the television suddenly go out. Alf hopes it is a power cut, so it will ruin their party, but to his dismay he finds that the meter has run out, and he hasn't even got a shilling to put in it ... Standing in the darkness, he hears the crowd singing 'Auld Lang Syne' and moans that even if he went to bed he couldn't sleep with all the noise. Then he accidentally steps in Else's anti-mouse water. Utterly miserable, he sits down, head in hands. Happy New Year ...

ARGUMENTS, ARGUMENTS

The Mahareshi and meditation; religion; slum properties and extortion; De Gaulle; the Royals; Harold bloody Wilson; Harold Macmillan; James Callaghan; Roy Jenkins; Karl Marx.

BLOODY LANGUAGE

Twenty-five 'bloodies', a 'Scouse git', a 'silly little bitch', an 'atheistic Scouse git', one 'bleeding'.

FUNNY BUSINESS

Alf's malapropism of 'Marjorie Anna' (for 'marijuana'); Else's pleasure in finding that she has come second in a beauty contest and won £10; Alf blaming Else for not waking him at Christmas so he could go to church; Alf declaring that the local vicar is an embarrassment with his stuttering (surely a self-reference by Johnny Speight); Else's logic regarding mice not being able to swim; the neighbour's rambling monologue about borrowing, repeating 'I said' seemingly at the end of every sentence; Alf on bloody Wilson borrowing more than a cup of sugar, and reminding his wife about James Callaghan's departure from No 11 (Callaghan, the Chancellor, had swapped posts with Roy Jenkins, the Home Secretary, on 30 November 1967, shortly after the government's catastrophic devaluation of the pound); Else asserting that the Queen might lend money to ''Ogg'; Alf mentioning foot and mouth disease, prompting Else to remark that his father suffered from that – Alf responds that it was trench foot he suffered from, during the War, and that only animals get foot and mouth, and Else agrees: his father was a pig, just like him …

WHAT ELSE?

Mrs Moore is also mentioned in 'The Phone'. George Wigg, criticised by Alf in the episode, was a well-connected Labour politician who had been appointed Chairman of the Horserace Betting Levy Board in November 1967. The foot and mouth references recall the epidemic that hit Britain that year. At one point, Alf loosely quotes Robert Walpole (1739) – 'Today they ring the bells. Tomorrow they will wring their hands' – as he warns about darlin' 'Arolds new year.

35.0% of the UK viewing audience watched this episode on its first showing, 34.0% on its repeat. The *Radio Times* synopsis stated: 'In most families, a quiet parlour game would not lead to bitter argument. But when Alf Garnett is one of the players …'

The events of this episode would be referred to in 1974's 'Strikes and Blackouts', which would use some similar dialogue, including lines about capitalist landlords extorting rents on slum properties.

Mr J S Donaldson of Newport complained to the BBC regarding the trailer for this episode, which was shown on 14 Sunday January 1968, on the grounds that it presented clips from the 'vile Alf Garnett show *Till Death Us Do Part*', complete with cursing and blasphemy, without warning just after the movie *Sitting Pretty*. 'How dare BBC Wales …' he wrote, adding that the Welsh did not like that kind of language at all …

3.4: THE FUNERAL

Recorded 15 January 1968
First transmitted Friday 26 January 1968 at 8.20 pm, with an RI of 61
Repeated Saturday 25 January 1969 at 9.35 pm, with an RI of 63

With Joan Sims (Gran), Bill Fraser (Mr Williams), Frank Howard (Neighbour)

In the Garnetts' living room, the family sit in darkness and silence, the elder generation with an air of smug solemnity, the younger fidgeting and restless. The stillness is suddenly broken by Mike and Rita. They despair of their parents' dour adherence to tradition and total hypocrisy when it comes to funerals, especially since its only Mrs Weatherby down the street who has died. Why keep the curtains drawn and the telly off? Is it because Alf wants to be invited to the booze up at the wake? Mike tries to persuade his in-laws to change their minds by reminding Alf that West Ham are on telly later ... However, the collection for the deceased and the post-funeral buffet have been arranged by Alf and Else, and they have to show respect for the dead. Mike says that there is too much talk about death and not enough about life amongst the working classes. Then Mr Williams the local grocer arrives to complain that the dear departed has departed without paying her bill, having had the temerity to die on a Wednesday, when she usually paid her bills on a Friday. He hints that maybe the collection money could be used to pay off some of the deceased's debts to him ... Alf responds that he will be paid for his ham destined for the buffet and that is sufficient. Else, however, suggests that Mrs Weatherby would not have wanted to die in debt to someone. She tells Mr Williams that he could collect the cans of food from the deceased's house – after all, she won't be needing them – and this seems to console the shopkeeper. After he leaves, Rita and Mike note that his shop is not known for its food hygiene, but Alf says that having a few flies on the ham doesn't hurt anyone. The youngsters praise supermarkets with their hermetically sealed food. Then they go off to bed, leaving their elders to talk about ham and flies. Upstairs, Rita wonders if she and Mike will end up like their parents: 'All Dad thinks about is beer and football; and Mum, I don't think she thinks at all.' Mike insists that he and Rita are different; their love will thrive. However, he then hears that the telly has been switched on in the living room and, realising that Else's self-imposed purdah must have ended, rushes downstairs, deserting his wife ...

The mourners arrive for the buffet. Gran waxes sentimental over the course of several gins, proudly proclaiming that her mother was laid up in her house for nearly a week before they screwed her down ... She starts to sing, and the others join her, drowning out Alf's attempt at a speech. Else comments that when Alf goes, she'll be dancing on his grave ...

ARGUMENTS, ARGUMENTS

Labour inefficiency; corporate competition; shop hygiene; traditional funerals and their hypocrisies.

BLOODY LANGUAGE

Twenty-one 'bloodies', a 'great hairy Scouse pillock', a 'Scouse git', a 'silly great pudden', an 'old ragbag', an 'ignorant swine'.

FUNNY BUSINESS

The solemn expressions of Alf and Else at the beginning, contrasting with the boredom and exasperation of Mike and Rita; Else and Alf moaning about the neighbours; Alf's look of doubt as Mike reminds him that West Ham are on telly that evening playing Fulham; Bill Fraser's lugubrious shopkeeper whinging about Mrs Weatherby's inconsiderately-timed demise; a bizarre conversation between Alf and Else about 'our flies' on Williams's ham; Rita saying she hopes her marriage with Mike will not decay like that of her parents; Mike assuring her that it will not, then rushing out to watch football on the telly downstairs, leaving his wife on her own; Alf pinching drinks meant for other people; Gran, getting drunk, getting maudlin and 'singing' (the same song as always – see 'Gran's Watch'); Else's savage parting shot.

WHAT ELSE?

Mrs Weatherby's terminal status was mentioned in 'The Phone', as was Mrs Williams' caring behaviour toward the old lady, which prevented Mike from placing Alf's bets over the public phone. Is Bill Fraser's character the same Mr Williams as is heard over the phone (played by Lewis Ward) in 'A Woman's Place Is in the Home' ...? The revered status of Tinto Road funerals is noted again (see 'A House With Love In It').

Bernard Cribbins was considered on 4 December 1967 for the role of Mr Williams. According to *Radio Times*, Gran was originally to have been played by Beryl Reid.

32.8% of the viewing population watched this episode on its first showing, 30.1% on its second.

The Listener: 'In drama and comedy, any writer must compete with scripts as good as Johnny Speight's look at a dockland funeral in *Till Death Us Do Part*.'

3.5: FOOTBALL

Recorded 29 January 1968
First transmitted Friday 2 February 1968 at 8.20 pm, with an RI of 64
Repeated Saturday 30 November 1968 at 9.35 pm, with an RI of 63

With Bobby Moore (Himself), Reg Pratt (Himself), Roland MacLeod (Father).

Alf has confiscated a football from two kids playing outside and is now suffering practical jokes and insults directed at him in retribution. He answers the door to be greeted by the kids shouting 'Baldy' and 'Four eyes', then trips over a concealed rope as he tries to chase them. Fuming, he returns inside to the others, who suggest he hands the ball back. Then the phone rings, Alf answers it and finds to his fury that the callers are the kids, happily repeating their insults.

Alf blames the welfare state for these infernal offspring, while Mike and Rita blame society and the older generation's opposition to the pill. Alf replies that nowadays the young want all the pleasure but not the responsibility. Mike insists that Tory policies of using people as factory fodder and then dispensing with them have created this mess, but Alf counters that it is Wilson's policies that are creating unemployment. Else interrupts to ask if Rita is on the pill, and her daughter replies that she doesn't want a baby now because this is a terrible area in which to bring up children. This upsets her parents, leading to a general debate about work prospects in the area. Alf hits out at the unions causing strife and unemployment. His ranting is interrupted by a phone call. Else picks up the receiver and calmly hands it to her husband – and Alf is subjected to another stream of invective from those bloody kids. Else goes on to regale the others with embarrassing tales of her husband's childhood, saying that he was unwanted and unloved, used a dummy until he was seven, was scared of the dark ... The phone rings again, and Alf screams down it – only to find it is the vicar asking him to help train the local boys' parish football team ... Mike scoffs at the idea of Alf as a football manager, but Alf insists that he could have played for West Ham ... He daydreams of a match in which a TV commentator declares that 'this man Garnett' has already scored 55 goals before half time ...

But at the training ground, Alf is completely humiliated by his lack of footballing prowess. To make matters worse, he then accidentally kicks the ball through his own front window, ruining his dinner in the process. The phone rings, bringing more cries of 'Baldy'. Exasperated, Alf calls the operator and orders him to stop the bloody kids bloody phoning him and calling him bloody names. The operator vehemently suggests he does the right thing and return their bloody ball ...

At another training session, Mike remarks on the ability of one teenager, suggesting that he should be signed by a major club, and Alf's eyes light up at the thought of a nice little earner as the boy's manager ... He visits West Ham, nearly being run over by his hero Bobby Moore in his Rolls **en route**. *Meeting the Chairman, Mr Pratt, Alf tells him that it was his team that was responsible for England winning the World Cup, but then admonishes him for allowing them to falter so badly in the league. The Chairman demands to know why he is there. Alf tells him of the teenage prodigy and asks if he is interested in seeing the lad. Pratt says he will send someone down to view the potential star. However, when Alf returns to the training ground and asks the boy to sign a contract, with him as manager, he finds he is too late – the boy's dad has already signed him with Chelsea. Returning home, Alf is hit by a missile launched by the two boys and tells Else he will kill those bloody kids. Then the boys' father comes in, glares at Alf and retrieves the ball, leaving Alf helpless …*

ARGUMENTS, ARGUMENTS

Labour policies creating unemployment; Tory policies creating factory fodder.

BLOODY LANGUAGE

At least 44 'bloodies', a 'big-headed little swine', one 'silly moo', a 'Scouse git'.

FUNNY BUSINESS

Alf's anger at the 'bloody kids'; Mike shocking Alf into silence by saying that he agrees with his assertion that Wilson has caused unemployment; Else worrying that her daughter is on the pill; Alf's comment that if Mike had his way, the chinless wonders would work the docks and buses, the workers would live in big houses and Buckingham Palace would be hidden by lines of washing; Else gleefully telling the others that Alf's mother hated him as a child; the longest 'Look …' ever from Alf as he tries to stop his wife's embarrassing monologue; the local boys running rings around Alf at the training session; Alf's conversation with the telephone operator; Bobby Moore's Agincourt salute to Alf; Alf telling an increasingly irritated Mr Pratt how to run his team; the child prodigy stating that when Alf wrote 'complete power and authority', he should have spelt 'authority' with a 'th' and not an 'f' …

WHAT ELSE?

The boys who torment Alf are not named on screen but are called David and Tony in the script. The scene where Alf kicks the football and smashes his own window – then tells Else it was those bloody kids who did it – would be repeated with modifications in the first movie.

The football sequences were filmed on 24 January 1968 at Caterley Sports Ground, with members of the Italia Conti stage school playing the footballers, trained by a proper football coach, David Underwood. Bobby Moore makes a guest appearance on film, in a non-speaking, two-finger-gesturing role, while seated in his Rolls.

Measures were taken to borrow and insure West Ham's TV award, two silver cups and a World Cup replica.

The *Radio Times* previewed the repeat: 'An ardent football supporter and loyal fan of the Hammers, Alf Garnett tries to teach the younger generation how to play football and keep off the streets'.

The episode attracted 31.4% of the UK viewing audience on its first showing and 28.3% on its repeat.

3.6: THE PUPPY aka THE DOG

Recorded 22 January 1968
First transmitted Friday 9 February 1968 at 8.20 pm, with an RI of 69
Repeated Saturday 7 December 1968 at 9.50 pm, with an RI of 67

With Pickles (Bob)

Sunday afternoon, and as the others hungrily await their delayed roast dinner, Alf returns with a new addition to the family – a mongrel dog called Bob, bought for a pound from a 'professional dog breeder' in the pub. He explains that his father trained his dog as a ratter to such a high pitch that his old mate , the Prince of Wales, offered him £4,000 for it, without success. He says that he may have to dock the tail (otherwise the dog may go mad or blind or both), recalling that it was traditional for the dustman to bite it off, and that he will discipline the animal by hitting it over the head with a broomstick. Mike demands to see the pedigree, but Alf, making a mess of carving the roast, dismisses this as unnecessary and asserts that he is determined to train his prize pooch, following in his father's footsteps by not pampering it. Later, much to Alf's amusement, Bob tears up Mike's new £5 shirt. He is much less happy, however, when the animal keeps him awake all night with its howling.

The next day, Alf returns from work to find the house empty but with one of Else's homemade pies in the oven. He starts to eat it, but then his wife arrives back and accuses him of stealing Bob's dinner – the pie filling is dog meat, although the pastry is handmade as a special doggie treat. Alf furiously – and rather stupidly – demands that either Bob goes or he goes. When he realises that the others would prefer to keep the canine, he makes to leave. On the doorstep, however, he sees that it is snowing heavily outside, and diplomatically decides to give the pooch another chance. Then he finds that Bob has chewed his favourite pipe and threatens to dump him out into the snow, but Else protects her new pet and browbeats her husband into submission.

Alf is forced to resort to subterfuge ... He returns home the following evening after taking the dog for a walk, but without Bob, who he claims wandered off, having slipped his leash. Else glares at him, filled with suspicion. But then Mike comes in with Bob in his arms. The clever little creature has found his own way home. Else cradles the mongrel in her arms and thrusts him into Alf's frustrated and bewildered face ...

ARGUMENTS, ARGUMENTS

None really, except about the dog.

BLOODY LANGUAGE

Sixteen 'bloodies'. three 'silly moos' (including one insult by Mike towards Else)

FUNNY BUSINESS

Alf spitting out the dog meat, and Mike telling him that it will do his coat a world of good; Alf demolishing the joint of meat; Else remarking that if horses are measured in hands, surely dogs must be measured in paws; Alf saying that his father's dog could smell him from four streets away as was coming home and Else' perfect rejoinder 'Everyone could ...'; Alf and Else manoeuvrings in the bed, replete with Else' leaking hot water bottle; Else happily chatting to the dog; Alf's pathetic attempts to train the dog and threatening to throw Bob out of the window; Alf's reaction as he realises he's eaten the dogfood; Alf warning his wife, to absolutely no avail; Else' final gesture to her husband.

WHAT ELSE?

Pickles was named after the pooch who found the World Cup when it was stolen in 1966; he was trained by John Holmes of Formakin animal training, who had a contract with the BBC to train animals for shows. (Other programmes that Holmes worked on included *Out of the Unknown*, *The Forsyte Saga* and the 1972 *Till Death Us Do Part* episode 'Women's Lib and Bournemouth'.)

The *Radio Times* synopsis on the repeat declared: 'A dog is a man's best friend. Whether Alf Garnett is a dog's best friend is highly debatable.'

31.5% of the UK viewing population saw the first transmission, 27.8% the second. The last five minutes of this episode survives.

3.7: AUNT MAUD

Recorded 12 February 1968
Transmitted Friday 16 February 1968 at 8.20 pm, with an RI of 65
Repeated Saturday 14 December 1968 at 9.50 pm, with an RI of 66

With Ann Lancaster (Maud), Edward Evans (Mr Pringle), Pickles (Bob)

Else is in bed, stricken with bronchitis, and her sister Maud has arrived to look after her. Alf and Maud loathe each other with a passion and constantly argue. Alf at one point reminds Maud that when she was a young girl, she would show anyone her knickers for a bite of her toffee apple. Maud bursts into tears, saying that her mother was right: Alf is a lying, foul-mouthed swine and her sister Else should never have married him. She gets her revenge by refusing to cook Alf meals and telephoning her husband Bert in Southend so that he can give him a piece of his mind over the slurs he has cast on his wife. The strain tells on Alf, who is forced to buy fish and chips every night while he gazes on the meat puddings that Maud prepares for Mike and Rita; and of course Else is totally unsympathetic. Alf, outraged by the monstrous regiment of women, resorts to citing Biblical precedent and the story of Adam's rib, which proves simultaneously that women are subservient to men and that Mike's mate Darwin was talking rubbish ... Mike and Rita tease him mercilessly about God and about his piscine dinners. Mike declares that God is a fire-and-brimstone monster, an invention of the gullible. When a friend, George Pringle, arrives and enquires about Else's health, Maud sees an opportunity to get her revenge on Alf. She informs him that Pringle and Else once slept on Southend beach together, but it didn't really matter because they were planning to get married anyway ... Rita mock-innocently asks Alf if that means Pringle was her dad. Alf swings a punch at her, but she ducks out of the way.

Alf demands the truth from his wife, but first she feigns a lack of understanding and then blatantly ignores him. When he has gone, Else tells Maud that she didn't sleep with Pringle, but she isn't going to let her husband know that, is she? Alf later presents his wife with a bunch of daffodils and says that he has forgiven her – only for her to reveal that Dr Kelly has recommended that she go down to Southend with Maud in order to recuperate. Alf storms out, leaving Else with a nasty smile playing over her lips ...

ARGUMENTS, ARGUMENTS

The Bible; Darwin; God; Lyndon Johnson; Harold Wilson.

BLOODY LANGUAGE

Thirty 'bloodies', a 'silly little bitch', a 'bloody selfish bitch', a 'bloody blasphemous swine', a 'bloody old cow', a 'dirty git', a 'Scouse git', one 'bleeding'. Alf mispronounces 'fracas' as 'fracarse' three times ...

FUNNY BUSINESS

The lengthy silence at the beginning of the episode as Alf can barely restrain his fury; Alf mouthing something regarding Maud behind his newspaper; Maud saying that her Bert never resorted to drink, which Alf remarks is a bloody surprise considering his wife; Maud aping Else and calling Alf a pig; Alf brimming with *braggadocio* during his telephone conversation with Bert, until Mike reminds him that *he* is paying for the call; Rita mimicking Alf's boxing gestures on the phone to Bert; Alf spitting a piece of fish across the table and then throwing the custard dish and currant duff against the wall; Alf reading aloud from the Bible, to the others' hilarity; Alf's assertion that God made hands on the end of our arms so that they would be ... well, *handy*; Mike mimicking his father-in-law's 'I only 'ope he can hear you'; Alf's malapropism – 'righteousnessness' (for 'righteousness'); Alf declaring that Harold Wilson is a plague and pestilence, and Mike's 'You're potty!' reaction, miming the smoking of marijuana; Alf's basilisk stare as Pringle's one-time liaison with Else is made public; Else's sly smirk at her husband's questions regarding Pringle; Alf's self-pitying rant about trying to keep virginal and pure, apparently to no avail, thanks to Else.

WHAT ELSE?

As originally scripted, the episode was to have centred more on George Pringle, a former lover of Else's who returns home a very erudite and civilized man – everything that Alf is not. When Dandy Nichols succumbed to bronchitis, however, this forced a radical change. After the episode was transmitted, the Honeyglo Health Centre Special Massage Team based in Wiltshire wrote to the Controller of BBC One enclosing free medication for 'the dear lady's' bronchitis, having heard that the actress had been unable to play a full part in the recording.

A sequence where Mike drinks his beer from a glass with the broken handle, only to learn that this is where Maud usually puts her false teeth, was originally written for, but cut from, the *Comedy Playhouse* pilot. A joke of Mike's about an aristocratic ' Lord God' was first used in *If There Weren't Any Blacks, You'd Have to Invent Them*. The 'toffee apple' euphemism was to be reused by Gran in the colour series.

This episode marks our last sighting of Bobby the dog. Ann Lancaster was also to play Aunt Maud in the first *Till Death Us Do Part* movie, while Edward Evans was to reappear in 'Women's Lib and

Bournemouth' in the 1972 series as a train ticket collector. The show was rehearsed at North Paddington Boys' Club, 235 Lanarch Rd, Maida Vale.

36% of the UK viewing population watched the first transmission, 33.3% the repeat. Much of this episode survives: only the first four minutes and the closing credits are missing.

The *All in The Family* adaptation featured Aunt Maude (a very left wing, intelligent Democrat) visiting the Bunkers to assist the Dingbat in looking after the rest of her family, who are all sick with the flu.

A letter from 'a Believer' of Washwood Heath in the *Birmingham Evening Mail*: 'I think *Till Death Us Do Part* had a fair amount of amusing entertainment, but the things that were said about religion should not have been allowed on the air.'

Another reader's letter in the same newspaper: 'The fact that there are still legal penalties for blasphemy only demonstrates how stupidly out of date and undemocratic many of our laws still are. What about our right of free speech?'

TILL DEATH US DO PART

Retitled *Alf 'n' Family* in the US.

Starring Warren Mitchell (Alf Garnett), Dandy Nichols (Else), Anthony Booth (Mike), Una Stubbs (Rita), Brian Blessed (Sergeant), Bill Maynard (Bert), Michael Robbins (Fred the Landlord), Cleo Sylvestre (Girl at Wedding Party), Liam Redmond (Mike's Father), Shelagh Fraser (Mike's Mother), Geoffrey Hughes (Mike's Brother), Bob Grant (Pubgoer), Edward Evans (Jim the Shopkeeper), Sam Kydd (Pubgoer), Frank Thornton (Valuation Officer), Ann Lancaster (Maud), Tommy Godfrey (Man in Pub), John D Collins (RAF Man at Tube Station), Michael Wolf (German Football Fan), Davilla O'Connor (Maternity Nurse), Kate Williams (Sergeant's Girlfriend), with Pat Coombs, Madge Brindley, Bill Ward, Leslie Noyes, Brenda Kempner, Jack Jordan, Sulky Gowers.

Story and screenplay by Johnny Speight. Directed by Norman Cohen. Produced by Jon Pennington. Executive Producer: Beryl Vertue. Director of Photography: Harry Waxman. Film Editor: Anthony Lenny. Music composed and conducted by Wilfred Burns. Title song 'Till Death Us Do Part' composed by Ray Davies, sung by Chas Mills. Design by Terence Knight.

Made at Shepperton Studios, London, England. Running time: 100 minutes

Preview showings in London from 12 December 1968, and on general UK release from 12 January 1969. *Alf 'n' Family* released in the USA on 13 August 1972.

The story of Alf and Else, from 1939 to the present, suffering from war, rationing, poverty, the swinging '60s and finally the redevelopers …

WHAT ELSE?

The Garnetts' address is shown as number 25, as would be the case in the 1974 TV series. The final demolition of the house is scheduled for 10 July 1968 – approximately the same time that the original house in Garnet Street as used in the television title sequence was knocked down. Nassau Terrace, seen in the movie, is actually in Putney. The tower block is Denham House in Roehampton.

Speight's script for the film reuses various pieces of dialogue and comedy business from the TV episodes: jokes between Alf and Else about sex drive originated in the *Comedy Playhouse* pilot; a quip by Cleo Sylvestre about her colour coming off was first heard in 'Till Closing Time Us Do Part'; Alf's theft of a baby's milk bottle repeats Patrick Rawlins' actions in 'From Liverpool with Love'; the description of Edward Heath as a 'grammar school twit' had been used several times before; the idea of Alf kicking a football through a window and then blaming some nearby kids was first exploited in 'Football'; Alf's quarrel with a German football fan is lifted from 'Intolerance'; a joke about Harold Wilson and the England football team's red shirts was first used in 'Peace and Goodwill'; a fantasy scene with the Queen was previously attempted in 'The Blood Donor'(where the Garnetts' telephone number, Stepney Green 1098, had its initial mention); Else's reference to famous black stars such as Al Jolson in *Sonny Boy* originated in 'Intolerance' (and would return with Min in the final episode of the entire series); a sequence with Alf in the bath is a partial repeat of an incident from 'Two Toilets – That's Posh!'; and the 'God-in-a-glass' scene that was cut from 'Aunt Maud' before recording finally appears here. A comment by Alf about Hitler not being all bad would be reused in the 1975 episode 'The Wake'.

UP THE POLLS! (THE CAMPAIGN'S OVER)

Recorded and transmitted Thursday 18 June 1970, between 10.05 pm and 10.25 pm, as part of *Election '70*.

Starring Warren Mitchell (Alf Garnett), Eric Sykes (Arthur Blenkinsopp), Spike Milligan (Paki-Paddy), Joan Sims (Gran). With Lorna Wilde (Barmaid)

On General Election night, Alf Garnett, Arthur Blenkinsopp and Paki-Paddy, with Gran lurking over her gin, discuss the state of the nation, including the Common Market, immigration, the World Cup …

WHAT ELSE?

This sketch was produced and directed by Dennis Main Wilson. Mitchell was paid £600 for his appearance. Sykes and Milligan resumed their *Curry and Chips* characters, Blenkinsopp and Paki-Paddy. Milligan was to appear in episodes in the 1972 and 1974 *Till Death Us Do Part* series, and the show itself was to fill an Election Night slot again on 28 February 1974.

The script featured what was to be Mitchell's favourite line of Speight dialogue, spoken by Sykes, about his father being so poor that he had to walk eight miles using borrowed boots to vote Tory. Although the 1970 World Cup was still ongoing, the England team had been eliminated from the competition; 'Back Home', the team's hit single, was used as the playout. Someone – surely either Milligan or Mitchell? – throws an egg at the on-screen closing titles, to strong approval from the studio audience.

BBC executives in a written memo stated that the sketch reflected 'a failure to execute properly [what was] a basically sound idea'.

25.4 % of UK viewers watched the show. Never repeated, it survives incomplete (the first few minutes are missing) and in poor quality on a monochrome early home video recording format.

CHRISTMAS NIGHT WITH THE STARS

Recorded 12 December 1971
Transmitted Saturday 25 December 1971

With Warren Mitchell, Dandy Nichols, Mark Heath (Vicar) and seven carol singers

It is Christmas Eve. Else is busy stoning raisins and placing them in the Christmas pudding bowl, while Alf paces up and down the room, anxiously waiting for news of Rita, who is expecting her first child. Alf is fed up – the telly's broken down, the bloody engineer hasn't come and he wants his grandchild to be a Garnett, not a Rawlings. His temper does not improve when Else answers the phone and accepts the charges for Gran – calling from Newcastle. He hears a knock on the door and angrily goes to open it, expecting carol singers, only to find it is a vicar – and a black one, at that – with some of his parishioners, asking for aid for Africa. He returns to the living room to find

Else still on the phone, which he takes from her and slams down. Alf ponders the mysteries of this world – bloody merry Christmas, bloody prosperous New Year, bloody Newcastle, bloody black vicars with bloody white collars … He decides to write a letter to the Queen on the basis that if his grandson is born on Christmas Day, then Her Majesty will send a telegram. Else suggests that he telephone as it's much quicker, prompting howls of derision from Alf and then a debate on whether or not the Queen will get her mooted one million pound rise. He reads the letter aloud, naturally interrupted by Else:

Your dearest Majesty,

Why I am writing is to wish you and yours a Merry Christmas and a prosperous New Year, and to let you know that my little girl will be giving birth to my grandson, Alfred, Winston, Alec Douglas, Enoch Garnett, and as it is your custom, Your Majesty, to send a telegram to the first born child on Christmas Day, I am enclosing my address.

Your loyal subject,

Yours, Alf Garnett Esq

PS. Mummy sends her regards to you and yours and we are both looking forward to seeing you tomorrow on your Christmas show.

Else reminds him that they won't be able to watch the Queen's Speech if the telly is still broken. Alf proudly shows her his gift for his grandson, a carrier bag proclaiming Bobby Moore's Sports Shop, and containing a full West Ham kit. Else points out that they don't know if it will be a boy or a girl as yet. Then the phone rings again, and she picks it up. She tells Alf the good news: he was right, he now has a grandson, weighing ten and a half pounds, and his mother is doing well. Alf sits down, thunderstruck. Ten and a half pounds! That's the size of their turkey. With that weight, the boy will dominate the midfield … Then another, darker realisation dawns. He looks at his watch. It is 11.55 pm. The randy Scouse git couldn't even wait five minutes! No telegram from the Queen for him!

ARGUMENTS, ARGUMENTS

The Queen's prospective pay rise, and the possibility of Her Majesty moving to the USA if she doesn't receive it.

BLOODY LANGUAGE

At least 15 'bloodies', a 'randy Scouse git', a 'Shirley Temple', one 'silly moo'.

FUNNY BUSINESS

Else mixing up 'Monty' the general with 'Marty' (Feldman) the comedian, whom Alf refers to as a 'pop eyed git'; Alf commenting that the pudding bowl is being filled with so many coins it will make the pudding go rusty; Alf's rage as Else spells out with excruciating slowness the name of Rita's hospital to Gran in Newcastle while on the phone; Alf's idea that the Yanks will pay millions for the Queen so that they can be called Lord Nixon or Sir Spiro Agnew; Else recommending a royal name, Angus, for their grandson, and Alf dismissing this as fit only for steakhouses.

WHAT ELSE?

This sketch, directed by Duncan Wood, formed part of the annual *Christmas Night With the Stars* compilation, which ran from 6.40 pm to 10.00 pm on BBC One. Mitchell and Nichols each received £100 for their performance.

The script contained references to the second series episode 'In Sickness and in Health' (copper coins in Christmas puddings) and to Marty Feldman, who had appeared in Speight's plays 'The Compartment' and 'Playmates' in *The Wednesday Play*, originally transmitted in 1969 and repeated earlier in 1971, and for whom Speight was to write a series in 1973. The business with the vicar and the carollers was lifted straight from the 1966 'Peace and Goodwill' episode, and was to be used again in a Christmas episode of the follow-on series *In Sickness and in Health*.

The next series of *Till Death Us Do Part* would follow directly on from this sketch, but the Christmas birth date of Rita's baby – ultimately named Michael, after his father – would be forgotten about in favour of a late summer setting. This show does not survive either on video or on audio.

THE ALF GARNETT SAGA
aka *The Garnett Saga*

Starring Warren Mitchell (Alf Garnett), Dandy Nichols (Else), Paul Angelis (Mike), Adrienne Posta (Rita), Tom Chadbon (Jim), John Le Mesurier (Mr Frewin), Patsy Byrne (Mrs Frewin), Patricia Quinn (Jim's Girlfriend), Ken Wynne (Passenger), Cleo Sylvestre (Bus Conductress), J G Devlin (Irishman), Derek Griffiths (Rex), Ellis Dale (Clerk), John Bird (Willis), Roy Kinnear (Wally), Joan Sims (Gran), Roy Hudd (Milkman), Arnold Diamond (Policeman), Julie Ege (Herself), Eric Sykes (Himself), Kenny Lynch (Himself), Max Bygraves (Himself), Arthur Askey (Himself), George Best (Himself), Bobby Moore (Himself), Salmaan Peer (unknown). With Sam Kydd (unknown), Nosher Powell (Ginger), Mary Pratt (Receptionist),

Johnny Speight (Barmy Harry), Will Stampe (Barman), Richard Speight (unknown)

Story and screenplay by Johnny Speight. Directed By Bob Kellett. Produced By Ned Sherrin. Executive Producer: Beryl Vertue. Music by Georgie Fame. Art Director: Terence Knight.

Preview showings in London from late August 1972, and on general UK release from 10 September 1972.

Made at Shepperton Studios, London, England. Running time: 93 minutes

A week in the lives of the Garnetts. Alf goes to work in Wapping, buying illicit whisky, getting drunk with the bank manager who lives next door and finally taking LSD by mistake. Else barely ventures out of their new flat, except to meet Gran. Mike and his mate continue an idyllic work-shy existence with lady friends, gambling and drugs, until his actions upset Rita, who sleeps with a black singer in revenge.

WHAT ELSE?

The Garnetts' new tower block home is John Walsh Tower, Montague Road, Leytonstone. Alf's reference to 'Saint Bernadette' is a sarcastic nod toward Bernadette Devlin, noted IRA propagandist; his declaration that he is 'smoking for England' is a direct lift from 'I Can Give It Up Anytime I Like'; his reference to Stalin the 'American spy' is taken from 'Two Toilets – That's Posh'; and his fears about 'Eyeties' and the EEC stem from the same episode. Else's confusion regarding 'Monty' Feldman first surfaced in the 1971 *Christmas Night With the Stars* sketch. The 'stocking on the head' insult to Alf was originally used in 'Till Closing Time Us Do Part', which was also where Gran's favourite tipple was first mentioned. The sandwich-dipping routine derived from 'Up The Polls! (The Campaign's Over)'. A cheery milkman akin to those seen in episodes of the first two TV series appears, this time in a much more camp form. Reg Pratt (uncredited) and Bobby Moore, having previously guested in 'Football', are seen again here. And is that racing driver Graham Hill glimpsed in the crowd at West Ham?

References to 'Morning Cloud' and the Queen needing her money would reappear in the fourth series, and the idea of the bank manager getting drunk would be repeated in 'Party Night'. George Best was to guest again in the penultimate *Till Death Us Do Part* episode in 1975.

In a notable continuity error, the headline on Alf's copy of the *Daily Mirror* changes from 'Stay In Jail Till You Die' to 'Wilson Calls Heath A Liar' in a matter of moments.

During production of the movie, Bobby Moore, his wife Tina and Speight had dinner with Ned Sherrin at the Alvaro restaurant in the King's Road. George Best was invited but turned up very late, a little worse for wear, enjoyed a sambuca and started to flirt with Tina Moore. Moore and Best then embarked on a bacchanalia of glass after glass of sambuca. Best eventually passed out. Speight remarked that, despite Best's stamina, it was sambuca that floored him. The following week, in Moore's regular newspaper column, the headline was 'Sam Booka floors Best', generating debate about who this mystery footballer was ... In the meantime, Best did not turn up for filming the following day, forcing Sherrin to shoot his scene later in a public toilet in Manchester ...

In June 1973, when the England football team were in the USSR, instead of Moore and co spending the last night of their tour seeing *Sleeping Beauty* at the Bolshoi, Sir Alf Ramsey arranged for them to view an 'old Alf Garnett film' at the British Embassy Club – it was almost certainly this one.

SERIES FOUR

This series was shown on Wednesdays at 9.25 pm, after the watershed, opposite a new run of *Van Der Valk* on ITV (with two exceptions, an edition of *Playhouse* starring Tom Bell on 25 October 1972 and *The Val Doonican Show* on Boxing Day). A total of about 222 'bloodies' spattered the series, but thanks to the march of time (and the new scheduling) this elicited hardly any public criticism. After an attempt to 'sepiatise' the original '60s title sequence was deemed unsuccessful, a new sequence was filmed from the balcony of 79 Bow Sprit, West Ferry Rd, London E14 – a 20-floor high-rise block of flats – between 6.00 am and 7.00 pm on 30 August 1972; the occupier, Mrs Hazell, received £10 for the privilege. A new arrangement of the theme music was recorded early in September. There were further audio innovations: the use of music cues in each episode was discontinued, and the sound of a squealing baby was added over the closing credits. Three babies were used as Michael during production: Joanne Martie (recorded on Friday 14 July for the first episode); Toby Andrews (filmed on Sunday 16 July at the Royal Bath Hotel in Bournemouth for 'Women's Lib and Bournemouth'); and William Wilson (filmed on Sunday 23 July at West Ham FC for 'Up The 'Ammers!'). The parents of each baby received a £5 fee. As for the stars, Warren Mitchell received £913 per episode, Dandy Nichols £779, Anthony Booth £337 and Una Stubbs £315. Dennis Main Wilson again directed most of the episodes. The original transmissions had a BBC voiceover during the closing credits stating that Una Stubbs was 'appearing by the permission of the Mermaid Theatre Trust'; she was starring in a Mermaid production of *Cowardy Custard* at the time. RI figures are unavailable for this series; the BBC had by this point adopted a new style of audience appreciation measurement.

4.1: TO GARNETT A GRANDSON

Recorded 30 July 1972
Transmitted Wednesday 13 September 1972 at 9.25 pm

With Carolyn Moody (First Nurse/Receptionist), Cleo Sylvestre (Second Nurse), Joan Sims (Gran), Bob Murphy (Flower Seller)

Alf is now a grandfather. He visits Rita in the hospital with Mike and Else, where he finds that the baby is to be christened Michael Patrick Rawlins, and that Mike wants it baptised in the Roman Catholic faith, even though Mike is an atheist, to please his mother …

ARGUMENTS, ARGUMENTS

The BBC weather forecast; the iniquities of the NHS; the merits of Edward Heath's sailing activities (at least he tried to win the Admiral's Cup for Britain) versus Harold Wilson's labrador, two new bloody houses, trips to the Scilly Isles and wife's bloody rubbishy poetry; capitalism; flower sellers' 'spivvery'; darling 'Arold's attempts to reduce the Royals to penury; Her Majesty's wage claim, and the possibility that she might have to sell her corgis, and Prince Philip his polo ponies; the wage claims of coalminers, rail workers etc; the dockers being subsidised by the IRA (the Industrial Relations Court being punned with the Irish Republican Army); the rogue dockers being fined £50,000, imprisoned and subsequently freed by the Solicitor General; Bobby Moore and his 'fair late tackle' against Germany in the 1970 World Cup; Wapping and the Blitz; Prince Charles; the perils of being a pensioner; the French charging the British army rent for the use of trenches in the Great War; De Gaulle.

BLOODY LANGUAGE

Seventy-five 'bloodies', three 'Shirley Temples', two 'Greta Garbos', two 'bleedings', a 'moon-faced moron', a 'big Sheila', an 'Edna' (after novelist Edna O Brien?), two 'traitorous Scouse gits', a 'red-faced Micks', a 'scandal-mongering old bitch', a 'silly old moo', a 'silly moo', a 'long-nosed git', a 'Supermouse', a 'tit', an 'arse'. Not forgetting 'cobblers' and 'double cobblers' …

FUNNY BUSINESS

Else's recollection that it took six days for Alf to see baby Rita, who was only upstairs, and that he was so drunk that he thought she had had twins; Mike's fab gear; Alf appealing to the women at the bus stop for sympathy over his awful son in law; Alf's rant about the Royal Navy blowing up Ireland, followed by maniacal laughter; Else wondering if the Queen dreams of winning the pools or bingo; Else engaging in baby talk with little Michael; Else settling down to eat the chocolates she has brought for Rita; Alf's reaction to Rita breastfeeding; Else thinking that the Royal Family name, 'Gotzberg', means that they are Jewish; Gran musing about her husbands, and comparing them with Alf.

WHAT ELSE?

Filming for this episode took place near Speight's home, at the Mount Vernon Hospital, Northwood Hill and Northwood Station bus stop, on the morning of 12 July 1972. (The crew then moved on to the local Co-op shop to shoot scenes the same afternoon for the intended second episode, 'Up The 'Ammers!'.) Certain scenes of Una Stubbs and baby Joanne Martie in the hospital ward were recorded on Friday 14 July (and some outtakes from these, in which Dennis Main Wilson can be heard directing his young star, still survive). The Christening of the baby was also set to be filmed at Ealing on 14 July, but with the ominous proviso 'Dialogue to be written'; ultimately, although photographs of a Christening were used to publicise the show in the *Radio Times*, the actual filming was never completed. Consideration had been given earlier in 1972 to having Cyril Cusack (of *Them* fame) appear as the priest at the Christening, and to perhaps ending with a drunken brawl featuring Mike's parents and others, but these plans seem not to have been progressed beyond the initial ideas stage. A couple of lines concerning David Frost's relationship with singer and actress Diahann Carroll were cut from the script because of fears of legal action. Mike's 'trendy' apparel leads Alf to liken him to Hetty King, a female impersonator of men, famed for the song 'All the Nice Girls Love a Sailor'. (King would die on 29 September 1972, while the series was being broadcast.)

Rehearsals for the studio recording were held at St Mary Abbot Hall between 25 and 29 July, and the recording itself took place the following day. The integration of the studio material with the pre-filmed inserts is pretty terrible at times – there is, for instance, an obvious lack of rain when Else is holding up her umbrella in the studio recreation of the hospital exterior, and the length of Warren Mitchell's hair differs noticeably between the two. Carolyn Moody reprised the nurse part she had played in 'The Blood Donor' and received a £70 fee. She was also to appear in 'Up the 'Ammers!', as a passer-by. Cleo Sylvestre received a £50 fee for reprising her role as a nurse in 'In Sickness and in Health'. She had also been seen as Kenny Lynch's girlfriend in 'Till Closing Time Us Do Part'. Joan Sims received £300 for her appearance as Gran.

32.4% of the viewing population tuned in to the episode, as opposed to 8.8% to ITV and 7.3% to BBC Two. A new-style audience research report presented the following data on respondents' opinions:

Very funny	41%	27%	18%	8%	6%	Thoroughly unfunny
Script excellent	32%	27%	20%	12%	9%	Script poor
Very well cast	67%	22%	9%	1%	1%	Poorly cast
Sets and costumes excellent	43%	37%	16%	3%	1%	Sets and costumes poor

Despite some reservations regarding the script, most respondents were happy to see the return of the show, 40% being highly enthusiastic: 'So true to life, so funny, so marvellous; thanks for a real good laugh again'; 'the script was absolutely brilliant; the best laugh I have had this year'; 'Always a marvellous programme; everyone involved 100%'. However, many thought that the show did not need to have so much bad language to sustain hilarity: 'We expect Alf to swear, but he overdid it in this episode.' A few dismissed the episode as tasteless rubbish, saying that Speight seemed to have made Alf worse than before; some considered the political rows 'boring', others that the script could have been so much funnier. Praise for the cast was high: Mitchell was said to be 'terrific', 'a scream', and Nichols 'smashing, a real pudding, [with] such a marvellous face'. There was some criticism of the artificial settings and the crude transition between film and studio recording.

Birmingham Evening Mail: 'As foul-mouthed and racist, as ignorant and intolerant as ever, Alf Garnett re-erupted on BBC One like some eternal Colonel Bogeyman. Doubts [that] the parting had been too long proved as groundless as Alf's own arguments on royalty and politicians, West Ham and Ireland. The years might never have passed.'

4.2: THE PIGEON FANCIER

Recorded 13 August 1972
Transmitted Wednesday 20 September 1972 at 9.25 pm

With Bill Maynard (Bert), George Tovey (George), Joan Sims (Gran), Will Stampe (Fred), David Healy (American on Train), Joseph Greig (Barman on Train).

Alf returns home from work, Else knowing of his imminent arrival since baby Michael begins to cry as soon as he turns the street corner. After the usual arguments, Mike asks Alf if he is going up the pub to celebrate his £82 post-war credit rebate (which is promptly halved by Else taking her share). At the local hostelry, Gran mourns the fact that she will never know the identity of a man who groped her on the bus generations earlier, George complains that his new-high rise home is not conducive to keeping his chickens, and Bert marvels at the homing abilities of his six pigeons, which he swears could be released in Liverpool and still reach home in Wapping before him. Alf scoffs at this, so Bert challenges him and states that he will prove it. The two place bets using the proceeds from their post-war credits, then journey to Liverpool, release the pigeons and return to London, in an increasingly inebriated state while ensconced in the British Rail restaurant car. Alf finds that the pigeons have got back three minutes before them, having hitched a ride on top of first the train carriage and then the taxi ...

ARGUMENTS, ARGUMENTS

The current status of the Holy Family; the possibility of Alf Ramsey selling the national football team to the Germans; the idiocy of Chamberlain starting a war without bothering to cost it beforehand; Canterbury (Kent) versus Canterbury (New Zealand); Labour subsidises and featherbedding of farmers; home rule for Wales and Scotland; the debt America owes England for the sale of slaves.

BLOODY LANGUAGE

Thirty-five 'bloodies', five 'bleedings', two 'silly moos', one 'ignorant Scouse git', one 'blasphemous Scouse git', one 'heathen Scouse pillock', a 'bleeding silly cow'.

FUNNY BUSINESS

Else's contention that baby Michael can sense when Alf approaches home; Alf's business with some salt and a knife; Else mixing up the Ramseys (Alf and Archbishop); Mike's joke that the Canterbury Cloisters is a pub down the Old Kent Road; a smiling Else's question to Alf, '*Are* you having a heart attack?', as he experiences heartburn; Alf's malapropism – 'metrolopis' (for 'metropolis'); George's gripes about his chickens in their new environment; the drunken interplay between Alf and Bert; the tale of Gran's grope in 1914, between Aldgate Pump and the Causeway Wapping; Alf's final declaration of '*I'm going dahn the pub*', only for Fred to point out that he's there already – and its closed.

WHAT ELSE?

This episode was originally intended to be transmitted third in the series' running order. Filming for the scenes of Alf's and Bert's journey to Liverpool took place on 10 July and 11 July. The outward train left London Euston Station 1.00 pm and arrived at Liverpool Lime Street at 3.52 pm. The return, the following day, departed Lime Street at 12.30 pm and arrived at Euston at 3.28 pm. British Rail was paid a £100 facility fee for the use of its premises and trains. Thirty-six pigeons were required for the filming in Liverpool on 11 July. Some other scenes involving the pigeons were prerecorded on the 14 July. George's 'pigeon run' (mentioned in the pub to Rita) was apparently constructed and set to be filmed in his high-rise residence on 12 July, but this was either cut or never completed due to time dictates. Rehearsals for the main studio recording took place between 10 and 12 August 1972 at the North Acton rehearsal block.

An expensively-produced sepia-tinted version of the third series titles was used for this episode, then dropped in favour of the new titles. Mike is seen reading Colin Wilson's *The God of the Labyrinth* (1970). There are so many shots of Golden Wonder crisp packets in the episode that it seems almost as if there must be some sort of product placement deal going on.

Post-war credits, mentioned in the script, were devised as a part of the financing of the Second World War. The additional tax paid as a result of a lowering of personal allowances was recorded and credited to the taxpayer, and finally repaid to those who had kept their post-war credit certificates by 1973.

Bill Maynard received £219 for his appearance in the episode, Joan Sims £300, David Healy £100 and George Tovey £84. Johnny Speight's son Richard was contracted but not used, while Winnie Sabina was filmed but had her role cut.

Dennis Main Wilson's press release for the episode stated: 'Johnny Speight uses the train journey for his main theme, which is a devastating attack upon nationalism on the one hand and parochialism (Garnett's of course) on the other.'

An unedited studio recording spool survives for this episode, capturing everything that was taped between 8.00 pm and 22.00 pm on 13 August 1972. During the count-in to the start of recording, we hear Warren Mitchell declaring that the bloody aspidistra needs watering. Then we see the whole of the first scene in the Garnett living room prior to the departure for the pub. There is a retake here, with lines about Georgie Best and booze and girls redone, and then Mike's mention of the post-war credits. Mitchell seems to act as orchestrator of the proceedings: he gets his chin made up again with remnants of soon food he spat out earlier, he sings out in a posh voice, he suggests that Tony Booth (smiling throughout) is being 'a bit premature' again, and he enquires about Dandy Nichols' health. Then he suggests that the audience talk amongst themselves, and even does a vocal impression of a camera breaking down. Nichols says that she was given the wrong cue, for which Geoff Jowitt, production assistant, apologises. We move on to the pub scenes, with shots of customers drinking, and then George Tovey's lines about his chickens, which he is asked to perform again. There is another break, with Mitchell saying that he will have to go back to the khazi again and Joan Sims doing some facial exercises. There is another retake as Sims says that she is confused as to the order of the glasses 'Tony' has provided – big glass or small glass first? Off screen, Mitchell shouts something about her knickers and Sims laughs, gets up, rearranges her dress and sits down again. Tovey's scene is then re-shot, along with the remainder of the pub scenes. The filmed insert of Liverpool follows, then the sequence featuring Alf and Bert aboard the train, complete with blue screen for the addition of Colour Separation Overlay effects, for which Mitchell tells the studio audience to watch their own screens in order to obtain the best view. He asks if there are any 'Scots, Welsh or coons' in the audience, and reminds them that the opinions he is soon to voice are not his but Mr Garnett's and Mr Speight's. (Maynard says 'Coward!' in response.) He picks out one audience member and asks him where he is from. The reply is Jamaica, and Mitchell assures him that his nationality is not mentioned in the following sequence, but then gets a laugh as he asks if it's true that they are all limboing under the toilet doors down in Ladbroke Grove ... There is a further retake when the conversation switches to Mary, Queen of Scots, and Mitchell 'loses his thread', distracted by scene shifters. He calls for more crisps for Maynard, and jokingly assures the audience that the recording will be finished by 1.00 am. One woman in the audience appears to get up, so he tells her to sit down, as the doors are locked and she can't escape. Maynard asks was it something they said, and Mitchell reiterates this and insists he didn't say 'Piss off' ... Finally, more shots of Gran waking up and then going off to sleep again are taken, eliciting raucous applause from the audience. Then its Nichols' turn, as she gives a masterclass in performing a range of expressions from disdain, boredom, smirking, puzzlement, frowning and more consumption of crisps. The audience wildly applaud, and Sims bursts out laughing.

The episode attracted 31% of the viewing population. The audience research report on the series' final episode, 'Euthanasia', presented the following breakdown of respondents' reactions to 'The Pigeon Fancier':

Very funny : Unfunny	76 : 24
Script excellent : Script poor	70 : 30
Very well cast : Poorly cast	93 : 7
Sets and costumes excellent : Sets and costumes poor	86 : 14

Birmingham Evening Mail: '... Alf as usual marched crunch-crunch over sensitive toes, but had a whole new pigeon joke going for him in what was undoubtedly one of his funniest of all scripts.'

4.3: WOMEN'S LIB AND BOURNEMOUTH
aka 'Holiday in Bournemouth'

Recorded 27 August 1972
Transmitted Wednesday 27 September 1972 at 9.25 pm

With Arnold Diamond (Train Passenger), Spike Milligan (Train Passenger), Edward Evans (Train Inspector), Harold Berens (Taxi Driver), Norman Bird

(Hotel Owner), Rita Webb (Hotel Owners)

The Garnetts, complete with the new family member, go to Bournemouth for a holiday. En route, they get turfed out of a first class train coach, meet a pompous hotel landlady, her put-upon husband and her yapping Poochy, talk to a coloured gentleman who hates Pakistanis and a Jewish taxi driver who believes Alf to be a Yiddisher boy. Finally, Alf receives an accidental soaking at the hotel swimming pool and returns home to find his choice of meal at the Garnett residence is not available.

ARGUMENTS, ARGUMENTS

Television ruining things by giving women ideas of liberation; the theory of Adam's rib proving that God created women to cook/wash/clean for men (see also 'Aunt Maud'); Enoch Powell's prediction of race war in Britain in 1978; the India-Pakistan war of 1971; the business prowess of Jews buying up chicken cheap at the market, sticking a kosher label on it and selling it at 10p per pound extra; whether or not the sea at Bournemouth is the same sea as at Wapping …

BLOODY LANGUAGE

Fifty-one 'bloodies', one 'bleeding', a 'Peruvian Ponce', one 'Shirley Temple', a 'Goldilocks'.

FUNNY BUSINESS

Else ironing Alf's long-johns, discussing her husband's dirt; Spike's 'Bloody white wog!' reaction to Alf; the taxi driver calling Alf Jewish; Rita Webb's Mae West-like turn as the landlady, and Alf's and Mike's enjoyment in taunting her; John Bird's performance as the laconic, henpecked husband; Alf – 'You wouldn't care if I was dying would you?' Else – 'Well, I wouldn't let it spoil my holiday'; Else and Alf (wearing a knotted handkerchief on his head, *a la Monty Python's* gumbies) on the beach discussing the water at Wapping; Alf's inebriated comments to Harold the landlord – his wife is ugly (no offence) and there ought to be a law against ugly women, because the most ugly are also the fattest (no offence); Else's impression of the landlady and Poochy.

WHAT ELSE?

Location filming was carried out in Bournemouth. The cast and crew departed on the 12.30 pm train from London Waterloo to Bournemouth on 15 July 1972 and cast rehearsals took place the following day at the Round

House Hotel, prior to filming that afternoon at the swimming pool of the Royal Bath Hotel, starting at 2.30 pm. The hotel charged a fee of £25 for this. More filming, of the Garnetts arriving at Bournemouth Station, began at 9.30 am on 17 July. Last to be shot, on 18 July, were the scenes featuring Harold Berens, Dandy Nichols and Warren Mitchell alighting from the taxi ride from Bournemouth to the hotel.

Rehearsals for the studio recording took place in North Acton between 22 and 26 August.

John Holmes of Formakin Animal Centre Wimborne was again engaged to train the Boston terrier that played Poochy, and apart from his fee also received two tickets to the studio recording. The sound of Poochy yapping is obviously overdubbed in one scene, being out of synch with the movements of the dog's mouth.

Mitchell's friend Arnold Diamond received £75 for his role as a train passenger; Johnny Speight's friend Spike Milligan £175 for his, while as the hotel owners, Norman Bird received £160 and Rita Webb £105. Edward Evans, the ticket collector here, had played Mr Pringle in 'Aunt Maud'. A cameo by Henry McGee for £100 as an officious waiter at the hotel pool was cut due to time constraints. Speight's son Richard is the boy in the swimming pool who ensures that Alf falls in. Locals from the Pavilion Theatre Bournemouth acted as hotel guests at the pool.

Apart from the usual problems, the studio recording started three minutes late and overran by 15 minutes. Mike reads *Steps* (1968) by Jerzy Kosinski. Mention is made by Else of her sister Maud moving out of her home in Southend.

'Ikey', the insult delivered by the taxi driver to Alf in response to his tip, is a derivative of Victorian insult to Jews, 'Ikey-Mo' ('Isaac-Moses').

The episode was watched by 32.8% of the viewing population. The audience research report on 'Euthanasia' recorded the following reactions to 'Women's Lib and Bournemouth':

Very funny : Unfunny	83 : 17
Script excellent : Script poor	80 : 20
Very well cast : Poorly cast	94 : 6
Sets and costumes excellent : Sets and costumes poor	89 : 11

Someone did not do their homework regarding the naming of the Commodore Hotel in the show, forcing the BBC in the shape of Bill Cotton to make a public statement following transmission (rather late in the day, on 11 October) alerting the public to the fact that there was a real hotel of the same name – an AA two star-registered establishment with 20 rooms in the Southbourne area of Bournemouth …

Dennis Main Wilson's press release for the episode remarked: 'The holiday is a peg on which Alf Garnett attacks women's lib.'

4.4: IF WE WANT A DEMOCRACY WE'VE GOT TO START SHOOTING A FEW PEOPLE
aka 'Dock Pilfering'

Recorded 20 August 1972
Transmitted Wednesday 11 October 1972 at 9.25 pm

With Roy Kinnear (Dockworker), George Tovey (Dockworker)

The Garnetts are seated at breakfast, and Alf is pleased to read in the newspaper that some of the properties in Wapping may be worth £20,000 under this Tory government, whereas under Wilson the figure was only £600. This leads to Mike and Alf arguing over the post-War policies of Clement Attlee, treacherously handing over East Germany and India to Molotov while Churchill talked to Stalin at Yalta. Else chips in with her theories on Communism. They then debate God, and Mike questions His existence and challenges Him to strike him down within ten seconds.

At work, Alf sits down for his lunch while his colleagues pilfer tomatoes from the boxes they have unloaded. He then finds to his fury that Else has forgotten to pack him any food. He argues that recent laws against the dockers are only fair, while his mate states that all the Tories are doing is attempting to do the dockers down – first by politics and then by criminalising their perfectly lawful activities. Alf returns home in a fury to find that not only did Else forget to pack his lunch, but she has now also eaten his dinner …

ARGUMENTS, ARGUMENTS

Rising property values; the race relations board; inflation; post-War politics; Labour corruption; Gandhi and Jesus; God the capitalist owning the world; the BBC; prison trade unions; Billy Butlin; Labour giving the colonies away; the recent case of the imprisonment of five dockers; Communism; the Conservative government's attempt to restrain the dockers.

BLOODY LANGUAGE

Sixty-five 'bloodies', five 'bleedings', a 'bloody thieving bastards', one 'two-faced bolshie bastard', one 'pissed down', one 'Shirley Temple', two 'silly moos', a 'blasphemious Scouse git', a 'dirty, scruffy peroxide blonde', and a 'Scouse ponce'.

FUNNY BUSINESS

Else's recollections about the bombing in the War, thinking that the Luftwaffe specifically targeted the Jews in their road; Alf's logic about rent and inflation; Else's impressions of Churchill; Alf's Biblical confusion – 'It's harder for the rich man to pass through the eye of a camel … than for the needle … as the Lord Jesus sayeth …'; Mike challenging God to strike him down, and then hiding under the table when he hears a bang outside; Else talking about the hypocrisy of Communism; a brilliant scene where Alf elaborately prepares for his dinner in total silence only to find that Else has forgotten to put anything in his lunch box; Roy Kinnear's stomach-churning denunciation of the evils of Toryism as he stuffs his sandwiches down his mouth and Alf looks on enviously; Else's logic regarding her husband's dinner.

WHAT ELSE?

This episode was rehearsed between 15 and 19 August 1972 at the North Acton Rehearsal Block. The reference to Stalin having been an American spy evokes 'Two Toilets – That's Posh', as does the discussion of the value of Alf's house. It is said that Mike and Rita pay £2 per week to Alf for their room (double the amount in 'Caviar on the Dole').

Roy Kinnear received £250 and George Tovey £84 for their roles.

Dennis Main Wilson described the episode in his press release, commenting: '[It] reflects in terms of comedy the general mood of violence and anarchy that is prevalent in the world today.' He embellished this with a litany of the current concerns of the nation: the conflict over defined jobs in the docks; criminals in jail forming their own trade union; the idea of Billy Butlin taking over HM Prisons; the argument that growing violence is due to the baleful influence of television; and the riots and industrial violence that had occurred during the summer. 'Viewers will have to decide whether it is Garnett's point of view or whether it is Johnny Speight's, but this script says quite clearly that if you want a democracy, you have to shoot someone …'

31.7% of the viewing population tuned in this time. The audience reaction report on 'Euthanasia' records the following data for this earlier episode:

Very funny : Unfunny	73 : 27
Script excellent : Script poor	68 : 32
Very well cast : Poorly cast	92 : 8
Sets and costumes excellent : Sets and costumes poor	87 : 13

A clip of the scene in which Alf and the others discuss the value of the house was shown on BBC One's early evening news round-up *Nationwide* in

September 1973 in a report about the rising cost of housing.

Birmingham Evening Mail: 'Any new viewer who took a peek at *Till Death* … expecting the Garnetts to break further barriers of taste and offer fresh shocks might have been disappointed. Not that Alf was short of vulgarities or expletives, but there actually seemed a limit to what he was prepared to say. We even had a subdued Alf virtually silent through a complete sequence.'

4.5: UP THE 'AMMERS!

Recorded 6 August 1972
Transmitted Wednesday 18 October 1972 at 9.25 pm

With Bobby Moore (Himself), Alan Ball (Himself), Martin Peters (Himself), Joan Sims (Gran), Carolyn Moody (Neighbour) (uncredited), William Wilson (Baby), Johnny Speight (Barmy Harry) (uncredited)

Alf proudly puts up a picture of the previous Royal Family – Queen Victoria, Edward Prince of Wales, George V and Edward Duke Of Windsor – which he has found in a junk shop. This prompts memories of the glory days of Empire, leading ineluctably to a discussion of the glories of football. After the men argue yet again the relative merits of West Ham and Liverpool, Rita blows her top – she is worn out looking after the baby and demands that Mike serves his turn tomorrow. Her husband replies that he has to go to Arsenal to see his team play, and Alf is going to see West Ham …

Over breakfast the next morning, arguments rage again, this time over Alf's contention that it is a well known fact that Germans cannot function on the left side of the brain … They muse on the Boche elements present in the Royal Family and this sparks in Alf the thought that if Edward hadn't met Mrs Simpson, he would have given West Ham a royal licence … While Alf gets ready to go to the match, he has a daydream of the three kings of West Ham – Bobby Moore, Alan Ball and Martin Peters – playing in front of yer actual King Edward, waving his royal approval. Then he discovers that Mike and Rita have been defacing the Royal portrait with Alf's features and a caption emblazoned with 'Up Yer Hammers!'

Else and her daughter leave the baby in its pram outside the local shop, only to discover on emerging minutes later that the pram has vanished. While Rita is hysterical, Alf is happily looking after the baby, feeding whisky into its bottle, while watching the West Ham game … Late that night, as Rita sobs, waiting for news of her baby, consoled by her husband and her mother, Alf turns up drunk in charge of Michael. Else promptly locks him out in fury …

ARGUMENTS, ARGUMENTS

Football (Liverpool, West Ham, Lord Harewood, Don Revie, Leeds, Reg

Pratt); the Empire; religion causing wars; the Raj banning *suttee*[47]; strikes; the Great War; the identity of Alf's father; the Royal family.

BLOODY LANGUAGE

Twenty-eight 'bloodies', five 'bleedings', a 'stupid little bitch', two 'silly great moos', a 'daft great pie can'; two 'Shirley Temples'; an 'ignorant Scouse git' and a 'silly old rat bag'.

FUNNY BUSINESS

Alf's questionable football knowledge – 'a *3-4-3… or a 3-3-4 … dominant wings with an orthodox cross …*'; Else's reaction to Alf's comments on *suttee* – 'I'd burn for you any day, pig!'; Rita turning on Mike, saying that he's no better than her father; Else's soliloquy about prices always going *up, up, up,* defying the laws of gravity; Gran's litany of terrible things that could have happened to Rita's baby – 'Someone's taken him … someone mental … someone a bit touched … one who's a bit loony … someone off their head … with a screw loose … one of them mad people … probably gypsies …'

WHAT ELSE?

This episode was the second of the series to be made and was originally scheduled as second in the running order. Filming of the scenes of Rita losing the baby took place at the Co-op, 91 South Ealing Rd, on the afternoon of Wednesday 12 July 1972, after early closing, with extra shooting scheduled for 26 July. Some of this material was cut from the episode before transmission, as Una Stubbs' performance was thought to be too convincingly harrowing. The fantasy football scene was filmed at West Ham FC between 11.00 am and 12.30 pm on Sunday 23 July. Stock footage of West Ham versus Stoke City (possibly from 26 January 1972) was inserted for the scenes of Alf and the baby at the Arsenal versus West Ham match. (The real match was played on Tuesday 29 August 1972; Alf would not have been happy, as his team lost by one goal. The match Mike is said to be attending, Arsenal versus Liverpool, actually took place on 16 September 1972.) Rehearsals for the studio recording took place at St Mary Abbotts Hall between 1 and 5 August 1972.

For the first time, we see that the Garnetts live at number 27 (as opposed to number 25 as in *The Alf Garnett Saga* and later in the 1974 series). The picture of royalty and the reference to a junk shop evoke 'A Wapping Mythology'.

Speight repeated his cameo from *The Alf Garnett Saga* as Barmy Harry at the football match – the second time he had guested uncredited in the series –

---

[47] The Indian custom of a woman burning herself on her husband's funeral pyre.

for a fee of £150. For their own cameo roles, Bobby Moore received £50, Alan Ball £40 and Martin Peters £40.

The total cost of the production was £12,000. On 14 July, the designer was changed on medical grounds from Ian Rawnsley to Barrie Dobbins.

Dennis Main Wilson, editing this episode on 18 September, complained about the complexity of the BBC's new computer editing system. This may have been the cause of its rescheduling.

The episode was watched by 32.9% of viewing population and, according to the audience research report on 'Euthanasia', drew the following reactions:

Very funny : Unfunny	70 : 30
Script excellent : Script poor	67 : 33
Very well cast : Poorly cast	92 : 8
Sets and costumes excellent : Sets and costumes poor	86 : 14

4.6: EUTHANASIA
aka 'Alf's Broken Leg'

Recorded 3 September 1972
Transmitted Wednesday 25 October 1972 at 9.25 pm

With Joan Sims (Gran), Richard Speight (Kid), Clive Moss (Kid), Balfour Sharpe (Kid), Will Stampe (Fred), Alf Mangan (walk-on), Edith Raye (walk-on)

Alf has broken his leg in two places, having (whilst drunk) slipped on a mat that Else had replaced over a newly-polished floor; now confined to a wheelchair, he is even more insufferable than usual, with a nagging suspicion that Else has tried to kill him and claim on the insurance. A visit from Gran, who contends that doctors are dangerous and keen to amputate the odd limb or so, does nothing to improve Alf's mood. Else takes up the theme, talking of the recent visit of a life insurance agent to the Garnett home. Then Mike steps in and suggests euthanasia on the NHS – 'Join Up and Get Put Down!'. Desperate to go to the pub, Alf allows his wife to push both him and the baby's pram, until three kids kindly offer to help out and take Mr Garnett to the pub themselves. At the pub, they put sleeping tablets in Alf's beer. Then, while he slumbers, they paint his face and ask passersby for a 'Penny for the Guy'. Mike takes over and brings his drowsy father-in-law home. At first Alf is amused by the others' mirth, but then Else shows him a mirror ... Alf is furious, but his wife insists that there is still work to be done earning money for the Guy.

ARGUMENTS, ARGUMENTS

The War; marriage; overpopulation.

BLOODY LANGUAGE

Forty-two 'bloodies', one 'silly moo', a 'dirty Scouse git', a 'daft great peroxide pillock', and one 'bastards'.

FUNNY BUSINESS

Else's cruel reaction to her husband's demands for assistance; the struggle getting Alf down the stairs; Gran getting stuck over Alf's leg; Alf listening with mounting terror to the whispering by Rita and Else about the dangers of hospitals; Mike's case for euthanasia; Gran recounting the sorry state of Mrs Jones, dying stuck on a potty, and musing philosophically that one starts life as a baby, on a potty, and ends it, like a baby, on a potty; Fred's reaction to the boys telling him about Alf's accident – 'Good, serves him right!'; Mike's lightning transition from hysterical laughter at the sight of his painted father-in-law to down-to-earth business, asking for pennies for the Guy …

WHAT ELSE?

Rehearsals for this episode took place at North Acton Rehearsal Block between 29 August and 2 September 1972, with some pre-recording being done on 29 August. The studio session on 3 September overran by 15 minutes due to Alf's wheelchair breaking five minutes into recording, despite a specially-strengthened one having been obtained in light of Warren Mitchell having already broken two wheels on the one used during rehearsals. Twenty minutes of recording time were lost due to the necessary repairs. To add to what Dennis Main Wilson would later refer to as this 'major disaster', the main boom microphone went down during recording.

Will Stampe received £70 for his appearance. Johnny Speight's son Richard plays one of Alf's tormentors for the second time in this series (see 'Women's Lib and Bournemouth' for details of the first). Alf says of the kids that he knows the father of the 'little blonde one, [who] wears yellow trousers and stutters' – a clear reference to Speight senior.

The face painting idea is repeated from 'Hair Raising!' (and was later to be reused, with a twist, in episode two of the follow-up series *Till Death* …). The references to toffee apples and Southend beach echo some notorious dialogue from 'Aunt Maud', Else mourning that she married Alf rather than enjoying Bertie Knight's toffee apple … A recent edition of the *Radio Times* with a picture of racing driver Jackie Stewart on the front cover can be seen draped on the Garnetts' television set. Mike is reading *Collages* by Anais Nin. Reference is made to David Mackay, the Scottish footballer, who broke his leg in 1964 when playing for Tottenham Hotspur. Alf and Else emerge from the house next to number 25, which would be seen as the number of the Garnetts' own residence in the next series ...

Dennis Main Wilson to Duncan Wood: 'I agree that programme six ... is all right from a programme content point of view – macabre though the subject is.'

Wilson summed up the episode: 'Old Gran discusses hospitals, amputations, death and funerals.'

An audience research report was commissioned for this episode, which attracted 31.4% of the viewing population compared to 10.3% for ITV and 1.1% for BBC Two. The following reactions were recorded:

Very funny	43%	30%	17%	8%	2%	Thoroughly unfunny
Script excellent	35%	31%	23%	6%	5%	Script poor
Very well cast	66%	24%	8%	2%	0%	Poorly cast
Sets and costumes excellent	48%	34%	15%	2%	1%	Sets and costumes poor

Most respondents thought the episode extremely funny and, as usual, true to life. Some felt that the reduction in the show's controversial political comment had enhanced it. Many however deplored the swearing, which they saw as monotonous and unnecessary, and said that they were becoming bored with the attacks on royalty and the political content. A few stated that Speight had become too dependent on bad language (described as 'quite unnecessary, as the situations are humorous anyway'). There was wide agreement on the excellence of the script, comments including: 'Johnny Speight excelled himself. The script included a number of risqué remarks but somehow they all seemed right – just a part of the Garnett way of life'; 'The script lent itself to laughs readily. The last ten minutes were, by far, the best in the whole series'. There was praise for the cast, especially Mitchell, Nichols and Sims, although several respondents thought that Booth and Stubbs could have been given more to do. 'Good character acting from the four main stars,' said one, 'and Joan Sims was brilliant as Gran. She should definitely be retained for future series.'

THE ROYAL VARIETY PERFORMANCE

Recorded Monday 30 October 1972
Broadcast Sunday 5 November 1972

The Garnetts watch the television presentation of the Royal Variety performance, with a swear box at hand – to which, naturally, Alf contributes frequently. Else wants her husband to shut up so that she can watch the show and suggests that he go to the pub. When he replies that he now has no money, she breaks her own taboo by telling him to take it out of the bloody swear box. Mike then gives Alf a few ripe suggestions of his own, having contributed 20 pence in advance … and Alf is totally unable to reply …

ARGUMENTS, ARGUMENTS

Is Max Bygraves older than the Queen Mother?; Edward Heath; Harold Wilson; the BBC; Jack Jones.

BLOODY LANGUAGE

One 'foul mouthed git', one 'bloody Scouse git', one 'Scouse git', a 'bloomin great pudden' and two other 'bloodies'.

FUNNY BUSINESS

Alf thinking that Jack Jones' inclusion on the bill of the show is a sop to the trade unions; Else's conviction that the use of the phrase 'opening your bowels' constitutes swearing; Alf's presumption that Prince Philip swears a lot if those corgis get under his feet or the band plays outside the Palace when he's got a hangover; the idea of Her Majesty having a quiet drink from the Royal Bottle and thus avoiding queues at the bar and signing all those autographs; the idea that many in the audience have come with a view to gaining knighthoods, but that Her Majesty will not grant any that night as she hasn't brought her sword along.

WHAT ELSE?

Alf's suggestion that Prince Philip should be Prime Minister derives from the series two episode 'I Can Give It Up Anytime I Like', while the reference to Lord Hill being the first to swear on the BBC is surely Speight's reprisal for the Chairman's recent apology to 'Mary Whitewash'. 'Facetious' makes a return, as does the description of Heath as a 'grammar school twit'. The Prime Minister is also referred to in a gag about 'having his bottom scraped' at Broadstairs, where his yacht 'Morning Cloud' was undergoing repairs.

Max Bygraves, also referred to in the script, had just appeared as himself in *The Alf Garnett Saga*; 'Sir Bernard Delafonte' – Bernard Delfont, the organiser of the show – was indeed later rewarded for his efforts …

CHRISTMAS SPECIAL

Recorded 4 and 5 December 1972
Transmitted Tuesday 26 December 1972 at 9.10 pm

With Bill Maynard (Bert), Paul Nicholas (Himself), Dana Gillespie (Herself), Brian Leeson (Himself), Sally Riggs (Herself), Derek Griffiths (Watch Seller), Will Stampe (Fred), Maureen Lane (Barmaid), Carolyn Moody

The Garnetts visit the West End production of Jesus Christ Superstar *and then chat to some of the cast in the local pub, Alf expressing horror that a man playing Jesus could be living with a woman who is not his lawful wife.*

Back home on Christmas morning, Else is depressed at the thought of Christmas with all the work it entails for her, while Alf is keen to go out drinking, Rita is tired from looking after young Michael and his father is suffering from imbibing too much liquor at the midnight mass. Worse still, the turkey is too big to fit in the oven, and Alf suddenly realises he hasn't bought his wife a gift.

In the local hostelry, Bert introduces Alf to a black man who may be able to sell him a watch. He knocks the watch down from a fiver to 30 bob. Bert, Alf and Mike return home and discuss the following day's football match, amongst many things – the Biblical world, Jewish television, and Alf's opinion that England has given so much to the world it deserves a good rest … Just to make the day complete, the watch Alf has given his wife falls apart, much to Else's contempt …

ARGUMENTS, ARGUMENTS

Jesus' crucifixion, resurrection and return; alcohol; marriage; Christmas; the Queen; Idi Amin forcing the Asians from Uganda; sport on television; Jews; the Bible; the nature of Jesus.

BLOODY LANGUAGE

Twenty-six 'bloodies', two 'bleedings', a 'stupid bitch', a 'bloody Jew-nosed coon', an 'ignorant Scouse git', a 'blasphemous Scouse git' and a 'silly moo'.

FUNNY BUSINESS

Alf's sense of wonder as he views Jesus on stage; Else embarrassing Alf in the pub; Alf's horror at hearing the opening strains of Chuck Berry's 'My

Ding-a-Ling' on the radio; Mike looking well and truly wrecked, to Alf's amusement and the others' disgust; Mike's inspiring speech about making women feel they are the most important person in the world, to which Alf replies that he'll buy Else a packet of fags; Else's musings about a government conspiracy to subdue the population with drugs and diseases implanted in food and water; Derek Griffiths as a racist black marketer – 'They're Swiss – none of yer foreign rubbish'; Alf's comments about 'yer Jewish ITV' with Jimmy Hill as their rabbi (an oft-repeated clip); the discussion about the Boxing Day match between Tottenham Hotspur (with their large Jewish fan base) and West Ham; Bert's Biblical knowledge; Else's contention that the Holy family had to stay in a stable because it is always crowded at Christmas …

WHAT ELSE?

The filming of yer actual *Jesus Christ Superstar* show took place at the Cambridge Theatre on 19 November 1972. Rehearsals for the studio recording took place between 27 November and 3 December. This episode is unusual in having no introductory music and different opening titles: a series of shots of a church and a scanning of the Stations of the Cross.

As with 'Peace and Goodwill', much of the episode is set on Christmas Day. Prime Minister Heath is yet again referred to as a 'grammar school twit'. A line about workers sitting on the bog smoking recalls similar comments in series one and two, especially in 'Sex Before Marriage'; and Alf's musings on God making the world in seven days echo dialogue from the same episode. Alf's contention that the BBC clock is wrong is reminiscent of his complaints about Big Ben in the *Comedy Playhouse* pilot.

A number of members of the cast of *Jesus Christ Superstar* appear as themselves, including stars Paul Nicholas and Dana Gillespie. Gillespie later tried a solo musical career with RCA Mainman under the auspices of David Bowie. Derek Griffiths' character here is similar to the one he played in *The Alf Garnett Saga* and akin to that of Kenny Lynch in *Curry and Chips* – indeed, they speak some of the same lines, for example, 'They tell me to go 'ome, coon – but I am 'ome.' Griffiths so impressed the producer and writer that they attempted to create a regular role for him in the following series.

Warren Mitchell appears positively hirsute on this occasion. He received £1,150 for the show; Dandy Nichols received £950; Anthony Booth was paid £355; and Una Stubbs got £325 – a sure sign of the widening gulf in status between the regulars. This was the second *Till Death Us Do Part* Boxing Day episode, and was watched by 31.4% of the viewing population.

SERIES FIVE

The first four episodes of the fifth series were shown in the same peak slot as those of the previous run, Wednesdays at 9.25 pm, just before *Sportsnight*, starting on 2 January 1974. There was a week's break to make way for a *Sportsnight* special on 16 January, then the fifth and sixth episodes were shown on consecutive Tuesdays. The seventh episode was deliberately held back for transmission on Thursday 28 February at 9.30 pm as part of the BBC's coverage of the snap General Election called by the Heath government in response to the industrial unrest that had paralysed the nation. The choice of viewing on ITV included documentary series *The World at War* on Wednesdays, an edition of *Playhouse* on Tuesday 5 February, a documentary on racing driver Graham Hill the following week, and an episode of *Special Branch* on Election Night.

Speight's creation was seen as a very political animal, and the Election Night scheduling of the final episode followed that of 'Up The Polls! (The Campaign's Over)' four years earlier. As the national crisis worsened, producer Dennis Main Wilson adjusted the running order of the episodes so as to give Speight's scripts maximum political relevance. Note that the audience percentage figures quoted below must be seen in the context of extensive national and local power cuts during the period, which meant that some potential viewers were forced to miss certain episodes.

The seven episodes contained about 489 'bloodies', the highest number of the show's entire run. A new, brassier version of the theme tune was commissioned. Mitchell received £1000 per episode, Nichols £775, Booth £300 and Stubbs £250, with Sims on a fee of £300 and Speight receiving £1100 per script. Felix Bowness was commissioned at £25 per session to warm up the audience before recording for at least the last four studio sessions (on 6, 13, 20 and 27 January respectively), and possibly for the first three as well. Approximate cost per show was £12,000.

For the first time since 'The Blood Donor', the Reaction Index figures fell in three cases to the mid '50s, suggesting that the love affair between public and Garnetts was beginning to wane.

5.1: THE TV LICENCE

Recorded 9 December 1973
Transmitted Wednesday 2 January 1974 at 9.25 pm, with an RI of 56

With Gordon Kaye (TV Licence Man)

Saturday afternoon in the Garnett household. As Else collates her Green Shield stamps and the others idly watch wrestling on the TV, arguments rage over sport, TV, race, the Tories, Mary Whitehouse, Lord Longford, the Middle East conflict … As Alf gets ready to go out, he graciously allows Else and the others to continue watching the TV, even though he knows he has no licence, having refused to pay for it due to his low opinion of the rubbishy BBC and its Liberal Party propaganda. Next morning, over breakfast, Alf forces the others to watch the Remembrance Day ceremony at the Cenotaph, while he regales them with his theories on Empire, war and Europe. Then the TV licence inspector arrives and demands to see his licence. When Alf is threatened with a £50 fine or one year in prison, Mike comes to his father-in-law's rescue and proffers the licence in his name – but in return, he unplugs the TV to take it upstairs, and Alf is unable to protest. To cap it all, Alf finds that Else has eaten his breakfast …

ARGUMENTS, ARGUMENTS

TV; racism; the NHS; the Arab-Israeli conflict pushing up the price of oil; the 'Whitechapel Mob'; Whitehouse; Longford; Enoch Powell; wrestling; pensioners; sex out of wedlock; the War; home rule for Wales and Scotland.

BLOODY LANGUAGE

112 'bloodies', one 'bleeding', a 'middle-aged peroxide clunk click albino ponce' (i.e. disc jockey Jimmy Saville, who at the time was fronting the 'clunk clink' public information campaign encouraging car users to wear seatbelts), one 'tit', two 'Shirley Temples', one 'great, hairy, filthy Scouse git', one 'ignorant Scouse git', one 'silly moo', one 'Goldilocks', one 'lazy bloody moo', one 'slant eyed Micks'.

FUNNY BUSINESS

A particularly electrifying row as Alf denies that he sat up to 10.30 pm not to actually watch the Andy Warhol programme on TV but simply to be able to complain about it; Mike's contention that Mary Whitehouse and Lord Longford are tipsters of porn; Mike gazing upwards, crossing himself and speaking of Mary and virgin birth – a sign of Speight hitting back over the events of 1972; Alf's rants about yer *evil Top of the Pops* and Jimmy Saville, the BBC's Liberal Party propaganda and yer Russian bloody Mick, yer Ludovic bleeding Kennedy; Mike's reference to Enoch Powell being barmy and his mock Nazi salute; Alf reiterating that he is *not bloody Jewish*; talk of Ginger George the raver and the wrestling 'nancy boys'; Else's logic regarding the BBC and the telly (telling them not to send their programmes, except Bruce Forsyth's *The Generation Game*); allegations of the BBC bugging the nation, just like Nixon and Watergate …

WHAT ELSE?

The action of this episode is set on Saturday 10 November and Remembrance Sunday 11 November 1973. The Andy Warhol play mentioned was actually a documentary shown in March 1973. A reference to Enoch Powell and excreta stems from Powell's 1968 speech in Birmingham when he related the story of one of his Wolverhampton constituents who had apparently received excreta through her letterbox from neighbouring immigrants. We learn that Alf's grandfather was lost in the Crimea, and his mother was illegitimate. Else is saving up for a deckchair by collecting Green Shield stamps. (These stamps were given away with purchases by many stores in the '60s and '70s as a promotional device to encourage savings; they were very popular, until inflation decimated their value and the idea was abandoned by the end of the decade.) The Green Shield company allowed the use of the stamps in the production in return for a donation to a charity of the cast's choice. It appears from this episode that the local hostelry run by Fred, and never named previously, may be The Three Pigeons. Gordon Kaye, who received £70 for his role, later recalled in his autobiography that he was aware of rumours that Warren Mitchell was 'difficult', but that he had found him very professional. This episode holds the record for the number of 'bloodies', surely a deliberate reaction to Mrs Whitehouse again.

An Audience Research Report was commissioned for the episode, which attracted 32.2% of the viewing population, compared to 14.5% for ITV and 1.7% for BBC Two. This recorded the following reaction scores:

A+	A	B	C	C-
9%	32%	37%	17%	5%

This equated to an RI of 56, the lowest for the show so far. Many respondents received the return of the show with little enthusiasm, finding the Remembrance Day theme and bad language distasteful and overshadowing the usual wit and humour. They were also disappointed with the lack of a common theme, except Alf's bigotry. A substantial number on the other hand found some of Alf's comments contained a great deal of truth, and enjoyed the acting, especially from Mitchell and Nichols. A few thought Mitchell was now overacting, and the characters less convincing. The production was found satisfactory if a little static, and some enjoyed the addition of the photo of Anne and Mark Phillips on the Garnetts' wall. For some, however, the casting, performance and production were 'wasted on a "played out" series, which in their opinion, should never have been resurrected.'

5.2: THE ROYAL WEDDING

Recorded 16 December 1973
Transmitted Wednesday 9 January 1974 at 9.25 pm, with an RI of 56

With Roy Kinnear (Sid), Pat Coombs (Woman Next Door), Will Stampe (Fred), Joan Sims (Gran)

Alf cajoles the others into decorating the house in celebration of the imminent wedding of Princess Anne to Mark Phillips, 'the poor man's Harvey Smith', as Rita calls the groom. After arguments on the class divide, Alf wants to go to the pub and tries to borrow 50p out of the box used to pay for the phone but finds Else has taken it, having lent Mike some money and then found she had run out of housekeeping … Alf laments the fact that although he's the only capitalist amongst them, he seems to be the only one without any money … Later, the Garnetts watch a television interview with the royal couple and argue about royal manners. Alf and Mike then venture up the pub, only to find that Sid is mourning the lack of enthusiasm for a street party. Next day, Alf and Sid carry a piano into the street, prior to watching the ceremony on the television with Gran and the others. They then discover that no-one there can play the piano, although Else manages some scales, rather badly. The Garnetts and Sid find that they are the only people on the street taking part in the party. When Alf insults Else's awesome piano playing, the others decide to go indoors, Sid decides to go home and Alf is left alone …

ARGUMENTS, ARGUMENTS

The Army; Poland putting England out of the running for the 1974 World Cup, despite Great Britain having helped their nation in 1939; the end of the British Empire and the working and upper classes; anti-royalist MP Willie Hamilton; previous royal weddings, and the cost of these ceremonies when the country is bankrupt.

BLOODY LANGUAGE

Sixty-four 'bloodies', a 'lazy git', two 'Scouse gits', one 'silly moo' and one 'Shirley Temple'.

FUNNY BUSINESS

Else decorating the Christmas crib with red, white and blue bunting and a Union Flag; Mike's comment, 'Jesus saves but the Pope invests'; Alf the Tory finding that he is the only one without any money; Else playing the piano scales hopelessly out of tune; Alf's malapropism as he refers to Phillips having a 'batsman' to look after his needs; Rita's posh impressions – 'Is one orf up one's pub?'; Mike's fake Cockney aside, 'I can talk proper'; Alf saying that Else kept herself pure before their wedding, and she replying 'So you say' …

WHAT ELSE?

This episode, for unspecified reasons, probably illness on Dennis Main Wilson's part, was co-produced by David Croft. It is set over three days: Sunday 12 November, with the Garnetts making preparations for celebrating the Royal Wedding; the night of Tuesday 13 November when, after watching the *Panorama* TV interview with the royal couple, Alf and Mike go down the pub; and the wedding day itself, Wednesday 14 November, which was a national holiday for most workers. Thus the opening scenes are set on the same day as 'TV Licence'; but the continuity is not followed. The episode follow a structure similar to that of 'Monopoly' from the third series, in that Alf is left alone at the end. There is a reference to Centrepoint, the tower block built in 1964 at 101 Oxford Street in conditions of immense secrecy on land acquired by Harry Hyams, the property developer. By 1973, its estimated market value was an astonishing (for the time) £20 million, sustained purely because its capital appreciation (and the fact that because it was empty it was not liable for rates) was greater than any possible rental income. The husband of Pat Coombs' character is called Ron here, but by the last episode of *Till Death Us Do Part* in 1975 he would be named Wally. Mike and Rita are said to pay £1.50 rent per week to Alf, a 50p increase on the 1967 amount as revealed in 'Caviar on the Dole', but a 50p decrease compared with 'If We Want a Democracy We've Got to Start Shooting a Few People'. We learn that when Mike and Rita got married, Rita's car had to go eight times around the church waiting for Mike, as he was so boozed up. The character played by Roy Kinnear is revealed to be called Sid, the only time in the show he is clearly named. There is a possible in-joke reference to 'The Bulldog Breed', as Else and Pat Coombs' character complain about the piano blocking out their light, just as the lorry driven by Kinnear's (different) character did in the 1967 episode. Mike reads *The Workers' Press*. The Garnetts now apparently live at number 29, rather than number 25! Film of the real Royal Wedding was used for the TV feed. George Tovey was scheduled to reprise his role as the milkman, but this was cut. Roy Kinnear received £250 for his role, Pat Coombs £125, Will Stampe £70 and Joan Sims £300, which was equal to Tony Booth's fee and £50 more than Una Stubbs'. The episode was seen by 33.9% of the viewing population. Its original mastertape was wiped, but it still exists as a restored domestic VHS recording.

5.3: STRIKES AND BLACKOUTS

Recorded 6 January 1974
Transmitted Wednesday 23 January 1974 at 9.25 pm, with an RI of 64

With Olu Jacobs (TV Repair Man)

The Garnetts are playing Monopoly because the telly has broken down again. Else is being breathtakingly slow and indecisive, much to her husband's intense irritation. They argue about the current political crisis, Alf reflecting that Labour's much-vaunted USSR is evidence of the grey face of socialism, and Mike and Rita insisting that Heath is to blame for the crisis – everyone wants to pay the miners except him. Mike's vision of the Prime Minister as an old woman infuriates his wife, who launches into a scathing attack on 'fatso' Heath, reducing her parents to stunned silence. Then Alf notices his wife is prodding something in a matchbox. Else reveals that the box contains bees, which Mrs Coker has recommended as cure for her rheumatism, the stings to be directed at the vulnerable points as therapeutic medicine … The family continue to row, over Alf's suggestion that only mass unemployment will bring prosperity to the country and the possibility that the army will help out by working down the mines. They are interrupted by the arrival of the TV repair man, who – much to Alf's consternation – is black. The man gets the telly working again, but then there is a power cut. As Else tries to recall where she left the candles, Alf opens a box of matches – and promptly gets stung. Nursing his pain, Alf rails at the political situation that has brought about his agony. Mike meanwhile tries to light a fire, and Rita mercilessly lampoons her father's appearance.

Later, Else comes downstairs to find that the living room light is off; convinced there is a power cut, she says she cannot cook kippers for her husband's tea. Mike and Rita come in and the arguments resume, this time focusing on the cessation of credit during the emergency, Alf pointing out that the Mooneys across the road will suffer because they have always lived on credit. When the woman's husband died, she left him in the house and went and spent all the insurance money up the pub, leaving the council to bury him. Mike suddenly notices that the street lights are on and realises that actually there is no power cut – the light bulb has gone. Alf is furious and orders his wife to go in the kitchen and make the dinner. Else turns and tells him that when he dies, she will go up the pub and spend all the money and let the council put him *down – and she won't want them to tell her where he is buried, either! Then another power cut strikes, and Else says, 'Serves you right, you pig!'*

ARGUMENTS, ARGUMENTS

Phase Three of the government's wages' and salaries' progression framework; Heath; the economy; the government's exhortation to families to have heating in one room only; Boots taking over Harrods; MP Cyril Smith; the three day week; the miners.

BLOODY LANGUAGE

Sixty-three 'bloodies', a 'bolshie bastards', five 'silly moos', one 'silly great pudden', one 'bloody Scouse ponce', one 'Shirley Temple'.

FUNNY BUSINESS

Another explosive row between Mike and Alf; Else and her bees; Rita's stunning outburst regarding fat people and Tories, and Alf's stunned reaction; Rita saying 'All rich people are fat', and Alf pointing to Else and responding 'She isn't rich'; Mike jokingly making out that one of the Monopoly cards reads that Labour have been re-elected with a huge majority and that all land will be nationalised and property developers will have their profits taken off them – saying which, he grabs all Alf's Monopoly money; Alf suddenly realising, after a racist rant regarding Enoch Powell and the mines, that the black TV repair man has entered the room behind him; the repair man's triumphant 'Magic … Black magic!' on fixing the TV set; Mike spelling out his father-in-law's name, 'A – L – F', when Alf hesitates over signing the repair man's invoice; Mike and Rita giving black power salutes; Rita making bunny impressions with the handkerchief she has wrapped around Alf's head as a makeshift bandage; Alf's moan that he can't hold anything now, thanks to the bee stings, and Else's rejoinder that his hand will be all right when it sees a glass; Alf's malapropism – 'adrenalinin' (for 'adrenaline'); the discovery that the cats have been on the coal …

WHAT ELSE?

References to 'Monopoly' from the third series abound: mention is made of Mrs Moore's New Year's Eve party several years ago, and some scenes are essentially repeated from the earlier episode, including Alf waiting for Else to make a decision, Else asking Rita for help, Alf landing on Marlborough Street, which he wants to buy, while Else offers Euston Road in exchange. Else's water trap for mice in 'Monopoly' is replaced here by her equally demented matchbox full of bees.

Mike reads *Militant* again. Olu Jacobs, who received £50 for his performance, would reappear in the same role in *Till Death …* in 1981, similarly charging £3 to repair the Garnetts' TV set.

Warren Mitchell was interviewed from the set of this episode for *Pebble Mill at One* on 8 January 1974 – the clip does not exist.

The episode was seen by 21.1% of the viewing population, a considerable decrease on the series' usual audience, due – ironically, in view of the subject matter – to the localised power cuts at the time.

5.4: THREE DAY WEEK

Recorded 13 January 1974
Transmitted Wednesday 30 January 1974 at 9.25 pm, with an RI of 66

Alf returns home late one evening after work, pleased that he's been to the garage to fill up his lighter, and saying how the garage owner is making a lot of business out of the petrol rationing. Then he finds that his dinner isn't waiting for him on the table, and demands to know why. Else replies that since the country is on a three day week, she is too. Alf endeavours to explain that Mr Heath meant workers … workers in industry … important industry. Else argues that she's all of these. Alf again demands a dinner, but Else replies that she had no money and the queues at the shops were like those during the War. She says that there's some bacon and cheese in the pantry, and when her husband demands a hot dinner, she suggests he put mustard on it. An infuriated Alf is helpless in the face of this resistance, while Else proudly tells Rita that whereas the country is losing £40 million a week, she's actually saving, and can use the money to buy a new coat. Alf clatters around in the kitchen, and Rita asks her mother what food remains. Her mother replies that there's only some bacon, cheese and bread. At this point, Mike says that he took the bacon and cheese for sandwiches that morning. Else complains that she hasn't enough money, relying on the tallyman to get by, and suggests Alf get something from the shops, but Rita says that the only place open at this time is the local Chinese, and Alf adamantly refuses to eat from there. The trouble is, says Else, everyone helps themselves to food from the kitchen. Alf plugs the electric fire in, despite warnings from his wife that Mr Heath has said they should save energy. He and Mike bicker over Wilson and Heath not suffering the same privation as themselves, but Else states that she has seen 11 Prime Ministers come and go yet she has been hard up under all of them. Alf is disgusted – he's worked hard all his life … Else retorts that all their furniture is old and he can't even afford to buy a new coat. Alf, much to Rita's indignation, replies that if she asked for new furniture or a new coat, he would provide. Mike dismisses him as a typical Tory with 'old fashioned, Victorian, Stone Age philosophies'. Alf appeals to his daughter, asserting that he has always done his best for the family, working hard all his life. He may have been wrong, but are Mike's ideas right? Rita and Alf begin to get tearful, but Else gives her husband one of her most baleful looks. The others remind him that he has promised to pay for a coat, and Alf agrees, with his wife admitting that of course she's not on strike. It will cost £10, says Else, who gets up to go in the kitchen. Alf now thinks that they have been kidding him all along, and expects his dinner. He is speechless when Else emerges resplendent in a blue coat, explaining that she had no money to buy any food because she had paid the tallyman a deposit – for £16 – the shoes included in the deal. Still dazed, Alf looks on as Else pulls some cash from his wallet and suggests that they go up to the Chinese for a meal. Then Rita realises that someone will have to stay and look after the baby. She, Mike and Else all leave, promising to bring something back for Alf.

ARGUMENTS, ARGUMENTS

Petrol rationing; the miners; army recruitment; Heath; Wilson.

BLOODY LANGUAGE

Sixty-three 'bloodies', two 'silly moos', two 'great puddens', one 'Shirley Temple'.

FUNNY BUSINESS

Else's logic – in Mr Heath's three day week, the country is losing £40 million per week, while in hers, she is actually saving money; Alf warning his wife, without any reaction; the debate about the food in the house; Alf shouting that he doesn't want cheese because he isn't a mouse and Else replying that she wishes he was, and then she could put a trap down for him; Alf's response to his wife's reminder about the Prime Minister's energy saving exhortations: 'Sod Mr Heath'; Alf losing his thread thanks to Else, before imparting his economic knowledge – 'Yer balance of payments ... yer fiscal putting in and yer takeouts'; the analogy of the ship of state – Alf saying that the nation will pull together and bail the boat out, Mike retorting that the workers are chained to the oars while the rest enjoy themselves on deck; Rita's anger at her father, then her mock quivering lower lip as he explains how he has done his best for the family, only for her to be moved almost to tears later; Else's blank reaction to her husband's appeals for understanding; Alf becoming the helpless victim in the story's final payoff.

WHAT ELSE?

This episode was originally scheduled for transmission as the fifth in the series' running order. Mike reads a book called *The Satanic Man*. It is stated that Else's sister Maud has left for Australia, selling – or giving – her sofa to the Garnetts. Visible in the Garnetts' living room is a copy of the 5 January edition of the *TV Times*, with a *Man About the House* cover. Charles Clore, the financier, is mentioned, as in the original *Comedy Playhouse* pilot. The episode attracted 25.5% of the viewing population. It was repeated on 13 February 1986 in tribute to Dandy Nichols, who had just died. This saw her estate receive £2,790, Mitchell £3,600, Booth £1,080, Stubbs £900 and Speight £3,960 in repeat fees.

5.5: GRAN'S WATCH

Recorded 20 January 1974
Transmitted 5 February 1974 at 9.25 pm, with a RI of 60

With Joan Sims (Gran)

The Garnetts are having breakfast one Saturday morning when Alf asks his son-in-law if he is going with him to see West Ham. Before long, they are arguing about football, Mike lamenting the quality of the game in London, Alf in turn moaning that there is nothing worth having outside the capital. The row moves on to include Alf's regional prejudice. Else meanwhile meticulously counts up her money, finding that she hasn't enough to balance the books, or to pay for her husband's insurance. Alf talks of the past glories of England, with Drake and company ruling the seas and the harsh punishment being meted out to thieves, but Mike calls him a hypocrite. Heated debate on the miners and immigration follows, until Else brings things down to a personal level and her relationship with Alf, commenting on his family's poverty and the fact that he was last on her list of desirable men ... Else says she must see Gran, who is lying ill in bed in her lodgings, and Alf decides to go with her, much to Rita's bemusement.

As Gran, consoled by Else, feverishly remembers her mother's worries about religion, Alf searches the room and finds a gold watch that once belonged to Gran's husband Harry. He purloins it, fitting it to his gold chain, deluding himself that this is justified as Gran has promised Else all her bits and pieces should she die. While Else goes out to phone the doctor, he hands the old woman his old watch in exchange.

Later, on his return from the football match, Alf is shocked to find Gran being led into the living room by Else and complaining that she's been robbed of her Harry's gold watch. Mike says that he now agrees with Alf – anyone robbing a dying woman deserves the worst punishment possible ... Gran recalls that when she was dying, she saw two figures at her bedside, one the very image of the Holy Mother, the other the very Devil himself. And seeing Satan looming over her, touching her watch and taking away all the gold, she came back from death's door, refusing to go with him ... The others guess what has happened. Alf claims he saved the watch for her, but a glowering Else suggests that he give it back. The others stand silently in disgust, and Alf explodes and says that he's going down the pub.

ARGUMENTS, ARGUMENTS

Liverpool FC manager Bill Shankly; the miners; Enoch Powell; immigration; Liverpool.

BLOODY LANGUAGE

Forty 'bloodies', one 'Shirley Temple', one 'bloody blond ponce' and one 'bloody Scouse git'.

FUNNY BUSINESS

Alf talking about his cultural background; the vision of a young Alf hanging around on street corners pretending to be a film star (King Kong, says Mike); Rita's mimic of a Victorian master, using her hair as a fake moustache; Alf's assertion 'I've been a good husband, I have,' and Else's reply, 'Good at what?'; Else's logic over the phone money – Mike pays her 3p to phone Liverpool, including an extra penny because it's outside London, therefore she charges Gran 4p when she phones her friend in Glasgow, because Scotland's that little bit further away; Gran recounting her salvation from death by the angel and the devil, imbuing her with the strength to carry on.

WHAT ELSE?

Mike reads *The Militant*, *The New Statesman* and the *Morning Star*, and Alf reads the *Daily Mail* and the *Daily Express*. The match between West Ham and Hereford, mentioned by the two men, actually took place on 5 January 1974, with Bobby Moore being injured in his last ever game for the Hammers; the teams drew one all. We learn that Alf started wearing his homburg and growing his moustache when he was inspired by Clark Gable in the film *San Francisco*. (Min will opine that he looks 'Clark Gabley' too, at least in the antiperspirant department, in the second episode of series six.) The episode was seen by 26.9% of the viewing population.

5.6: PARTY NIGHT
aka 'The Demon Drink'

Recorded 23 December 1973
Transmitted Tuesday 12 February 1974 at 10.10 pm, with an RI of 62

With Will Stampe (Fred), Rita Webb (Ruby), Adrienne Posta (Milly), Roy Kinnear (Sid), Joan Sims (Gran)

Alf is suffering at the breakfast table after a night on the booze. Else has no sympathy, and neither has Rita, who calls her father an alcoholic. Alf strenuously denies this, citing the case of Mr Fraybourne the bank manager, who daren't touch a drop in case he reverts to his old boozy ways. Else says that Alf was drunk on their wedding night and has been drunk ever since, guzzling the bonded whisky at the docks, sleeping it off in a warehouse and then claiming overtime. Alf states that Churchill was a good example of a man who liked a drink and could still function. He then searches for some beer as 'the hair of the dog' and, unable to find it, goes back to bed in a rage, while Else mutters 'Drunken pig!'

At the pub later that night, Else, Mike and Rita sit at a table with Gran having a drink, while Alf and Sid stand at the bar discussing the old days. Then Ruby and her daughter Milly the local prostitute arrive, and Milly orders Fred's entire consignment of champagne in order to celebrate her mum's birthday. Alf is disgusted at 'the wages of sin' and calls Milly a whore, but Sid helps out – and helps himself – with the bubbly. It is not long before Else and Rita are quite drunk, leading the group in singing 'She Loves You' and 'Yellow Submarine'. Else tries to get her husband to drink out of her shoe, then asks him to dance and finally flashes her bloomers at him. A black chauffeur enters and tells Milly that his boss wants her. As the girl leaves, Rita becomes very sentimental with her husband, and the drink continues to flow.

Alf is snoring in bed and Else, wide awake but totally inebriated, wakes him up with champagne and shouts to Rita through the walls. Alf then attempts to sleep on the sofa downstairs, because tomorrow is one of his three days at work, but the monstrous regiment of women descend to torment him, soaking a very sober Mike in the process.

ARGUMENTS, ARGUMENTS

Alcoholism; the good old days when there was so much business in the docks that the bosses were totally at the workers' mercy; the wages of sin.

BLOODY LANGUAGE

Seventy-one 'bloodies', one 'bleeding', one 'Shirley Temple'.

FUNNY BUSINESS

Else's description of sausages making someone ill as an analogy for the effects of alcohol; the pub discussion in which Sid and Alf hypocritically state that the power workers, miners and rail workers abuse the right to strike; Millie Milligan's stark question, 'Had yer penn'eth?', to a leering Alf and Sid; Gran's glum recollection that she gave her sexual favours away for nothing; the scenes of Rita and Else getting blind drunk on the champagne; Else's bedside rendition of 'I Wonder Why You Keep Me Waiting'.

WHAT ELSE?

This, the only 'non-political' episode of the fifth series, was the third to be recorded. It was originally scheduled for transmission on Wednesday 23

January but postponed until Tuesday 12 February, when it and shown at 10.10 pm, just prior to the closedown curfew. Mike has very little dialogue throughout; an uncharacteristic state of affairs. Martin Chivers was a famous Tottenham Hotspur player in the '70s, and the chant, uttered by Else and Rita, based on his name, was well known. The talk of Mr Fraybourne may be the last vestige of the idea to create a regular role in the 1972 series for John Le Mesurier's bank manager character, Mr Frewin, from *The Alf Garnett Saga*. Adrienne Posta had played Rita in the same film, when she had become a mistress to a wealthy black singer – not a million miles from her situation as Millie in this episode. She had also appeared on the same *It's Lulu* show as Warren Mitchell performing his Alf solo spot in 1973. (In those days, Lulu was a neighbour of Mitchell's.) Rita Webb had appeared in similar roles (but not named) in 'Arguments, Arguments' and 'Till Closing Time Us Do Part'. This episode marked Will Stampe's last appearance on the show, which had seen him making regular appearances since, again, 'Arguments, Arguments'. Else mentions 'Ogg (Quintin Hogg) again. The episode was seen by 15.7% of the viewing population.

5.7: PAKI-PADDY

Recorded 27 January 1974
Transmitted Thursday 28 February 1974 at 9.30 pm, with an RI of 57

With Joan Sims (Gran), Maureen Lane (Barmaid), Spike Milligan (Paki-Paddy)

The Garnetts have just finished dinner, but Alf and Mike, fuelled by generous amounts of whisky bought by Alf at a knockdown rate, are embarked on yet another course of arguments, the subjects this time including: the value of the house and Alf's idea that no less a personage than Harry Hyams might buy it as part of his planned 30-mile stretch of entertainment blocks from Tower Bridge to Southend; the decline of the docks; immigrants, and Alf's contention that they're in Britain only to get their false teeth and false eyeballs and wooden legs; the miners; Enoch Powell; the Jews; the Arabs; Russia; Rhodesia; race riots; the US army ... When Alf orders Mike to 'Switch Off Something' in obedience to Mr Heath, both Mike and Rita do exactly the opposite, turning on every appliance in the house in support of the miners – until Alf takes the fuse out and goes up the pub ...

Gran, Alf, Else and Rita are drinking in the pub. Here Gran and Alf discuss, amid peals of merriment, a well-dressed Asian gentleman at the bar. The man comes over and offers them some champagne. Then the reason for Gran's amusement is clarified, as she tells Alf that he is the Garnetts' new neighbour ... The man introduces himself as Kevin O'Grady and Alf starts to insult him, mixing up Pakistan and India in the process. Kevin replies that he's half Muslim on his mother's side and half Irish by an old friend of his father's. He says that he would accept Enoch's two grand and go home – home to Dublin … Kevin proclaims his vision of Britain, much to Alf's anger, then tries to sell him and Else some watches. Alf suggests he goes home, and Kevin states that indeed he will. As he leaves the pub, however, there is a loud explosion, and he returns, clothing in tatters, complaining about the bloody Irish …

Back home, Alf finds Mike slumped on his chair, having drunk all the whisky, and with every conceivable electrical appliance activated. Else tells her husband with glee that Mike has beaten him. Then there is a power cut, and Else says, 'Now, you've beat him'.

ARGUMENTS, ARGUMENTS

See above …

BLOODY LANGUAGE

Seventy-six 'bloodies', one 'silly moo', one 'great soft twit', one 'silly sod'.

FUNNY BUSINESS

Alf proudly announcing 'This property is mine!', just as the photo of Princess Anne and Mark Phillips falls from the wall to the floor; Rita denouncing the slum they live in, and Else saying that she told Alf not to buy it; Alf reading from the Bible – 'advise them … chastise them …' – and Rita chipping in – '… circumcise them', her father having again protested that he is *'not bloody Jewish!'*; Rita teasing Alf by asking if God will send down a leader who will deal with the miners (and mend the soap rack, adds Else); Enoch Powell's divine revelation, as recounted to Robin Day on TV; Else filling in the previous week's football pools coupon, found inside the Bible; Alf slurring his speech as he and Mike consume the whisky (75p a bottle off the back of a lorry) and Else devours crisps and celery; Alf referring to the world chess champion, Boris Spassky, as 'Boris Plastic'; Mike's version of Heath's 'SOS' – 'Silly Old Sod'; Alf's battle to save energy; Gran's constant cackling in the pub, before she reveals that Paki-Paddy is Alf's new neighbour; Paki-Paddy's vision of Britain; Else's final words.

WHAT ELSE?

This episode was hurriedly rescheduled from 19 or 20 February to the night of the (first) General Election of 1974. The closing titles include the credit, 'The part of Spike Milligan was played by Paki-Paddy'. 'Ikey-Mo' is again referred to by Alf as one of the insults directed at Jews. A few lines of dialogue, for example a reference to Paki-Paddy coming from 'Burnt Cork' and a statement by Alf that he has heard of all types of Irish but never Pakistani Irish, derived from the debut episode of *Curry and Chips*.

An audience research report was commissioned for the episode, which was seen by only 17.1% of the viewing population, as opposed to 17.5% tuning in to ITV and 2.8% to BBC Two. The RI was 57, compared with an average for the current series of 61. The breakdown of audience reaction was given as follows:

A+	A	B	C	C-
9%	33%	35%	21%	2%

In general, the report found, there was no great enthusiasm for the episode, which was considered to have too much bad language – 'almost every other word was a "bloody", they pointed out' – and too little plot, with too much tiresome monologue from Alf. Some, however, found it 'a pleasant bit of light relief for Election Night' and enjoyed the confrontation between Alf and Paki-Paddy. Production was considered reasonable, and there was praise for Mitchell, Nichols ('the star of the show, as she sits calmly through raging family arguments') and Milligan, one or two hoping that the latter's character might be retained for future series.

SERIES SIX

This series was scheduled on Wednesdays at 9:25 pm, except for episode one, which went out on New Year's Eve, a Tuesday, at 10.30 pm. In opposition, ITV offered *The Wheeltappers' and Shunters' Club* on New Year's Eve, then *Kung Fu* (8 and 15 January) and *The Jimmy Tarbuck Show* (22 January to 19 February). All seven episodes were directed by Colin Strong. At least 263 'bloodies' were present in total. Leslie Noyes, one of the Arthur Haynes crew, who had also appeared in 'Sex Before Marriage' and the first movie, features uncredited in certain episodes as the pub landlord. Patricia Hayes and Alfie Bass were billed as guest stars for this series. Reaction Indices for this series were the lowest ever for *Till Death Us Do Part*, although viewing numbers improved as it went on. Two voiceover credits (repeated in the *Radio Times*) stated that Una Stubbs was a member of the Mermaid Theatre Trust, where she was appearing in *Cole*, and that Patricia Hayes was a member of the Royal Shakespeare Company. Dandy Nichols appears only in the first two episodes, in film inserts.

6.1: OUTBACK BOUND
aka 'Else to Australia'

Recorded 24 November 1974
Transmitted Tuesday 31 December 1974 at 10.30 pm, with an RI of 53

With Jane Hayden (Airport Ticket Clerk), Ray Miller (Qantas Passenger), Ranjit Nakara (Cleaner), George Tovey (Man in Airport Lounge)[48], Johnny Wade (Security Man), Tommy Wright (Security Man)

Alf is beside himself with rage. Else's sister Maud – whom Alf loathes – is very ill in Australia, and her husband, Uncle Ted, has paid for Else to go and stay with her until she recovers. Rita tries to persuade him that he cannot stop Else, but Alf repeatedly orders his wife not to go. Else, however, is already packing her suitcase. Alf pursues her to the airport, demanding that she stay, but in vain. As the Qantas flight departs for Sydney, with Else having a wonderful time drinking champagne with the other passengers, Alf, Mike and Rita debate the wonders of flight – and the sheer nerve of Alf, who has paid out £2 on a life insurance policy that would net him £10,000 if anything happened to Else. Back home, Alf, alone for the first time in over 30 years, asks Him to look after her ...

---

[48] Cut from the episode as transmitted.

ARGUMENTS, ARGUMENTS

The price of food; Labour giving South Africa to the Russians, oilfields to Scotland, and coal back to Wales; Arthur 'Scarface' and his alleged ballot rigging.

BLOODY LANGUAGE

Thirty-seven 'bloodies', one 'silly moo', one 'mooooo!', and a 'pissed off'.

FUNNY BUSINESS

Rita's 'Utter loneliness is better than living with you; utter, desolate loneliness'; Alf's idea that if Maud is in a coma there is no need for Else to go – Uncle Ted could parade anyone in front of his wife and tell her it's Else; Mike's suggestion that a person can be in a coma for years – and Alf's rejoinder that seeing him, he can well believe it; Else packing that rare commodity, sugar, into her suitcase; the Garnetts trying to explain how an aircraft from up in England could possibly land down under in Australia; Alf's final appeal to God to protect Else …

WHAT ELSE?

The film sequences were shot at Heathrow Terminal 3. Dandy Nichols received £950 for her performance in this episode and the next, all of which was on film. Anthony Booth received £383.

A scene involving a bomb scare was cut out, allegedly for timing reasons. In this, after Else sings 'Waltzing Matilda', Mike points out a nearby parcel and suggests that Alf should have obtained some insurance for himself. When a puzzled Alf asks why, Mike goes 'Tick tock, tick tock'. Alf then picks up the parcel and dumps it into a cleaner's bucket of water. A man played by George Tovey emerges from the toilet to inquire what happened to his parcel – in reality, another bag of sugar. At this point a sheepish Alf nods toward the cleaner, and while the man is distracted, he and the others clear off. Other sequences were also cut, including one in which Alf uses a press cutting of Harold Wilson as toilet paper. Comments about Maud giving the convicts of Australia bad blood were cut from the script before recording, as was an insult between neighbours, 'Sod next door', 'Sod you too'. Canned laughter was added to the airport film scenes.

Notable is the incredible speed with which Else says farewell to her husband and then boards the plane. A much bigger living room set than usual was provided in the studio, to emphasise the amount of space available in the Garnett household after Else departs. Mike reads the *Socialist*

Worker. George Tovey can be heard as Alf's toilet neighbour, and is credited at the end of the episode, although his airport appearance was excised.

Warren Mitchell had already filmed an advert for 'Quaint-Arse' in the guise of Alf earlier that year.

An audience research report was prepared for this episode, which was seen by 11.8% of the viewing audience, while ITV secured 14.5% and BBC Two received 9.3%. This was the lowest percentage figure the show had received since the first series. The RI was 53, the lowest for *Till Death Us Do Part* so far, based on the following breakdown:

A+	A	B	C	C-
10%	26%	38%	18%	8%

Reaction, said the report, was very mixed. 40% found the show only moderately entertaining, and less funny than normal, and there were the usual complaints regarding bad language ('not so unusual now on British television') and comments to the effect that the show could be just as effective without the 'bloodies' ('If Americans can make comedy shows without even a suggestion of bad language or "blue" jokes, why can't we?'). They were unhappy with the departure of Else, wanting her back before the series ended, and found this compromised the reality of the show, with the two men remaining proving 'impossible'. A quarter of the respondents found the show 'offensive' and 'unfunny' and Alf a 'distasteful bore', and again thought there had been a failure in reality ('Surely no-one really behaves like him?'). According to these respondents, the lack of plot and extreme antagonism became 'rather horrid' and 'extremely tedious'. A third however still thought Alf convincing ('Alf is an insensitive, uncouth bloke, but expresses much of what is feared by many of us'), the script clever in depicting the reactions of a self-centred man being left to his own resources, and the airport scenes hilarious. Most regretted the brevity of Dandy Nichols' appearance and many praised Mitchell, even though they felt that he should change his pitch a little ('This was 30 minutes of uncontrollable frenzy'), while Booth and Stubbs were seen to have little to do. The camera work at the airport was widely praised.

6.2: PHONE CALL TO ELSE

Recorded 8 December 1974
Transmitted Wednesday 8 January 1975 at 9.25 pm, with an RI of 54

Else has been gone only a week and already Alf is missing her – or at least the meals she used to cook for him when he got home from work. Min, the next door neighbour, arrives and informs him that Rita has asked her to help out, and here she is, because Mike and Rita have gone to the pictures. She allays Alf's rage by saying that she will give him dinner – on the one hand seeming to promise the untold pleasures of one of her meat puddings yet simultaneously merely offering to open the tins of ravioli and kosher barley soup she has provided. She also wants Alf to help fill out a questionnaire on antiperspirants, expressing her wonder at their efficacy on her husband. After Min admits that there's no dinner for him except the two tins, Alf loses his temper – and his chance of any meal, as Min storms out in protest at his behaviour. Bloody women!

Up the pub, Alf chats to Bert about his missus and her eccentricities, hinting that if Bert conveys his apologies, Min might give him half of her fabled meat pudding. Mike comes in, lamenting that now Else has gone, he finds it hard to scrounge any money. He states that they have fish and chips warming in the oven back home, prompting Alf to tell Bert he can instruct his wife to stick her puddings. Then Alf finds out there is no fish and chips for him …

Alf is reduced to messily eating a combination of baby food and tomato sauce, before launching into yet another diatribe against his wife's departure to Australia, of all places – an uncivilised land of deadly spiders and sharks. Rita suggests he telephone Else, and reluctantly – considering the cost, a pound a minute – he does, setting his watch to make sure that they don't stay on the line too long. He gets through to Sydney – after a crossed line – only for his wife to pick up the phone and then leave it for several minutes while she chats to the milkman. As Alf realises he is wasting £4, he repeatedly shouts down the line at his wife, who promptly hangs up.

ARGUMENTS, ARGUMENTS

BBC filth – the cause of all yer violence; 'darlin' 'Arold' mollycoddling everyone so there's no-one willing to work.

BLOODY LANGUAGE

Fifty-two 'bloodies', two 'bleedings', three 'silly moos', two 'silly great puddens', a 'toffee nosed git' and a 'pissed'.

FUNNY BUSINESS

Patricia Hayes steals the show. The opening dialogue between Min and Alf regarding dinner and Bert's body odour; Alf's malapropisms – 'afrodaisyriac' (for 'aphrodisiac'); 'ariasol' (for 'aerosol'); 'abo-reginals' (for 'aboriginals'); Alf and Min declaring that they only watch TV seven days a week, that's all – they're 'not avid'; Min's rambling conversation regarding Bert's TV habits and his shirts; Min mouthing the same questions Alf asks her; Alf's Freudian slip of 'couldn't' to 'puddent'; the disgusting scene with Alf eating baby food and pouring tomato sauce, prompting Rita to give him a bib; Alf and the crossed line with the two posh ladies; Else talking to the milkman, oblivious of the telephone call … and her delighted smile as she hangs up on her husband.

WHAT ELSE?

The emptiness of the house without Else is emphasised in the opening shot. It is established that Else has been gone for almost a week. Leslie Noyes appears as the barman, but is not credited. The fish and chips for two idea recalls 'A Woman's Place Is in the Home'. Mike is reading *The Workers' Press*. Note that Australia not only suffers from deadly spiders and sharks but also terrible CSO. The episode was seen by 14.9% of the viewing population, an increase on the previous episode thanks no doubt to its more sensible scheduling.

6.3: MARITAL BLISS

Recorded 15 December 1974
Transmitted Wednesday 15 January 1975 at 9.25 pm, with an RI of 56

Alf, Mike and Rita are trying to eat dinner, but Alf is becoming increasingly frustrated by the simple task of retrieving pickled onions from a jar, resulting in a chaotic swirl of activity, at the end of which they become suddenly aware that they have a new arrival – Bert, who has calmly walked in with a meat pudding dinner and silently sat down to eat it. Soon, the reason for this becomes clear as Min shouts through the walls about her ungrateful husband, threatening to leave him and go to her mother's. Apparently, Bert is failing to comply with his wife's demands for lovemaking. As the others watch amusedly, Min arrives with a raspberry pie and custard and forces him to eat it, complaining that he thinks more about his pigeons than her … Then she storms out, leaving the Garnetts crippled with mirth and Bert saying that he really should put his foot down.

At the pub, the Garnetts and Bert discuss the mysteries of marriage, as Bert recalls his youth in the navy when there was a girl in every port, and he could obtain lots of duty free. Alf muses that Else was quite good around the house, and a good cook, but he could never give her more money, as that would have broken the social contract. Anyway, wives have to be kept busy, unlike the workers, rendered bone idle under Labour. Wives cannot be sacked, but cannot expect the same working conditions as others. They could perhaps have unemployment benefit, he concedes, but a better simbly [sic] is football: rather than sack a bad player, you simply transfer him, and that's how it should be with a wife – swap her for cash, or for one who will be a better cook, for example.

Later, Bert and Alf have had rather too much to drink, and they are thrown out of the pub at closing time. Min returns home to find Bert in bed with another figure. She is outraged that he has left her for another woman, but then realises that the figure is actually Alf. Bert, she declares, didn't tell her he had become a pansy …

ARGUMENTS, ARGUMENTS

The Labour government; marriage; the social contract.

BLOODY LANGUAGE

Twenty-two 'bloodies', a 'pisses off', an 'arse' and a 'randy Scouse git'.

FUNNY BUSINESS

The hilarious scene with the pickled onions; Min shouting through the wall at her husband; the talk of annulling the marriage; Bert's line after his wife stomps out – 'I can see I'm gonna have to put my foot down with her'; the conversation about wives and their purpose in life; Rita's bitter reference to her husband's redundancy; Alf winking at the barmaid; a discussion of West Ham getting rid of Bobby Moore to Fulham, where they play a more sedate game.

WHAT ELSE?

Leslie Noyes again appears uncredited as the barman.

An audience research report was prepared for this episode, which secured 18.5% of the population, as opposed to 16.4% for ITV and 4% for BBC Two. An RI of 56 was achieved, with the following breakdown:

A+	A	B	C	C-
11%	31%	36%	16%	6%

It was generally felt that the show had improved, with less bad language, a better script, more realistic dialogue and 'a more amusing true to life storyline with the addition of the neighbours'. It was perceived by respondents that there was a close correlation between a paucity of ideas and a surfeit of 'bloodies', and here Alf was quieter, and more 'fascinating when mellow'. The cast were on top form, it was said, with Patricia Hayes threatening to overshadow the others; and some considered that the episode was 'brilliant all the way through'. Over half the respondents missed Else, however, feeling that with her departure the show had lost its point, and lamenting the loss of her 'silences [that] spoke more than all Alf's words'. A fifth of the respondents found that the bad language and aggression levels were still too high, and the comedy – especially the table manners – too crude. A good proportion found the episode amusing in parts, but several thought the show was running out of ideas, one viewer stating that it contained 'no jokes, no social comment, nothing'. Some did not appreciate the newcomers and thought Mike and Rita ill-used.

6.4: WEDGIE BENN

Recorded 12 January 1975
Transmitted Wednesday 22 January 1975 at 9.25 pm, with an RI of 53

The Garnetts and their neighbours are ensconced in the living room and engaged in argument. Alf rails about the fact that Tony Benn talks like a Tory and lives in a stately home despite his Labour credentials and preoccupation with nationalising everything. He should have been smothered at birth, he declares. Bert says that Benn has mad eyes like Hitler, and this leads to a discussion of the relative merits of Churchill's and Hitler's painting talents, the nationality of Picasso, the cowardice of the French, Franco, and the half-built hotels in Spain that British workers seem to enjoy when really they should be forced to stay at home and get rewarded with a holiday in Margate. There are filthy beaches in Spain, opines Alf, and one can catch all manner of diseases, including yer BBC (Barcelona beach crabs), yer Trinidad trots and yer Paki pox … Mike remarks on the QE2, with its new cruises priced at £42,000, which he declares is obscene. Alf rants on about Heath lying to the public about the Common Market; the plight of Africa under Kaunda and Smith; Cilla Black; Keith Joseph; the use of birth control to limit the working class (because they are not fit to bring up their own kids); Else being a political cabbage; and the immorality of dock pilfering … It is left to Bert to wisely sum up by observing that it's a funny old world – Alf living here in Wapping, a Tory surrounded by socialists, while Wedgwood Benn lives in a stately home, a socialist surrounded by Tories. Maybe Alf could write to him and try to arrange a swap …

ARGUMENTS, ARGUMENTS

See above!

BLOODY LANGUAGE

Sixty-nine 'bloodies', one 'daft great pillock', a 'bolshie bastard', two 'Shirley Temples', a 'silly twit', a 'daft great tit', a 'silly Scouse git' and a 'Sleeping Beauty'.

FUNNY BUSINESS

Alf's contention that Benn is an educated man '… apart from his ideas and the things he says'; Alf's idea of French: *'Kamerad! Kamerad! Silver Play'*; Bert's 'No, no, no, no, no, you're wrong there, Alf'; Min's rubber soles finished with tyre tread to grip the road; the near explosion into violence when Mike gets up from the sofa to go to bed.

WHAT ELSE?

God made pigs/sheep/cows/fish/vegetables – echoes of series three's 'Aunt Maud' again. This episode is unusual in that the script, a whirlwind of dialogue surveying a wide range of contemporary issues, is not supported by much in the way of improvised business. The line 'Look! Look! It moves! It moves!' as Mike gets off the sofa was however an improvisation by Warren Mitchell. A clue to the faltering of the comic business needed to sustain the script may be seen when Bert asks what day it is.

Tony Booth was of course a friend of Anthony Wedgwood Benn.

The episode was recorded sixth in sequence and seen by 20.7% of the viewing population, a big increase on the earlier episodes of this series, although the RI figure was still low.

Birmingham Evening Mail: 'With Patricia Hayes' Min taking the bluster out of Warren Mitchell's Alf and pretty near all the applause last week … dear old Dandy Nichols isn't going to be so badly missed.'

6.5: THE WAKE

Recorded 22 December 1974
Transmitted Wednesday 29 January 1975 at 9.25 pm, with an RI of 54

Alf and Bert escort a distraught Min to the Garnett household following the funeral of her mother. She believes that the recently deceased will be reincarnated as a blackbird, as her father was, while her uncle Fred was reborn as a goldfish. Later, Min brings her uncle in with Bert in order to watch the TV broadcast of the Ali versus Foreman boxing match; all have been careful that day to avoid any news of the outcome. Alf and Bert even developed coughs so that they didn't have to go to work … But as the match starts, Else rings from Sydney, and tells Alf that Ali knocks his opponent out in the eighth round.

ARGUMENTS, ARGUMENTS

The high cost of dying; the Empire; the Royals; Jews; Arabs; Indians; Ali's refusal to fight in Vietnam.

BLOODY LANGUAGE

Forty-five 'bloodies', one 'silly moo', one 'bleeding', one 'silly great pudden', one 'red-faced Mick'.

FUNNY BUSINESS

Min and her goldfish bowl; Bert's 'No, no, no' then 'Yeeeeeeeeees'; Mike's mock Nazi salute; Min talking about Alf's imminent death; Alf ranting about Labour ruining the pound and giving away the Empire, and the Arabs being happily ignorant sitting in their desert with their flies until the 'four by twos' moved in next door with their fur coats and flash cars and ruined everything – just as the Indians were happy with their frankincense and myrrh but now get £30 per week shouting 'Mind the doors' at the station; the idea that the Irish troubles were caused by the Irish never forgiving Henry VIII for standing up to the Pope and his mafia; Alf's assertion that Hitler did some bad things but wasn't all bad; Mike's suggestion that Princess Anne's big hooter might suggest Jewish blood in the Royal Family; the idea of Min feeding her goldfish uncle jam sponge and ice cream; Mike's thought that if Alf had been reincarnated as a blackbird, he would have bought a cat.

WHAT ELSE?

The 'Rumble in the Jungle' boxing match between Mohammed Ali and George Foreman took place on 29 October 1974. Patricia Hayes kept the goldfish used in the recording as she felt sorry for it when told that it would be thrown away afterwards. Alf points a toy rifle at Mike at one point (shades of *Who's Afraid of Virginia Woolf?*?), but it is not highlighted by the direction. One scripted sequence was cut from the episode. In this, when Alf accuses Mike of being in the IRA, Mike replies that merely being Catholic does not equate to membership of that organisation. There is then a loud bang outside, resembling an explosion, although it just a clap of thunder.

This episode was recorded fourth in sequence and was seen by 21.3% of the viewing population.

6.6: CHRISTMAS CLUB BOOKS

Recorded 5 January 1975
Transmitted Wednesday 5 February 1975 at 9.25 pm, with an RI of 54

With Rita Webb, Felix Bowness, Stanley Meadows, Roland MacLeod, Godfrey Jackman, Leslie Noyes (Pub Landlord)

Alf is desperately trying to work out the local hostelry's Christmas club accounts, which he has looked after since he is their treasurer, but the pub-goers are getting impatient. This is the fourth night running they have waited for him to pay out – and they have even sent Bert round to his house to see what he is up to. Alf insists

that it's a very difficult job, what with 'fluidity … and not too much liquidity …'.
The men at the pub wonder if Alf is embezzling the proceeds so he can afford to join
his wife in Australia, and begin to spy on him. Rita tries to help out, but eventually
Alf is forced to go to the pub to give an explanation of his actions, having had to rob
Peter (the darts club fund) to pay Paul … The natives are restless as Alf sits down to
hand out the cash, but half way through, an officer from the CID removes all the
books and minutes, leaving the pub in uproar.

ARGUMENTS, ARGUMENTS

No political or social arguments.

BLOODY LANGUAGE

Twenty-eight 'bloodies', a 'nosey old cow', a 'Shirley Temple' and two
'bleedings'.

FUNNY BUSINESS

Mike's impression of 'yer darlin 'Arold'; Alf catching Bert and the others
watching him through the window; Mike and Alf harmonising on 'You're
my father-in-law – *worse luck!*'; Alf's speech regarding trust – 'People …
neighbours … friends …'('Countrymen', adds Rita, as if in *Carry On Cleo*);
Rita's cheery 'Hello leg!' when Alf points out that they know his 'leg
problems' that will prevent him from attending the pub; the sight of Alf and
Bert trying to calculate seven times 12 …

WHAT ELSE?

Recorded fifth in sequence, this episode seems to have suffered from an even
later than usual script delivery. Apart from it being possibly the least
interesting episode in the entire history of *Till Death Us Do Part*, evidence of
haste is shown by a note on the script to the effect that there were 'many
retakes'. The final scripted scene, in which Alf is forced to pay back all the
money, was not recorded at all. Stanley Meadows at one point mistakenly
calls Alfie Bass's character 'Fred' rather than 'Bert'.

The idea of the Chancellor living next door to the PM so that he can keep
an eye on him stems from 'State Visit'. Rita Webb makes a reappearance, for
the first time since 1972. Roland MacLeod had previously featured in series
three's 'Football'.

This episode was seen by 22.5% of the viewing population.

6.7: THE LETTER

Recorded 19 January 1975
Transmitted Wednesday 12 February 1975 at 9.25 pm, with an RI of 53

While enjoying a bevy or two in the pub, Alf and Bert again discuss the subject of marriage. Alf advises Bert that women require a lot of training, like dogs, although they are considerably more useful around the house. They need to know who is master, and should always be kept on a short leash. On returning home, Alf decides to write a letter to his wife. While attempting to do so, he overhears through the walls that Min has seen a letter from Else addressed to Rita, declaring that she does not want to come back to England. A row breaks out between Rita, Mike and Alf on one side and Min on the other, which ends in Alf tearing up the living room in order to find the letter. A tearful Rita tells him that they had kept this quiet so as not to upset him. Else has suggested that Mike, Rita and their son should go out to a new life in Australia. Alf demands to know what they will do about him. *Mike suggests that he sell the house to pay for the others' fares, then he can stay in a home until Mike has earned enough money to bring him over to live with them. Enraged, self-pitying, Alf goes back to the pub, where Bert suggests that he sell up the house and move in with him and Min. They have always admired his three-piece suite and colour telly, and Else has forfeited all her 'conjugals' by deserting Alf …*

A temporarily revitalised Alf returns, determined to sell up the house and move in with the neighbours, but then flops down in his armchair. Rita tells him that they cannot afford to go to Australia, and that they will stay with him until Else returns. Rita and Mike sit either side of Alf, who is exhausted, while Min in turn sits with her husband and ponders the future.

ARGUMENTS, ARGUMENTS

See above.

BLOODY LANGUAGE

Forty-seven 'bloodies', a 'peroxide ponce', a 'randy Scouse git', a 'nosy little cow', a 'poor old cow', an 'old rat bag', a 'silly little twit', a 'piss off' and three 'sods'.

FUNNY BUSINESS

The conversation between Alf and Bert about how to handle wives and women; talk about the Queen, who, although gracious, is still a woman and therefore not as good as a man; Alf's 'Have you ever heard of a *woman* Prime Minister,' to which Bert replies, 'That Jewboy woman, Goldwyn Mayer'; the effort needed for Alf to write a letter; the hysterical laughter of two studio audience members drowning out the letter-writing scene; Alf insisting 'I can still open a beer bottle with my teeth', only for Mike to offer him the opportunity to prove it; the sheer violence of Alf's rage, beautifully contrasted with his depression at the pub; 'She is my wife and it's till death, till death us do part ...'; Alf's assertion that when Else agreed to marriage, they both made that 'contract in His eyes ...'; the grandstanding row through the walls; Min working herself up into an emotional frenzy; Bert saying that the only good thing about Min is her cooking, but that's preferable in a marriage to 'you-know-what ...'; the beautiful symmetry of the closing scene in both households.

WHAT ELSE?

Alf uses salt and a pinch of coal dust to clean his teeth. Mary Whitehouse gets another mention. Min is said to like a gin and port. Alf was the first person in the street to buy a colour telly.

This episode was watched by 22.1% of the viewing population.

SERIES SEVEN

This series was again scheduled on Wednesdays at or around 9.25 pm. No episode was shown on 10 December 1975 because the slot was given over to the *Sportsnight* review of the year. ITV's opposition this time came in the form of the glossy film series *The Zoo Gang* for the first three weeks, then *Tully*, a filmed play starring Anthony Valentine, on 26 November; the spy spoof film *In Like Flint* on 3 December; and the second part of a documentary on Mongolia on 17 December. The regular cast billing now put Patricia Hayes and Alfie Bass higher than Anthony Booth and Una Stubbs. All episodes were directed by Dennis Main Wilson. There were 92 'bloodies' in total. This series saw the show experiencing an unusual dichotomy in terms of public appreciation, with regular rises in RI figures accompanied by equally regular falls in viewing numbers.

7.1: MOVING IN WITH MIN

Recorded 1 November 1975
Transmitted Wednesday 5 November 1975 at 9.25 pm, with an RI of 53

Alf, frustrated in his attempts to make young Michael's model train set run properly, smashes it up. He furiously contrasts the old days, when kids were brought up properly, with today, when even his own grandson insults him as 'baldy git', 'four eyes' and 'Kojak' … Alf blames the parents. He goes on to announce that he is determined to divorce Else, sell the house and move in next door with Min and Bert. Rita insists that half of the house is her mother's, and Mike asserts that Alf cannot ignore their feelings as they are sitting tenants. Alf decides to try things out as a lodger first. Armed only with a bottle of whisky and a portrait of the Queen, he is welcomed by Min rather too warmly: having sent Bert down to the shops, she attempts to seduce him in the bedroom, leading him to make a panic-stricken exit. Later, Min punishes Alf by offering him only sardines on toast, while Bert receives a huge dinner including her celebrated meat pudding. At the pub that evening, the naïve Bert thinks his wife is angry because Alf didn't bring his colour telly with him. Alf expresses doubts about Min's sanity, and Bert agrees, stating that her mother was 'doolally'. They talk about Gran, now in the 'funny farm' with all the other amusing loonies. Alf and Bert get plastered and return home, but Min will not admit Alf, the drunken pig, into her home. Alf thus returns to his own house, falling flat on his face as Rita opens the door. Then he climbs into bed and tries to cuddle Mike, thinking Else has come back from the Antipodes …

ARGUMENTS, ARGUMENTS

Society.

BLOODY LANGUAGE

Twenty-eight 'bloodies', a 'Scouse gits', a 'malevolent toad', a 'lying moo', a 'Minnie moo', a 'Shirley Temple', two 'arses', one 'Scouse ponce', one 'bolshie bastards'.

FUNNY BUSINESS

The business with the train set and the teddy bear; Alf's derision at Mike's insistence that he's a 'sitting tenant'; the photo of Else staring balefully – 'a malevolent old toad,' as Alf calls her; the clever symmetry of Alf putting up a picture of his real icon, the Queen, in his new quarters, in contrast to the photo of his wife; Min's seduction, following a period of virtual silence from Alf – 'Close intimacy can lead to things wot is beyond our control'; Bert's rejoinder of 'certstificate' [sic] to everything Alf says about 'loonies'; Alf's response to the voice that tells him to go to bed; Bert's rendition of 'Come Inside', suggesting to Alf that Bert as well as Min is trying to seduce him; Alf hurtling through the front door when Rita opens it; Mike's slurred 'Not again, love … Oh, all right, then,' as Alf mistakenly cuddles him; the brief moment of poignancy as Alf thinks his wife has returned from Australia.

WHAT ELSE?

The sequence where Alf is enticed to become a lodger next door is restaged, rather than repeated from the equivalent scene in 'The Letter'. Alf's mention of West Ham beating Birmingham by five goals refers to an away match that took place on 1 November 1975, the day the episode was recorded – how's that for topicality? Liz Taylor and Richard Burton are mentioned in the context of marriage break-ups. Gran is revealed as not being even a distant relative of the Garnetts. There is a very noticeable wobble of the set as Alf bangs on the door of his neighbours' house.

Dandy Nichols may have quit *Till Death Us Do Part*, but she could be seen on ITV, alongside Tommy Cooper, one hour earlier on the night of this episode's transmission.

An audience research report was compiled for the episode, which was seen by 16.3% of the UK viewing audience, while the figure for ITV was 19.5% and that for BBC Two was 4.2%. The RI figure of 53 equalled the average for series six. The breakdown of viewer responses was as follows:

A+	A	B	C	C-
8%	29%	39%	16%	8%

Two out of five respondents found the show only moderately entertaining, for the same reasons as before – thin plot, wearing verbal abuse, bad language, and the absence of Else, 'the perfect counterfoil' to Alf. A more worrying development was the general feeling that the format was the same as ever, with dreary settings and predicable plotting, and that the show was losing its sense of reality, as the neighbours were perceived to be 'artificial'. Many erstwhile fans were now tired of the formula, while diehard dissidents as always found everything too crude. Some respondents still enjoyed the show despite its increasing familiarity, citing the scenes of Min seducing Alf and of Alf and Bert as two maudlin drunks in the pub as highlights of the episode, almost making up for the absence of the dear departed Else. Alfie Bass and Patricia Hayes were praised along with Mitchell for their acting.

7.2: MIN THE HOUSEKEEPER

Recorded 8 November 1975
Transmitted Wednesday 12 November 1975 at 9.35 pm, with an RI of 57

With Pat Coombs

A weary Alf returns one evening to find Min reclining on the sofa watching his colour telly and surrounded by the detritus of a house that has no-one to tidy it now that Else has left. Min has been let in by Rita in order to clear up, light a fire for when Alf gets back and make the beds, but it is perfectly evident that she has done none of these things; and indeed she makes Alf himself take the crockery into the kitchen and make a cup of tea. Alf even finds that Min – along with the dustmen – has quaffed most of his bottles of rum and whisky … Min then has the temerity to suggest that he give her ten shillings as payment for her services. Before he can say anything, Min hands him an opened letter, which she says is from Else – who wants a divorce, she helpfully adds … Alf loses his temper and Min walks out, angry at his ingratitude. Alf rails against the monstrous regiment of women, makes a fire in the hearth, moans about the woman they've put in charge of the Tories, then hurts himself touching the hot kettle …Then he finds to his fury that the opened letter is addressed not to him but to Rita. He hollers through the walls at Min, only to knock a picture off its hook and onto his head.

Next door, a sex-crazed Min watches Bert eat the dinner she has cooked for him, and tells him it has filosan sprinkled on it to fortify his passion. Now she wants his body –- but all he wants is her meat pudding …

Rita is shocked to find the mess in the house, including a sinkful of smashed crockery and the opened letter addressed to her, which Alf has now read. Alf resumes his tirades against women and says that half-wits like Min should be denied the vote.

Mike calls him a Capitalist dupe, and they argue about strikes, Harold Wilson's advertising of HP sauce and Mike's habitual horizontal position on the sofa. Alf says that despite his age, he can still beat his son-in-law in a race around the block. He backs down, however, when Mike calls his bluff; and Rita then defeats him easily in a spontaneous bout of arm wrestling.

Later, up the pub, Alf and Bert talk industrial relations, before Bert asks why Alf looks so fed up. Alf replies that he is tired, and his friend declares that he is tired as well, for different reasons ... When do women stop making demands? When he and Min went on honeymoon, he lost two stone in weight because she would not let him out of the bedroom ...

Alf returns home to find Min on the sofa chatting to her two friends, drinking his liquor, and gossiping about Else wanting a divorce. Not noticing that Alf is there, Min blithely talks of having heard screams from Else in the past, saying she knows that Alf repeatedly thumped his wife, although there were never any marks because he beat her where it didn't show ... She suddenly sees Alf and declares that she is babysitting while Mike and Rita have gone out ... Would he like to sit down? Alf looks at her, speechless.

ARGUMENTS, ARGUMENTS

Mrs Thatcher in charge of the Tory party; the Labour government; the 'brain drain'; the miners; the railway workers; Wilson getting backhanders (advertising beer for Weight Watchers and HP sauce); strikes and unemployment.

BLOODY LANGUAGE

Thirty-five 'bloodies', a 'lying bloody rat bag', a 'stupid little ragbag', a 'bleeding, interfering, nosey bloody parker', a 'stupid little moo', an 'arse', a 'bolshie bastard', a 'bastards'.

FUNNY BUSINESS

Min's non-existent cleaning prowess; Alf's helplessness in the face of Min's constant gibbering and outrage at his ingratitude; Alf almost immolating himself while trying to light a fire, then demolishing the dinner plates in the kitchen; Min's rapt attention as she watches Bert eat his meal; Rita's comments about the 'exodus of the eggheads'; Mike's Tarzan impression; Alf's reaction when Mike takes up his challenge to race him around the block; Rita's arm-wrestling victory over her father; Bert's tale of woe regarding unemployment – he was one of the moderates in the strike at his place, then they gave up and went back to work, only to find that the firm had beggared off; Bert's despair at his wife's continual demands – ' I hear [your wife] wants a divorce. I wish mine did'; Bert – 'She wouldn't let me touch her before we got married', Alf – 'You was the only one, mate'; Bert's tale about his honeymoon and his new bride's sexual needs.

WHAT ELSE?

The fire-lighting incident replicated one in 'A Woman's Place Is in the Home'.

This episode was seen by 16.9% of the viewing population.

7.3: DRUNK IN CHARGE OF A BICYCLE

Recorded 15 November 1975
Transmitted Wednesday 19 November 1975 at 9.25 pm, with an RI of 60

With James Ellis (Sergeant), Oscar James (Policeman), Keith Jackman (Policeman), Ahmed Khalil (Doctor), Robert Keegan (Bus Driver)

Alf argues about the identity of Jack the Ripper – it was Gladstone the Jew, he says – while Min says that the Ripper's crimes were the result of curdled passion, of a wife failing to fulfil his demands, subsequently causing mayhem … She likens this to Alf's lovelorn state, created by his wanting Else to return. Alf continues to assert that the Ripper was the former Prime Minister – the ideal disguise. Everyone in Wapping knew this, as did Disraeli and Queen Victoria; Her Majesty wouldn't leave Windsor Castle when Gladstone was around, and demanded of Disraeli that he restrain that notorious Jew … The intellectual debate is interrupted by the arrival of Bert, resplendent in a tracksuit. Min declares that she has persuaded her husband to go running, having been inspired by a Charles Atlas bodybuilding book. She orders Bert to go on a 10 mile run and asks Alf to pace him and 'bring him back a man'.

The pair leave the house, Alf on a bicycle and a breathless Bert jogging alongside, but get only as far as the Jolly Sailor round the corner. Hours later, completely drunk, the dynamic duo ride tandem down the middle of a street, falling foul of a Number 67 bus with a black driver and then being stopped by a black policeman, who orders them to go home. When Alf offensively states that he is home and that the policeman should go home instead, another officer steps up and they take the pair to the nearest police station to charge them. The Sergeant at the desk gives them the choice of either a blood or urine test, but they refuse. Alf is angry that the black policeman and the bloody white liberal are telling him what to do, then he insults the Asian police doctor and continues his racist rant.

Later, at the pub, Rita gleefully points out that her father will be charged with being drunk in charge of a bicycle. Alf blames Barbara Castle's introduction of the breathalyser for ruining the British car industry – after all, if you can't drink and drive, what is the point of owning a car. He feels that his arrest was deeply hypocritical when there are so many drunks in charge of the country. They should breathalyse Parliament, he moans. Then he sees the policeman who arrested him at the bar and goes over to try to bribe him with money and a double whisky. The officer accepts the whisky, but tells Alf he will see him in court …

ARGUMENTS, ARGUMENTS

The Ripper; Jesus; British history; Disraeli; Hansard; Henry VIII and his wives; Barbara Castle; the Labour government; Idi Amin; Jim Callaghan; Churchill.

BLOODY LANGUAGE

Thirty-seven 'bloodies', three 'bleedings', one 'atheist git', one 'Shirley Temple' and a 'piss off'.

FUNNY BUSINESS

Talk of Julius Caesar and his 'hokey-pokey, penny-a-lump Eyeties' running the world; Alf's *'Look…'* in response to Min's drivel about curdled passion and Henry VIII; Alf's conspiracy theory regarding Gladstone the Jew as Jack the Ripper and the origins of the Gladstone bag; Min fondling Mike's hair then turning his legs over as she demonstrates the principle of isometrics using a frog as an example; Bert's sudden anger at his wife; the idea that Bert's brother won't get into a car until he's drunk because of his nerves; Alf's contention that Parliament won't be televised because the MP's are drunk; the final riposte by the policeman in the pub.

WHAT ELSE?

Alf refers to Bert as 'Bruce Woodcock', the English heavyweight boxer (1921-1997), and to the policeman played by Oscar James as 'Clyde Best', the Bermudan footballer who played for West Ham. Alf says he used to be a PT instructor.

Filming for this episode took place outside the Jolly Sailor pub near Garnet Street, around Sampson Street and near Tower Bridge.

James Ellis was known for his role in *Z Cars*; Ahmed Khalil was to appear in the BBC series *Gangsters* the following year.

This episode was seen by 13.5% of the viewing population.

7.4: WINDOW
aka 'Stuck'

Recorded 22 November 1975
Transmitted Wednesday 26 November 1975 at 9.25 pm, with an RI of 60

With Felix Bowness (Mr Felix), Pat Coombs (Ethel), Tom McCall (Pianist), George Tovey (Carpenter), Bill Ward (Bill the Landlord)

It's Vegas Nite at the Jolly Sailor, and Alf complains loudly to Rita, Mike, Bert and Min about the 'fairy' – 'Mr Felix' – who is singing 'Delilah'. He blames the government for making 'it' legal. The singer shouts abuse back at this heckler, saying that Evel Knievel couldn't ride across his mouth. Alf then expresses his disgust at Charles Aznavour's recent show of 'making love to himself' in the Royal Variety Performance, and again criticises 'queers'. Rita comments sarcastically that what he wants is a world full of Alf Garnetts with everyone hating everybody else. Min mentions that the singer cleans her windows, always apparently catching her in a state of undress, every Wednesday at 12.30. Rita says that their windows need cleaning and asks Min how much the man charges. But Alf pooh-poohs the very reasonable fee of £1.50. If Rita wants the windows cleaning, he says, he will do it himself and save the money. He doesn't want that 'pansy' cleaning his windows.

The following day, Alf, moaning that the Scouse git hasn't the brains to understand how he intends to clean the windows, backs out onto the window ledge of the upstairs bedroom – and suddenly finds himself trapped out there when the window gets stuck. To make matters worse, Mike and Rita have gone out. Alf spies Min returning from the shops and Ethel emerging from her house across the road. The two women ask why he is sitting out there, before totally ignoring him and chatting about Ethel's husband, the NHS, a world cruise … After a small eternity, Alf manages to convince them that he needs help. The intrepid ladies gain entry to the Garnett household, but as they open the upstairs window, Alf falls back and is left hanging from the ledge by his legs. The ladies try to comfort him by supporting his head with a stepladder, placing a cushion on the top of it, and plying him with tea.

Alf is beset not just by the elements but also by the inanity of Min and Bert, and by his son-in-law trying to watch the colour telly that Bert has thoughtfully placed upstairs to keep Alf entertained. Mike is somewhat dilatory in his attempts to assist Alf thanks to his father-in-law's insults. Eventually, Rita brings in a carpenter, who takes out the window but dislodges Alf rather too successfully, sending him plunging to the ground, where he is administered the kiss of life by an enthusiastic Min. Later that night, Rita sees that her father is tucked up in bed, telling him that the carpenter will replace the window the next day. As she leaves and turns out the lights, Alf has a desperate need to use the toilet. He gets out of bed, only to stumble and defenestrate himself yet again …

ARGUMENTS, ARGUMENTS

Homosexuals; the Royal Variety Performance; the NHS.

BLOODY LANGUAGE

Thirty-two 'bloodies', a 'silly great beanpole', a 'randy Scouse git', a 'stupid Scouse git', and two 'thick Micks'.

FUNNY BUSINESS

Alf's invective directed at that 'Froggie', 'Charles Arse-navour'; the mind-numbing discussion between Min and Ethel about the merits of a world cruise – around the Isle of Wight – and the NHS; Ethel's tale about her Wally being off work with stress because he worries so much about the political situation and the health service; Min and Ethel finishing each other's sentences; Min and Ethel climbing in Alf's downstairs window, then discussing the state of his house; Min's primal shriek and shedding of tears as she sees Alf defenestrated; Alf, upside down, drinking tea; Min administering the kiss of life to a helpless Alf.

WHAT ELSE?

Felix Bowness makes another appearance (as 'Mr Felix'), having first warmed up the studio audience. Alf has apparently moved to number 13 this week. The mike boom makes an unscheduled appearance in the pub, and in the street. Alf's moan about Charles Aznavour refers to the French singer's act at the twenty-seventh Royal Variety Performance at the London Palladium on 16 November 1975. Warren Mitchell used to be a window cleaner – could he have provided the inspiration for this story ...? The episode was seen by 12.7% of the viewing population.

7.5: GOLF
aka 'A Hole In One'

Recorded 29 November 1975
Transmitted Wednesday 3 December 1975 at 9.25 pm, with an RI of 63

With Roy Castle (Himself), George Best (Himself), Ballard Berkeley (Golf Club Member), Philip Gilbert (Golf Club Member), Peter Welch (Golf club Member)

Alf, watching a golf tournament on television, remarks that he wouldn't mind trying to play the game himself. As he observes Ronnie Corbett on the links, he wonders if the man is really that small … or is it a trick? Television personalities are not necessarily real people, he declares – Lulu is definitely not real; a bloke 'acts her'. Min wonders if that Ted Heath, seen sometimes on the Mike Yarwood show, is the same one who used to be Prime Minister. The conversation wanders from golf to Shakespeare, apparently the author of **Scrooge**, *which according to Alf is not the same work as* **A Christmas Carol**, *written by Charles Dickens. Alf explains the storyline to Bert and Min, who is at first rather restless but settles down when her husband masterfully asserts that Alf is teaching her something. They move on to discuss* **Othello**, *and Alf's opinion that blacks are emotionally unstable when it comes to sexual jealousy, before settling on* **Hamlet**, *the storyline of which proves that your permissive society brings only tragedy … Finally, Alf again expresses an interest in taking up golf, inspired by the footage on the telly.*

Alf and Bert, with Min in tow, venture to the golf club, where Alf attempts a round of golf, fortified by several rounds of whisky. Alf's antics delay two other golfers, Roy Castle and George Best, getting on the course. Alf tells Best how he urges him on at West Ham, inspirationally calling him a 'stupid Mick'. After a while, Alf and his two companions retire to the bar, where club rules conveniently mean that Min has to stand outside, drinking her port and bewailing her fate. Alf meanwhile sees that a pair of golfers are celebrating a hole in one by handing out champagne to everyone. He learns that the seventeenth hole cannot be seen from the ridge where the golfers tee off, and in the old days the kids used to hide in the woods and wait for the ball to appear, then place it in the hole and claim part of the prize. This gives Alf an idea. Soon, an increasingly intoxicated Alf and Bert are placing the ball in the blind hole, running back to the bar and enjoying the fruits of the club tradition whenever there is a hole in one – champagne all round.

ARGUMENTS, ARGUMENTS

Strikes and workers.

BLOODY LANGUAGE

Twenty 'bloodies', one 'bleeding' and one 'Minnie moo'.

FUNNY BUSINESS

The entire conversation about television and reality, Shakespeare and Dickens; Alf's malapropism – 'permissivesnessess' (for 'permissiveness'); the observation about Arthur Mullard 'not torkin nothin' like' a real Cockney such as Alf; Bert ordering Min to listen to Alf, and Min settling down respectfully, pleased by her husband's dominating behaviour; Min irritating Alf by simultaneously miming the last word of every sentence he utters; Bert rambling on to himself; Bert hiding the snot on his sleeve from Rita; Min going on about the Isle of Wight again; Min sobbing in the doorway to the bar, moaning about being banned and left with a 'bloody arrowroot biscuit'; Alf ending up – for only the second time in the show's history – on a high, as he and Bert stagger around the seventeenth hole.

WHAT ELSE?

Min mentions again that she is 'not avid' as regards watching television.

Some scripted dialogue was cut prior to transmission. This came shortly after the talk about the incest in *Hamlet*, a tale of a royal coming back from his holiday in Denmark to find that his uncle has poisoned his father and is now having it away with his mother. In the cut sequence, Alf offers the comparison of 'young prince Charles' coming home from the navy on leave and finding 'that his father, Prince Philip, has had a dose of arsenic ...' – 'in the ear 'ole,' interrupts Mike – '... and his mother ...' – 'the Queen,' interjects Mike again – ... at which point Alf peters out, saying that of course she would never do anything like that, since she is above all that ..

Philip Gilbert, seen here as the golf club barman, is better known as the voice of the computer 'Tim' in *The Tomorrow People*, while Ballard Berkeley is famous for the role of the Major in *Fawlty Towers*.

This episode had the highest RI of the last two series, but was seen by only 9.7% of the viewing population.

7.6: UNEMPLOYED

Recorded 6 December 1975
Transmitted Wednesday 17 December 1975 at 9.40 pm (RI unknown)

With Pat Coombs (Ethel Carey), Hugh Lloyd (Wally Carey), Joan Sims (Gran), Richard Speight (Telegram Messenger)

Alf returns to an apparently empty house. He laments that not only does he miss Else but he has also just been made redundant – and on his birthday, too. To add to his problems, he hears noises in the house; believing them to be made by burglars, he cowers in the corner and begs his unseen visitors not to hurt him ...Then the lights go up and Alf finds himself instead the recipient of a surprise birthday party, attended by Min, Bert, Ethel, her henpecked husband Wally, Gran, Rita and Mike, who of course is gleeful at having witnessed Alf's abject terror. Alf prepares a surprise of his own for his son-in-law – a sandwich laced with cigar ash and mustard – but finds this backfires on him, much to everyone's amusement. The older generation reminisce about the good old days as they imbibe alcohol under the unforgiving gaze of Else's photo. They chat about the delights of drenching the lower stalls with lemonade from the upper gallery in the Roxy cinema, in the days when they made much better films with stars such as Marie Lloyd and Rudolph Valentino.

Things take a more sinister turn when Gran suggests that maybe Else hasn't gone down under after all, but reclines six feet under in the back yard. Gran also accuses Ethel of beating her husband. Despite Ethel's denials, Min casually mentions that Wally does seem to have a habit of walking into doors … Wally throughout the conversation remains totally silent, nursing a black eye. Ethel proudly proclaims that she buys meat that is fit only for the dog, yet cooks it for her husband, who never notices … And then there's Alf's redundancy, a terrible betrayal for a man who fought a world war, or would have done had he not been in a reserved occupation. The conversation turns to home rule for Scotland, and Alf lets the household know exactly what he thinks about his Caledonian cousins, which prompts the seemingly trappist Wally to break silence with a Scottish brogue and challenge him to a fight outside. Alf again cowers on the perimeter until Wally agrees to forgive him, and they shake hands … at which point a telegram arrives for Mr Garnett, which Min obligingly reads. It's from Else. She wants a divorce.

ARGUMENTS, ARGUMENTS

Home rule for Scotland; redundancies of workers and generals, caused by Mike's socialist policies; the NHS and private medicine.

BLOODY LANGUAGE

Forty 'bloodies', an 'old rat bag', a 'thick Mick' and a 'Scouse pillock'.

FUNNY BUSINESS

Alf failing to blow out the candles on his cake, then lunging at Mike; Ethel's memories of a grope at the pictures; Min waxing tearful over memories of *Sonny Boy*; Bert singing 'Mame'; Alf singing to the photograph of the malevolent toad; Min's closing line, 'Thoughtful of her to send it greetings, wasn't it? Didn't want to upset anyone.'

WHAT ELSE?

This episode reuses the joke about the womenfolk believing Al Jolson to be black, at least in *Sonny Boy* (although this time it is Min who says so and not Else). Then there's the gross sight of Gran dipping her sandwich in her gin, repeated from 'Up The Polls! (The Campaign's Over)', *The Alf Garnett Saga* and others. Gran sings the same song as in 'Gran's Watch', while Alf sings 'My Old Dutch', as he did at the wedding anniversary do in 'A House with Love in It' in 1966 and in 'Till Closing Time Us Do Part'. Gran must have left the 'funny farm' (mentioned by Alf in the first episode of this series) especially for Alf's birthday. Mike's taunt about 'Jack Solomons' as the fight is about to break out between Alf and Wally refers to Britain's foremost boxing match promoter from the late 1930s to the 1960s. The fact that Else wants a divorce should not come as a surprise to Alf, as he discovered this in 'Min the Housekeeper' earlier in the series.

Johnny Speight's son Richard plays the telegram delivery boy.

The episode was watched by 18.9% of the viewing population.

APPENDICES

Appendix A

ALL IN THE FAMILY ON THE BBC

First Series (selected episodes) – shown on Thursdays at 7.50 pm on BBC One, except 'Edith's Jury Duty' which was shown at 7.55 pm

Meet the Bunkers	8 July 1971
Mike's Hippy Friends Come to Visit	15 July 1971
Judging Books by Covers	22 July 1971
Lionel Moves Into the Neighbourhood	29 July 1971
Edith Has Jury Duty	5 August 1971
The First and Last Supper	19 August 1971
Archie is Worried About His Job	26 August 1971
Oh, My Aching Back	2 September 1971
Archie Gives Blood	9 September 1971

Second Series (selected episodes) shown at various times on Saturdays between 11.15 pm and 11.30 pm on BBC One

The Blockbuster	3 June 1972
Sammy's Visit	10 June 1972
Flashback – Mike Meets Archie	17 June 1972
Edith Writes a Song	24 June 1972
Insurance Is Cancelled	1 July 1972
Edith's Accident	8 July 1972

Appendix B

THE MISSING EPISODES

During the '60s, all but five episodes of *Till Death Us Do Part* were repeated (the exceptions being 'Sex Before Marriage', 'A Woman's Place Is In The Home', 'Alf's Dilemma', 'Till Closing Time Us Do Part' and 'The Blood Donor'). After this, the master tapes were erased during the early '70s in line with BBC policy at that time. It seems that by 1972 only 'The Blood Donor' could be found when producer Dennis Main Wilson enquired about the possibility of a further repeat season. Thankfully, due to the hard work of private collectors and the BBC archivists, the position has improved considerably since then – the recovered material consists mainly of film recordings made for overseas sales purposes – although huge gaps remain. Below is a list of the episodes that, as of 2016, are still missing or incomplete.

As far as the '70s episodes are concerned, these all remain complete. Still missing however is the 1971 *Christmas Night with the Stars* sketch in which Alf and Else await the birth of their grandchild. In addition, 'Up The Polls! (The Campaign's Over)' exists only in poor quality monochrome format, with the first few minutes missing. The original master tape of 'The Royal Wedding' episode from the fifth series does not survive; the best copy now existing is a restored domestic recording. Certain other appearances by members of the cast – Alf on the Petula Clark show in 1971, Warren Mitchell being interviewed on the set of the 1974 series for an edition of *Nationwide*, interviews with Booth and Mitchell to promote the 1968 film and so on – also seem not to have survived in any condition.

COMEDY PLAYHOUSE

'Till Death Us Do Part' (a two minute clip is extant from a 1966 *Late Night Line-Up* programme)

FIRST SERIES

'Hair Raising!'
'Two Toilets – That's Posh!'
'From Liverpool With Love'
'Claustrophobia'

SECOND SERIES

'Sex Before Marriage' (clips survive from the 1972 *Late Night Line-Up* special)
'I Can Give It Up Any Time I Like'
'The Bulldog Breed'
'Caviar On The Dole'
'A Wapping Mythology (The Workers' King)' (a clip survives from the 1972 *Late Night Line-Up* special)
'A Woman's Place Is In The Home'
'Alf's Dilemma' (some studio footage survives; ten minutes of material, including film sequences, does not)

THIRD SERIES

'Monopoly'
'The Funeral'
'Football'
'The Puppy' (the last five minutes remains, having been recorded by Galton and Simpson)
'Aunt Maud' (most of this remains, but a few minutes at the beginning are missing, as are the end titles)

Index

About the Author

Mark Ward was only seven when Alf Garnett hit our screens but he remembers being allowed to stay up and watch the show despite the language, using the excuse that his parents' laughter kept him awake. He wishes he had been born earlier so that he could have enjoyed the 'swinging' bit of the '60s and seen Hendrix and Cream in the flesh but does not blame his parents for this. He continues a love affair with any rock music created between 1965 and 1975 and more recent offerings such as Bjork. His love for old telly resulted in his first book, *Out of the Unknown: A Guide to the legendary BBC Series*, in 2004. His other interests include reading ancient and medieval history, the cinema and travelling as much of the world as he can afford.

Printed in Great Britain
by Amazon